Better Homes and Gardens®

Simple Slow Cooker Recipes

Meredith® Books
Des Moines, Iowa

SIMPLE SLOW COOKER RECIPES

Editor: Carrie E. Holcomb
Senior Associate Design Director: John Eric Seid
Contributing Designer: Joyce DeWitt
Contributing Editors: Spectrum Communication Services, Inc., Winifred Moranville
Copy Chief: Terri Fredrickson
Copy and Production Editor: Victoria Forlini
Editorial Operations Manager: Karen Schirm
Managers, Book Production: Pam Kvitne, Marjorie J. Schenkelberg, Rick von Holdt
Recipe Developers: Juliana Hale, Linda Henry, Maryellyn Krantz, Tami Leonard,
    Shelli McConnell, Marcia Stanley, Colleen Weeden
Contributing Copy Editor: Kim Catanzarite
Contributing Proofreaders: Lisa Baker, Emmy Clausing, Gretchen Kauffman
Indexer: Elizabeth Parson
Contributing Illustrator: Jim Swanson
Editorial and Design Assistants: Karen McFadden, Mary Lee Gavin
Test Kitchen Director: Lynn Blanchard
Test Kitchen Product Supervisor: Marilyn Cornelius
Test Kitchen Home Economists: Juliana Hale; Laura Harms, R.D.;
    Jennifer Kalanowski, R.D.; Maryellyn Krantz; Jill Moberly;
    Colleen Weeden; Lori Wilson

Meredith® Books
Editor in Chief: Linda Raglan Cunningham
Design Director: Matt Strelecki
Executive Editor, Food and Crafts: Jennifer Dorland Darling

Publisher: James D. Blume
Executive Director, Marketing: Jeffrey Meyers
Executive Director, New Business Development: Todd M. Davis
Executive Director, Sales: Ken Zagor
Director, Operations: George A. Susral
Director, Production: Douglas M. Johnston
Business Director: Jim Leonard

Vice President and General Manager: Douglas J. Guendel

Better Homes and Gardens® **Magazine**
Editor in Chief: Karol DeWulf Nickell
Deputy Editor, Food and Entertaining: Nancy Hopkins

Meredith Publishing Group
President, Publishing Group: Stephen M. Lacy
Vice President-Publishing Director: Bob Mate

Meredith Corporation
Chairman and Chief Executive Officer: William T. Kerr

In Memoriam: E. T. Meredith III (1933-2003)

Our Better Homes and Gardens® Test Kitchen seal on the back cover of this book assures you that every recipe in *Simple Slow Cooker Recipes* has been tested in the Better Homes and Gardens® Test Kitchen. This means that each recipe is practical and reliable, and meets our high standards of taste appeal. We guarantee your satisfaction with this book for as long as you own it.

All of us at Better Homes and Gardens® Books are dedicated to providing you with the information and ideas you need to create delicious foods. We welcome your comments and suggestions. Write to us at: Better Homes and Gardens Books, Cookbook Editorial Department, 1716 Locust St., Des Moines, IA 50309-3023.

If you would like to purchase any of our cooking, crafts, gardening, home improvement, or home decorating and design books, check wherever quality books are sold. Or visit us at: bhgbooks.com

TABLE OF CONTENTS

BONUS CHAPTERS
Simple
Slow Cooker
Recipes
BONUS CHAPTERS

INTRODUCTION

You already know that when it comes to getting satisfying home-cooked meals on the table, slow cookers can't be beat. You simply mix together the food, plug in the pot, and go on your merry way. What you might not know is this: Many of the dishes you crave can be cooked in a slow cooker. From Herbed Philly Steak Sandwiches to Chicken Curry, this book presents clever ways to bring slow cooker ease to lots of your favorite meals, plus some intriguing surprises too.

Many of the recipes call for today's terrific convenience products—canned soups, bottled salsas, pesto, refrigerated diced potatoes, and others—which help you get on your way even sooner.

Because slow cookers are making a splash at potlucks, an entire chapter focuses on recipes that are perfect for such gatherings. The whole idea of slow cooking is simplicity, so an entire chapter features swiftly made side dishes that round out a slow cooked meal.

Whether you're looking for a family-pleasing supper for tonight, a special dinner-party entrée for this weekend, or party fare for the gang, your slow cooker can do the trick deliciously.

APPETIZERS, SNACKS & BEVERAGES

1

With only five ingredients, this crowd-pleasing party appetizer is incredibly simple yet tastes deceptively complex.

CRANBERRY-CHIPOTLE MEATBALLS

PREP:

15 minutes

COOK:

4 to 5 hours

MAKES:

16 servings

1   16-ounce package frozen cooked plain meatballs, thawed

1   16-ounce can jellied cranberry sauce

1   15½-ounce can pineapple chunks, drained

¼   cup packed brown sugar

1   to 2 tablespoons canned chipotle chile peppers in adobo sauce, chopped

1 In a 1½-quart slow cooker place meatballs. In a medium bowl combine cranberry sauce, pineapple, brown sugar, and chipotle peppers. Pour over meatballs in cooker.

2 Cover and cook for 4 to 5 hours. Serve meatballs and pineapple with wooden toothpicks.

Nutrition Facts per serving: 161 cal., 7 g total fat (3 g sat. fat), 10 mg chol., 233 mg sodium, 21 g carbo., 1 g fiber, 4 g pro. **Daily Values:** 4% vit. C, 2% calcium, 2% iron

*Note: Some 1½-quart slow cookers include variable heat settings; others offer only one standard (low) setting. The 1½-quart slow cooker recipes in this book were only tested on the low-heat setting, if one was present.

Made of ground ham, ground pork, and apricots, this meatball recipe takes an all-time favorite to new gourmet heights.

APRICOT-GLAZED HAM BALLS

1	slightly beaten egg
½	cup graham cracker crumbs
2	tablespoons unsweetened pineapple juice
1	teaspoon dry mustard
¼	teaspoon salt
8	ounces ground cooked ham
8	ounces lean ground pork
½	cup snipped dried apricots
1	18-ounce jar apricot preserves
⅓	cup unsweetened pineapple juice
1	tablespoon cider vinegar
½	teaspoon ground ginger

PREP:
25 minutes

BAKE:
20 minutes

COOK:
4 to 5 hours (low) or 1½ to 2 hours (high)

OVEN:
350°F

MAKES:
30 servings

1 For meatballs, in a large bowl combine egg, graham cracker crumbs, the 2 tablespoons pineapple juice, the dry mustard, and salt. Add ground ham, ground pork, and dried apricots; mix well. Shape into 30 meatballs. In a 15×10×1-inch baking pan arrange meatballs in a single layer. Bake, uncovered, in a 350° oven for 20 minutes. Drain well. Transfer meatballs to a 3½- or 4-quart slow cooker.

2 For sauce, in a medium bowl combine apricot preserves, the ⅓ cup pineapple juice, the vinegar, and ginger. Pour over meatballs in cooker.

3 Cover and cook on low-heat setting for 4 to 5 hours or on high-heat setting for 1½ to 2 hours.

4 Serve immediately or keep warm on low-heat setting for up to 2 hours. Stir gently before serving. Serve ham balls with wooden toothpicks.

Nutrition Facts per serving: 86 cal., 2 g total fat (1 g sat. fat), 15 mg chol., 151 mg sodium, 15 g carbo., 0 g fiber, 3 g pro. **Daily Values:** 3% vit. A, 3% vit. C, 1% calcium, 2% iron

Somehow cocktail meatballs and weenies are always among the first treats to disappear from the appetizer table. This recipe boasts a festive cranberry spark and flavorful ground ham instead of beef.

CRIMSON HAM BALLS & SMOKIES

PREP:

30 minutes

BAKE:

15 minutes

COOK:

2 to 3 hours (high)

OVEN:

350°F

MAKES:

25 servings

1	slightly beaten egg
½	cup graham cracker crumbs
¼	cup finely chopped onion
2	tablespoons snipped dried cranberries
2	tablespoons milk
	Dash ground cloves
8	ounces ground cooked ham
8	ounces lean ground pork
	Nonstick cooking spray
1	16-ounce can jellied cranberry sauce
1	12-ounce bottle chili sauce
1	tablespoon vinegar
½	teaspoon dry mustard
1	16-ounce package small cooked smoked sausage links

1 For meatballs, in a large bowl combine egg, graham cracker crumbs, onion, dried cranberries, milk, and cloves. Add ground ham and ground pork; mix well. Shape into 50 meatballs.

2 Lightly coat a 15×10×1-inch baking pan with cooking spray. Arrange meatballs in a single layer in prepared pan. Bake, uncovered, in a 350° oven for 15 minutes. Drain well.

3 Meanwhile, for sauce, in a medium saucepan stir together cranberry sauce, chili sauce, vinegar, and dry mustard. Cook over medium heat until cranberry sauce is melted, stirring occasionally.

4 In a 3½- to 5-quart slow cooker combine meatballs and sausage. Pour sauce over mixture in cooker. Cover and cook on high-heat setting for 2 to 3 hours. Serve immediately or keep warm on low-heat setting for up to 2 hours. Serve meatballs and sausage with wooden toothpicks.

Nutrition Facts per serving: 138 cal., 7 g total fat (2 g sat. fat), 29 mg chol., 524 mg sodium, 13 g carbo., 1 g fiber, 6 g pro. Daily Values: 2% vit. A, 4% vit. C, 1% calcium, 3% iron

This appetizer holds up well for an hour—but don't be surprised if it's long gone by then!

TURKEY KIELBASA BITES

1   16-ounce package cooked turkey kielbasa, cut in 1-inch pieces

1   12-ounce carton cranberry-orange or cranberry-raspberry crushed fruit

1   tablespoon Dijon-style mustard

¼   teaspoon crushed red pepper

1 In a 1½-quart slow cooker combine kielbasa, cranberry-orange crushed fruit, Dijon mustard, and crushed red pepper.

2 Cover and cook for 2½ to 3 hours. Serve immediately or keep warm for up to 1 hour. Serve kielbasa with wooden toothpicks.

Nutrition Facts per serving: 126 cal., 4 g total fat (1 g sat. fat), 28 mg chol., 441 mg sodium, 15 g carbo., 0 g fiber, 7 g pro. **Daily Values:** 3% iron

*Note: Some 1½-quart slow cookers include variable heat settings; others offer only one standard (low) setting. The 1½-quart slow cooker recipes in this book were only tested on the low-heat setting, if one was present.

PREP:
10 minutes

COOK:
2½ to 3 hours

MAKES:
10 to 12 servings

Here's a unique take on the ever-popular cocktail weenie. The three ingredients meld beautifully, resulting in a mysteriously good sauce.

BOURBON-GLAZED COCKTAIL SAUSAGES

PREP:

10 minutes

COOK:

4 hours

MAKES:

12 servings

1   16-ounce package cocktail wieners or small cooked smoked sausage links

½   cup apricot preserves

¼   cup pure maple syrup

1   tablespoon bourbon or orange juice

1 In a 1½-quart slow cooker combine cocktail wieners, apricot preserves, maple syrup, and bourbon. Cover and cook for 4 hours.

2 Serve immediately or keep warm for up to 1 hour. Serve wieners with wooden toothpicks.

Nutrition Facts per serving: 170 cal., 10 g total fat (4 g sat. fat), 23 mg chol., 383 mg sodium, 14 g carbo., 0 g fiber, 5 g pro. **Daily Values:** 2% vit. C, 3% calcium, 3% iron

*Note: Some 1½-quart slow cookers include variable heat settings; others offer only one standard (low) setting. The 1½-quart slow cooker recipes in this book were only tested on the low-heat setting, if one was present.

INCREASING THE RECIPE

Double the ingredient amounts, using 1 package cocktail wieners and 1 package sausage links. Cover and cook in a 3½- or 4-quart slow cooker on low-heat setting for 4 hours.

A bold mix of vegetables, spices, and sweet mango fills these cute appetizer-size tacos with big flavor.

ZESTY BEEF-FILLED TACOS

1	medium onion, cut into wedges
1	medium carrot, quartered
1	12-ounce beef flank steak
¼	cup snipped fresh cilantro
½	to 1 teaspoon crushed red pepper
½	teaspoon salt
1	14½-ounce can diced tomatoes with roasted garlic, undrained
½	cup water
24	miniature taco shells
1	cup finely chopped mango
	Assorted toppings (such as snipped fresh cilantro, sliced green onion, chopped tomato, and/or finely shredded lettuce)

PREP:

25 minutes

COOK:

*7 to 9 hours (low) or
4 to 5 hours (high),
plus 15 minutes (high)*

MAKES:

24 servings

1 In a 3½- or 4-quart slow cooker place onion and carrot. Trim fat from meat. Add meat to cooker. Sprinkle with the ¼ cup cilantro, the crushed red pepper, and salt. Pour tomatoes and water over mixture in cooker.

2 Cover and cook on low-heat setting for 7 to 9 hours or on high-heat setting for 4 to 5 hours. Remove meat from cooker.

3 Using two forks, pull meat apart into shreds; if desired, cut into shorter shreds. Drain vegetable mixture, discarding cooking liquid. Transfer vegetable mixture to a food processor bowl or blender container. Cover and process or blend with several on/off pulses until chopped. Return meat and vegetable mixture to cooker. If using low-heat setting, turn to high-heat setting. Cover and cook for 15 to 30 minutes more or until heated through.

4 Spoon meat mixture into taco shells. Add mango and toppings.

Nutrition Facts per serving: 53 cal., 2 g total fat (1 g sat. fat), 6 mg chol., 145 mg sodium, 5 g carbo., 1 g fiber, 4 g pro. Daily Values: 14% vit. A, 5% vit. C, 1% calcium, 2% iron

No last-minute hassles here. This easy version of the ever-popular sports-bar favorite is ready to go long before your guests arrive.

BUFFALO-STYLE CHICKEN WINGS

PREP:

20 minutes

BAKE:

20 minutes

COOK:

*4 to 5 hours (low)
or 2 to 2½ hours (high)*

OVEN:

375°F

MAKES:

16 servings

3 pounds chicken wings (about 16)

1½ cups bottled hot-style barbecue sauce

2 tablespoons butter or margarine, melted

1 to 2 teaspoons bottled hot pepper sauce

⅔ cup bottled blue cheese or ranch salad dressing

1 If desired, using a sharp knife, carefully cut off tips of chicken wings; discard wing tips. In a foil-lined 15×10×1-inch baking pan arrange chicken wings in a single layer. Bake, uncovered, in a 375° oven for 20 minutes. Drain well.

2 For sauce, in a 3½- or 4-quart slow cooker combine barbecue sauce, melted butter, and hot pepper sauce. Add chicken wings, stirring to coat with sauce.

3 Cover and cook on low-heat setting for 4 to 5 hours or on high-heat setting for 2 to 2½ hours.

4 Serve immediately or keep warm on low-heat setting for up to 2 hours. Serve chicken wings with salad dressing.

Nutrition Facts per serving: 204 cal., 16 g total fat (4 g sat. fat), 64 mg chol., 371 mg sodium, 4 g carbo., 0 g fiber, 11 g pro. **Daily Values:** 6% vit. A, 3% vit. C, 1% calcium, 1% iron

Five-spice powder is a blend often used in Asian cooking, especially Chinese-inspired dishes like this tantalizing appetizer. Look for five-spice powder on your supermarket spice shelf or in the Asian foods aisle.

FIVE-SPICE CHICKEN WINGS

3   pounds chicken wings (about 16)

1   cup bottled plum sauce

2   tablespoons butter or margarine, melted

1   teaspoon five-spice powder

1 If desired, using a sharp knife, carefully cut off tips of chicken wings; discard wing tips. In a foil-lined 15×10×1-inch baking pan arrange chicken wings in a single layer. Bake, uncovered, in a 375° oven for 20 minutes. Drain well.

2 For sauce, in a 3½- or 4-quart slow cooker combine plum sauce, melted butter, and five-spice powder. Add chicken wings, stirring to coat with sauce.

3 Cover and cook on low-heat setting for 4 to 5 hours or on high-heat setting for 2 to 2½ hours.

4 Serve immediately or keep warm on low-heat setting for up to 2 hours. If desired, garnish with orange wedges and pineapple slices.

Nutrition Facts per serving: 176 cal., 13 g total fat (3 g sat. fat), 70 mg chol., 82 mg sodium, 6 g carbo., 0 g fiber, 12 g pro. **Daily Values:** 1% vit. A, 2% calcium

PREP:

20 minutes

BAKE:

20 minutes

COOK:

4 to 5 hours (low)
or 2 to 2½ hours (high)

OVEN:

375°F

MAKES:

16 servings

For some people, it isn't a party unless wings are served. If you're one of that crowd, try this whiskey-laced twist on the classic.

CHICKEN WINGS IN MAPLE SAUCE

PREP:

20 minutes

BAKE:

20 minutes

COOK:

*4 to 5 hours (low)
or 2 to 2^1/$_2$ hours (high)*

OVEN:

375°F

MAKES:

16 servings

3   pounds chicken wings (about 16)

^{1}/$_2$ cup pure maple syrup or maple-flavored syrup

^{1}/$_2$ cup whiskey or orange juice

2   tablespoons butter or margarine, melted

1 If desired, using a sharp knife, carefully cut off tips of chicken wings; discard wing tips. In a foil-lined 15×10×1-inch baking pan arrange chicken wings in a single layer. Bake, uncovered, in a 375° oven for 20 minutes. Drain well.

2 For sauce, in a 3^1/$_2$- or 4-quart slow cooker combine maple syrup, whiskey, and melted butter. Add chicken wings, stirring to coat with sauce.

3 Cover and cook on low-heat setting for 4 to 5 hours or on high-heat setting for 2 to 2^1/$_2$ hours.

4 Serve immediately or keep warm on low-heat setting for up to 2 hours.

Nutrition Facts per serving: 180 cal., 11 g total fat (3 g sat. fat), 62 mg chol., 67 mg sodium, 7 g carbo., 0 g fiber, 10 g pro. **Daily Values:** 1% vit. A, 1% calcium, 1% iron

PARTY TIME

Looking for an easy way to entertain? Host an appetizer buffet with the help of a slow cooker. Start with one or two of the appetizer recipes in this section and borrow another cooker, if necessary. Complement the slow cooker recipes with purchased dips, chips, crackers, cheese, fresh fruits or vegetables, and a selection of beverages.

Few hot party dips are easier—and few will disappear more quickly—than this fantastic, four-ingredient crowd-pleaser.

SUPER SIMPLE BEAN DIP

2   16-ounce cans refried beans

1   11-ounce can condensed nacho cheese soup

½   cup bottled salsa

¼   cup sliced green onions

1 In a 1½-quart slow cooker combine refried beans, nacho cheese soup, and salsa. Cover and cook for 3½ to 4 hours.

2 Sprinkle with green onions. Serve dip with tortilla chips.

Nutrition Facts per serving (dip only): 53 cal., 1 g total fat (0 g sat. fat), 2 mg chol., 330 mg sodium, 8 g carbo., 2 g fiber, 3 g pro. **Daily Values:** 3% vit. A, 2% vit. C, 3% calcium, 4% iron

*Note: Some 1½-quart slow cookers include variable heat settings; others offer only one standard (low) setting. The 1½-quart slow cooker recipes in this book were only tested on the low-heat setting, if one was present.

PREP:
10 minutes

COOK:
3½ to 4 hours

MAKES:
22 (¼-cup) servings

Skip the chips and serve this dip with something unexpected: Corn Bread Dippers. Your guests will rave about the combination of crunchy sticks and spicy dip.

CHEESY BEER-SALSA DIP

PREP:

15 minutes

COOK:

*3 to 4 hours (low)
or 1 1/2 to 2 hours (high)*

MAKES:

22 (1/4-cup) servings

CORN BREAD DIPPERS
Prepare one 8 1/2-ounce package corn muffin mix according to package directions. Spread batter in an 8×8×2-inch baking pan. Bake in a 400°F oven about 20 minutes or until a wooden toothpick inserted in center comes out clean. Cool bread in pan on a wire rack for 5 minutes. Remove bread from pan; cool completely. Cut into 1/2-inch slices; cut each slice into 3 pieces. Place in a single layer on a large baking sheet. Bake in a 425°F oven about 10 minutes more or until crisp, turning once. Remove from baking sheet; cool on wire rack. Makes 48 dippers.

1   16-ounce jar salsa

2/3   cup beer or milk

4   cups shredded American cheese (1 pound)

2   cups shredded Monterey Jack cheese (8 ounces)

1   8-ounce package cream cheese, cut up

1   recipe Corn Bread Dippers or tortilla chips

1 In a 3 1/2- or 4-quart slow cooker combine salsa and beer. Stir in American cheese, Monterey Jack cheese, and cream cheese.

2 Cover and cook on low-heat setting for 3 to 4 hours or on high-heat setting for 1 1/2 to 2 hours.

3 Serve immediately or keep warm on low-heat setting for up to 2 hours. Stir before serving. Serve dip with Corn Bread Dippers.

Nutrition Facts per serving: 264 cal., 17 g total fat (8 g sat. fat), 55 mg chol., 1,114 mg sodium, 18 g carbo., 0 g fiber, 10 g pro. **Daily Values:** 12% vit. A, 5% vit. C, 25% calcium, 5% iron

Here's another sports-bar favorite deliciously adapted to the slow cooker. Process Swiss cheese is the ticket here—the natural cheeses called for in oven-baked versions do not become as smooth when slow-cooked in the cooker.

SWISS-ARTICHOKE DIP

1   8- or 9-ounce package frozen artichoke hearts, thawed and chopped

2   3-ounce packages cream cheese, cut up

2   ounces process Swiss cheese slices, torn into small pieces

¼   cup snipped dried tomatoes (not oil-packed)

¼   cup mayonnaise

¼   cup milk

1   teaspoon dried minced onion

1   clove garlic, minced

Crackers or baguette slices, toasted

PREP:
15 minutes
COOK:
2 to 3 hours
MAKES:
8 (¼-cup) servings

1 In a 1½-quart slow cooker combine artichoke hearts, cream cheese, Swiss cheese, dried tomatoes, mayonnaise, milk, dried onion, and garlic. Cover and cook for 2 to 3 hours.

2 Stir before serving. Serve dip with crackers.

Nutrition Facts per serving (dip only): 169 cal., 15 g total fat (7 g sat. fat), 33 mg chol., 261 mg sodium, 5 g carbo., 2 g fiber, 4 g pro. **Daily Values:** 9% vit. A, 5% vit. C, 9% calcium, 3% iron

*Note: Some 1½-quart slow cookers include variable heat settings; others offer only one standard (low) setting. The 1½-quart slow cooker recipes in this book were only tested on the low-heat setting, if one was present.

The basic picadillo is a quartet of garlic, onion, tomatoes, and meat. This sassy picadillo dip, however, mingles with olives, almonds, and raisins, establishing a Mediterranean flair.

PICADILLO PITA DIP

PREP:

20 minutes

COOK:

*6 to 8 hours (low)
or 3 to 4 hours (high)*

MAKES:

16 servings

1	pound lean ground beef
1	16-ounce jar salsa
1	medium onion, chopped
$\frac{1}{2}$	cup raisins
$\frac{1}{4}$	cup chopped pimiento-stuffed green olives
2	tablespoons red wine vinegar
$\frac{1}{2}$	teaspoon ground cinnamon
$\frac{1}{2}$	teaspoon ground cumin
3	cloves garlic, minced
$\frac{1}{4}$	cup slivered almonds, toasted

1 In a large skillet cook ground beef until meat is brown. Drain off fat. Transfer meat to a $3\frac{1}{2}$- or 4-quart slow cooker. Stir in salsa, onion, raisins, olives, vinegar, cinnamon, cumin, and garlic.

2 Cover and cook on low-heat setting for 6 to 8 hours or on high-heat setting for 3 to 4 hours. Stir in almonds.

3 Sprinkle with additional almonds. Serve dip with toasted pita wedges.

Nutrition Facts per serving (dip only): 94 cal., 5 g total fat (2 g sat. fat), 18 mg chol., 190 mg sodium, 6 g carbo., 1 g fiber, 6 g pro. **Daily Values:** 4% vit. A, 8% vit. C, 2% calcium, 6% iron

GARLIC IN JARS

Bottled minced and bottled chopped garlic are handy products found in the produce section of the supermarket (you get great garlic flavor with none of the fuss). One teaspoonful is the equivalent of two cloves of fresh garlic. Store opened jars in the refrigerator.

When faced with a hungry crowd, you can't beat this hot and hearty dip. Just for fun (and especially if you're serving little folks who aren't used to dipping), spoon the mixture into mini buns and serve them hot from a tray.

CHEESEBURGER DIP

2	pounds lean ground beef
1½	cups chopped onions
2	cloves garlic, minced
1	15-ounce jar cheese dip
½	cup catsup
¼	cup prepared mustard
¼	cup sweet pickle relish

PREP:

15 minutes

COOK:

*3 to 4 hours (low)
or 1½ to 2 hours (high)*

MAKES:

22 (¼-cup) servings

1 In a large skillet cook ground beef, onions, and garlic until meat is brown. Drain off fat. Transfer meat mixture to a 3½-quart slow cooker. Stir in cheese dip, catsup, mustard, and pickle relish.

2 Cover and cook on low-heat setting for 3 to 4 hours or on high-heat setting for 1½ to 2 hours.

3 Serve immediately or keep warm on low-heat setting for up to 2 hours. Serve dip with chips.

Nutrition Facts per serving (dip only): 134 cal., 8 g total fat (4 g sat. fat), 38 mg chol., 447 mg sodium, 5 g carbo., 0 g fiber, 10 g pro. **Daily Values:** 5% vit. A, 3% vit. C, 7% calcium, 5% iron

Is the dip hot enough for you? If not, you'll find extra heat in hot Italian sausage, hot salsa, and Monterey Jack cheese with jalapeño peppers.

RIO GRANDE DIP

PREP:

15 minutes

COOK:

*3 to 4 hours (low)
or 1 1/2 to 2 hours (high)*

MAKES:

24 (1/4-cup) servings

8   ounces bulk Italian sausage

1   small onion, finely chopped

2   15-ounce cans refried black beans

1 1/2   cups bottled salsa

1   4-ounce can diced green chile peppers, undrained

1 1/2   cups shredded Monterey Jack cheese (6 ounces)

1   In a large skillet cook Italian sausage and onion until meat is brown. Drain off fat. Transfer sausage mixture to a 3 1/2- or 4-quart slow cooker. Stir in refried black beans, salsa, and green chile peppers. Stir in Monterey Jack cheese.

2   Cover and cook on low-heat setting for 3 to 4 hours or on high-heat setting for 1 1/2 to 2 hours.

3   Serve immediately or keep warm on low-heat setting for up to 2 hours. Stir before serving. Serve dip with chips.

Nutrition Facts per serving (dip only): 90 cal., 5 g total fat (2 g sat. fat), 13 mg chol., 238 mg sodium, 6 g carbo., 2 g fiber, 5 g pro. **Daily Values:** 2% vit. A, 5% vit. C, 8% calcium, 4% iron

A trip to an upscale deli that serves a stacked ham, apple, and melted Swiss cheese sandwich on rye bread was the inspiration here. The combination of flavors is well-suited to a dip.

HAM-SWISS DIP

8	ounces cooked ham, finely chopped
4	ounces process Swiss cheese slices, torn into small pieces
1	3-ounce package cream cheese, cubed
1	medium onion, chopped
¼	cup hard apple cider or apple juice
1	tablespoon Dijon-style mustard
¼	teaspoon caraway seeds

PREP:
15 minutes
COOK:
2 to 3 hours
MAKES:
8 (¼-cup) servings

1 In a 1½-quart slow cooker combine ham, Swiss cheese, cream cheese, onion, cider, mustard, and caraway seeds. Cover and cook for 2 to 3 hours.

2 Stir before serving. Serve dip with rye crackers and apple wedges.

Nutrition Facts per serving (dip only): 143 cal., 10 g total fat (6 g sat. fat), 40 mg chol., 621 mg sodium, 2 g carbo., 0 g fiber, 9 g pro. **Daily Values:** 6% vit. A, 1% vit. C, 12% calcium, 3% iron

*Note: Some 1½-quart slow cookers include variable heat settings; others offer only one standard (low) setting. The 1½-quart slow cooker recipes in this book were only tested on the low-heat setting, if one was present.

Your guests will feel as if they have been treated to something truly special when they taste this spicy shrimp dip.

CAJUN SPINACH-SHRIMP DIP

PREP:

15 minutes

COOK:

2 to 3 hours

MAKES:

12 (1/4-cup) servings

1   10¾-ounce can condensed cream of shrimp or cream of chicken soup

1   10-ounce package frozen chopped spinach, thawed and well drained

1   8-ounce package cream cheese, cubed

1   4-ounce can tiny shrimp, drained

¼   cup finely chopped onion

¼   to ½ teaspoon Cajun seasoning

2   cloves garlic, minced

1 In a 1½-quart slow cooker combine shrimp soup, spinach, cream cheese, shrimp, onion, Cajun seasoning, and garlic. Cover and cook for 2 to 3 hours.

2 Stir before serving. Serve dip with vegetables and/or crackers.

Nutrition Facts per serving (dip only): 103 cal., 8 g total fat (5 g sat. fat), 40 mg chol., 290 mg sodium, 4 g carbo., 1 g fiber, 5 g pro. **Daily Values:** 41% vit. A, 7% vit. C, 5% calcium, 6% iron

*Note: Some 1½-quart slow cookers include variable heat settings; others offer only one standard (low) setting. The 1½-quart slow cooker recipes in this book were only tested on the low-heat setting, if one was present.

This rich crab dip—perfectly spiced with horseradish and Worcestershire sauce and given smoky depth with bacon—stands out on an appetizer spread.

HORSERADISH-CRAB DIP

2   6- or 6½-ounce cans crabmeat, drained, flaked, and cartilage removed

1   8-ounce package cream cheese, cubed

1   4-ounce can mushroom stems and pieces, drained and chopped

¼   cup finely chopped onion

2   slices bacon, crisp-cooked, drained, and crumbled

2   teaspoons prepared horseradish

1   teaspoon Worcestershire sauce

PREP:
15 minutes
COOK:
1½ to 2½ hours
MAKES:
10 (¼-cup) servings

1 In a 1½-quart slow cooker combine crabmeat, cream cheese, mushrooms, onion, bacon, horseradish, and Worcestershire sauce. Cover and cook for 1½ to 2½ hours.

2 Stir before serving. Serve dip with crackers and/or celery.

Nutrition Facts per serving: 223 cal., 14 g total fat (6 g sat. fat), 57 mg chol., 426 mg sodium, 14 g carbo., 1 g fiber, 11 g pro. **Daily Values:** 8% vit. A, 4% vit. C, 8% calcium, 9% iron

*Note: Some 1½-quart slow cookers include variable heat settings; others offer only one standard (low) setting. The 1½-quart slow cooker recipes in this book were only tested on the low-heat setting, if one was present.

For a completely luscious pleasure, dip fruit, berries, cake, or brownies into this rum-laced confection. It's a sweet finish to your appetizer table.

BUTTERSCOTCH FONDUE

PREP:

10 minutes

COOK:

3 hours (low)

MAKES:

20 servings

2   14-ounce cans (2½ cups) sweetened condensed milk

2   cups packed brown sugar

1   cup butter, melted

⅔   cup light-colored corn syrup

1   teaspoon vanilla

¼   cup rum or milk

Assorted dippers (such as apple slices, strawberries, sponge cake cubes, and/or brownie cubes)

1 In a 3½- or 4-quart slow cooker combine sweetened condensed milk, brown sugar, melted butter, corn syrup, and vanilla. Cover and cook on low-heat setting for 3 hours. Whisk in rum until smooth. Serve immediately or keep warm on low-heat setting for up to 2 hours, stirring occasionally.

2 To serve, spear dippers with fondue forks. Dip into butterscotch mixture, swirling as you dip.

Nutrition Facts per serving: 317 cal., 13 g total fat (8 g sat. fat), 38 mg chol., 163 mg sodium, 49 g carbo., 0 g fiber, 3 g pro. **Daily Values:** 9% vit. A, 2% vit. C, 13% calcium, 3% iron

All of the intensely flavored ingredients that make the Reuben sandwich a universal favorite are here. Slather this party-perfect spread on top of rye bread or crackers.

REUBEN SPREAD

1	pound cooked corned beef, finely chopped
1	16-ounce can sauerkraut, rinsed, drained, and snipped
1	cup bottled Thousand Island salad dressing
1½	cups shredded Swiss cheese (6 ounces)
1	3-ounce package cream cheese, cut up
1	tablespoon prepared horseradish
1	teaspoon caraway seeds
	Party rye bread slices, toasted, or rye crackers

1 In a 3½- or 4-quart slow cooker combine corned beef, sauerkraut, and salad dressing. Stir in Swiss cheese, cream cheese, horseradish, and caraway seeds. Cover and cook on low-heat setting for 2½ to 3 hours.

2 Serve immediately or keep warm on low-heat setting for up to 2 hours. Stir before serving. Serve spread with toasted bread slices.

Nutrition Facts per serving (spread only): 157 cal., 13 g total fat (5 g sat. fat), 38 mg chol., 531 mg sodium, 3 g carbo., 1 g fiber, 7 g pro. **Daily Values:** 4% vit. A, 6% vit. C, 10% calcium, 5% iron

PREP:
15 minutes
COOK:
2½ to 3 hours (low)
MAKES:
20 (¼-cup) servings

You'll love this dish warm, but it's great at room temperature too. If it fits your schedule better, make the dip ahead, then chill. Return to room temperature before serving.

WHITE BEAN SPREAD

PREP:

15 minutes

COOK:

3 to 4 hours

MAKES:

16 servings

2	15-ounce cans Great Northern or white kidney (cannellini) beans, rinsed and drained
$1/2$	cup chicken or vegetable broth
1	tablespoon olive oil
1	teaspoon snipped fresh marjoram or $1/4$ teaspoon dried marjoram, crushed
$1/2$	teaspoon snipped fresh rosemary or $1/8$ teaspoon dried rosemary, crushed
$1/8$	teaspoon black pepper
3	cloves garlic, minced
	Pita bread wedges or baguette slices, toasted

1 In a $1 1/2$-quart slow cooker combine Great Northern beans, chicken broth, olive oil, marjoram, rosemary, pepper, and garlic. Cover and cook for 3 to 4 hours. Using a potato masher, mash bean mixture slightly.

2 Serve spread warm or at room temperature with toasted pita wedges. (Mixture thickens as it cools.)

Nutrition Facts per serving (spread only): 70 cal., 1 g total fat (0 g sat. fat), 0 mg chol., 33 mg sodium, 11 g carbo., 3 g fiber, 4 g pro. **Daily Values:** 1% vit. C, 3% calcium, 5% iron

*Note: Some $1 1/2$-quart slow cookers include variable heat settings; others offer only one standard (low) setting. The $1 1/2$-quart slow cooker recipes in this book were only tested on the low-heat setting, if one was present.

MAKE-AHEAD DIRECTIONS
Prepare as directed through Step 1. Cover and chill for up to 24 hours. Bring to room temperature before serving.

Once the punch has simmered, set the slow cooker on low. Doing so will keep the drinks at the perfect sipping temperature down to the very last serving.

SPICY CRANBERRY PUNCH

8	inches stick cinnamon, broken into 1-inch pieces
6	whole cloves
5	cups white grape juice
2⅔	cups water
1	12-ounce can frozen cranberry juice concentrate

1 For spice bag, cut a double thickness of 100-percent-cotton cheesecloth into a 6-inch square. Place cinnamon and cloves in center of cloth. Bring corners together and tie with a clean string. In a $3\frac{1}{2}$- to 5-quart slow cooker combine spice bag, grape juice, water, and cranberry juice concentrate.

2 Cover and cook on low-heat setting for 4 to 6 hours or on high-heat setting for 2 to $2\frac{1}{2}$ hours. Remove spice bag.

3 Serve immediately or keep warm on low-heat setting for up to 2 hours. Ladle punch into cups. If desired, garnish with additional stick cinnamon.

Nutrition Facts per serving: 44 cal., 0 g total fat (0 g sat. fat), 0 mg chol., 12 mg sodium, 11 g carbo., 0 g fiber, 0 g pro. **Daily Values:** 17% vit. C

PREP:

10 minutes

COOK:

4 to 6 hours (low)
or 2 to $2\frac{1}{2}$ hours (high)

MAKES:

18 (4-ounce) servings

The little dab of butter floating on top of each cup places this hot drink on the list of most comforting comfort foods.

HOT BUTTERED CIDER

PREP:

10 minutes

COOK:

4 to 6 hours (low)
or 2 to 3 hours (high)

MAKES:

12 (8-ounce) servings

Peel from 1 medium lemon, cut into strips

4   inches stick cinnamon, broken into 1-inch pieces

1   teaspoon whole allspice

1   teaspoon whole cloves

8   cups apple cider or apple juice

2   tablespoons brown sugar

2   tablespoons butter

1 For spice bag, cut a double thickness of 100-percent-cotton cheesecloth into a 6-inch square. Place lemon peel, cinnamon, allspice, and cloves in center of cloth. Bring corners together and tie with a clean string. In a 3½- or 4-quart slow cooker combine spice bag, apple cider, and brown sugar.

2 Cover and cook on low-heat setting for 4 to 6 hours or on high-heat setting 2 to 3 hours. Remove spice bag.

3 Serve immediately or keep warm on low-heat setting for up to 2 hours. Ladle cider into mugs. Top each serving with ½ teaspoon of the butter.

Nutrition Facts per serving: 101 cal., 2 g total fat (1 g sat. fat), 5 mg chol., 26 mg sodium, 21 g carbo., 0 g fiber, 0 g pro. **Daily Values:** 2% vit. A, 2% vit. C, 1% calcium, 4% iron

INCREASING THE RECIPE

Place the peel from 1 large lemon; 6 inches stick cinnamon, broken into 1-inch pieces; 1½ teaspoons whole allspice; and 1½ teaspoons whole cloves in center of cloth as in Step 1. In a 5½- or 6-quart slow cooker combine spice bag, 16 cups apple cider, and ¼ cup packed brown sugar. Continue as in Step 2. Top each serving with ½ teaspoon butter (¼ cup butter total). Makes 24 (8-ounce) servings.

This wassail, a Norse word which means "be in good health," is bound to become a holiday favorite. Garnish each serving with a slice of fresh orange.

HOLIDAY WASSAIL

6	inches stick cinnamon, broken into 1-inch pieces
12	whole cloves
6	cups water
1	12-ounce can frozen cranberry juice concentrate
1	12-ounce can frozen raspberry juice blend concentrate
1	12-ounce can frozen apple juice concentrate
1	cup brandy, rum, or orange juice
⅓	cup lemon juice
¼	cup sugar
	Orange slices (optional)

1 For spice bag, cut a double thickness of 100-percent-cotton cheesecloth into a 6-inch square. Place cinnamon and cloves in center of cloth. Bring corners together and tie with a clean string.

2 In a 4- to 6-quart slow cooker combine spice bag, water, juice concentrates, brandy, lemon juice, and sugar.

3 Cover and cook on low-heat setting for 4 to 6 hours or on high-heat setting for 2 to 3 hours. Remove spice bag.

4 Serve immediately or keep warm on low-heat setting for up to 2 hours. Ladle beverage into cups. If desired, float an orange slice on each serving.

Nutrition Facts per serving: 178 cal., 0 g total fat (0 g sat. fat), 0 mg chol., 12 mg sodium, 37 g carbo., 0 g fiber, 0 g pro. **Daily Values:** 85% vit. C, 1% calcium, 2% iron

PREP:

10 minutes

COOK:

4 to 6 hours (low)
or 2 to 3 hours (high)

MAKES:

16 (6-ounce) servings

To add an extra festive touch, garnish each cup or glass of this ruby punch with a few cranberries threaded onto a cocktail skewer.

HOT SCARLET WINE PUNCH

PREP:

10 minutes

COOK:

*3 to 4 hours (low)
or 1 to 1½ hours (high),
plus 30 minutes (high)*

MAKES:

14 (4-ounce) servings

2   inches stick cinnamon, broken into 1-inch pieces

4   whole cloves

1   32-ounce bottle cranberry juice (4 cups)

⅓   cup packed brown sugar

1   750-ml bottle white Zinfandel or dry white wine

     Whole fresh cranberries (optional)

1 For spice bag, cut a double thickness of 100-percent-cotton cheesecloth into a 6-inch square. Place cinnamon and cloves in center of cloth. Bring corners together and tie with a clean string. In a 3½- or 4-quart slow cooker combine spice bag, cranberry juice, and brown sugar.

2 Cover and cook on low-heat setting for 3 to 4 hours or on high-heat setting for 1 to 1½ hours. Remove spice bag.

3 If using low-heat setting, turn to high-heat setting. Stir wine into mixture in cooker. Cover and cook for 30 minutes more.

4 Serve immediately or keep warm on low-heat setting for up to 2 hours. Ladle punch into cups. If desired, garnish with cranberries.

Nutrition Facts per serving: 99 cal., 0 g total fat (0 g sat. fat), 0 mg chol., 6 mg sodium, 16 g carbo., 0 g fiber, 0 g pro. **Daily Values:** 43% vit. C, 1% calcium, 2% iron

SPICE BAG

It's easy to remove whole spices and fruit peel from a mixture when they are bundled together. Simply follow the directions in each recipe for creating a cotton cheesecloth bag.

Use a vegetable peeler to carefully peel the orange. You want to get only the outer orange layer and as little as possible of the bitter white layer.

GLOGG

Peel from 1 medium orange

8   inches stick cinnamon, broken into 1-inch pieces

6   whole cloves

2   cardamom pods, opened

1   750-ml bottle dry red wine

½   cup raisins

½   cup gin, vodka, or aquavit

⅓   cup sugar

¼   cup blanched whole almonds

PREP:

10 minutes

COOK:

3 hours (low)

MAKES:

8 (4-ounce) servings

1 For spice bag, cut a double thickness of 100-percent-cotton cheesecloth into a 6-inch square. Place orange peel, cinnamon, cloves, and cardamom in center of cloth. Bring corners together and tie with a clean string. In a 3½- or 4-quart slow cooker combine spice bag, wine, raisins, gin, and sugar.

2 Cover and cook on low-heat setting for 3 hours. Remove spice bag.

3 Serve immediately or keep warm on low-heat setting for up to 2 hours. Just before serving, stir in almonds.

Nutrition Facts per serving: 182 cal., 2 g total fat (0 g sat. fat), 0 mg chol., 6 mg sodium, 18 g carbo., 1 g fiber, 1 g pro. Daily Values: 2% calcium, 4% iron

The unusual combination of fruit juices and wine is what makes this delicious drink so memorable.

PINEAPPLE-ORANGE SIPPER

PREP:

10 minutes

COOK:

*5 to 7 hours (low)
or 2¹/₂ to 3 hours (high)*

MAKES:

12 (6-ounce) servings

    Peel from 1 medium lemon, cut into strips

5   inches stick cinnamon, broken into 1-inch pieces

1   teaspoon whole allspice

1   teaspoon whole cloves

4   cups water

1   12-ounce can frozen pineapple-orange juice concentrate

¼   cup honey

1   750-ml bottle dry white wine

① For spice bag, cut a double thickness of 100-percent-cotton cheesecloth into a 6-inch square. Place lemon strips, cinnamon, allspice, and cloves in center of cloth. Bring corners together and tie with a clean string. In a 3¹/₂- to 6-quart slow cooker combine spice bag, water, juice concentrate, and honey. Stir in wine.

② Cover and cook on low-heat setting for 5 to 7 hours or on high-heat setting for 2¹/₂ to 3 hours. Remove spice bag.

Nutrition Facts per serving: 121 cal., 0 g total fat (0 g sat. fat), 0 mg chol., 15 mg sodium, 20 g carbo., 0 g fiber, 1 g pro. **Daily Values:** 95% vit. C, 2% calcium, 1% iron

A perfect starter for the next cool-weather brunch or tailgate party, this sipper has just the right amount of spicy warmth. Garnish with celery sticks or dill pickle spears.

SPICY TOMATO SIPPER

1	46-ounce can vegetable juice
1	stalk celery, halved crosswise
2	tablespoons brown sugar
2	tablespoons lemon juice
1½	teaspoons prepared horseradish
1	teaspoon Worcestershire sauce
½	teaspoon bottled hot pepper sauce
	Celery sticks or dill pickle spears (optional)

1 In a 3½- or 4-quart slow cooker combine vegetable juice, halved celery stalk, brown sugar, lemon juice, horseradish, Worcestershire sauce, and hot pepper sauce.

2 Cover and cook on low-heat setting for 4 to 5 hours or on high-heat setting for 2 to 2½ hours. Discard halved celery stalk.

3 Ladle beverage into cups. If desired, garnish each serving with a celery stick.

Nutrition Facts per serving: 46 cal., 0 g total fat (0 g sat. fat), 0 mg chol., 456 mg sodium, 10 g carbo., 1 g fiber, 1 g pro. **Daily Values:** 29% vit. A, 75% vit. C, 3% calcium, 5% iron

PREP:

10 minutes

COOK:

4 to 5 hours (low)
or 2 to 2½ hours (high)

MAKES:

8 (6-ounce) servings

Consider setting up a cocoa bar at your next wintertime party. Prepare a batch of basic cocoa and have coffee crystals and spices available to stir into individual servings. Offer marshmallows or whipped cream to spoon on top.

THREE-WAY COCOA

PREP:

10 minutes

COOK:

3 to 4 hours (low)
or 1¹/₂ to 2 hours (high)

MAKES:

10 (6-ounce) servings

³/₄ cup sugar

¹/₂ cup unsweetened cocoa powder

8 cups milk

1 tablespoon vanilla

Marshmallows or whipped cream (optional)

1 In a 3¹/₂- to 5-quart slow cooker combine sugar and unsweetened cocoa powder. Stir in milk.

2 Cover and cook on low-heat setting for 3 to 4 hours or on high-heat setting for 1¹/₂ to 2 hours.

3 Serve immediately or keep warm on low-heat setting for up to 2 hours. Before serving, stir in vanilla. If desired, carefully beat cocoa with a rotary beater until frothy. Ladle cocoa into mugs. If desired, top each serving with marshmallows.

Nutrition Facts per serving: 174 cal., 4 g total fat (2 g sat. fat), 15 mg chol., 98 mg sodium, 26 g carbo., 0 g fiber, 8 g pro. **Daily Values:** 8% vit. A, 3% vit. C, 29% calcium, 4% iron

SPICY COCOA

Prepare Three-Way Cocoa as directed, except add 1 teaspoon ground cinnamon and ¹/₈ teaspoon ground nutmeg with the cocoa powder.

MOCHA COCOA

Prepare Three-Way Cocoa as directed, except stir ³/₄ teaspoon instant coffee crystals into each mug of cocoa.

SOUPS & STEWS

2

One pound of beef stew meat easily makes six servings of hearty soup when you add tummy-filling ingredients like wild rice and rutabaga.

WILD RICE & VEGETABLE BEEF SOUP

PREP:

20 minutes

COOK:

8 to 10 hours (low) or 4 to 5 hours (high)

MAKES:

6 servings

1	pound lean beef stew meat
1	tablespoon olive oil (optional)
3	14-ounce cans beef broth
2	cups rutabaga cut into ½-inch pieces
1	cup sliced carrots
1	cup frozen whole kernel corn
½	cup chopped onion
⅓	cup uncooked wild rice, rinsed and drained
1½	teaspoons dried thyme, crushed
¼	teaspoon black pepper
4	cloves garlic, minced

1 Cut meat into 1-inch pieces. If desired, in a large skillet brown meat, half at a time, in hot oil. Drain off fat.

2 Transfer meat to a 3½- or 4-quart slow cooker. Stir in beef broth, rutabaga, carrots, corn, onion, wild rice, thyme, pepper, and garlic.

3 Cover and cook on low-heat setting for 8 to 10 hours or on high-heat setting for 4 to 5 hours.

Nutrition Facts per serving: 203 cal., 4 g total fat (1 g sat. fat), 45 mg chol., 747 mg sodium, 21 g carbo., 3 g fiber, 21 g pro. **Daily Values:** 109% vit. A, 22% vit. C, 5% calcium, 17% iron

Here's a classic home-style winter warmer. Store extra barley in tightly covered containers in a cool, dry place for up to 1 year.

BEEF & BARLEY SOUP

1½	pounds boneless beef sirloin steak, cut ¾ inch thick
2	14-ounce cans beef broth
1	14½-ounce can stewed tomatoes, undrained
3	medium carrots, cut into ½-inch slices
2	small onions, cut into wedges
½	cup regular barley
½	cup water
1	bay leaf
1	teaspoon dried thyme, crushed
2	cloves garlic, minced

1 Trim fat from meat. Cut meat into ¾-inch pieces. In a 3½- or 4-quart slow cooker combine meat, beef broth, tomatoes, carrots, onions, barley, water, bay leaf, thyme, and garlic.

2 Cover and cook on low-heat setting for 9 to 11 hours or on high-heat setting for 4½ to 5½ hours. Remove bay leaf.

Nutrition Facts per serving: 261 cal., 6 g total fat (2 g sat. fat), 53 mg chol., 660 mg sodium, 23 g carbo., 5 g fiber, 29 g pro. **Daily Values:** 155% vit. A, 9% vit. C, 6% calcium, 22% iron

PREP:

20 minutes

COOK:

9 to 11 hours (low)
or 4½ to 5½ hours (high)

MAKES:

6 servings

This soup's robust Italian flavors call for a loaf of crusty bread. Try wedges of focaccia or thick slices of buttery garlic bread.

BEEF & TORTELLINI SOUP

20 minutes

COOK:

7 to 8 hours (low) or 3¹/₂ to 4 hours (high), plus 30 minutes (high)

MAKES:

4 servings

8	ounces boneless beef round steak, cut 1 inch thick
1	tablespoon all-purpose flour
¹/₂	teaspoon salt
¹/₂	teaspoon black pepper
¹/₂	cup chopped onion
1	tablespoon butter or margarine
1	14-ounce can beef broth
1	14-ounce jar roasted garlic pasta sauce
1	cup sliced carrots
¹/₂	cup water
¹/₂	teaspoon dried Italian seasoning, crushed
1	medium zucchini, cut in thin bite-size strips (1¹/₄ cups)
1	9-ounce package refrigerated cheese-filled tortellini

1 Trim fat from meat. Cut meat into 1-inch pieces. In a plastic bag combine flour, salt, and pepper. Add meat pieces, a few at a time, shaking to coat. In a large skillet cook meat and onion in hot butter until meat is brown and onion is tender. Drain off fat.

2 Transfer meat mixture to a 3¹/₂- or 4-quart slow cooker. Stir in broth, pasta sauce, carrots, water, and Italian seasoning. Cover and cook on low-heat setting for 7 to 8 hours or on high-heat setting for 3¹/₂ to 4 hours.

3 If using low-heat setting, turn to high-heat setting. Stir in zucchini and tortellini. Cover and cook for 30 minutes more.

Nutrition Facts per serving: 383 cal., 11 g total fat (4 g sat. fat), 71 mg chol., 1,252 mg sodium, 45 g carbo., 3 g fiber, 26 g pro. **Daily Values:** 165% vit. A, 19% vit. C, 20% calcium, 22% iron

Store-bought salsa is the shortcut to the bold flavors in this soup. Simply choose your favorite brand to make your own "house specialty."

SOUTHWEST STEAK & POTATO SOUP

1½	pounds boneless beef sirloin steak, cut 1 inch thick
2	medium potatoes, cut into 1-inch pieces
2	cups frozen cut green beans
1	small onion, sliced and separated into rings
1	16-ounce jar thick and chunky salsa
1	14-ounce can beef broth
1	teaspoon dried basil, crushed
2	cloves garlic, minced
	Shredded Monterey Jack or Mexican blend cheese (optional)

PREP:

25 minutes

COOK:

*8 to 10 hours (low)
or 4 to 5 hours (high)*

MAKES:

6 servings

1 Trim fat from meat. Cut meat into 1-inch pieces. Set aside. In a 3½- or 4-quart slow cooker place potatoes, green beans, and onion. Add meat. In a medium bowl stir together salsa, beef broth, basil, and garlic. Pour over mixture in cooker.

2 Cover and cook on low-heat setting for 8 to 10 hours or on high-heat setting for 4 to 5 hours. If desired, sprinkle each serving with cheese.

Nutrition Facts per serving: 206 cal., 4 g total fat (1 g sat. fat), 68 mg chol., 624 mg sodium, 16 g carbo., 3 g fiber, 27 g pro. **Daily Values:** 13% vit. A, 37% vit. C, 6% calcium, 27% iron

Use curly dried Chinese egg noodles rather than rice sticks or rice noodles for this recipe.

TERIYAKI BEEF-NOODLE SOUP

PREP:

20 minutes

COOK:

*6 to 8 hours (low)
or 3 to 4 hours (high)*

STAND:

5 minutes

MAKES:

6 servings

1   pound beef stir-fry strips

2   14-ounce cans beef broth

2   cups water

2   medium red or green sweet peppers, cut into ½-inch pieces

1   8-ounce can sliced water chestnuts, drained and chopped

6   green onions, cut into 1-inch pieces

3   tablespoons soy sauce

1   teaspoon ground ginger

¼   teaspoon black pepper

5   to 6 ounces dried Chinese noodles

1 In a 3½- or 4-quart slow cooker combine meat, broth, water, sweet peppers, water chestnuts, green onions, soy sauce, ginger, and pepper.

2 Cover and cook on low-heat setting for 6 to 8 hours or on high-heat setting for 3 to 4 hours. Turn off cooker. Stir in noodles. Cover and let stand for 5 minutes.

Nutrition Facts per serving: 232 cal., 4 g total fat (1 g sat. fat), 46 mg chol., 1,588 mg sodium, 27 g carbo., 3 g fiber, 22 g pro. **Daily Values:** 44% vit. A, 112% vit. C, 3% calcium, 18% iron

Give your family a change of pace. Replace the usual spaghetti night with a night of Italian soup.

EASY ITALIAN SOUP

12	ounces boneless beef round steak, cut ¾ inch thick
1	16-ounce package loose-pack frozen zucchini, carrots, cauliflower, lima beans, and Italian beans
1	1¼-ounce envelope spaghetti sauce mix
3	cups water
1	14½-ounce can diced tomatoes with basil, oregano, and garlic, undrained
1	14-ounce can reduced-sodium chicken broth
4	ounces dried gemelli pasta or medium shell macaroni
⅓	cup finely shredded Parmesan cheese

1 Trim fat from meat. Cut meat into ¾-inch pieces. In a 3½- or 4-quart slow cooker combine meat and frozen vegetables. Sprinkle with spaghetti sauce mix. Stir in water, tomatoes, and chicken broth.

2 Cover and cook on low-heat setting for 8 to 10 hours or on high-heat setting for 4 to 5 hours.

3 If using low-heat setting, turn to high-heat setting. Stir in pasta. Cover and cook about 30 minutes more or until pasta is tender. Sprinkle each serving with Parmesan cheese.

Nutrition Facts per serving: 233 cal., 3 g total fat (1 g sat. fat), 28 mg chol., 1,032 mg sodium, 29 g carbo., 3 g fiber, 20 g pro. Daily Values: 54% vit. A, 17% vit. C, 13% calcium, 16% iron

PREP:

15 minutes

COOK:

8 to 10 hours (low)
or 4 to 5 hours (high),
plus 30 minutes (high)

MAKES:

6 servings

TYPES OF COOKERS

● **Continuous slow cooker:** This type of slow cooker, the type for which all the recipes in this book are intended, cooks foods at a very low wattage. The heating coils or elements wrap around the sides of the cooker and remain on continuously. The low-heat setting cooks at about 200°F and the high-heat setting, at about 300°F. The cooker's ceramic liner may or may not be removable.

● **Intermittent slow cooker:** This type of slow cooker has the heating element or coil located below the food container. It cycles on and off during operation and has a dial that indicates temperatures in degrees. Because it works sporadically, this type of cooker is insufficient for recipes in this book.

Burgundy wines are made from Pinot Noir grapes. If you don't want to splurge on an expensive Burgundy wine from France, simply choose a good Pinot Noir from California.

BURGUNDY BEEF STEW

PREP:

20 minutes

COOK:

*10 to 12 hours (low)
or 5 to 6 hours (high)*

MAKES:

6 servings

2	pounds boneless beef chuck
1	teaspoon salt
¼	teaspoon black pepper
2	tablespoons cooking oil (optional)
2	tablespoons quick-cooking tapioca
6	large carrots, cut into 1-inch pieces
1	9-ounce package frozen cut green beans
½	of a 16-ounce package (2 cups) frozen small whole onions
1	14-ounce can beef broth
1	cup Burgundy
2	cloves garlic, minced
5	slices bacon, crisp-cooked, drained, and crumbled

1 Trim fat from meat. Cut meat into 1-inch pieces. Sprinkle with salt and pepper. If desired, in a large skillet brown meat, half at a time, in hot oil. Drain off fat.

2 Transfer meat to a 3½- or 4-quart slow cooker. Sprinkle with tapioca. Stir in carrots, green beans, onions, beef broth, wine, and garlic.

3 Cover and cook on low-heat setting for 10 to 12 hours or on high-heat setting for 5 to 6 hours. Sprinkle each serving with crumbled bacon.

Nutrition Facts per serving: 339 cal., 9 g total fat (3 g sat. fat), 95 mg chol., 862 mg sodium, 19 g carbo., 5 g fiber, 37 g pro. **Daily Values:** 416% vit. A, 22% vit. C, 9% calcium, 29% iron

Chipotle chile peppers are dried, smoked jalapeño peppers. Canned in piquant adobo sauce, they're packed with flavor and convenient for seasoning stews. You'll find them in the ethnic foods aisle of supermarkets or in Hispanic food markets.

NEW MEXICO BEEF STEW

1½	pounds boneless beef chuck
2	cups fresh corn kernels or one 10-ounce package frozen whole kernel corn, thawed
2	cups chopped peeled celery root or 1 cup sliced celery
1	15-ounce can garbanzo beans (chickpeas), drained
1	cup chopped onion
2	to 3 canned chipotle chile peppers in adobo sauce, chopped
3	cloves garlic, minced
1	teaspoon salt
1	teaspoon dried thyme, crushed
½	teaspoon black pepper
1	28-ounce can tomatoes, undrained and cut up

1 Trim fat from meat. Cut meat into ¾-inch pieces; set aside. In a 4- to 5½-quart slow cooker place corn, celery root, garbanzo beans, onion, chipotle peppers, and garlic. Add meat. Sprinkle with salt, thyme, and black pepper. Pour tomatoes over mixture in cooker.

2 Cover and cook on low-heat setting for 12 to 14 hours or on high-heat setting for 6 to 7 hours. Stir before serving. Season to taste with additional salt and black pepper.

Nutrition Facts per serving: 367 cal., 8 g total fat (2 g sat. fat), 54 mg chol., 1,078 mg sodium, 42 g carbo., 7 g fiber, 33 g pro. **Daily Values:** 19% vit. A, 48% vit. C, 10% calcium, 27% iron

PREP:

25 minutes

COOK:

12 to 14 hours (low) or 6 to 7 hours (high)

MAKES:

6 servings

If Steak Diane—a classic French dish—is one of your favorites, you'll love this hearty stew of the same name.

MUSHROOM STEAK DIANE STEW

PREP:

20 minutes

COOK:

8 to 10 hours (low)
or 4 to 5 hours (high)

MAKES:

6 servings

1½	pounds boneless beef round steak
2	medium onions, cut into thin wedges
3	cups sliced fresh button mushrooms (8 ounces)
1	10¾-ounce can condensed golden mushroom soup
¼	cup tomato paste
2	teaspoons Worcestershire sauce
1	teaspoon dry mustard
½	teaspoon cracked black pepper
3	cups hot cooked noodles

1 Trim fat from meat. Cut meat into 1-inch pieces. Set aside. In a 3½- or 4-quart slow cooker place onions; top with mushrooms. Add meat. In a medium bowl stir together mushroom soup, tomato paste, Worcestershire sauce, mustard, and pepper. Pour over mixture in cooker.

2 Cover and cook on low-heat setting for 8 to 10 hours or on high-heat setting for 4 to 5 hours. Serve over hot cooked noodles.

Nutrition Facts per serving: 314 cal., 7 g total fat (2 g sat. fat), 92 mg chol., 569 mg sodium, 30 g carbo., 3 g fiber, 33 g pro. **Daily Values:** 12% vit. A, 11% vit. C, 2% calcium, 25% iron

Perfect for a cozy dinner with friends, all this stew needs for accompaniment is some crusty bread, olives, and hearty red wine.

PROVENÇAL BEEF STEW

1½	pounds boneless beef chuck
8	tiny new potatoes
1	pound small carrots with tops, peeled and trimmed, or one 16-ounce package peeled baby carrots
1	large onion, cut into wedges
½	cup pitted green or ripe olives
1	cup beef broth
1	tablespoon quick-cooking tapioca
1	teaspoon dried herbes de Provence, crushed
¼	teaspoon salt
¼	teaspoon cracked black pepper
4	to 6 cloves garlic, minced
¼	cup dry red wine or beef broth
	Snipped fresh parsley (optional)
	Capers (optional)

PREP:

20 minutes

COOK:

10 to 12 hours (low) or 4 to 5 hours (high), plus 30 minutes

MAKES:

6 servings

1. Trim fat from meat. Cut meat into 2-inch pieces. Set aside. Remove a narrow strip of peel from center of each new potato. In a 3½- or 4-quart slow cooker place potatoes, carrots, onion, and olives. Add meat. In a small bowl combine beef broth, tapioca, herbes de Provence, salt, pepper, and garlic. Pour over mixture in cooker.

2. Cover and cook on low-heat setting for 10 to 12 hours or on high-heat setting for 4 to 5 hours. Stir in wine. Cover and cook for 30 minutes more.

3. If desired, sprinkle each serving with parsley and capers.

Nutrition Facts per serving: 198 cal., 5 g total fat (2 g sat. fat), 54 mg chol., 308 mg sodium, 16 g carbo., 3 g fiber, 20 g pro. **Daily Values:** 293% vit. A, 17% vit. C, 4% calcium, 18% iron

*Bacon and tomatoes are a match made in food heaven (ask any BLT lover!).
Here the duo works its magic on a rib-sticking stew.*

BACON BEEF STEW

PREP:

30 minutes

COOK:

*9 to 10 hours (low)
or 4½ to 5 hours (high)*

MAKES:

6 servings

6	slices bacon, cut into 1-inch pieces
1½	pounds boneless beef sirloin steak, cut 1 inch thick
2	medium potatoes, peeled and cut into ¾-inch pieces
2	cups packaged peeled baby carrots
1½	cups frozen small whole onions
1	14½-ounce can diced tomatoes with basil, oregano, and garlic, undrained
1	12-ounce jar brown gravy

1 In a large skillet cook bacon over medium heat until crisp. Drain bacon on paper towels, reserving 1 tablespoon drippings in skillet. Wrap bacon and chill until ready to serve. Trim fat from meat. Cut meat into 1-inch pieces. In the same skillet brown meat, half at a time, in hot drippings. Drain off fat. Set aside.

2 In a 3½- or 4-quart slow cooker place potatoes, carrots, and onions. Add meat. In a medium bowl combine tomatoes and gravy. Stir into mixture in cooker.

3 Cover and cook on low-heat setting for 9 to 10 hours or on high-heat setting for 4½ to 5 hours. Sprinkle each serving with bacon.

Nutrition Facts per serving: 326 cal., 12 g total fat (4 g sat. fat), 77 mg chol., 883 mg sodium, 26 g carbo., 4 g fiber, 30 g pro. **Daily Values:** 213% vit. A, 28% vit. C, 11% calcium, 26% iron

Cumin, cayenne, cinnamon, and dried fruits are what give this stew its interesting North African angle. What to serve with it? Couscous, of course, a quintessential Moroccan staple.

NORTH AFRICAN BEEF STEW

1½	pounds lean beef stew meat
2	medium sweet potatoes, peeled, halved lengthwise, and sliced ½ inch thick
1	medium onion, cut into wedges
1	cup water
1	teaspoon instant beef bouillon granules
¾	teaspoon ground cumin
¼	teaspoon cayenne pepper
⅛	teaspoon ground cinnamon
4	cloves garlic, minced
1	14½-ounce can diced tomatoes, undrained
½	cup dried apricots or pitted dried plums (prunes), quartered
	Hot cooked couscous (optional)
¼	cup chopped peanuts

PREP:

20 minutes

COOK:

7½ to 8½ hours (low) or 3½ to 4 hours (high), plus 30 minutes

MAKES:

6 servings

1 Cut meat into 1-inch pieces. In a 3½- or 4-quart slow cooker combine meat, sweet potatoes, and onion. Stir in water, bouillon granules, cumin, cayenne pepper, cinnamon, and garlic.

2 Cover and cook on low-heat setting for 7½ to 8½ hours or on high-heat setting for 3½ to 4 hours. Stir in tomatoes and dried apricots. Cover and cook for 30 minutes more.

3 If desired, serve meat mixture over hot cooked couscous. Sprinkle each serving with peanuts.

Nutrition Facts per serving: 274 cal., 7 g total fat (2 g sat. fat), 67 mg chol., 373 mg sodium, 24 g carbo., 4 g fiber, 27 g pro. **Daily Values:** 173% vit. A, 28% vit. C, 6% calcium, 23% iron

This traditional soup is plenty filling. It's also plenty easy thanks to canned beets (no peeling!) and sweet-and-sour cabbage (no slicing!).

BEEF, CABBAGE & BEET STEW

PREP:

15 minutes

COOK:

*8 to 10 hours (low)
or 4 to 5 hours (high)*

MAKES:

4 servings

12 ounces boneless beef chuck

1 tablespoon cooking oil

2 large carrots, finely chopped

1 large onion, cut into thin wedges

1 16-ounce jar sweet-and-sour red cabbage, drained

1 16-ounce can diced beets, drained

1 14-ounce can beef broth

Dairy sour cream (optional)

1 Trim fat from meat. Cut meat into $\frac{1}{2}$-inch pieces. In a large skillet brown meat in hot oil. Drain off fat. Transfer meat to a $3\frac{1}{2}$- or 4-quart slow cooker. Add carrots and onion. Top with cabbage and beets. Pour beef broth over mixture in cooker.

2 Cover and cook on low-heat setting for 8 to 10 hours or on high-heat setting for 4 to 5 hours.

3 If desired, top each serving with sour cream.

Nutrition Facts per serving: 281 cal., 8 g total fat (2 g sat. fat), 50 mg chol., 1,118 mg sodium, 33 g carbo., 7 g fiber, 20 g pro. **Daily Values:** 231% vit. A, 17% vit. C, 4% calcium, 21% iron

Here's the perfect supper to warm up with after a day of raking leaves or sledding. For dessert, serve some good old-fashioned cupcakes or spiced pumpkin bars purchased from the bakery.

FIRESIDE BEEF STEW

1	pound boneless beef chuck
2	tablespoons all-purpose flour
2	tablespoons cooking oil
1	pound tiny new potatoes, quartered
1	pound butternut squash, peeled, seeded, and cut into 1-inch pieces (about 2½ cups)
2	small onions, cut into wedges
2	cloves garlic, minced
1	14-ounce can beef broth
1	cup vegetable juice
2	tablespoons Worcestershire sauce
1	tablespoon lemon juice
½	teaspoon sugar
½	teaspoon paprika
¼	teaspoon black pepper
⅛	teaspoon ground allspice
1	9-ounce package frozen Italian green beans or 2 cups frozen peas

PREP:

25 minutes

COOK:

10 to 12 hours (low) or 5 to 6 hours (high), plus 15 minutes (high)

MAKES:

6 servings

1 Trim fat from meat. Cut meat into 1-inch pieces. Place flour in a plastic bag. Add meat pieces, a few at time, shaking to coat. In a large skillet brown meat in hot oil. Drain off fat.

2 Transfer meat to a 3½- to 4½-quart slow cooker. Add potatoes, squash, onions, and garlic. In a large bowl combine beef broth, vegetable juice, Worcestershire sauce, lemon juice, sugar, paprika, pepper, and allspice. Pour over mixture in cooker.

3 Cover and cook on low-heat setting for 10 to 12 hours or on high-heat setting for 5 to 6 hours.

4 If using low-heat setting, turn to high-heat setting. Stir in green beans. Cover and cook for 15 minutes more.

Nutrition Facts per serving: 304 cal., 13 g total fat (4 g sat. fat), 48 mg chol., 456 mg sodium, 30 g carbo., 4 g fiber, 19 g pro. **Daily Values:** 74% vit. A, 65% vit. C, 7% calcium, 24% iron

Hungarian paprika is lighter in color and more pungent in flavor than ordinary paprika. It may be labeled as sweet (mild) or hot. Look for it in specialty markets.

HUNGARIAN-STYLE GOULASH

PREP:

15 minutes

COOK:

10 to 12 hours (low) or 5 to 6 hours (high)

STAND:

10 minutes

MAKES:

6 servings

1½ pounds lean beef stew meat

3 medium potatoes, cut into 1-inch cubes

2 medium onions, chopped

2 cloves garlic, minced

1 14-ounce can beef broth

1 14-ounce can chunky tomatoes with garlic and spices, undrained

1 6-ounce can tomato paste

2 tablespoons hot-style Hungarian or regular paprika

1 teaspoon caraway or fennel seeds

½ teaspoon salt

1 8- or 9-ounce package frozen artichoke hearts, thawed

3 cups hot cooked noodles

⅓ cup dairy sour cream

1 Cut meat into 1-inch pieces. Set aside. In a 3½- to 5-quart slow cooker place potatoes, onions, and garlic. Add meat. In a medium bowl combine beef broth, tomatoes, tomato paste, paprika, caraway seeds, and salt. Pour over mixture in cooker.

2 Cover and cook on low-heat setting for 10 to 12 hours or on high-heat setting for 5 to 6 hours.

3 Turn off cooker. Stir in artichokes. Cover and let stand for 10 minutes. Serve over hot cooked noodles. Top each serving with sour cream.

Nutrition Facts per serving: 501 cal., 13 g total fat (5 g sat. fat), 121 mg chol., 820 mg sodium, 58 g carbo., 5 g fiber, 38 g pro. **Daily Values:** 29% vit. A, 64% vit. C, 9% calcium, 53% iron

Chipotle in adobo is doubly delicious: The smoky jalapeño is a direct hit of heat, while the adobo sauce is a slow burn. Together they flavor this chili with a deep richness only slow cooking provides.

BEEF & RED BEAN CHILI

1	cup dry red beans or kidney beans
2	pounds boneless beef chuck
1	large onion, coarsely chopped
1	tablespoon olive oil
1	15-ounce can tomato sauce
1	14½-ounce can diced tomatoes with mild green chiles, undrained
1	14-ounce can beef broth
1	or 2 canned chipotle chile peppers in adobo sauce, finely chopped, plus 2 teaspoons adobo sauce
2	teaspoons dried oregano, crushed
1	teaspoon ground cumin
½	teaspoon salt
1	medium red sweet pepper, chopped
¼	cup snipped fresh cilantro

PREP:

40 minutes

STAND:

1 hour

COOK:

10 to 12 hours (low) or 5 to 6 hours (high)

MAKES:

6 servings

1 Rinse beans. In a large saucepan combine beans and enough water to cover beans by 2 inches. Bring to boiling; reduce heat. Simmer, uncovered, for 10 minutes. Remove from heat. Cover and let stand for 1 hour. Drain and rinse beans.

2 Trim fat from meat. Cut meat into 1-inch pieces. In a large skillet cook half of the meat and the onion in hot oil until meat is brown. Transfer meat mixture to a 3½- or 4-quart slow cooker. Repeat with remaining meat. Stir beans, tomato sauce, tomatoes, beef broth, chipotle peppers and adobo sauce, oregano, cumin, and salt into meat mixture in cooker.

3 Cover and cook on low-heat setting for 10 to 12 hours or on high-heat setting for 5 to 6 hours. Top each serving with sweet pepper and cilantro.

Nutrition Facts per serving: 516 cal., 26 g total fat (9 g sat. fat), 98 mg chol., 1,162 mg sodium, 32 g carbo., 8 g fiber, 38 g pro. **Daily Values:** 34% vit. A, 91% vit. C, 7% calcium, 34% iron

Looking for a chili that is a little off beat? You found it. This recipe is from Gainesville, Florida, a fact that helps explain the funny name. It also could be called "everything but the kitchen sink" chili, as it boasts three different meats and a variety of chili seasonings.

SWAMP CHILI

PREP:

30 minutes

COOK:

*8 to 10 hours (low)
or 4 to 5 hours (high)*

MAKES:

6 servings

8	ounces bulk Italian sausage
1½	pounds boneless beef chuck
1	large onion, chopped
1	medium green sweet pepper, chopped
1	clove garlic, minced
2	cups water
1	14½-ounce can diced tomatoes, undrained
1	6-ounce can tomato paste
6	slices bacon, crisp-cooked, drained, and crumbled
1	to 2 fresh jalapeño chile peppers, seeded and finely chopped
1	small dried red chile pepper, seeded and crumbled
1	tablespoon chili powder
¼	teaspoon salt
¼	teaspoon dried oregano, crushed
1	15-ounce can pinto or red kidney beans, rinsed and drained

1 In a 4-quart Dutch oven cook Italian sausage until meat is brown. Using a slotted spoon, transfer sausage to a 3½- or 4-quart slow cooker, reserving drippings. Trim fat from beef. Cut beef into ½-inch pieces. Cook half of the beef in hot drippings until brown; transfer beef to cooker. Add remaining beef, the onion, sweet pepper, and garlic to Dutch oven. Cook until meat is brown and onion is tender. Drain off fat. Transfer beef mixture to cooker.

2 Stir in water, tomatoes, tomato paste, bacon, jalapeño peppers, dried chile pepper, chili powder, salt, and oregano.

3 Cover and cook on low-heat setting for 8 to 10 hours or on high-heat setting for 4 to 5 hours. Stir in beans; heat through.

Nutrition Facts per serving: 430 cal., 19 g total fat (4 g sat. fat), 78 mg chol., 658 mg sodium, 25 g carbo., 6 g fiber, 37 g pro. **Daily Values:** 28% vit. A, 87% vit. C, 9% calcium, 33% iron

HANDLING HOT CHILE PEPPERS
Because hot chile peppers contain volatile oils that can burn your skin and eyes, avoid direct contact with chiles as much as possible. When working with chile peppers, wear plastic or rubber gloves. If your bare hands do touch the chile peppers, wash your hands well with soap and water.

The Old World and New World hook up in this one-dish meal that melds favored Italian ingredients (Italian sausage, basil, and oregano) with the stuff of quintessential Tex-Mex chili.

HAMBURGER-BEAN SOUP

1	pound lean ground beef
8	ounces bulk Italian sausage
1	cup chopped onion
1	cup chopped green sweet pepper
3	cloves garlic, minced
1	28-ounce can whole Italian-style tomatoes, undrained and cut up
1	15-ounce can garbanzo beans (chickpeas), rinsed and drained
1	15-ounce can light red kidney beans, rinsed and drained
1	cup water
3	tablespoons Worcestershire sauce
2	to 3 tablespoons chili powder
2	teaspoons dried basil, crushed
2	teaspoons dried oregano, crushed
½	teaspoon bottled hot pepper sauce (optional)
¼	teaspoon salt
	Hot cooked rice (optional)
	Shredded cheddar cheese (optional)

PREP:

20 minutes

COOK:

6 to 8 hours (low) or 3 to 4 hours (high)

MAKES:

6 to 8 servings

1 In a large skillet cook ground beef, sausage, onion, sweet pepper, and garlic until meat is brown. Drain off fat.

2 Transfer meat mixture to a 3½- or 4-quart slow cooker. Stir in tomatoes, garbanzo beans, kidney beans, water, Worcestershire sauce, chili powder, basil, oregano, hot pepper sauce (if desired), and salt.

3 Cover and cook on low-heat setting for 6 to 8 hours or on high-heat setting for 3 to 4 hours.

4 If desired, serve over hot cooked rice and sprinkle each serving with cheddar cheese.

Nutrition Facts per serving: 436 cal., 20 g total fat (7 g sat. fat), 72 mg chol., 992 mg sodium, 36 g carbo., 10 g fiber, 29 g pro. **Daily Values:** 38% vit. A, 71% vit. C, 14% calcium, 28% iron

Italian wedding soup derives its name from the blissful union of its meats and greens. The different varieties are based on the local availability of ingredients.

ITALIAN WEDDING SOUP

PREP:

30 minutes

COOK:

8 to 10 hours (low) or 4 to 5 hours (high), plus 15 minutes (high)

MAKES:

6 servings

1	large onion
1	slightly beaten egg
¼	cup fine dry bread crumbs
3	oil-packed dried tomatoes, finely chopped
2	teaspoons dried Italian seasoning, crushed
1	pound lean ground beef
2	teaspoons olive oil
1	large fennel bulb
4	14-ounce cans chicken broth
½	teaspoon freshly ground white pepper
6	cloves garlic, thinly sliced
1	cup dried orzo pasta (rosamarina)
5	cups shredded fresh spinach

1 Finely chop one-third of the onion; thinly slice remaining onion. In a medium bowl combine the chopped onion, egg, bread crumbs, dried tomatoes, and 1 teaspoon of the Italian seasoning. Add ground beef; mix well. Shape into 12 meatballs. In a large skillet brown meatballs in hot oil. Drain off fat. Transfer meatballs to a 4½- to 5½-quart slow cooker. Add the sliced onion.

2 Cut off and discard upper stalks of fennel. If desired, save some of the feathery leaves for garnish. Remove any wilted outer layers; cut off a thin slice from fennel base. Cut fennel into thin wedges. Stir fennel, chicken broth, white pepper, garlic, and remaining 1 teaspoon Italian seasoning into mixture in cooker.

3 Cover and cook on low-heat setting for 8 to 10 hours or on high-heat setting for 4 to 5 hours.

4 If using low-heat setting, turn to high-heat setting. Gently stir in orzo. Cover and cook about 15 minutes more or until orzo is tender. Stir in spinach. If desired, garnish each serving with reserved fennel leaves.

Nutrition Facts per serving: 308 cal., 12 g total fat (4 g sat. fat), 83 mg chol., 1,034 mg sodium, 24 g carbo., 5 g fiber, 25 g pro. **Daily Values:** 31% vit. A, 30% vit. C, 9% calcium, 29% iron

Cinnamon, apples, almonds, and raisins (as a final touch, if you opt for them) are not your usual chili ingredients and this is not your usual chili.

FRUIT & NUT CHILI

1½	pounds lean ground beef
2	cups chopped onions
2	cups coarsely chopped green, red, and/or yellow sweet peppers
2	cups coarsely chopped cooking apples
1	15-ounce can red kidney beans, rinsed and drained
1	14½-ounce can diced tomatoes, undrained
1	14-ounce can chicken broth
1	8-ounce can tomato sauce
2	4-ounce cans diced green chile peppers, undrained
3	tablespoons chili powder
2	tablespoons brown sugar
½	teaspoon ground cinnamon
3	cloves garlic, minced
⅔	cup slivered almonds, toasted
	Raisins, shredded cheddar cheese, and/or dairy sour cream (optional)

PREP:

25 minutes

COOK:

8 to 10 hours (low) or 4 to 5 hours (high)

MAKES:

8 servings

1 In a large skillet cook ground beef until meat is brown. Drain off fat. Transfer meat to a 4½- or 5-quart slow cooker.

2 Stir onions, sweet peppers, apples, kidney beans, tomatoes, chicken broth, tomato sauce, green chile peppers, chili powder, brown sugar, cinnamon, and garlic into meat in cooker.

3 Cover and cook on low-heat setting for 8 to 10 hours or on high-heat setting for 4 to 5 hours. Stir in almonds. If desired, top each serving with raisins, cheese, and/or sour cream.

Nutrition Facts per serving: 372 cal., 18 g total fat (5 g sat. fat), 53 mg chol., 663 mg sodium, 33 g carbo., 8 g fiber, 25 g pro. **Daily Values:** 24% vit. A, 83% vit. C, 13% calcium, 22% iron

This recipe was developed with large slow cookers—and a housefull of friends—in mind. You'll love having leftovers. Spoon them over baked potatoes or make chili dogs with your favorite franks.

SOUTHWEST CHILI

PREP:

20 minutes

COOK:

8 to 10 hours (low) or 4 to 5 hours (high)

MAKES:

8 servings

2	pounds lean ground beef
2	cups chopped onions
1/2	cup chopped green or red sweet pepper
6	cloves garlic, minced
3 1/2	cups water
1	12-ounce can tomato paste
1	15-ounce can dark red kidney beans, rinsed and drained
1	15-ounce can Great Northern beans, rinsed and drained
1	14 1/2-ounce can diced tomatoes, undrained
1	tablespoon prepared mustard
1	teaspoon chili powder
1	teaspoon black pepper
1/2	to 1 teaspoon cayenne pepper
1/2	teaspoon salt
1/2	teaspoon ground cumin

1 In a 12-inch skillet cook ground beef, onions, sweet pepper, and garlic until meat is brown. Drain off fat.

2 Transfer meat mixture to a 4 1/2- to 6-quart slow cooker. In a medium bowl stir together the water and tomato paste; pour over meat mixture in cooker. Stir in kidney beans, Great Northern beans, tomatoes, mustard, chili powder, black pepper, cayenne pepper, salt, and cumin.

3 Cover and cook on low-heat setting for 8 to 10 hours or on high-heat setting for 4 to 5 hours.

Nutrition Facts per serving: 414 cal., 18 g total fat (7 g sat. fat), 75 mg chol., 772 mg sodium, 36 g carbo., 9 g fiber, 32 g pro. **Daily Values:** 25% vit. A, 54% vit. C, 9% calcium, 27% iron

COOKER SIZES

When deciding what size cooker you should buy, consider how many people you usually cook for and the type of cooking you do. For singles, a 1 1/2-quart cooker is best. Choose a 3 1/2-quart cooker for a couple. A family of three or four will need a 3 1/2- to 4 1/2-quart cooker; families of four or five, a 4 1/2- or 5-quart cooker. A 6-quart cooker is the best option for larger families, preparing potluck meals, or cooking to have enough food to freeze for another meal. If you frequently cook large roasts, keep in mind that they fit better in a 5- to 6-quart cooker.

Cincinnati is famous for its chili parlors, where intriguingly spiced mixtures like this one are served over spaghetti and often topped with cheese.

CINCINNATI CHILI

1	bay leaf
½	teaspoon whole allspice
½	teaspoon whole cloves
2	pounds lean ground beef
2	cups chopped onions
1	15-ounce can dark red kidney beans, rinsed and drained
1	15-ounce can tomato sauce
1½	cups water
3	tablespoons chili powder
1	teaspoon Worcestershire sauce
¾	teaspoon ground cumin
¾	teaspoon ground cinnamon
½	teaspoon salt
¼	teaspoon cayenne pepper
4	cloves garlic, minced
½	ounce unsweetened chocolate, chopped
12	ounces dried spaghetti, cooked and drained
1	cup shredded cheddar cheese (4 ounces)

PREP:

30 minutes

COOK:

8 to 10 hours (low) or 4 to 5 hours (high)

MAKES:

6 servings

1 For spice bag, cut a double thickness of 100-percent-cotton cheesecloth into a 4-inch square. Place bay leaf, allspice, and cloves in center of cloth. Bring corners together and tie with a clean string.

2 In a large skillet cook ground beef until meat is brown. Drain off fat. Transfer meat to a 3½- or 4-quart slow cooker.

3 Stir onions, kidney beans, tomato sauce, water, chili powder, Worcestershire sauce, cumin, cinnamon, salt, cayenne pepper, and garlic into meat in cooker. Stir in spice bag.

4 Cover and cook on low-heat setting for 8 to 10 hours or on high-heat setting for 4 to 5 hours, stirring in chocolate the last 30 minutes of cooking. Remove spice bag.

5 Serve chili over hot cooked spaghetti. Sprinkle each serving with cheddar cheese.

Nutrition Facts per serving: 701 cal., 28 g total fat (12 g sat. fat), 115 mg chol., 889 mg sodium, 66 g carbo., 8 g fiber, 48 g pro. **Daily Values:** 31% vit. A, 10% vit. C, 21% calcium, 40% iron

Balsamic vinegar and roasted red peppers add a new Italian angle to this utterly up-to-date soup. Both were once hard-to-find ingredients that are now widely available.

PORK & RED PEPPER SOUP

PREP:

25 minutes

COOK:

*6 to 8 hours (low)
or 3 to 4 hours (high),
plus 15 minutes (high)*

MAKES:

6 servings

1½   pounds boneless pork shoulder

2   14-ounce cans beef broth

1   14½-ounce can diced tomatoes with basil, oregano, and garlic, undrained

1   7-ounce jar roasted red sweet peppers, drained and cut into bite-size strips (1 cup)

½   cup chopped onion

2   tablespoons balsamic vinegar

¼   teaspoon black pepper

2   medium zucchini, halved lengthwise and sliced ¼ inch thick

1 Trim fat from meat. Cut meat into 1-inch pieces. In a 3½- or 4-quart slow cooker combine meat, beef broth, tomatoes, roasted sweet peppers, onion, vinegar, and pepper.

2 Cover and cook on low-heat setting for 6 to 8 hours or on high-heat setting for 3 to 4 hours.

3 If using low-heat setting, turn to high-heat setting. Stir in zucchini. Cover and cook about 15 minutes more or until zucchini is crisp-tender.

Nutrition Facts per serving: 177 cal., 6 g total fat (2 g sat. fat), 51 mg chol., 887 mg sodium, 12 g carbo., 2 g fiber, 18 g pro. **Daily Values:** 13% vit. A, 133% vit. C, 7% calcium, 15% iron

Thanks to some peanut butter and a sprinkling of peanuts, this luscious soup has an unmistakably nutty flavor. Serve it with breadsticks and a refreshing green salad made with crinkly napa cabbage.

PORK & PEANUT SOUP

1½   pounds boneless pork shoulder
1   15-ounce can hominy, drained
1   cup chopped carrots
1   medium green sweet pepper, cut into ¾-inch pieces
1   medium onion, chopped
1   stalk celery, chopped
1   cup reduced-sodium chicken broth
¼   cup peanut butter
1   14½-ounce can stewed tomatoes, undrained
2   tablespoons chopped peanuts

1 Trim fat from meat. Cut meat into 1-inch pieces. Set aside.

2 In a 3½- or 4-quart slow cooker combine hominy, carrots, sweet pepper, onion, and celery. Add meat. In a medium bowl gradually whisk chicken broth into peanut butter; stir in stewed tomatoes. Pour over mixture in cooker.

3 Cover and cook on low-heat setting for 7 to 9 hours or on high-heat setting for 3½ to 4½ hours. Sprinkle each serving with peanuts.

Nutrition Facts per serving: 290 cal., 13 g total fat (3 g sat. fat), 51 mg chol., 522 mg sodium, 23 g carbo., 5 g fiber, 21 g pro. **Daily Values:** 116% vit. A, 39% vit. C, 7% calcium, 13% iron

PREP:

15 minutes

COOK:

7 to 9 hours (low)
or 3½ to 4½ hours (high)

MAKES:

6 servings

This sophisticated soup is a winter vegetable extravaganza. Fresh spinach added just prior to serving boosts the nutritional value.

SPICY PORK & VEGETABLE SOUP

PREP:

30 minutes

COOK:

*10 to 11 hours (low)
or 5 to 5¹/₂ hours (high)*

MAKES:

6 servings

1   pound lean pork or beef stew meat

1   tablespoon cooking oil

¹/₂   cup chopped onion

1   teaspoon paprika

2   cloves garlic, minced

3   cups water

8   ounces winter squash, peeled and cut into ¹/₂-inch pieces

3   medium parsnips or carrots, cut into ¹/₄-inch slices

1   medium sweet potato, peeled and cut into ¹/₂-inch pieces

1   8³/₄-ounce can whole kernel corn, undrained

4   teaspoons instant beef bouillon granules

¹/₂   teaspoon salt

¹/₄   teaspoon cayenne pepper

2   cups torn fresh spinach

1 Cut meat into ¹/₂-inch pieces. In a large skillet cook half of the meat in hot oil until brown. Transfer meat to a 3¹/₂- or 4-quart slow cooker. Add remaining meat, the onion, paprika, and garlic to skillet. Cook until meat is brown and onion is tender. Drain off fat. Transfer meat mixture to cooker.

2 Stir water, squash, parsnips, sweet potato, corn, bouillon granules, salt, and cayenne pepper into meat mixture in cooker. Cover and cook on low-heat setting for 10 to 11 hours or on high-heat setting for 5 to 5¹/₂ hours.

3 Just before serving, stir in spinach.

Nutrition Facts per serving: 243 cal., 9 g total fat (2 g sat. fat), 51 mg chol., 907 mg sodium, 25 g carbo., 5 g fiber, 18 g pro. **Daily Values:** 146% vit. A, 32% vit. C, 7% calcium, 15% iron

Eat this Asian-influenced soup with both taste and nutrition in mind. Green soybeans (edamame) are great sources of soy, which is associated with a reduced risk of some types of cancer and the promotion of good bone health.

PORK & EDAMAME SOUP

2	pounds boneless pork shoulder
1	tablespoon cooking oil
2	14-ounce cans chicken broth
1	12-ounce package frozen green soybeans (edamame)
1	8-ounce can sliced water chestnuts, drained
1	cup chopped red sweet pepper
2	tablespoons light soy sauce
1	tablespoon bottled hoisin sauce
2	teaspoons grated fresh ginger
$1/4$	to $1/2$ teaspoon crushed red pepper
6	cloves garlic, minced
1	3-ounce package ramen noodles, broken

PREP:

25 minutes

COOK:

7 to 8 hours (low) or $3^{1}/_{2}$ to 4 hours (high), plus 5 minutes

MAKES:

6 servings

1 Trim fat from meat. Cut meat into 1-inch pieces. In a large skillet brown meat, half at a time, in hot oil. Drain off fat.

2 Transfer meat to a $3^{1}/_{2}$- to $4^{1}/_{2}$-quart slow cooker. Stir in chicken broth, soybeans, water chestnuts, sweet pepper, soy sauce, hoisin sauce, ginger, crushed red pepper, and garlic.

3 Cover and cook on low-heat setting for 7 to 8 hours or on high-heat setting for $3^{1}/_{2}$ to 4 hours. Skim off fat. Stir in ramen noodles (reserve seasoning packet for another use). Cover and cook for 5 minutes more.

Nutrition Facts per serving: 400 cal., 15 g total fat (4 g sat. fat), 111 mg chol., 906 mg sodium, 22 g carbo., 7 g fiber, 41 g pro. **Daily Values:** 29% vit. A, 85% vit. C, 8% calcium, 23% iron

Sweet-and-sour pork, an all-time favorite Chinese standby, is high in fat because the pork is battered and fried. Here's a soup with the same basic flavoring, but not nearly as much fat.

SWEET-SOUR PORK STEW

PREP:

20 minutes

COOK:

7 to 9 hours (low)
or 3½ to 4½ hours (high)

MAKES:

4 to 6 servings

1½	pounds lean pork stew meat
3	tablespoons all-purpose flour
½	teaspoon salt
¼	teaspoon black pepper
1	tablespoon cooking oil
1	cup chopped onion
5	medium carrots, cut into ½-inch slices
1	14½-ounce can diced tomatoes, undrained
¼	cup packed brown sugar
¼	cup vinegar
2	tablespoons quick-cooking tapioca
1	tablespoon Worcestershire sauce

1 Cut meat into 1-inch pieces. In a plastic bag combine flour, salt, and pepper. Add meat pieces, a few at a time, shaking to coat. In a large skillet cook half of the meat in hot oil until brown. Transfer meat to a 3½- or 4-quart slow cooker. Add remaining meat and the onion to skillet. Cook until meat is brown and onion is tender. Drain off fat. Transfer meat mixture to cooker. Add carrots.

2 In a medium bowl combine tomatoes, brown sugar, vinegar, tapioca, and Worcestershire sauce. Pour over mixture in cooker.

3 Cover and cook on low-heat setting for 7 to 9 hours or on high-heat setting for 3½ to 4½ hours.

Nutrition Facts per serving: 394 cal., 10 g total fat (3 g sat. fat), 95 mg chol., 619 mg sodium, 41 g carbo., 4 g fiber, 34 g pro. **Daily Values:** 386% vit. A, 36% vit. C, 11% calcium, 18% iron

Tortilla chips make a fun accompaniment to this south-of-the-border spiced stew.

TACO PORK STEW

1½	pounds lean pork stew meat
1	tablespoon cooking oil
1	15-ounce can red kidney beans, rinsed and drained
1½	cups frozen whole kernel corn
1	cup frozen small whole onions
1	14½-ounce can diced tomatoes, undrained
1	8-ounce can tomato sauce
1	cup water
1	1¼-ounce envelope taco seasoning mix
½	teaspoon ground cumin
⅓	cup shredded cheddar cheese
⅓	cup dairy sour cream

1 Cut meat into 1-inch pieces. In a large skillet brown meat, half at a time, in hot oil. Drain off fat. Transfer meat to a 3½- or 4-quart slow cooker. Stir in kidney beans, corn, and onions. In a medium bowl combine tomatoes, tomato sauce, water, taco seasoning mix, and cumin. Stir into mixture in cooker.

2 Cover and cook on low-heat setting for 8 to 10 hours or on high-heat setting for 4 to 5 hours. Top each serving with cheese and sour cream.

Nutrition Facts per serving: 360 cal., 15 g total fat (5 g sat. fat), 85 mg chol., 1,171 mg sodium, 30 g carbo., 7 g fiber, 33 g pro. Daily Values: 4% vit. A, 16% vit. C, 13% calcium, 15% iron

PREP:

15 minutes

COOK:

8 to 10 hours (low)
or 4 to 5 hours (high)

MAKES:

6 servings

Two kinds of pork make this hearty stew extra flavorful. Sop up the wine-flavored gravy with chunks of Italian bread or rolls.

ITALIAN PORK STEW

PREP:

30 minutes

STAND:

1 hour

COOK:

7 to 8 hours (low) or 3 1/2 to 4 hours (high), plus 15 minutes (high)

MAKES:

6 servings

2	cups dry Great Northern beans
8	ounces bulk Italian sausage
1	pound lean boneless pork
1 1/2	cups coarsely chopped onions
3	medium carrots, cut into 1/2-inch slices
1	teaspoon instant beef bouillon granules
1/2	teaspoon dried thyme, crushed
1/2	teaspoon dried oregano, crushed
3	cloves garlic, minced
1/4	cup dry red wine or water
1/2	of a 6-ounce can (1/3 cup) tomato paste
1/4	cup snipped fresh parsley

1 Rinse beans. In a large saucepan combine beans and 6 cups water. Bring to boiling; reduce heat. Simmer, uncovered, for 10 minutes. Remove from heat. Cover and let stand for 1 hour. Drain and rinse beans. Transfer beans to a 4- to 5-quart slow cooker.

2 In a large skillet cook Italian sausage until meat is brown. Using a slotted spoon, transfer sausage to cooker, reserving drippings. Trim fat from pork. Cut pork into 1/2-inch pieces. Cook pork, half at a time, in hot drippings until brown. Drain off fat. Transfer pork to cooker. Stir in onions, carrots, bouillon granules, thyme, oregano, and garlic. Stir in 3 cups *fresh water.*

3 Cover and cook on low-heat setting for 7 to 8 hours or on high-heat setting for 3 1/2 to 4 hours.

4 If using low-heat setting, turn to high-heat setting. In a small bowl stir wine into tomato paste; add to cooker. Stir in parsley. Cover and cook for 15 minutes more.

Nutrition Facts per serving: 473 cal., 13 g total fat (5 g sat. fat), 73 mg chol., 566 mg sodium, 49 g carbo., 15 g fiber, 37 g pro. **Daily Values:** 164% vit. A, 29% vit. C, 15% calcium, 24% iron

Here boneless pork shoulder—an everyday cut of meat—gets a bistro-style update with fresh fennel, sweet peppers, and an herb-cream base.

RED PEPPER, PORK & FENNEL STEW

3	medium onions, cut into thin wedges
2	small fennel bulbs, trimmed and cut into ½-inch wedges
1	14-ounce can beef broth
4	teaspoons quick-cooking tapioca
½	teaspoon dried marjoram or savory, crushed
¼	teaspoon salt
¼	teaspoon cracked black pepper
1½	pounds boneless pork shoulder
1	tablespoon olive or cooking oil
1	7-ounce jar roasted red sweet peppers, drained and cut into thin strips (1 cup)
⅓	cup whipping cream
3	cups hot cooked rice

PREP:

20 minutes

COOK:

8 to 10 hours (low)
or 4 to 5 hours (high)

MAKES:

6 servings

1 In a 3½- or 4-quart slow cooker combine onions and fennel. Stir in beef broth, tapioca, marjoram, salt, and pepper.

2 Trim fat from meat. Cut meat into 1-inch pieces. In a large skillet brown meat, half at a time, in hot oil. Drain off fat. Transfer meat to cooker.

3 Cover and cook on low-heat setting for 8 to 10 hours or on high-heat setting for 4 to 5 hours. Stir in roasted sweet peppers and cream. Serve over hot cooked rice.

Nutrition Facts per serving: 387 cal., 16 g total fat (7 g sat. fat), 95 mg chol., 425 mg sodium, 32 g carbo., 9 g fiber, 26 g pro. **Daily Values:** 4% vit. A, 125% vit. C, 7% calcium, 12% iron

The few extra minutes it takes to brown the pork are well spent. Browning brings out the flavor of the meat and results in an appealing color.

GREEN CHILE STEW

PREP:

25 minutes

COOK:

*7 to 8 hours (low)
or 3 1/2 to 4 hours (high)*

MAKES:

5 or 6 servings

2	pounds boneless pork sirloin or shoulder
1	tablespoon cooking oil
1/2	cup chopped onion
4	medium potatoes, peeled and cut into 1/2-inch cubes
3	cups water
1	15-ounce can hominy or whole kernel corn, drained
2	4-ounce cans diced green chile peppers, undrained
2	tablespoons quick-cooking tapioca
1	teaspoon garlic salt
1/2	teaspoon salt
1/2	teaspoon black pepper
1/2	teaspoon ground cumin
1/8	teaspoon dried oregano, crushed
	Snipped fresh cilantro (optional)

1 Trim fat from meat. Cut meat into 1/2-inch pieces. In a large skillet cook half of the meat in hot oil until brown. Transfer meat to a 3 1/2- to 4 1/2-quart slow cooker. Add remaining meat and the onion to skillet. Cook until meat is brown and onion is tender. Drain off fat. Transfer meat mixture to cooker.

2 Stir in potatoes, water, hominy, green chile peppers, tapioca, garlic salt, salt, black pepper, cumin, and oregano. Cover and cook on low-heat setting for 7 to 8 hours or on high-heat setting for 3 1/2 to 4 hours. If desired, sprinkle each serving with cilantro.

Nutrition Facts per serving: 414 cal., 11 g total fat (3 g sat. fat), 102 mg chol., 980 mg sodium, 40 g carbo., 5 g fiber, 40 g pro. **Daily Values:** 1% vit. A, 55% vit. C, 7% calcium, 24% iron

VOLUME IS VITAL

The slow cooker must be at least half full but not more than two-thirds full in order for the food to cook to proper doneness in the time range given. If you decide to skip an ingredient (for example, you want to leave out the potatoes in a stew recipe), replace that ingredient with something else or increase another ingredient (such as the carrots) to keep the volume in the slow cooker at the correct level. When choosing a recipe, be sure it is intended for the size of slow cooker you own.

Satay is an Indonesian specialty of spicy marinated meat that's skewered, then broiled or grilled. Bring its lively flavors home with this easy, full-flavored stew.

PORK SATAY STEW

1½	pounds boneless pork shoulder
2	medium red and/or green sweet peppers, cut into 1-inch pieces
1	large red onion, cut into wedges
1	cup bottled thick and chunky salsa
½	cup creamy peanut butter
1	tablespoon reduced-sodium soy sauce
1	tablespoon lime juice
1½	teaspoons grated fresh ginger
½	teaspoon ground coriander
¾	cup half-and-half or light cream
3	cups hot cooked rice
⅓	cup chopped dry roasted peanuts
¼	cup sliced green onions

1 Trim fat from meat. Cut meat into 1-inch pieces. In a 3½-quart slow cooker combine meat, sweet peppers, onion, salsa, peanut butter, soy sauce, lime juice, ginger, and coriander.

2 Cover and cook on low-heat setting for 7 to 8 hours or on high-heat setting for 3½ to 4 hours. Stir in cream. Serve over hot cooked rice. Sprinkle each serving with peanuts and green onions.

Nutrition Facts per serving: 502 cal., 25 g total fat (7 g sat. fat), 84 mg chol., 462 mg sodium, 36 g carbo., 3 g fiber, 34 g pro. **Daily Values:** 46% vit. A, 112% vit. C, 8% calcium, 19% iron

PREP:

15 minutes

COOK:

7 to 8 hours (low) or 3½ to 4 hours (high)

MAKES:

6 servings

Dried apricots and pumpkin pie spice, a balance of sweetness and zest, enliven the pork and winter squash mix. Any type of winter squash will do, although butternut is easiest to peel.

PORK & SQUASH STEW

PREP:

20 minutes

COOK:

*7 to 8 hours (low)
or 3½ to 4 hours (high)*

MAKES:

4 servings

1½   pounds boneless pork shoulder

2   tablespoons cooking oil

1½   pounds winter squash (such as butternut, hubbard, or acorn), peeled, seeded, and cut into 1-inch pieces

½   cup sliced onion

½   cup dried apricots

2   tablespoons raisins

3   tablespoons instant flour or ¼ cup packaged instant mashed potato flakes

1   tablespoon brown sugar

¾   teaspoon pumpkin pie spice

¼   teaspoon salt

1   14-ounce can chicken broth

1   tablespoon bottled steak sauce

1 Trim fat from meat. Cut meat into 1-inch pieces. In a large skillet brown meat, half at a time, in hot oil. Drain off fat. Set aside.

2 In a 3½- or 4-quart slow cooker combine squash, onion, apricots, and raisins. Add meat. Sprinkle with instant flour, brown sugar, pumpkin pie spice, and salt. In a medium bowl combine chicken broth and steak sauce; pour over mixture in cooker.

3 Cover and cook on low-heat setting for 7 to 8 hours or on high-heat setting for 3½ to 4 hours. Stir gently before serving.

Nutrition Facts per serving: 469 cal., 21 g total fat (6 g sat. fat), 115 mg chol., 771 mg sodium, 33 g carbo., 2 g fiber, 38 g pro. **Daily Values:** 131% vit. A, 22% vit. C, 8% calcium, 22% iron

Here you need only six rustic ingredients to prove once again that sometimes the most satisfying recipes are also the simplest.

PEASANT-STYLE PORK & CABBAGE STEW

1½	pounds boneless pork shoulder
2	medium carrots, thinly sliced
1	15-ounce can white kidney (cannellini) or Great Northern beans, rinsed and drained
1	14½-ounce can diced tomatoes with onion and garlic, undrained
¼	cup dry white wine or water
3	cups shredded cabbage

1 Trim fat from meat. Cut meat into 1-inch pieces. Set aside.

2 In a 3½- or 4-quart slow cooker place carrots. Add meat, kidney beans, tomatoes, and wine.

3 Cover and cook on low-heat setting for 7 to 8 hours or on high-heat setting for 3½ to 4 hours. If using low-heat setting, turn to high-heat setting. Stir in cabbage. Cover and cook for 30 minutes more.

Nutrition Facts per serving: 377 cal., 12 g total fat (4 g sat. fat), 113 mg chol., 568 mg sodium, 28 g carbo., 7 g fiber, 41 g pro. **Daily Values:** 172% vit. A, 56% vit. C, 12% calcium, 23% iron

PREP:

15 minutes

COOK:

7 to 8 hours (low) or 3½ to 4 hours (high), plus 30 minutes (high)

MAKES:

4 servings

You'll enjoy this boldly flavored chili even more if you eat it with a soothing side dish. Creamy Apple Salad (page 344) is a fruity, fluffy option.

SOUTHWEST TWO-MEAT & BEER CHILI

PREP:

20 minutes

COOK:

8 to 10 hours (low) or 4 to 5 hours (high)

MAKES:

6 servings

12	ounces boneless beef sirloin steak, cut 1 inch thick
12	ounces lean pork stew meat
¼	cup all-purpose flour
1	tablespoon cooking oil
2	14½-ounce cans diced tomatoes with basil, oregano, and garlic, undrained
1	15-ounce can red kidney beans, rinsed and drained
1	12-ounce can beer or 1½ cups beef broth
1	8-ounce can tomato sauce
1	medium onion, chopped
2	tablespoons chili powder
1	teaspoon ground cumin
¼	teaspoon ground cinnamon

1. Trim fat from beef. Cut beef and pork into 1-inch pieces. In a plastic bag place flour. Add meat pieces, a few at a time, shaking to coat. In a large skillet brown meat, half at a time, in hot oil. Drain off fat.

2. Transfer meat to a 4- to 5-quart slow cooker. Stir in tomatoes, kidney beans, beer, tomato sauce, onion, chili powder, cumin, and cinnamon. Cover and cook on low-heat setting for 8 to 10 hours or on high-heat setting for 4 to 5 hours.

Nutrition Facts per serving: 339 cal., 8 g total fat (2 g sat. fat), 71 mg chol., 1,105 mg sodium, 34 g carbo., 6 g fiber, 32 g pro. **Daily Values:** 34% vit. A, 21% vit. C, 13% calcium, 32% iron

If you've never had the pleasure of trying green salsa, look forward to it. It's made with tomatillos, a fruit that looks like a green tomato but has citrus and apple-flavor tones. Along with the cilantro, the green salsa adds color and appeal. Corn bread is the perfect accompaniment.

WHITE & GREEN CHILI

1½	pounds lean ground pork
1	cup chopped onion
2	15-ounce cans Great Northern beans, rinsed and drained
1	16-ounce jar green salsa
1	14-ounce can chicken broth
1½	teaspoons ground cumin
2	tablespoons snipped fresh cilantro
⅓	cup dairy sour cream (optional)

1 In a large skillet cook ground pork and onion until meat is brown and onion is tender. Drain off fat.

2 Transfer meat mixture to a 3½- to 4½-quart slow cooker. Stir in Great Northern beans, salsa, chicken broth, and cumin. Cover and cook on low-heat setting for 7 to 8 hours or on high-heat setting for 3½ to 4 hours. Stir in cilantro.

3 If desired, top each serving with sour cream and additional cilantro.

Nutrition Facts per serving: 348 cal., 9 g total fat (4 g sat. fat), 53 mg chol., 613 mg sodium, 39 g carbo., 9 g fiber, 26 g pro. **Daily Values:** 1% vit. A, 19% vit. C, 15% calcium, 18% iron

PREP:

20 minutes

COOK:

*7 to 8 hours (low)
or 3½ to 4 hours (high)*

MAKES:

6 servings

Ever notice how nacho cheese dips disappear quickly at parties? This similarly flavored soup has much the same effect at the dinner table.

NACHO CHEESE SOUP

PREP:

25 minutes

COOK:

*4 to 6 hours (low)
or 2 to 3 hours (high)*

MAKES:

8 servings

1   pound lean ground pork or beef

2   11-ounce cans whole kernel corn with sweet peppers, drained

2   11-ounce cans condensed nacho cheese soup

2   cups water

1   16-ounce jar salsa

2   4-ounce cans diced green chile peppers, undrained

1   cup crushed tortilla chips

$^1/_2$ cup dairy sour cream

1 In a large skillet cook ground pork until meat is brown. Drain off fat.

2 Transfer meat to a 3$^1/_2$- or 4-quart slow cooker. Stir in corn, cheese soup, water, salsa, and green chile peppers.

3 Cover and cook on low-heat setting for 4 to 6 hours or on high-heat setting for 2 to 3 hours. Top each serving with chips and sour cream.

Nutrition Facts per serving: 396 cal., 23 g total fat (9 g sat. fat), 55 mg chol., 1,252 mg sodium, 33 g carbo., 5 g fiber, 17 g pro. **Daily Values:** 30% vit. A, 43% vit. C, 14% calcium, 14% iron

Bake up some Bacon-Cheese Corn Muffins (page 363) to add extra homespun appeal to a dinner starring this legendary soup.

GREEN BEANS, HAM & LENTIL SOUP

1¼	cups dry lentils
2	14-ounce cans chicken broth
2	cups cubed cooked ham
1½	cups chopped carrots
1	9-ounce package frozen cut green beans
1	cup frozen small whole onions
1	cup water
1	teaspoon dried thyme, crushed
½	teaspoon dried marjoram, crushed

PREP:

15 minutes

COOK:

8 to 10 hours (low)
or 4 to 5 hours (high)

MAKES:

6 servings

1 Rinse and drain lentils. In a 3½- or 4-quart slow cooker combine lentils, chicken broth, ham, carrots, green beans, onions, water, thyme, and marjoram.

2 Cover and cook on low-heat setting for 8 to 10 hours or on high-heat setting for 4 to 5 hours.

Nutrition Facts per serving: 267 cal., 6 g total fat (2 g sat. fat), 26 mg chol., 1,198 mg sodium, 33 g carbo., 15 g fiber, 21 g pro. **Daily Values:** 160% vit. A, 16% vit. C, 8% calcium, 23% iron

Tuscans love their white beans, and you will too once you've experienced them in this varied and colorful soup.

TUSCAN HAM & BEAN SOUP

PREP:

25 minutes

COOK:

6 to 8 hours (low)
or 3 to 4 hours (high)

MAKES:

8 servings

3	15-ounce cans small white beans, rinsed and drained
2½	cups cubed cooked ham
1½	cups chopped carrots
1	cup thinly sliced celery
1	cup chopped onion
¼	teaspoon black pepper
2	14½-ounce cans diced tomatoes with garlic and herbs, undrained
2	14-ounce cans reduced-sodium chicken broth
8	cups torn fresh kale or spinach leaves
	Freshly shredded Parmesan cheese (optional)

1 In a 5- to 6-quart slow cooker combine beans, ham, carrots, celery, onion, and pepper. Stir in tomatoes and chicken broth.

2 Cover and cook on low-heat setting for 6 to 8 hours or on high-heat setting for 3 to 4 hours. Just before serving, stir in kale. If desired, sprinkle each serving with Parmesan cheese.

Nutrition Facts per serving: 323 cal., 3 g total fat (1 g sat. fat), 21 mg chol., 2,099 mg sodium, 53 g carbo., 12 g fiber, 25 g pro. **Daily Values:** 241% vit. A, 100% vit. C, 24% calcium, 35% iron

CHOPPING INGREDIENTS AHEAD
Cut or chop the vegetables and meat up to 24 hours ahead. Place vegetables and meat in separate containers; cover and refrigerate. The next day, place ingredients in the cooker in the order specified in the recipe. Cover and cook as directed.

Escaping south of the border is easy. Simply tap your pantry and freezer for these southern ingredients, toss them in the cooker, and you're there with each spoonful.

HAM & SALSA SOUP WITH LIME

2¼   cups dry black beans (about 1 pound)

2   cups diced cooked ham

1   cup chopped yellow and/or red sweet pepper

1   16-ounce jar lime-garlic salsa

Dairy sour cream (optional)

Lime wedges (optional)

1 Rinse beans. In a large saucepan combine beans and enough water to cover beans by 2 inches. Bring to boiling; reduce heat. Simmer, uncovered, for 10 minutes. Remove from heat. Cover and let stand for 1 hour. Drain and rinse beans.

2 In a 3½- or 4-quart slow cooker combine beans, ham, and sweet pepper. Stir in 3½ cups *fresh water.* Cover and cook on low-heat setting for 11 to 13 hours or on high-heat setting for 5½ to 6½ hours. If desired, using a potato masher, mash beans slightly. Stir in salsa.

3 If desired, top each serving with sour cream and lime wedges.

Nutrition Facts per serving: 341 cal., 4 g total fat (1 g sat. fat), 28 mg chol., 1,176 mg sodium, 49 g carbo., 12 g fiber, 29 g pro. **Daily Values:** 6% vit. A, 93% vit. C, 12% calcium, 24% iron

PREP:

25 minutes

STAND:

1 hour

COOK:

11 to 13 hours (low)
or 5½ to 6½ hours (high)

MAKES:

6 servings

This homey stew is quick to assemble because there's little measuring required. Cream-style corn thickens the flavorful broth.

HAM & VEGETABLE STEW

PREP:

10 minutes

COOK:

6 to 8 hours (low) or 3 to 4 hours (high)

MAKES:

5 servings

1	28-ounce can diced tomatoes, undrained
2½	cups diced cooked ham
1	15-ounce can navy beans, rinsed and drained
1	14¾-ounce can cream-style corn
1	cup chopped onion
¼	cup water
¼	teaspoon black pepper
	Dash bottled hot pepper sauce

1 In a 3½- or 4-quart slow cooker combine tomatoes, ham, navy beans, corn, onion, water, black pepper, and hot pepper sauce.

2 Cover and cook on low-heat setting for 6 to 8 hours or on high-heat setting for 3 to 4 hours.

Nutrition Facts per serving: 368 cal., 8 g total fat (3 g sat. fat), 50 mg chol., 2,190 mg sodium, 45 g carbo., 7 g fiber, 29 g pro. **Daily Values:** 2% vit. A, 43% vit. C, 12% calcium, 22% iron

Take note: This recipe calls for evaporated milk instead of regular. Not only does evaporated milk add creamy richness, but unlike regular milk, it won't break down during the slow cooking time.

SWISS, HAM & BROCCOLI CHOWDER

2   10¾-ounce cans cream of celery soup

1   12-ounce can (1½ cups) evaporated milk

½   cup water

1   16- to 20-ounce package refrigerated diced potatoes or 3 cups loose-pack frozen diced hash brown potatoes with onion and peppers, thawed

2   cups diced cooked ham

1   cup finely chopped celery

8   ounces process Swiss cheese slices, torn into small pieces

2   cups chopped fresh broccoli or frozen chopped broccoli, thawed

PREP:

15 minutes

COOK:

6 to 7 hours (low) or 3 to 3½ hours (high), plus 30 minutes (high)

MAKES:

6 servings

1 In a 3½- or 4-quart slow cooker combine celery soup, evaporated milk, and water. Gently stir in potatoes, ham, and celery.

2 Cover and cook on low-heat setting for 6 to 7 hours or on high-heat setting for 3 to 3½ hours. If using low-heat setting, turn to high-heat setting. Stir in cheese and broccoli. Cover and cook for 30 minutes more.

Nutrition Facts per serving: 460 cal., 24 g total fat (13 g sat. fat), 78 mg chol., 2,148 mg sodium, 34 g carbo., 4 g fiber, 24 g pro. **Daily Values:** 25% vit. A, 63% vit. C, 45% calcium, 8% iron

Minestra (mee-NAYS-truh) is the Italian word for soup,—and it usually describes one that contains meat and vegetables. With cannellini beans, Italian-style tomatoes, Italian sausage, escarole, and Asiago cheese, this recipe certainly lives up to its name!

MINESTRA

PREP:

15 minutes

COOK:

*5 to 6 hours (low)
or 2$\frac{1}{2}$ to 3 hours (high)*

MAKES:

6 servings

1   19-ounce can white kidney (cannellini) beans, rinsed and drained

2   medium potatoes, peeled and cut into $\frac{3}{4}$-inch pieces

1   14$\frac{1}{2}$-ounce can Italian-style stewed tomatoes, undrained

1   14-ounce can beef broth

8   ounces cooked Italian sausage links, cut into $\frac{1}{2}$-inch slices

$\frac{1}{4}$ teaspoon crushed red pepper

4   cloves garlic, minced

2   cups chopped escarole or Swiss chard leaves

$\frac{1}{3}$ cup shredded Asiago or Parmesan cheese

1 In a 3$\frac{1}{2}$- or 4-quart slow cooker combine kidney beans, potatoes, tomatoes, beef broth, sausage, crushed red pepper, and garlic.

2 Cover and cook on low-heat setting for 5 to 6 hours or on high-heat setting for 2$\frac{1}{2}$ to 3 hours. Just before serving, stir in escarole. Sprinkle each serving with Asiago cheese.

Nutrition Facts per serving: 263 cal., 12 g total fat (5 g sat. fat), 33 mg chol., 806 mg sodium, 26 g carbo., 6 g fiber, 15 g pro. **Daily Values:** 7% vit. A, 14% vit. C, 12% calcium, 12% iron

Kielbasa, a smoked pork sausage, comes in chubby links and usually is precooked. It's also called Polish sausage.

KIELBASA STEW

4	cups coarsely chopped cabbage
3	cups cubed peeled potatoes
1½	cups sliced carrots
1	pound cooked kielbasa, sliced
½	teaspoon dried basil, crushed
½	teaspoon dried thyme, crushed
½	teaspoon black pepper
2	14-ounce cans reduced-sodium chicken broth

1 In a 4- to 5-quart slow cooker combine cabbage, potatoes, and carrots. Add kielbasa. Sprinkle with basil, thyme, and pepper. Pour chicken broth over mixture in cooker.

2 Cover and cook on low-heat setting for 7 to 9 hours or on high-heat setting for 3½ to 4½ hours.

Nutrition Facts per serving: 522 cal., 34 g total fat (12 g sat. fat), 76 mg chol., 1,658 mg sodium, 34 g carbo., 5 g fiber, 23 g pro. **Daily Values:** 233% vit. A, 68% vit. C, 6% calcium, 13% iron

PREP:

20 minutes

COOK:

7 to 9 hours (low) or 3½ to 4½ hours (high)

MAKES:

4 or 5 servings

MEATS TO KEEP ON HAND

Preserved meats such as kielbasa, pepperoni, and packaged corned beef store longer than others, making them good choices for people who have hectic, ever-changing schedules. If you don't cook them the week you buy them, it's usually OK because they have longer shelf lives than other meats. Next time you shop, check the "sell by" and "use by" dates of such meats and be sure to refrigerate them.

Take advantage of prepared veggies: Baby-cut carrots come perfectly sized and already peeled, as do the small whole onions, relieving you of peeling and chopping duties.

SAVORY LAMB SOUP

PREP:

20 minutes

COOK:

10 to 12 hours (low) or 5 to 6 hours (high)

MAKES:

6 servings

1½	pounds lean lamb stew meat
1	tablespoon cooking oil
2	14-ounce cans beef broth
3	cups baby carrots, trimmed
2	cups frozen cut green beans
1½	cups frozen small whole onions
2	teaspoons dried thyme, crushed
½	teaspoon garlic powder
¼	teaspoon black pepper
½	cup dry white wine or water
	Snipped fresh parsley (optional)

1 Cut meat into 1-inch pieces. In a large skillet brown meat, half at a time, in hot oil. Drain off fat. Transfer meat to a 4- to 5-quart slow cooker. Stir in beef broth, baby carrots, green beans, onions, thyme, garlic powder, and pepper.

2 Cover and cook on low-heat setting for 10 to 12 hours or on high-heat setting for 5 to 6 hours. If necessary, skim off fat. Stir in wine. If desired, sprinkle each serving with parsley.

Nutrition Facts per serving: 234 cal., 7 g total fat (2 g sat. fat), 71 mg chol., 552 mg sodium, 14 g carbo., 4 g fiber, 26 g pro. **Daily Values:** 313% vit. A, 19% vit. C, 9% calcium, 18% iron

Easy-to-use lentils don't require presoaking or precooking. Just rinse them and they're ready to join the rest of the ingredients in the slow cooker.

LAMB-LENTIL SOUP

12	ounces lean boneless lamb or beef
1	tablespoon cooking oil
3¼	cups water
1	10½-ounce can condensed French onion soup
1	cup dry lentils, rinsed and drained
1	cup coarsely chopped carrots
1	cup thinly sliced celery
1½	teaspoons dried thyme, crushed
½	teaspoon salt
½	teaspoon black pepper

1 Trim fat from meat. Cut meat into ½-inch pieces. In a large skillet brown meat in hot oil. Drain off fat.

2 Transfer meat to a 3½- or 4-quart slow cooker. Stir in water, onion soup, lentils, carrots, celery, thyme, salt, and pepper. Cover and cook on low-heat setting for 7 to 8 hours or on high-heat setting for 3½ to 4 hours.

Nutrition Facts per serving: 379 cal., 10 g total fat (2 g sat. fat), 57 mg chol., 989 mg sodium, 38 g carbo., 17 g fiber, 33 g pro. **Daily Values:** 157% vit. A, 13% vit. C, 8% calcium, 35% iron

PREP:

20 minutes

COOK:

7 to 8 hours (low)
or 3½ to 4 hours (high)

MAKES:

4 or 5 servings

A long-time food editor in the Better Homes and Gardens® family of publications says that she has made this recipe so many times, she doesn't need to measure the ingredients anymore. That's high praise from someone who has seen a lot of recipes over the years!

COUNTRY BEAN STEW

PREP:

35 minutes

STAND:

1 hour

COOK:

4 to 5 hours (high), plus 15 minutes (high)

MAKES:

6 servings

2	cups dry Great Northern beans
3	large carrots, coarsely chopped
12	ounces lean boneless lamb
8	ounces bulk Italian sausage
3	medium onions, coarsely chopped
3	cloves garlic, minced
1	teaspoon instant beef bouillon granules
½	teaspoon dried thyme, crushed
½	teaspoon dried oregano, crushed
¼	cup dry red wine or water
½	of a 6-ounce can (⅓ cup) tomato paste
½	cup cubed cooked ham
¼	cup snipped fresh parsley

1 Rinse beans. In a large saucepan combine beans and 6 cups water. Bring to boiling; reduce heat. Simmer, uncovered, for 10 minutes. Remove from heat. Cover and let stand 1 hour. Drain and rinse beans. In a 3½- to 5-quart slow cooker combine beans and carrots.

2 Trim fat from lamb. Cut lamb into ¾-inch pieces. In a large skillet cook lamb, Italian sausage, onions, and garlic until meat is brown and onions are tender. Drain off fat. Transfer meat mixture to cooker. Stir in bouillon granules, thyme, and oregano. Stir in 3 cups *fresh water.*

3 Cover and cook on high-heat setting for 4 to 5 hours. In a small bowl stir wine into tomato paste; add to cooker. Stir in ham and parsley. Cover and cook for 15 minutes more.

Nutrition Facts per serving: 475 cal., 13 g total fat (5 g sat. fat), 72 mg chol., 769 mg sodium, 50 g carbo., 15 g fiber, 37 g pro. **Daily Values:** 241% vit. A, 29% vit. C, 14% calcium, 28% iron

For a change of pace, you can make this sweet and savory stew with beef.
Serve it with a crisp romaine salad and hot corn bread.

VENISON & CIDER STEW

1¼	pounds lean venison or beef stew meat
2	tablespoons cooking oil
4	medium carrots and/or parsnips, cut up
2	medium red-skinned potatoes, cut up
2	medium onions, quartered
1	cup apple cider or apple juice
1	cup beef broth
1	stalk celery, sliced
2	tablespoons quick-cooking tapioca
¼	teaspoon salt
¼	teaspoon dried marjoram, crushed
¼	teaspoon crushed red pepper (optional)
2	medium apples, cored and cut into wedges

PREP:

25 minutes

COOK:

10 to 12 hours (low)
or 5 to 6 hours (high),
plus 30 minutes (high)

MAKES:

6 servings

1 Cut meat into 1-inch pieces. In a large skillet brown meat, half at a time, in hot oil. Drain off fat. Transfer meat to a 3½- to 5-quart slow cooker. Stir in carrots, potatoes, onions, apple cider, beef broth, celery, tapioca, salt, marjoram, and, if desired, crushed red pepper.

2 Cover and cook on low-heat setting for 10 to 12 hours or on high-heat setting for 5 to 6 hours. If using low-heat setting, turn to high-heat setting. Stir in apple wedges. Cover and cook for 30 minutes more.

Nutrition Facts per serving: 286 cal., 7 g total fat (2 g sat. fat), 80 mg chol., 306 mg sodium, 32 g carbo., 4 g fiber, 24 g pro. **Daily Values:** 207% vit. A, 23% vit. C, 3% calcium, 24% iron

Two beloved cooking classics, white wine and garlic, take much of the credit for the delicious rich flavor of this wholesome soup.

BEAN & CHICKEN SOUP

PREP:

20 minutes

COOK:

*7 to 8 hours (low)
or 3$\frac{1}{2}$ to 4 hours (high)*

MAKES:

4 servings

8 skinless, boneless chicken thighs (about 1$\frac{1}{2}$ pounds total), cut into bite-size pieces

2 15-ounce cans navy beans, rinsed and drained

1 14$\frac{1}{2}$-ounce can diced tomatoes, undrained

1 cup chicken broth

$\frac{1}{2}$ cup chopped onion

$\frac{1}{3}$ cup dry white wine or chicken broth

2 tablespoons tomato paste

$\frac{1}{2}$ teaspoon salt

$\frac{1}{4}$ teaspoon dried thyme, crushed

$\frac{1}{4}$ teaspoon black pepper

6 cloves garlic, minced

Snipped fresh parsley (optional)

1 In a 3$\frac{1}{2}$- or 4-quart slow cooker combine chicken, navy beans, tomatoes, chicken broth, onion, wine, tomato paste, salt, thyme, pepper, and garlic.

2 Cover and cook on low-heat setting for 7 to 8 hours or on high-heat setting for 3$\frac{1}{2}$ to 4 hours. If desired, sprinkle each serving with parsley.

Nutrition Facts per serving: 516 cal., 4 g total fat (1 g sat. fat), 98 mg chol., 1,836 mg sodium, 56 g carbo., 13 g fiber, 59 g pro. **Daily Values:** 1% vit. A, 32% vit. C, 18% calcium, 35% iron

Pea pods, cabbage, and a well-beaten egg transform this version of classic chicken soup into distinctively Asian cuisine.

ASIAN-STYLE CHICKEN SOUP

1	pound skinless, boneless chicken breast halves, cut into bite-size pieces
2	14-ounce cans chicken broth
1	cup water
1	medium red sweet pepper, cut into 3/4-inch pieces
1	medium carrot, sliced
1/3	cup thinly sliced green onions
1	tablespoon soy sauce
1	teaspoon grated fresh ginger
1/8	teaspoon crushed red pepper
2	cups shredded Chinese (napa) cabbage
1	cup fresh pea pods, halved crosswise, or half of a 6-ounce package frozen pea pods, thawed and halved crosswise
1	well-beaten egg

PREP:

25 minutes

COOK:

5 to 6 hours (low) or 2 1/2 to 3 hours (high), plus 10 minutes (high)

MAKES:

4 servings

1 In a 3 1/2- or 4-quart slow cooker combine chicken, chicken broth, water, sweet pepper, carrot, green onions, soy sauce, ginger, and crushed red pepper. Cover and cook on low-heat setting for 5 to 6 hours or on high-heat setting for 2 1/2 to 3 hours.

2 If using low-heat setting, turn to high-heat setting. Stir in cabbage and pea pods. Slowly pour in well-beaten egg; stir gently. Cover and cook for 10 minutes more.

Nutrition Facts per serving: 208 cal., 5 g total fat (1 g sat. fat), 119 mg chol., 1,195 mg sodium, 8 g carbo., 3 g fiber, 32 g pro. **Daily Values:** 122% vit. A, 102% vit. C, 7% calcium, 9% iron

This soup is a compilation of the many hallmarks of a great Southeast Asian curry, including a delightful finish of a rich, nutty coconut milk. A side of rice tames the spiciness.

CURRIED CHICKEN SOUP

PREP:

25 minutes

COOK:

*7 to 8 hours (low)
or 3^1/$_2$ to 4 hours (high)*

MAKES:

6 servings

1   pound skinless, boneless chicken thighs, cut into 1-inch pieces

2   14-ounce cans chicken broth

3   cups cauliflower florets

4   medium carrots, sliced

2   medium potatoes, peeled (if desired) and cut into 1-inch pieces

3   stalks celery, sliced

1   small onion, chopped

1   tablespoon curry powder

^{1}/$_2$ teaspoon ground cumin

^{1}/$_4$ teaspoon crushed red pepper

2   cloves garlic, minced

1   13^1/$_2$-ounce can unsweetened coconut milk

    Hot cooked rice (optional)

    Peanuts, raisins, and/or coconut, toasted (optional)

① In a 3^1/$_2$- or 4-quart slow cooker combine chicken, chicken broth, cauliflower, carrots, potatoes, celery, onion, curry powder, cumin, crushed red pepper, and garlic.

② Cover and cook on low-heat setting for 7 to 8 hours or on high-heat setting for 3^1/$_2$ to 4 hours. Stir in coconut milk.

③ If desired, serve with hot cooked rice and sprinkle each serving with peanuts, raisins, and/or coconut.

Nutrition Facts per serving: 309 cal., 18 g total fat (13 g sat. fat), 63 mg chol., 661 mg sodium, 19 g carbo., 4 g fiber, 20 g pro. **Daily Values:** 207% vit. A, 56% vit. C, 6% calcium, 23% iron

For a French finish to this French supper, follow the main course with a cheese course—serve some Brie with a French baguette bread and fresh fruit.

EASY CASSOULET SOUP

2	medium carrots, cut into ½-inch slices
1	large onion, chopped
1	medium red or green sweet pepper, cut into ½-inch pieces
3	cloves garlic, minced
2	15-ounce cans white kidney (cannellini) or Great Northern beans, rinsed and drained
1	14½-ounce can Italian-style stewed tomatoes, undrained
8	ounces skinless, boneless chicken thighs, cut into 1-inch pieces
8	ounces cooked smoked turkey sausage, halved lengthwise and cut into ½-inch pieces
1½	cups chicken broth
½	cup dry white wine or chicken broth
1	tablespoon snipped fresh parsley
1	bay leaf
1	teaspoon dried thyme, crushed
⅛	to ¼ teaspoon cayenne pepper

1 In a 3½- to 5-quart slow cooker place carrots, onion, sweet pepper, and garlic. Top with kidney beans, tomatoes, chicken, and sausage. Add chicken broth, wine, parsley, bay leaf, thyme, and cayenne pepper.

2 Cover and cook on low-heat setting for 7 to 8 hours or on high-heat setting for 3½ to 4 hours. Remove bay leaf.

Nutrition Facts per serving: 248 cal., 6 g total fat (2 g sat. fat), 55 mg chol., 969 mg sodium, 31 g carbo., 9 g fiber, 23 g pro. **Daily Values:** 133% vit. A, 64% vit. C, 8% calcium, 17% iron

PREP:

20 minutes

COOK:

7 to 8 hours (low)
or 3½ to 4 hours (high)

MAKES:

6 to 8 servings

ADAPTING FAVORITE RECIPES

Follow these tips to prepare your favorite entrées in a slow cooker: Use recipes that call for less tender cuts of meat, which benefit from long cooking. Find a sample recipe in this book that is similar to your own; it will give you a feel for quantities and liquid amounts. Cut vegetables into similar-size pieces to those in the sample recipe; place them in the bottom of the cooker. Trim the meat and, if necessary, cut to fit into the cooker. Place the meat on top of the vegetables. Reduce the liquids in your original recipe by about half (unless the dish contains rice). Follow the cooking times listed in the sample recipe.

Deviled refers to a food that is seasoned with piquant ingredients such as red pepper, hot pepper sauce, or, as in this dish, mustard. Add more or less to your liking.

DEVILED CHICKEN & VEGETABLE SOUP

PREP:

20 minutes

COOK:

*8 to 10 hours (low)
or 4 to 5 hours (high)*

MAKES:

6 servings

1	pound skinless, boneless chicken thighs, cut into bite-size pieces
1½	cups frozen whole kernel corn
1	large red-skinned potato, chopped
1	medium onion, chopped
1	stalk celery, chopped
3	tablespoons Dijon-style mustard
¼	teaspoon black pepper
⅛	teaspoon garlic powder
2½	cups vegetable juice
1	14-ounce can reduced-sodium chicken broth

1 In a 3½- or 4-quart slow cooker combine chicken, corn, potato, onion, celery, mustard, pepper, and garlic powder. Pour vegetable juice and chicken broth over mixture in cooker.

2 Cover and cook on low-heat setting for 8 to 10 hours or on high-heat setting for 4 to 5 hours.

Nutrition Facts per serving: 192 cal., 5 g total fat (1 g sat. fat), 36 mg chol., 800 mg sodium, 23 g carbo., 1 g fiber, 15 g pro. **Daily Values:** 13% vit. A, 59% vit. C, 2% calcium, 12% iron

A can of cream of chicken soup gives you a head start, and the final touch of bacon brings home a contrast to the creaminess.

CREAMED CHICKEN & CORN SOUP

12	ounces skinless, boneless chicken thighs
1	26-ounce can condensed cream of chicken soup
1	14$\frac{3}{4}$-ounce can cream-style corn
1	14-ounce can reduced-sodium chicken broth
1	cup chopped carrots
1	cup finely chopped onion
1	cup frozen whole kernel corn
$\frac{1}{2}$	cup chopped celery
$\frac{1}{2}$	cup water
2	slices bacon, crisp-cooked, drained, and crumbled

PREP:
20 minutes

COOK:
*5 to 6 hours (low)
or 2$\frac{1}{2}$ to 3 hours (high)*

MAKES:
4 to 6 servings

1 In a 3$\frac{1}{2}$- or 4-quart slow cooker combine chicken, chicken soup, cream-style corn, broth, carrots, onion, frozen corn, celery, and water.

2 Cover and cook on low-heat setting for 5 to 6 hours or on high-heat setting for 2$\frac{1}{2}$ to 3 hours. Remove chicken from cooker; cool slightly. Chop chicken; stir into mixture in cooker.

3 Sprinkle each serving with bacon.

Nutrition Facts per serving: 469 cal., 19 g total fat (6 g sat. fat), 87 mg chol., 2,063 mg sodium, 50 g carbo., 5 g fiber, 28 g pro. **Daily Values:** 172% vit. A, 21% vit. C, 6% calcium, 12% iron

For a weeknight supper or weekend get-together, this hearty dish is sure to conjure rave reviews. The sunny yellow saffron-flavored rice is as beautiful as it is delicious.

CHICKEN & SAFFRON RICE SOUP

PREP:

15 minutes

COOK:

*4 to 5 hours (low)
or 2 to 2½ hours (high),
plus 15 minutes (high)*

MAKES:

4 to 6 servings

1   pound skinless, boneless chicken breast halves, cut into 1-inch pieces

1   14½-ounce can diced tomatoes, undrained

1   14-ounce can reduced-sodium chicken broth

1   14-ounce can artichoke hearts, drained and quartered

1   medium onion, chopped

½   of a 7-ounce jar roasted red sweet peppers, drained and cut into strips (½ cup)

1   clove garlic, minced

½   cup frozen peas

1   5-ounce package saffron-flavored rice mix

2   tablespoons slivered almonds, toasted

1   In a 3½- or 4-quart slow cooker combine chicken, tomatoes, chicken broth, artichoke hearts, onion, roasted sweet peppers, and garlic. Cover and cook on low-heat setting for 4 to 5 hours or on high-heat setting for 2 to 2½ hours.

2   If using low-heat setting, turn to high-heat setting. Stir in frozen peas. Cover and cook for 15 minutes more.

3   Meanwhile, prepare rice mix according to package directions.

4   To serve, ladle soup into bowls. Mound cooked rice in center of each bowl. Sprinkle with almonds.

Nutrition Facts per serving: 415 cal., 10 g total fat (1 g sat. fat), 66 mg chol., 1,315 mg sodium, 44 g carbo., 9 g fiber, 35 g pro. **Daily Values:** 6% vit. A, 129% vit. C, 10% calcium, 32% iron

This northern Midwest wild rice stew pleasantly surprises even those who grew up eating stew of the same name—the leeks and rosemary deviate from the classic ingredients.

CHICKEN & WILD RICE STEW

3	cups quartered fresh button mushrooms (8 ounces)
2	medium carrots, sliced
2	medium leeks, sliced
½	cup uncooked wild rice, rinsed and drained
½	cup uncooked regular brown rice
12	ounces skinless, boneless chicken breast halves, cut into ¾-inch pieces
1	teaspoon dried thyme, crushed
½	teaspoon dried rosemary, crushed
¼	teaspoon black pepper
3	14-ounce cans reduced-sodium chicken broth
1	10¾-ounce can condensed cream of mushroom soup

PREP:

20 minutes

COOK:

*7 to 8 hours (low)
or 3½ to 4 hours (high)*

MAKES:

6 servings

1 In a 3½- to 6-quart slow cooker place mushrooms, carrots, leeks, wild rice, and brown rice. Add chicken, thyme, rosemary, and pepper. Pour chicken broth over mixture in cooker.

2 Cover and cook on low-heat setting for 7 to 8 hours or on high-heat setting for 3½ to 4 hours. Stir in mushroom soup.

Nutrition Facts per serving: 264 cal., 6 g total fat (2 g sat. fat), 33 mg chol., 908 mg sodium, 32 g carbo., 3 g fiber, 22 g pro. **Daily Values:** 104% vit. A, 6% vit. C, 4% calcium, 10% iron

The chicken gravy mix is responsible for the down-home flavor of this satisfying soup. Sour cream lends its irresistible creaminess and a mild tang.

CREAMY CHICKEN & VEGETABLE STEW

PREP:

30 minutes

COOK:

8 to 9 hours (low)
or 4 to 4¹/₂ hours (high)

MAKES:

6 servings

1¹/₂	pounds boneless, skinless chicken thighs, cut into 1-inch pieces
1	tablespoon cooking oil
1	pound potatoes, peeled and cut into 1-inch pieces
2	cups baby carrots, trimmed
2	cups frozen cut green beans
1	medium onion, chopped
1	teaspoon dried thyme, crushed
¹/₂	teaspoon salt
¹/₂	teaspoon poultry seasoning
2	cups water
2	0.87-ounce envelopes chicken gravy mix
1	8-ounce carton dairy sour cream

1 In a large skillet brown chicken, half at a time, in hot oil. Drain off fat.

2 Transfer chicken to a 3¹/₂- or 4-quart slow cooker. Stir in potatoes, carrots, green beans, onion, thyme, salt, and poultry seasoning. In a small bowl stir together water and gravy mix; stir into mixture in cooker.

3 Cover and cook on low-heat setting for 8 to 9 hours or on high-heat setting for 4 to 4¹/₂ hours.

4 In a medium bowl gradually stir about 1 cup of the hot chicken mixture into sour cream. Add sour cream mixture to cooker, stirring gently until combined.

Nutrition Facts per serving: 344 cal., 14 g total fat (6 g sat. fat), 107 mg chol., 769 mg sodium, 26 g carbo., 4 g fiber, 26 g pro. **Daily Values:** 217% vit. A, 32% vit. C, 10% calcium, 12% iron

Store-bought frozen seasoned and cooked chicken strips heat through in the hot soup. The torn tortillas take the place of pasta or rice.

TEX-MEX SOUP

2	cups water
1	14½-ounce can diced tomatoes, undrained
1	14-ounce can beef broth
1	8-ounce can tomato sauce
½	cup chopped onion
1	4-ounce can diced green chile peppers, undrained
1	teaspoon ground cumin
1	teaspoon chili powder
1	teaspoon Worcestershire sauce
½	teaspoon garlic powder
1	9-ounce package frozen cooked Southwestern-flavor chicken breast strips, thawed
8	to 10 corn tortillas, torn into 1- to 2-inch pieces
¾	cup shredded cheddar cheese or Monterey Jack cheese with jalapeño peppers (3 ounces)

1 In a 3½- or 4-quart slow cooker combine water, tomatoes, beef broth, tomato sauce, onion, green chile peppers, cumin, chili powder, Worcestershire sauce, and garlic powder.

2 Cover and cook on low-heat setting for 8 to 10 hours or on high-heat setting for 4 to 5 hours.

3 If using low-heat setting, turn to high-heat setting. Stir in chicken strips. Cover and cook for 15 minutes more. Just before serving, stir in tortillas. Sprinkle each serving with cheddar cheese.

Nutrition Facts per serving: 189 cal., 6 g total fat (3 g sat. fat), 26 mg chol., 615 mg sodium, 22 g carbo., 2 g fiber, 13 g pro. **Daily Values:** 5% vit. A, 20% vit. C, 16% calcium, 14% iron

PREP:

20 minutes

COOK:

8 to 10 hours (low) or 4 to 5 hours (high), plus 15 minutes (high)

MAKES:

8 servings

Round out this meal with Cheese-Herb Biscuits (page 364) and a crisp green salad topped with citrus slices and your favorite vinaigrette.

SPINACH, CHICKEN & WILD RICE SOUP

PREP:

15 minutes

COOK:

7 to 8 hours (low)
or 3 1/2 to 4 hours (high)

MAKES:

6 servings

3   cups water

1   14-ounce can chicken broth

1   10¾-ounce can condensed cream of chicken soup

⅔   cup uncooked wild rice, rinsed and drained

½   teaspoon dried thyme, crushed

¼   teaspoon black pepper

3   cups chopped cooked chicken or turkey

2   cups shredded fresh spinach

1   In a 3½- or 4-quart slow cooker combine water, chicken broth, chicken soup, wild rice, thyme, and pepper.

2   Cover and cook on low-heat setting for 7 to 8 hours or on high-heat setting for 3½ to 4 hours. Just before serving, stir in chicken and spinach.

Nutrition Facts per serving: 263 cal., 9 g total fat (3 g sat. fat), 66 mg chol., 741 mg sodium, 19 g carbo., 2 g fiber, 25 g pro. **Daily Values:** 19% vit. A, 5% vit. C, 4% calcium, 10% iron

To save time on early-morning preparation, precook the beans the night before, drain at once, rinse, and store in the refrigerator. In the morning, put them into the slow cooker along with the vegetables and seasonings.

CHICKEN & VEGETABLE BEAN SOUP

1	cup dry Great Northern beans
1	cup chopped onion
1	cup chopped carrots
1	medium fennel bulb, trimmed and cut into ½-inch pieces
2	tablespoons snipped fresh parsley
1	teaspoon dried rosemary, crushed
¼	teaspoon black pepper
2	cloves garlic, minced
4½	cups chicken broth
2½	cups shredded or chopped cooked chicken or turkey
1	14½-ounce can diced tomatoes, undrained

1 Rinse beans. In a large saucepan combine beans and 6 cups water. Bring to boiling; reduce heat. Simmer, uncovered, for 10 minutes. Remove from heat. Cover and let stand for 1 hour. Drain and rinse beans.

2 Meanwhile, in a 3½- to 5-quart slow cooker combine onion, carrots, fennel, parsley, rosemary, pepper, and garlic. Add beans. Pour chicken broth over mixture in cooker.

3 Cover and cook on low-heat setting for 8 to 10 hours or on high-heat setting for 4 to 5 hours.

4 If using low-heat setting, turn to high-heat setting. Stir in chicken and tomatoes. Cover and cook about 30 minutes more or until heated through.

Nutrition Facts per serving: 426 cal., 10 g total fat (3 g sat. fat), 78 mg chol., 1,454 mg sodium, 46 g carbo., 15 g fiber, 40 g pro. **Daily Values:** 176% vit. A, 42% vit. C, 16% calcium, 26% iron

PREP:

20 minutes

STAND:

1 hour

COOK:

8 to 10 hours (low) or 4 to 5 hours (high), plus 30 minutes (high)

MAKES:

4 to 6 servings

COOKING DRY BEANS

Your slow cooker is handy for gently simmering dry beans to tasty tenderness. Because the beans cook more slowly than in a saucepan, you must precook them for 10 minutes instead of the two minutes typical of range-top recipes. Soaking dry beans overnight won't work for slow cooker recipes because the beans won't become tender in the slow cooker that way. Our recipes tell you exactly how to precook dry beans for best results.

These days, many bakeries sell bread bowls, and this chili tastes terrific served in one. You also can spoon it over crusty corn muffins.

CONFETTI WHITE CHILI

PREP:

25 minutes

COOK:

6 to 8 hours (low) or 3 to 4 hours (high), plus 15 minutes (high)

MAKES:

6 to 8 servings

3	15-ounce cans Great Northern, pinto, and/or white kidney (cannellini) beans
1½	cups chopped red, green, and/or yellow sweet peppers
1	cup coarsely shredded carrots
½	cup sliced green onions
2	teaspoons dried oregano, crushed
1	teaspoon ground cumin
½	teaspoon salt
2	cloves garlic, minced
2	14-ounce cans chicken broth
2½	cups chopped cooked chicken or turkey
	Shredded Monterey Jack cheese (optional)

1 Rinse and drain two cans of beans and place in a 3½- or 4-quart slow cooker. Using a potato masher or fork, mash beans. Rinse and drain remaining can of beans (do not mash). Stir unmashed beans, sweet peppers, carrots, green onions, oregano, cumin, salt, and garlic into mashed beans in cooker. Stir in chicken broth.

2 Cover and cook on low-heat setting for 6 to 8 hours or on high-heat setting for 3 to 4 hours.

3 If using low-heat setting, turn to high-heat setting. Stir in chicken. Cover and cook about 15 minutes more or until chicken is heated through.

4 If desired, sprinkle each serving with Monterey Jack cheese.

Nutrition Facts per serving: 397 cal., 7 g total fat (2 g sat. fat), 52 mg chol., 846 mg sodium, 51 g carbo., 12 g fiber, 35 g pro. **Daily Values:** 135% vit. A, 110% vit. C, 15% calcium, 26% iron

It's a perfectly balanced spice blend that brings the turkey and sweet potatoes to life in this anything but ho-hum soup.

CURRIED TURKEY & SWEET POTATO SOUP

1   pound turkey breast tenderloins, cut into ¾-inch pieces

4   cups peeled sweet potatoes cut into bite-size pieces

2   14-ounce cans chicken broth

1   cup chopped onion

1   cup thinly sliced celery

1   tablespoon red curry powder

½   teaspoon salt

⅛   teaspoon crushed red pepper

2   cloves garlic, minced

1   13½-ounce can unsweetened coconut milk

PREP:
25 minutes

COOK:
6 to 8 hours (low) or 3 to 4 hours (high)

MAKES:
6 servings

1 In a 3½- or 4-quart slow cooker combine turkey, sweet potatoes, chicken broth, onion, celery, curry powder, salt, crushed red pepper, and garlic.

2 Cover and cook on low-heat setting for 6 to 8 hours or on high-heat setting for 3 to 4 hours. Stir in coconut milk.

Nutrition Facts per serving: 333 cal., 15 g total fat (12 g sat. fat), 47 mg chol., 843 mg sodium, 28 g carbo., 4 g fiber, 23 g pro. **Daily Values:** 321% vit. A, 30% vit. C, 6% calcium, 21% iron

When you know the morning will be hectic, cut up the turkey and vegetables the night before and refrigerate them in separate plastic bags.

MUSHROOM, TURKEY & RICE SOUP

PREP:

25 minutes

COOK:

*8 to 10 hours (low)
or 4 to 5 hours (high)*

STAND:

5 minutes

MAKES:

6 servings

2	cups sliced fresh shiitake or button mushrooms
1½	cups sliced bok choy
2	medium carrots, cut into thin bite-size strips
1	medium onion, chopped
1	pound turkey breast tenderloins or skinless, boneless chicken breast halves, cut into 1-inch pieces
2	14-ounce cans reduced-sodium chicken broth
2	tablespoons reduced-sodium soy sauce
1	tablespoon toasted sesame oil (optional)
2	teaspoons grated fresh ginger
4	cloves garlic, minced
1	cup uncooked instant white rice

1 In a 3½- or 4-quart slow cooker place mushrooms, bok choy, carrots, and onion. Add turkey. In a medium bowl combine broth, soy sauce, sesame oil (if desired), ginger, and garlic. Pour over mixture in cooker.

2 Cover and cook on low-heat setting for 8 to 10 hours or on high-heat setting for 4 to 5 hours. Turn off cooker. Stir in rice. Cover and let stand for 5 to 10 minutes or until rice is tender.

Nutrition Facts per serving: 186 cal., 1 g total fat (0 g sat. fat), 47 mg chol., 584 mg sodium, 20 g carbo., 1 g fiber, 24 g pro. **Daily Values:** 62% vit. A, 19% vit. C, 4% calcium, 11% iron

INCREASING THE RECIPE
Double the ingredient amounts and use a 5- to 6-quart slow cooker.

Dried herbs and herb blends are preferred for slow cooking because they release their flavors gradually. Usually dried Italian seasoning is a fragrant blend of basil, oregano, rosemary, fennel seeds, and sometimes garlic powder and cayenne pepper.

HEARTY TURKEY SOUP

1	pound uncooked ground turkey or chicken
1	cup chopped celery
½	cup thinly sliced carrot
½	cup chopped onion
3	cups tomato juice
2	cups frozen French-cut green beans
1	cup sliced fresh mushrooms
½	cup chopped tomato
2	teaspoons dried Italian seasoning, crushed
1½	teaspoons Worcestershire sauce
1	bay leaf
¾	teaspoon garlic salt
½	teaspoon sugar
¼	teaspoon black pepper

PREP:

20 minutes

COOK:

5 to 6 hours (low) or 2½ to 3 hours (high)

MAKES:

4 or 5 servings

1 In a large skillet cook ground turkey, celery, carrot, and onion until turkey is brown. Drain off fat. Transfer turkey mixture to a 3½- or 4-quart slow cooker. Stir in tomato juice, frozen green beans, mushrooms, tomato, Italian seasoning, Worcestershire sauce, bay leaf, garlic salt, sugar, and pepper.

2 Cover and cook on low-heat setting for 5 to 6 hours or on high-heat setting for 2½ to 3 hours. Remove bay leaf.

Nutrition Facts per serving: 256 cal., 10 g total fat (3 g sat. fat), 90 mg chol., 970 mg sodium, 20 g carbo., 4 g fiber, 24 g pro. **Daily Values:** 106% vit. A, 80% vit. C, 9% calcium, 22% iron

Choose your favorite variety of smoked turkey sausage for this flavorful take on the classic split pea soup.

SPLIT PEA & SMOKED TURKEY SOUP

PREP:

20 minutes

COOK:

*10 to 12 hours (low)
or 5 to 6 hours (high)*

MAKES:

4 servings

2½	cups dry green split peas (1 pound)
2	cups chopped cooked smoked turkey or sliced cooked smoked turkey sausage (8 to 10 ounces)
1½	cups coarsely chopped carrots
1	cup coarsely chopped yellow or green sweet pepper
½	cup chopped onion
1	teaspoon dried basil, crushed
1	teaspoon dried oregano, crushed
2	cloves garlic, minced
3	14-ounce cans chicken broth

1 Rinse and drain split peas. In a 3½- or 4-quart slow cooker combine split peas, turkey, carrots, sweet pepper, onion, basil, oregano, and garlic. Pour chicken broth over mixture in cooker.

2 Cover and cook on low-heat setting for 10 to 12 hours or on high-heat setting for 5 to 6 hours. Stir before serving.

Nutrition Facts per serving: 551 cal., 5 g total fat (1 g sat. fat), 22 mg chol., 2,258 mg sodium, 86 g carbo., 33 g fiber, 45 g pro. **Daily Values:** 237% vit. A, 154% vit. C, 10% calcium, 35% iron

For a traditional trattoria presentation, purchase a wedge of Parmesan cheese and use a vegetable peeler to cut wide shavings to use as a garnish for the soup.

SAUSAGE & TORTELLINI SOUP

2   14½-ounce cans Italian-style stewed tomatoes, undrained

3   cups water

2   cups frozen cut green beans or Italian green beans

1   10½-ounce can condensed French onion soup

8   ounces cooked smoked turkey sausage, halved lengthwise and cut into ½-inch pieces

2   cups packaged shredded cabbage with carrot (coleslaw mix)

1   9-ounce package refrigerated cheese-filled tortellini
    Finely shredded Parmesan cheese (optional)

PREP:

10 minutes

COOK:

*8 to 10 hours (low)
or 4 to 5 hours (high),
plus 15 minutes (high)*

MAKES:

10 to 12 servings

1 In a 4- to 5-quart slow cooker combine tomatoes, water, frozen green beans, onion soup, and turkey sausage.

2 Cover and cook on low-heat setting for 8 to 10 hours or on high-heat setting for 4 to 5 hours.

3 If using low-heat setting, turn to high-heat setting. Stir in cabbage and tortellini. Cover and cook for 15 minutes more. If desired, sprinkle each serving with Parmesan cheese.

Nutrition Facts per serving: 176 cal., 5 g total fat (1 g sat. fat), 28 mg chol., 717 mg sodium, 23 g carbo., 2 g fiber, 9 g pro. **Daily Values:** 20% vit. A, 14% vit. C, 9% calcium, 9% iron

The yellow split peas garner an autumnal hue. During cooking, the peas soften and begin to fall apart, which helps bring about a pleasing—but not overly thick—consistency.

GOLDEN TURKEY-SPLIT PEA SOUP

PREP:

20 minutes

COOK:

*9 to 10 hours (low)
or 4½ to 5 hours (high)*

MAKES:

6 servings

2   cups dry yellow split peas

2   14-ounce cans reduced-sodium chicken broth

2   cups water

2   cups frozen whole kernel corn

3   medium carrots, sliced

1   10¾-ounce can condensed cream of chicken soup

8   ounces cooked smoked turkey sausage, halved lengthwise and sliced

½   cup sliced green onions

½   cup chopped red sweet pepper

2   teaspoons dried thyme, crushed

1 Rinse and drain split peas. In a 4½- or 5-quart slow cooker combine split peas, chicken broth, water, frozen corn, carrots, chicken soup, turkey sausage, green onions, sweet pepper, and thyme.

2 Cover and cook on low-heat setting for 9 to 10 hours or on high-heat setting for 4½ to 5 hours.

Nutrition Facts per serving: 409 cal., 8 g total fat (2 g sat. fat), 30 mg chol., 1,076 mg sodium, 60 g carbo., 19 g fiber, 27 g pro. **Daily Values:** 178% vit. A, 53% vit. C, 7% calcium, 21% iron

Diced hash brown potatoes (prepared and frozen so you don't have to peel or slice) fill up this stew with rib-sticking goodness. You'll also appreciate the smoky flavor the sausage brings to the mix.

EASY SAUSAGE & CHICKEN STEW

1	pound cooked smoked turkey sausage, halved lengthwise and sliced
2	cups packaged peeled baby carrots
1	14-ounce can reduced-sodium chicken broth
1½	cups loose-pack frozen diced hash brown potatoes
1	10¾-ounce can condensed cream of chicken soup
1	teaspoon dried oregano, crushed
2	cups chopped cooked chicken or turkey
1	9-ounce package frozen cut green beans, thawed

1 In a 3½- or 4-quart slow cooker combine turkey sausage, carrots, chicken broth, hash brown potatoes, chicken soup, and oregano.

2 Cover and cook on low-heat setting for 8 to 10 hours or on high-heat setting for 4 to 5 hours.

3 If using low-heat setting, turn to high-heat setting. Stir in chicken and green beans. Cover and cook for 30 minutes more.

Nutrition Facts per serving: 477 cal., 30 g total fat (13 g sat. fat), 79 mg chol., 1,238 mg sodium, 25 g carbo., 4 g fiber, 27 g pro. **Daily Values:** 214% vit. A, 22% vit. C, 5% calcium, 13% iron

PREP:

10 minutes

COOK:

8 to 10 hours (low) or 4 to 5 hours (high), plus 30 minutes (high)

MAKES:

6 to 8 servings

Doctor up some canned pork and beans with a flavorful smoked turkey sausage link to create a stew that reminds kids of beenie weenies and adults of French cassoulet!

TURKEY SAUSAGE & BAKED BEAN STEW

PREP:

15 minutes

COOK:

*6 to 8 hours (low)
or 3 to 4 hours (high)*

MAKES:

6 servings

1   pound cooked smoked turkey sausage, halved lengthwise and sliced

2   15-ounce cans pork and beans in tomato sauce

1   15-ounce can garbanzo beans (chickpeas), rinsed and drained

1   cup sliced carrots

¾   cup bottled barbecue sauce

1   small onion, sliced and separated into rings

2   tablespoons cooked bacon pieces

1 In a 3½- or 4-quart slow cooker combine turkey sausage, pork and beans, garbanzo beans, carrots, barbecue sauce, and onion.

2 Cover and cook on low-heat setting for 6 to 8 hours or on high-heat setting for 3 to 4 hours.

3 Sprinkle each serving with bacon pieces.

Nutrition Facts per serving: 369 cal., 11 g total fat (3 g sat. fat), 63 mg chol., 1,814 mg sodium, 47 g carbo., 11 g fiber, 24 g pro. **Daily Values:** 111% vit. A, 14% vit. C, 12% calcium, 37% iron

A meal in itself, this thick and chunky chowder satisfies whether you use halibut, haddock, or the cod suggested here.

HEARTY FISH CHOWDER

2	medium potatoes, finely chopped
1½	cups chicken broth
1	10¾-ounce can condensed cream of celery soup
1	10-ounce package frozen whole kernel corn
1	10-ounce package frozen baby lima beans
1	cup chopped onion
⅓	cup dry white wine or chicken broth
1	teaspoon lemon-pepper seasoning
2	cloves garlic, minced
1	pound fresh cod or other white fish fillets
1	14½-ounce can stewed tomatoes, undrained
⅓	cup nonfat dry milk powder

PREP:

25 minutes

COOK:

*6 to 7 hours (low)
or 3 to 3½ hours (high),
plus 1 hour (high)*

MAKES:

6 servings

1 In a 3½- or 4-quart slow cooker combine potatoes, chicken broth, celery soup, frozen corn, frozen lima beans, onion, wine, lemon-pepper seasoning, and garlic. Cover and cook on low-heat setting for 6 to 7 hours or on high-heat setting for 3 to 3½ hours.

2 If using low-heat setting, turn to high-heat setting. Add fish. Cover and cook for 1 hour more.

3 Add tomatoes and dry milk powder to mixture in cooker, stirring gently to break up fish.

Nutrition Facts per serving: 295 cal., 4 g total fat (1 g sat. fat), 39 mg chol., 955 mg sodium, 40 g carbo., 6 g fiber, 23 g pro. **Daily Values:** 8% vit. A, 25% vit. C, 12% calcium, 15% iron

Thanks to the dry scalloped potato mix used here, the prep work for this wonderful dill-infused salmon chowder is as quick and easy as can be.

EASY POTATO & SALMON CHOWDER

PREP:

15 minutes

COOK:

*6 to 8 hours (low)
or 3 to 4 hours (high),
plus 20 minutes (high)*

MAKES:

8 servings

2 14-ounce cans reduced-sodium chicken broth

1½ cups frozen whole kernel corn

1½ cups thinly sliced carrots

1½ cups water

½ cup chopped onion

1 4.9-ounce package dry scalloped potato mix

2 teaspoons dried dill

2 cups half-and-half or light cream

½ cup all-purpose flour

2 6-ounce cans skinless, boneless salmon, drained

1 In a 3½- or 4-quart slow cooker combine chicken broth, frozen corn, carrots, water, onion, potato mix (including seasoning packet), and dill. Cover and cook on low-heat setting for 6 to 8 hours or on high-heat setting for 3 to 4 hours.

2 If using low-heat setting, turn to high-heat setting. In a medium bowl whisk together cream and flour. Gradually stir cream mixture into mixture in cooker. Gently stir in salmon. Cover and cook for 20 to 30 minutes more or until thickened.

Nutrition Facts per serving: 269 cal., 10 g total fat (5 g sat. fat), 45 mg chol., 827 mg sodium, 32 g carbo., 2 g fiber, 14 g pro. **Daily Values:** 122% vit. A, 8% vit. C, 8% calcium, 8% iron

To save time and retain all the nutrients potatoes have to offer, don't peel them. Just scrub and cut into cubes.

MANHATTAN-STYLE CLAM CHOWDER

2	6½-ounce cans minced clams or one 10-ounce can whole baby clams
2	medium potatoes, peeled and cut into ½-inch cubes
1	14½-ounce can Italian-style stewed tomatoes, undrained
1½	cups hot-style tomato juice or vegetable juice
1	cup chopped onion
1	cup chopped celery with leaves
½	cup chopped green sweet pepper
1	bay leaf
½	teaspoon dried thyme, crushed
4	slices bacon, crisp-cooked, drained, and crumbled, or ¼ cup cooked bacon pieces

PREP:

20 minutes

COOK:

8 to 10 hours (low) or 4 to 5 hours (high), plus 5 minutes (high)

MAKES:

4 servings

1 Drain clams, reserving liquid (about ⅔ cup). Place clams in a small bowl; cover and chill until needed.

2 In a 3½- or 4-quart slow cooker combine reserved clam liquid, potatoes, tomatoes, tomato juice, onion, celery, sweet pepper, bay leaf, and thyme. Cover and cook on low-heat setting for 8 to 10 hours or on high-heat setting for 4 to 5 hours.

3 If using low-heat setting, turn to high-heat setting. Stir in clams. Cover and cook for 5 minutes more. Remove bay leaf. Sprinkle each serving with crumbled bacon.

Nutrition Facts per serving: 238 cal., 5 g total fat (1 g sat. fat), 34 mg chol., 719 mg sodium, 30 g carbo., 4 g fiber, 17 g pro. **Daily Values:** 19% vit. A, 92% vit. C, 10% calcium, 78% iron

Some like it hot! The Better Homes and Gardens® Taste Panel sure did, and so will the spicy-food lovers in your crowd.

SHRIMP CREOLE

PREP:

20 minutes

COOK:

*5 to 6 hours (low)
or 2½ to 3 hours (high)*

MAKES:

6 to 8 servings

1	14½-ounce can diced tomatoes, undrained
1	14-ounce can chicken broth
1½	cups chopped onions
1	cup chopped green sweet pepper
1	cup sliced celery
1	6-ounce can tomato paste
⅓	cup thinly sliced green onions
1	bay leaf
1½	teaspoons paprika
½	teaspoon black pepper
¼	teaspoon salt
⅛	teaspoon bottled hot pepper sauce
2	cloves garlic, minced
1½	pounds peeled and deveined cooked medium shrimp
3	cups hot cooked rice

1 In a 3½-quart slow cooker combine tomatoes, chicken broth, onions, sweet pepper, celery, tomato paste, green onions, bay leaf, paprika, black pepper, salt, hot pepper sauce, and garlic.

2 Cover and cook on low-heat setting for 5 to 6 hours or on high-heat setting for 2½ to 3 hours.

3 Remove bay leaf. Stir shrimp into mixture in cooker; heat through. Serve over hot cooked rice.

Nutrition Facts per serving: 344 cal., 3 g total fat (1 g sat. fat), 227 mg chol., 673 mg sodium, 39 g carbo., 3 g fiber, 37 g pro. **Daily Values:** 16% vit. A, 67% vit. C, 14% calcium, 34% iron

As summer gives way to fall, come home with a bumper crop of late-season vegetables at their freshest best, then simmer them slowly in this wonderfully varied soup.

FARMER'S MARKET VEGETABLE SOUP

½ of a small rutabaga, peeled and chopped (2 cups)

2 large roma tomatoes, chopped

2 medium carrots or parsnips, chopped

1 large red-skinned potato, chopped

2 medium leeks, chopped

3 14-ounce cans vegetable broth

1 teaspoon fennel seeds, crushed

½ teaspoon dried sage, crushed

¼ to ½ teaspoon black pepper

½ cup dried tiny bow tie pasta

3 cups torn fresh spinach

1 recipe Garlic Toast (optional)

1 In a 3½- or 4-quart slow cooker combine rutabaga, tomatoes, carrots, potato, and leeks. Add broth, fennel seeds, sage, and pepper.

2 Cover and cook on low-heat setting for 8 to 9 hours or on high-heat setting for 4 to 4½ hours. If using low-heat setting, turn to high-heat setting. Stir in pasta. Cover and cook for 20 to 30 minutes more or until pasta is tender. Just before serving, stir in spinach.

3 If desired, float a Garlic Toast on each serving.

Nutrition Facts per serving: 198 cal., 2 g total fat (0 g sat. fat), 0 mg chol., 1,313 mg sodium, 41 g carbo., 8 g fiber, 8 g pro. **Daily Values:** 200% vit. A, 77% vit. C, 11% calcium, 26% iron

PREP:

30 minutes

COOK:

8 to 9 hours (low)
or 4 to 4½ hours (high),
plus 20 minutes (high)

MAKES:

4 servings

GARLIC TOAST
Brush both sides of eight ½-inch baguette slices with 1 tablespoon garlic-flavor olive oil. Arrange on a baking sheet. Broil 3 to 4 inches from the heat for 1 minute. Turn; sprinkle with 2 teaspoons grated Parmesan cheese. Broil for 1 to 2 minutes more or until lightly toasted.

Serve up a large portion of this meatless soup for a main dish or a cup paired with a ham sandwich for lunch.

SWEET POTATO-LIMA BEAN SOUP

PREP:

15 minutes

COOK:

*8 to 10 hours (low)
or 4 to 5 hours (high)*

MAKES:

6 servings

2   14-ounce cans chicken or vegetable broth

2   medium sweet potatoes, peeled and cut into $\frac{1}{2}$-inch pieces

1   10-ounce package frozen baby lima beans

2   medium parsnips, peeled and sliced

1   large onion, chopped

1   cup apple juice

$\frac{1}{2}$ teaspoon dried sage, crushed

$\frac{1}{4}$ teaspoon black pepper

1   In a $3\frac{1}{2}$- or 4-quart slow cooker combine chicken broth, sweet potatoes, frozen lima beans, parsnips, onion, apple juice, sage, and pepper.

2   Cover and cook on low-heat setting for 8 to 10 hours or on high-heat setting for 4 to 5 hours.

Nutrition Facts per serving: 221 cal., 2 g total fat (0 g sat. fat), 0 mg chol., 592 mg sodium, 46 g carbo., 8 g fiber, 7 g pro. **Daily Values:** 275% vit. A, 42% vit. C, 6% calcium, 11% iron

This hearty soup is a delicious way to add healthful brown rice and beans to your family's diet.

HEARTY BEAN SOUP

1¼	cups dry pinto beans
1	cup finely chopped onion
1	teaspoon salt
½	teaspoon paprika
¼	teaspoon black pepper
2	cloves garlic, minced
3	slices bacon, chopped
1	14½-ounce can diced tomatoes, undrained
1½	cups cooked brown rice

1 Rinse beans. In a large saucepan combine beans and 6 cups water. Bring to boiling; reduce heat. Simmer, uncovered, for 10 minutes. Remove from heat. Cover and let stand for 1 hour. Drain and rinse beans.

2 In a 3½- or 4-quart slow cooker combine beans, onion, salt, paprika, pepper, and garlic. Stir in 4 cups *fresh water.* Cover and cook on low-heat setting for 8 to 10 hours or on high-heat setting for 4 to 5 hours.

3 Meanwhile, in the same saucepan cook bacon over medium heat until crisp. Drain on paper towels. Wrap bacon and chill until ready to serve.

4 Turn off cooker. Stir tomatoes and cooked rice into mixture in cooker. Cover and let stand about 5 minutes or until heated through. Sprinkle each serving with bacon.

Nutrition Facts per serving: 233 cal., 2 g total fat (1 g sat. fat), 3 mg chol., 562 mg sodium, 42 g carbo., 11 g fiber, 11 g pro. **Daily Values:** 2% vit. A, 20% vit. C, 8% calcium, 15% iron

PREP:

25 minutes

STAND:

1 hour

COOK:

8 to 10 hours (low) or 4 to 5 hours (high)

MAKES:

6 servings

Ratatouille is a saucy mix of garden vegetables and olives that originated in the South of France. As a soup, it's filled with rich, rustic flavor.

RATATOUILLE SOUP WITH BEANS

PREP:

20 minutes

COOK:

*8 to 10 hours (low)
or 4 to 5 hours (high)*

MAKES:

6 servings

1   medium onion, coarsely chopped

2   cups peeled eggplant cut into ¾-inch cubes

2   medium zucchini, halved lengthwise and sliced
    ¼ inch thick (2½ cups)

1   medium red sweet pepper, coarsely chopped

1   medium green sweet pepper, coarsely chopped

1   15- or 19-ounce can white kidney (cannellini)
    or Great Northern beans, rinsed and drained

1   14½-ounce can diced tomatoes with basil,
    oregano, and garlic, undrained

1   14-ounce can reduced-sodium chicken broth

1   cup hot-style or regular vegetable juice

1   2¼-ounce can sliced pitted ripe olives, drained

6   tablespoons finely shredded Parmesan cheese

1 In a 3½- or 4-quart slow cooker layer in the following order: onion, eggplant, zucchini, sweet peppers, and kidney beans. Pour tomatoes, chicken broth, and vegetable juice over mixture in cooker.

2 Cover and cook on low-heat setting for 8 to 10 hours or on high-heat setting for 4 to 5 hours. Stir in olives. Sprinkle each serving with Parmesan cheese.

Nutrition Facts per serving: 148 cal., 3 g total fat (1 g sat. fat), 6 mg chol., 945 mg sodium, 25 g carbo., 6 g fiber, 10 g pro. **Daily Values:** 43% vit. A, 101% vit. C, 15% calcium, 15% iron

The hardy barley grain gives this vegetable soup its bulk and staying power. You'll feel full and satisfied long after enjoying it.

BARLEY VEGETABLE SOUP

1	cup chopped onion
1	medium carrot, coarsely chopped
1	stalk celery, coarsely chopped
2	cups sliced fresh mushrooms
1	15-ounce can red beans, rinsed and drained
1	14½-ounce can stewed tomatoes, undrained
1	10-ounce package frozen whole kernel corn
½	cup regular barley
2	teaspoons dried Italian seasoning, crushed
¼	teaspoon black pepper
3	cloves garlic, minced
5	cups vegetable or chicken broth

PREP:

25 minutes

COOK:

8 to 10 hours (low) or 4 to 5 hours (high)

MAKES:

6 servings

1 In a 3½- to 5-quart slow cooker place onion, carrot, and celery. Add mushrooms, red beans, tomatoes, frozen corn, barley, Italian seasoning, pepper, and garlic. Pour vegetable broth over mixture in cooker.

2 Cover and cook on low-heat setting for 8 to 10 hours or on high-heat setting for 4 to 5 hours.

Nutrition Facts per serving: 220 cal., 2 g total fat (0 g sat. fat), 0 mg chol., 1,167 mg sodium, 47 g carbo., 9 g fiber, 12 g pro. Daily Values: 60% vit. A, 16% vit. C, 6% calcium, 11% iron

In a melody, Paul Simon and Art Garfunkel immortalized the seasonings in this lovely pantry soup: parsley, sage, rosemary, and thyme. Like the song, it's a truly memorable combination of herbs.

WINTER VEGETABLE SOUP

PREP:

30 minutes

COOK:

10 to 11 hours (low) or 4 1/2 to 5 hours (high)

MAKES:

6 servings

2   15-ounce cans Great Northern or navy beans, rinsed and drained

2   cups water

1   14 1/2-ounce can diced tomatoes, undrained

2   medium parsnips, peeled, halved lengthwise, and cut into 1-inch pieces

1   large onion, chopped

1   medium turnip, peeled and cut into 3/4-inch pieces

1   medium potato, cut into 3/4-inch pieces

1/4   cup dry red wine or water

1   teaspoon salt

1/2   teaspoon dried thyme, crushed

1/4   teaspoon dried sage, crushed

1/4   teaspoon dried rosemary, crushed

4   cloves garlic, minced

1/4   cup snipped fresh parsley

1 In a 3 1/2- or 4-quart slow cooker combine Great Northern beans, water, tomatoes, parsnips, onion, turnip, potato, wine, salt, thyme, sage, rosemary, and garlic.

2 Cover and cook on low-heat setting for 10 to 11 hours or on high-heat setting for 4 1/2 to 5 hours. Just before serving, stir in parsley.

Nutrition Facts per serving: 211 cal., 1 g total fat (0 g sat. fat), 0 mg chol., 853 mg sodium, 41 g carbo., 11 g fiber, 9 g pro. **Daily Values:** 3% vit. A, 44% vit. C, 18% calcium, 18% iron

This zesty soup passes on meat, but it's so full of flavor you'll never miss it.
Top each bowl with a spoonful of sour cream and pass warm rolled tortillas or tortilla chips.

MEXICAN MINESTRONE

2 cups chopped red-skinned potatoes

2 cups frozen cut green beans

2 15-ounce cans black beans, rinsed and drained

2 14½-ounce cans Mexican-style stewed tomatoes, undrained

2 14-ounce cans vegetable broth

1 15¼-ounce can whole kernel corn, rinsed and drained

1 15-ounce can garbanzo beans (chickpeas), rinsed and drained

1 cup bottled salsa

Dairy sour cream (optional)

1 In a 5- to 6-quart slow cooker combine potatoes and frozen green beans. Add black beans, Mexican-style tomatoes, vegetable broth, corn, garbanzo beans, and salsa.

2 Cover and cook on low-heat setting for 9 to 11 hours or on high-heat setting for 4½ to 5½ hours. If desired, top each serving with sour cream.

Nutrition Facts per serving: 199 cal., 4 g total fat (2 g sat. fat), 5 mg chol., 1,051 mg sodium, 37 g carbo., 7 g fiber, 10 g pro. Daily Values: 9% vit. A, 37% vit. C, 8% calcium, 12% iron

PREP:

10 minutes

COOK:

9 to 11 hours (low)
or 4½ to 5½ hours (high)

MAKES:

12 servings

Move over, chili powder: Jerk seasoning brings something new to the chili bowl. With a variety of beans and the roasted red peppers, color sparks fly.

CARIBBEAN PEPPER CHILI

PREP:

15 minutes

COOK:

*6 to 8 hours (low)
or 3 to 4 hours (high)*

MAKES:

6 servings

1   15-ounce can black beans, rinsed and drained

1   15-ounce can red kidney beans, rinsed and drained

1   15-ounce can small white beans, rinsed and drained

2   7½-ounce cans chopped tomatoes with jalapeño peppers, undrained

1   14-ounce can vegetable or chicken broth

1   12-ounce jar roasted red sweet peppers, drained and chopped

½   cup chopped onion

½   of a 6-ounce can (⅓ cup) tomato paste

1   to 3 teaspoons Jamaican jerk seasoning

4   cloves garlic, minced

1️⃣ In a 3½- or 4-quart slow cooker combine black beans, kidney beans, white beans, tomatoes, vegetable broth, roasted sweet peppers, onion, tomato paste, Jamaican jerk seasoning, and garlic.

2️⃣ Cover and cook on low-heat setting for 6 to 8 hours or on high-heat setting for 3 to 4 hours.

Nutrition Facts per serving: 183 cal., 1 g total fat (0 g sat. fat), 0 mg chol., 1,025 mg sodium, 41 g carbo., 12 g fiber, 15 g pro. **Daily Values:** 8% vit. A, 128% vit. C, 7% calcium, 19% iron

Top this dish with the optional prosciutto, and it will have an even greater Italian flair.

TRIPLE-ONION & TOMATO SOUP

- 2   14-ounce cans beef broth
- 1   14½-ounce can Italian-style stewed tomatoes, undrained
- 1   large sweet onion (such as Vidalia or Walla Walla), quartered and cut into thin slices
- ½   cup water
- 2   medium shallots, coarsely chopped
- 2   tablespoons tomato paste
- 1   teaspoon bottled minced roasted garlic
- ⅓   cup sliced green onions
- ⅓   cup finely shredded fresh basil
- ⅓   cup finely shredded Romano or Parmesan cheese
- ⅓   cup finely shredded prosciutto (optional)

1 In a 3½- or 4-quart slow cooker combine beef broth, tomatoes, onion, water, shallots, tomato paste, and roasted garlic.

2 Cover and cook on low-heat setting for 10 to 12 hours or on high-heat setting for 5 to 6 hours.

3 Sprinkle each serving with green onions, basil, Romano cheese, and, if desired, prosciutto.

Nutrition Facts per serving: 85 cal., 2 g total fat (1 g sat. fat), 5 mg chol., 709 mg sodium, 13 g carbo., 2 g fiber, 4 g pro. **Daily Values:** 12% vit. A, 15% vit. C, 9% calcium, 5% iron

PREP:

20 minutes

COOK:

10 to 12 hours (low) or 5 to 6 hours (high)

MAKES:

6 side-dish servings

If you enjoy cream of mushroom soup but want something more substantial, you'll appreciate this version that's made extra-filling with potatoes. Hint: If you choose the 20-ounce package of potatoes, it may come with onions—a welcome addition to this recipe.

POTATO-MUSHROOM CHOWDER

PREP:

10 minutes

COOK:

6 to 7 hours (low) or 3 to 3½ hours (high)

MAKES:

6 to 8 side-dish servings

1   16- to 20-ounce package refrigerated diced potatoes

2   6-ounce jars sliced mushrooms, drained

½   teaspoon dried dill

¼   teaspoon black pepper

4   cloves garlic, minced

2   10¾-ounce cans condensed cream of mushroom soup

2   cups water

Dairy sour cream (optional)

1 In a 3½- or 4-quart slow cooker combine potatoes, mushrooms, dill, pepper, and garlic. In a medium bowl combine mushroom soup and water. Stir into mixture in cooker.

2 Cover and cook on low-heat setting for 6 to 7 hours or on high-heat setting for 3 to 3½ hours. If desired, top each serving with sour cream.

Nutrition Facts per serving: 179 cal., 6 g total fat (2 g sat. fat), 2 mg chol., 996 mg sodium, 26 g carbo., 3 g fiber, 5 g pro. **Daily Values:** 1% vit. A, 9% vit. C, 2% calcium, 3% iron

You'll love the extra punch of flavor caraway seeds bring to this soup.

CAULIFLOWER-CHEESE SOUP

2 cups cubed peeled potatoes

3 medium leeks, halved lengthwise, rinsed, and sliced

6 cups cauliflower florets

¼ teaspoon black pepper

2 14-ounce cans reduced-sodium chicken broth

½ cup water

8 ounces process Swiss cheese slices, torn into small pieces, or American cheese, cubed

½ teaspoon caraway seeds, crushed

PREP:

20 minutes

COOK:

6 to 8 hours (low) or 3 to 4 hours (high), plus 10 minutes (high)

MAKES:

8 side-dish servings

1 In a 3½- or 4-quart slow cooker place potatoes and leeks. Add cauliflower and pepper. Pour chicken broth and water over mixture in cooker. Cover and cook on low-heat setting for 6 to 8 hours or on high-heat setting for 3 to 4 hours.

2 Remove about half of the mixture from cooker; cool slightly. Transfer half of the cooled mixture to a blender container or food processor bowl. Cover and blend or process until nearly smooth. Return to cooker. Repeat with remaining half of cooled mixture.

3 If using low-heat setting, turn to high-heat setting. Stir in cheese and caraway seeds. Cover and cook for 10 to 15 minutes more. Stir until cheese is melted.

Nutrition Facts per serving: 170 cal., 7 g total fat (5 g sat. fat), 25 mg chol., 713 mg sodium, 17 g carbo., 3 g fiber, 10 g pro. **Daily Values:** 7% vit. A, 60% vit. C, 24% calcium, 7% iron

This dish is an appropriate sit-down starter to an elegant fall meal.

GOLDEN SQUASH SOUP

PREP:

30 minutes

COOK:

*6 to 8 hours (low)
or 3 to 4 hours (high)*

MAKES:

6 to 8 side-dish servings

2 pounds butternut squash, peeled, seeded, and cut into 1-inch cubes

1 large onion, chopped

2 stalks celery, chopped

2 cloves garlic, minced

2 14-ounce cans chicken broth

¾ cup half-and-half or light cream

Purchased basil pesto

1 In a 3½- or 4-quart slow cooker place squash, onion, celery, and garlic. Pour chicken broth over mixture in cooker.

2 Cover and cook on low-heat setting for 6 to 8 hours or on high-heat setting for 3 to 4 hours. Turn off cooker. Cool slightly.

3 Add squash mixture, in batches, to a blender container or food processor bowl. Cover and blend or process until smooth. Stir in cream. Top each serving with pesto.

Nutrition Facts per serving: 179 cal., 10 g total fat (3 g sat. fat), 13 mg chol., 687 mg sodium, 21 g carbo., 1 g fiber, 5 g pro. **Daily Values:** 192% vit. A, 42% vit. C, 13% calcium, 6% iron

SLOW COOKED SIDES

3

Bet you didn't know traditional baked bean flavorings work great with lima beans too.

MAPLE BAKED LIMAS

PREP:

25 minutes

STAND:

1 hour

COOK:

7 to 9 hours (low)
or 3½ to 4½ hours (high)

MAKES:

10 servings

2½ cups dry baby lima beans (1 pound)

1½ cups chopped onions

1½ cups chopped celery

¾ cup pure maple syrup or maple-flavored syrup

½ cup catsup

1 tablespoon Worcestershire sauce

1 bay leaf

¾ teaspoon salt

⅛ teaspoon black pepper

Bacon, crisp-cooked, drained, and crumbled (optional)

1 Rinse beans. In a Dutch oven combine beans and 8 cups water. Bring to boiling; reduce heat. Simmer, uncovered, for 10 minutes. Remove from heat. Cover and let stand for 1 hour. Drain and rinse beans.

2 In a 3½- or 4-quart slow cooker combine beans, onions, celery, maple syrup, catsup, Worcestershire sauce, bay leaf, salt, and pepper. Stir in ¾ cup *fresh water.*

3 Cover and cook on low-heat setting for 7 to 9 hours or on high-heat setting for 3½ to 4½ hours. Remove bay leaf. If desired, sprinkle each serving with bacon.

Nutrition Facts per serving: 241 cal., 1 g total fat (0 g sat. fat), 0 mg chol., 361 mg sodium, 51 g carbo., 10 g fiber, 10 g pro. **Daily Values:** 3% vit. A, 7% vit. C, 6% calcium, 15% iron

Don't be surprised when people ask you if these are made from scratch. The correct response is a simple smile.

SHORTCUT BAKED BEANS

2   16-ounce cans pork and beans in tomato sauce

2   15-ounce cans red kidney beans, drained

1/2   cup catsup

1/4   cup packed brown sugar

2   tablespoons cooked bacon pieces

4   teaspoons dried minced onion

4   teaspoons prepared mustard

PREP:

10 minutes

COOK:

5 to 6 hours (low)
or 2½ to 3 hours (high)

MAKES:

8 to 10 servings

1 In a 3½- or 4-quart slow cooker combine pork and beans, kidney beans, catsup, brown sugar, bacon pieces, dried onion, and mustard.

2 Cover and cook on low-heat setting for 5 to 6 hours or on high-heat setting for 2½ to 3 hours.

Nutrition Facts per serving: 235 cal., 2 g total fat (1 g sat. fat), 9 mg chol., 894 mg sodium, 49 g carbo., 12 g fiber, 14 g pro. Daily Values: 6% vit. A, 10% vit. C, 10% calcium, 29% iron

*This might be the most famous potluck recipe. It has appeared in many Better Homes and Gardens®
books and magazines throughout the years—and for good reason!*

BAKED BEAN QUINTET

PREP:

15 minutes

COOK:

*10 to 12 hours (low)
or 4 to 5 hours (high)*

MAKES:

12 to 16 servings

1	large onion, chopped
6	slices bacon, cut up
1	clove garlic, minced
1	16-ounce can lima beans, drained
1	16-ounce can pork and beans in tomato sauce
1	15-ounce can red kidney beans, drained
1	15-ounce can butter beans, drained
1	15-ounce can garbanzo beans (chickpeas), drained
¾	cup catsup
½	cup molasses
¼	cup packed brown sugar
1	tablespoon prepared mustard
1	tablespoon Worcestershire sauce

1 In a large skillet cook onion, bacon, and garlic over medium heat until bacon is crisp. Drain off fat.

2 Transfer onion mixture to a 3½- or 4-quart slow cooker. Stir in lima beans, pork and beans, kidney beans, butter beans, garbanzo beans, catsup, molasses, brown sugar, mustard, and Worcestershire sauce.

3 Cover and cook on low-heat setting for 10 to 12 hours or on high-heat setting for 4 to 5 hours.

Nutrition Facts per serving: 245 cal., 3 g total fat (1 g sat. fat), 5 mg chol., 882 mg sodium, 47 g carbo., 9 g fiber, 10 g pro. **Daily Values:** 5% vit. A, 13% vit. C, 10% calcium, 22% iron

The children (and adults) will gladly eat their vegetables when this offering is on the table.

GREEN BEANS IN CHEESE-BACON SAUCE

2	16-ounce packages frozen cut green beans
½	cup finely chopped onion
1	4½-ounce jar sliced mushrooms, drained
1	4-ounce jar sliced pimiento, drained
1½	cups shredded cheddar cheese (6 ounces)
1	10¾-ounce can condensed cream of mushroom soup
¼	teaspoon black pepper
6	slices bacon, crisp-cooked, drained, and crumbled

PREP:

10 minutes

COOK:

*5 to 6 hours (low)
or 2½ to 3 hours (high)*

MAKES:

8 to 10 servings

1 In a 3½- or 4-quart slow cooker combine frozen green beans, onion, mushrooms, and pimiento. Add cheddar cheese, mushroom soup, and pepper. Sprinkle with bacon.

2 Cover and cook on low-heat setting for 5 to 6 hours or on high-heat setting for 2½ to 3 hours. Stir before serving.

Nutrition Facts per serving: 199 cal., 13 g total fat (6 g sat. fat), 27 mg chol., 536 mg sodium, 14 g carbo., 4 g fiber, 10 g pro. **Daily Values:** 19% vit. A, 32% vit. C, 21% calcium, 9% iron

The diced ham in this slow cooker side dish imparts a wonderfully rich flavor.

SIMPLE SUCCOTASH WITH HAM

PREP:

15 minutes

COOK:

*7 to 9 hours (low)
or 3^1/$_2$ to 4^1/$_2$ hours (high)*

MAKES:

8 to 10 servings

1	16-ounce package frozen baby lima beans, thawed
1	16-ounce package frozen whole kernel corn, thawed
2	cups diced cooked ham
1	cup coarsely chopped red or green sweet pepper
^{1}/$_2$	cup chopped onion
^{1}/$_2$	cup chopped celery
^{1}/$_4$	teaspoon black pepper
2	cloves garlic, minced
1	14-ounce can chicken broth

1 In a 3^1/$_2$- or 4-quart slow cooker combine lima beans, corn, ham, sweet pepper, onion, celery, black pepper, and garlic. Pour chicken broth over mixture in cooker.

2 Cover and cook on low-heat setting for 7 to 9 hours or on high-heat setting for 3^1/$_2$ to 4^1/$_2$ hours. Serve with a slotted spoon.

Nutrition Facts per serving: 191 cal., 4 g total fat (1 g sat. fat), 21 mg chol., 719 mg sodium, 26 g carbo., 5 g fiber, 15 g pro. **Daily Values:** 24% vit. A, 69% vit. C, 3% calcium, 9% iron

KEEP A LID ON IT!
Although it's tempting, resist lifting the slow cooker lid to see how the food is doing or to give it a stir. Because a slow cooker cooks food at such a low temperature, removing the lid reduces the temperature inside the cooker dramatically, especially when the low-heat setting is used. An uncovered cooker loses as much as 20 degrees of cooking heat in just 2 minutes. When you lift the cover to add ingredients, replace it as quickly as possible. Most recipes do not need stirring during cooking.

Brilliantly colored fruits and vegetables sparkle in this tart and tangy side dish, which also happens to be packed with nutritive value. Some call it beauty food.

CRANBERRY-ORANGE SAUCED BEETS

2	pounds medium beets, peeled and quartered
$1/2$	teaspoon ground nutmeg
1	cup cranberry juice
1	teaspoon finely shredded orange peel
2	tablespoons butter or margarine
2	tablespoons sugar
4	teaspoons cornstarch

1 In a $3^1/2$- or 4-quart slow cooker place beets. Sprinkle with nutmeg. Add cranberry juice and orange peel; dot with butter.

2 Cover and cook on low-heat setting for 6 to 7 hours or on high-heat setting for 3 to $3^1/2$ hours. If using low-heat setting, turn to high-heat setting.

3 In a small bowl combine sugar and cornstarch. Stir about $1/2$ cup of the hot cooking liquid into cornstarch mixture; gently stir into mixture in cooker. Cover and cook for 15 to 30 minutes more or until cranberry mixture is thickened.

Nutrition Facts per serving: 127 cal., 4 g total fat (3 g sat. fat), 11 mg chol., 117 mg sodium, 22 g carbo., 2 g fiber, 2 g pro. **Daily Values:** 4% vit. A, 31% vit. C, 2% calcium, 5% iron

PREP:

20 minutes

COOK:

*6 to 7 hours (low)
or 3 to $3^1/2$ hours (high),
plus 15 minutes (high)*

MAKES:

6 servings

Who would have thought to put pears and cabbage together? You'll be glad someone did—the two foods' divergent flavors and textures complement each other well!

RED CABBAGE WITH PEARS

PREP:

15 minutes

COOK:

*6 to 7 hours (low)
or 2½ to 3 hours (high)*

MAKES:

8 servings

3 tablespoons cider vinegar

2 tablespoons sugar

2 tablespoons water

1 tablespoon butter or margarine, melted

1 teaspoon caraway seeds, crushed

6 cups coarsely shredded red cabbage

2 medium pears, cored and sliced

1 In a 3½- or 4-quart slow cooker combine vinegar, sugar, water, melted butter, and caraway seeds. Add cabbage and pears.

2 Cover and cook on low-heat setting for 6 to 7 hours or on high-heat setting for 2½ to 3 hours. Stir before serving. Serve with a slotted spoon.

Nutrition Facts per serving: 65 cal., 2 g total fat (1 g sat. fat), 4 mg chol., 22 mg sodium, 13 g carbo., 2 g fiber, 1 g pro. **Daily Values:** 2% vit. A, 44% vit. C, 3% calcium, 2% iron

The classic cheesy cauliflower is already wonderful enough, but it's even better with corn, green onions, and a bonus of crisp bacon.

CHEESY CAULIFLOWER & CORN

4   cups cauliflower florets

2   cups frozen whole kernel corn

6   ounces American cheese, cut into cubes

1   10¾-ounce can reduced-fat and reduced-sodium condensed cream of celery soup

½   cup sliced green onions

¼   teaspoon black pepper

4   slices bacon, crisp-cooked, drained, and crumbled

PREP:
15 minutes
COOK:
6 to 7 hours (low) or 3 to 3½ hours (high)
MAKES:
8 to 10 servings

1 In a 3½- or 4-quart slow cooker combine cauliflower, frozen corn, American cheese, celery soup, green onions, and pepper.

2 Cover and cook on low-heat setting for 6 to 7 hours or on high-heat setting for 3 to 3½ hours. Before serving, stir in crumbled bacon.

Nutrition Facts per serving: 156 cal., 8 g total fat (5 g sat. fat), 23 mg chol., 559 mg sodium, 14 g carbo., 2 g fiber, 9 g pro. **Daily Values:** 6% vit. A, 36% vit. C, 19% calcium, 2% iron

A classic comfort food with a yummy foundation of cream cheese and chives, this vegetable serve-along is a no-miss hit.

CREAMED CORN

PREP:

10 minutes

COOK:

8 to 10 hours (low) or 4 to 5 hours (high)

MAKES:

12 servings

2   16-ounce packages frozen whole kernel corn

2   cups coarsely chopped red or green sweet peppers

1   cup chopped onion

1/4 teaspoon black pepper

1   10 3/4-ounce can condensed cream of celery soup

1   8-ounce tub cream cheese with chive and onion or cream cheese with garden vegetables

1/4 cup milk

1 In a 3 1/2- or 4-quart slow cooker combine frozen corn, sweet peppers, onion, and black pepper. In a medium bowl whisk together celery soup, cream cheese, and milk. Pour over mixture in cooker.

2 Cover and cook on low-heat setting for 8 to 10 hours or on high-heat setting for 4 to 5 hours. Stir before serving.

Nutrition Facts per serving: 166 cal., 8 g total fat (5 g sat. fat), 21 mg chol., 280 mg sodium, 22 g carbo., 2 g fiber, 4 g pro. **Daily Values:** 33% vit. A, 75% vit. C, 5% calcium, 3% iron

Next time you cook a Sunday dinner ham, make this cheesy corn to go with it.

CHEESY CORN WITH CHILES

2   16-ounce packages frozen white whole kernel corn (shoe peg), thawed

2   cups shredded Monterey Jack cheese (8 ounces)

1   14³/₄-ounce can cream-style corn

1   cup chopped tomatoes

1   4-ounce can diced green chile peppers, undrained

¹/₃   cup chopped onion

1¹/₂   teaspoons chili powder

¹/₂   teaspoon salt

1   16-ounce carton dairy sour cream

2   tablespoons snipped fresh cilantro

PREP:

15 minutes

COOK:

*5 to 6 hours (low)
or 2¹/₂ to 3 hours (high)*

STAND:

10 minutes

MAKES:

12 servings

① In a 3¹/₂- or 4-quart slow cooker combine whole kernel corn, Monterey Jack cheese, cream-style corn, tomatoes, green chile peppers, onion, chili powder, and salt.

② Cover and cook on low-heat setting for 5 to 6 hours or on high-heat setting for 2¹/₂ to 3 hours.

③ Turn off cooker. Gently stir in sour cream and cilantro. Cover and let stand for 10 minutes before serving.

Nutrition Facts per serving: 250 cal., 15 g total fat (9 g sat. fat), 33 mg chol., 350 mg sodium, 25 g carbo., 2 g fiber, 9 g pro. **Daily Values:** 15% vit. A, 21% vit. C, 20% calcium, 4% iron

Leave the red skins on the potatoes! They're not only thin and easy to chew but also pretty—especially when covered with the sprinkling of parsley.

ROSEMARY-SCENTED RED POTATOES

PREP:

20 minutes

COOK:

*7 to 8 hours (low)
or 3 to 3½ hours (high)*

MAKES:

6 to 8 servings

2½ pounds small red-skinned potatoes, quartered

2 tablespoons water

2 tablespoons butter or margarine, melted

½ teaspoon finely shredded lemon peel

1 tablespoon lemon juice

1 teaspoon dried rosemary, crushed

½ teaspoon salt

¼ teaspoon black pepper

2 cloves garlic, minced

2 tablespoons snipped fresh parsley

1 In a 3½- or 4-quart slow cooker combine potatoes, water, melted butter, lemon peel, lemon juice, rosemary, salt, pepper, and garlic.

2 Cover and cook on low-heat setting for 7 to 8 hours or on high-heat setting for 3 to 3½ hours. Transfer to a serving bowl. Stir in parsley.

Nutrition Facts per serving: 179 cal., 4 g total fat (3 g sat. fat), 11 mg chol., 249 mg sodium, 32 g carbo., 3 g fiber, 4 g pro. **Daily Values:** 5% vit. A, 52% vit. C, 3% calcium, 15% iron

If you like creamy potatoes but don't particularly enjoy making cream sauces, this recipe is for you.

CREAMY HERBED POTATOES

Nonstick cooking spray

1 28-ounce package loose-pack frozen diced hash brown potatoes with onion and peppers, thawed

1 10¾-ounce can condensed cream of chicken soup

1 8-ounce package cream cheese, cut into cubes

2 teaspoons dried Italian seasoning, crushed

¼ teaspoon salt

¼ teaspoon black pepper

1 Lightly coat a 3½- or 4-quart slow cooker with cooking spray; set aside. In a large bowl stir together hash brown potatoes, soup, cream cheese, Italian seasoning, salt, and pepper. Spoon into prepared cooker.

2 Cover and cook on low-heat setting for 5 to 6 hours. Stir potato mixture before serving.

Nutrition Facts per serving: 213 cal., 13 g total fat (7 g sat. fat), 34 mg chol., 490 mg sodium, 21 g carbo., 2 g fiber, 5 g pro. Daily Values: 11% vit. A, 19% vit. C, 4% calcium, 9% iron

PREP:
10 minutes
COOK:
5 to 6 hours (low)
MAKES:
8 servings

SLOW COOKED SIDES   133

Everyone who loves potatoes loves them even more when they're mixed with chopped prosciutto, leeks, and smoked Gouda and provolone.

EASY CHEESY POTATOES

PREP:

20 minutes

COOK:

5 to 6 hours (low)

MAKES:

12 servings

1   28-ounce package loose-pack frozen diced hash brown potatoes with onion and peppers, thawed

1   10¾-ounce can condensed cream of chicken with herbs soup

1   8-ounce package cream cheese, cut into cubes

1   cup finely shredded smoked Gouda cheese (4 ounces)

1   cup finely shredded provolone cheese (4 ounces)

¾   cup milk

¼   cup finely chopped leek or thinly sliced green onions

¼   cup chopped prosciutto or 4 slices bacon, crisp-cooked, drained, and crumbled

½   teaspoon black pepper

2   tablespoons snipped fresh chives

1 In a 3½- or 4-quart slow cooker combine hash brown potatoes, chicken soup, cream cheese, Gouda cheese, provolone cheese, milk, leek, prosciutto (if using), and pepper.

2 Cover and cook on low-heat setting for 5 to 6 hours. Before serving, gently stir in chives and, if using, crumbled bacon.

Nutrition Facts per serving: 216 cal., 14 g total fat (8 g sat. fat), 39 mg chol., 534 mg sodium, 16 g carbo., 2 g fiber, 8 g pro. **Daily Values:** 12% vit. A, 14% vit. C, 18% calcium, 6% iron

For the best contrast of textures, spoon the zesty, hot potatoes over the spinach leaves just before serving.

HOT GERMAN POTATO SALAD

2	pounds potatoes, peeled and cut into ¼-inch slices (about 6 cups)
1	cup chopped onion
1	cup chopped celery
¾	cup water
⅔	cup cider vinegar
¼	cup sugar
1	teaspoon salt
¾	teaspoon celery seeds
¼	teaspoon black pepper
6	slices bacon, crisp-cooked, drained, and crumbled
¼	cup snipped fresh parsley
1	10-ounce package prewashed spinach
	Snipped fresh dill (optional)

PREP:
20 minutes

COOK:
8 to 10 hours (low) or 4 to 5 hours (high)

MAKES:
8 servings

1 In a 3½- or 4-quart slow cooker combine potatoes, onion, and celery. In a small bowl combine water, vinegar, sugar, salt, celery seeds, and pepper. Pour over mixture in cooker.

2 Cover and cook on low-heat setting for 8 to 10 hours or on high-heat setting for 4 to 5 hours. Stir in crumbled bacon and parsley.

3 Line salad plates with spinach. Spoon potato mixture on top of spinach. If desired, garnish with dill.

Nutrition Facts per serving: 157 cal., 3 g total fat (1 g sat. fat), 4 mg chol., 426 mg sodium, 30 g carbo., 5 g fiber, 5 g pro. **Daily Values:** 40% vit. A, 48% vit. C, 5% calcium, 20% iron

For some, sweet potatoes are an indispensable part of the holiday season.
If you're a member of that club, try this new twist on the popular holiday tuber.

APPLE-CINNAMON SWEET POTATOES

PREP:

15 minutes

COOK:

5 to 6 hours (low)
or 2 1/2 to 3 hours (high)

MAKES:

8 servings

3 pounds sweet potatoes, peeled and cut into 3/4-inch pieces

1/2 cup packed brown sugar

1/2 cup apple juice

1/4 cup butter or margarine, cut into small pieces

1 teaspoon ground cinnamon

1 teaspoon vanilla

1/3 cup chopped walnuts, toasted

1 In a 3 1/2- or 4-quart slow cooker combine sweet potatoes, brown sugar, apple juice, butter, cinnamon, and vanilla.

2 Cover and cook on low-heat setting for 5 to 6 hours or on high-heat setting for 2 1/2 to 3 hours. Before serving, stir in walnuts.

Nutrition Facts per serving: 276 cal., 10 g total fat (4 g sat. fat), 16 mg chol., 83 mg sodium, 46 g carbo., 4 g fiber, 3 g pro. **Daily Values:** 447% vit. A, 43% vit. C, 5% calcium, 7% iron

Deep orange mashed sweet potatoes are undeniably beautiful both on the table and plate.
The addition of parsnips affects only their sophisticated taste.

MASHED SWEET POTATOES & PARSNIPS

Nonstick cooking spray

1½ pounds sweet potatoes, peeled and cubed (about 4 cups)

3 medium parsnips, peeled and cubed

½ cup chicken broth

2 tablespoons butter or margarine, melted

½ teaspoon ground sage

½ teaspoon onion salt

PREP:

20 minutes

COOK:

7 to 8 hours (low)
or 3½ to 4 hours (high)

MAKES:

6 to 8 servings

1 Lightly coat a 3½- or 4-quart slow cooker with cooking spray. Add sweet potatoes, parsnips, chicken broth, butter, sage, and onion salt.

2 Cover and cook on low-heat setting for 7 to 8 hours or on high-heat setting for 3½ to 4 hours. Using a potato masher, mash sweet potato mixture until fluffy.

Nutrition Facts per serving: 166 cal., 5 g total fat (3 g sat. fat), 11 mg chol., 273 mg sodium, 30 g carbo., 5 g fiber, 2 g pro. **Daily Values:** 298% vit. A, 35% vit. C, 4% calcium, 4% iron

Root vegetables and balsamic vinegar are two very popular ingredients on trendy bistro menus. You can take the idea home with this creative side dish.

BALSAMIC ROOT VEGETABLES

PREP:

15 minutes

COOK:

9 to 11 hours (low)
or 4^1/$_2$ to 5^1/$_2$ hours (high)

MAKES:

8 servings

3	medium potatoes, peeled and cut into 1-inch pieces
3	medium parsnips, peeled and cut into 1-inch pieces
1	16-ounce package peeled baby carrots
^{1}/$_2$	of a 16-ounce package (2 cups) frozen small whole onions
1	cup chicken broth
^{1}/$_4$	cup balsamic vinegar
2	tablespoons brown sugar
^{1}/$_4$	teaspoon salt
^{1}/$_4$	teaspoon black pepper
2	cloves garlic, minced

1 In a 3^1/$_2$- or 4-quart slow cooker combine potatoes, parsnips, carrots, onions, chicken broth, vinegar, brown sugar, salt, pepper, and garlic.

2 Cover and cook on low-heat setting for 9 to 11 hours or on high-heat setting for 4^1/$_2$ to 5^1/$_2$ hours.

Nutrition Facts per serving: 136 cal., 1 g total fat (0 g sat. fat), 0 mg chol., 235 mg sodium, 32 g carbo., 6 g fiber, 3 g pro. **Daily Values:** 287% vit. A, 32% vit. C, 8% calcium, 6% iron

Eggplant Parmesan was the model for this zesty zucchini side dish.

ITALIAN-STYLE ZUCCHINI

2½   to 3 pounds zucchini and/or yellow summer squash, halved or quartered lengthwise and cut into 1-inch pieces

2   14½-ounce cans Italian-style stewed tomatoes, drained

1   tablespoon quick-cooking tapioca, crushed

2   teaspoons sugar

½   teaspoon dried basil, crushed

2   cloves garlic, minced

½   cup shredded provolone or mozzarella cheese (2 ounces)

1 In a very large bowl stir together squash, tomatoes, tapioca, sugar, basil, and garlic. Transfer to a 3½- or 4-quart slow cooker.

2 Cover and cook on low-heat setting for 4 to 5 hours or on high-heat setting for 2 to 2½ hours. Transfer to a serving dish; sprinkle with provolone cheese.

Nutrition Facts per serving: 97 cal., 3 g total fat (1 g sat. fat), 5 mg chol., 285 mg sodium, 13 g carbo., 3 g fiber, 4 g pro. **Daily Values:** 11% vit. A, 23% vit. C, 10% calcium, 7% iron

PREP:

15 minutes

COOK:

*4 to 5 hours (low)
or 2 to 2½ hours (high)*

MAKES:

8 to 10 servings

Rich in flavor and color, this squash dish does a good job of accompanying many autumnal entrées such as roasted pork tenderloin or pork chops.

ACORN SQUASH & CRANBERRY-ORANGE SAUCE

PREP:

15 minutes

COOK:

6 to 7 hours (low) or 3 to 3$\frac{1}{2}$ hours (high)

MAKES:

4 to 6 servings

2   medium acorn squash (about 2 pounds)

1   16-ounce can jellied cranberry sauce

$\frac{1}{4}$ cup orange marmalade

$\frac{1}{4}$ cup raisins

$\frac{1}{4}$ teaspoon ground cinnamon

1 Cut each acorn squash in half lengthwise; remove seeds and membranes. Cut squash into 1-inch wedges. Arrange squash in a 3$\frac{1}{2}$- or 4-quart slow cooker.

2 In a small saucepan heat and stir cranberry sauce, orange marmalade, raisins, and cinnamon until smooth. Pour over squash in cooker.

3 Cover and cook on low-heat setting for 6 to 7 hours or on high-heat setting for 3 to 3$\frac{1}{2}$ hours. Season to taste with salt and black pepper.

Nutrition Facts per serving: 328 cal., 0 g total fat (0 g sat. fat), 0 mg chol., 220 mg sodium, 83 g carbo., 5 g fiber, 2 g pro. **Daily Values:** 12% vit. A, 30% vit. C, 7% calcium, 9% iron

This recipe has dual possibilities. For a side dish, cook the dressing in the slow cooker while the turkey or a chicken roasts in the oven. For a main dish, add cooked poultry to the dressing and serve as a hearty meal in itself.

HERBED DRESSING CASSEROLE

4½	cups sliced fresh mushrooms (12 ounces)
1	cup sliced celery
1	cup chopped onion
6	tablespoons butter or margarine
⅓	cup snipped fresh basil or 1 tablespoon dried basil, crushed
½	teaspoon black pepper
12	cups dry bread cubes
1	14-ounce can chicken broth
¾	cup chopped pecans, toasted

1 In a 12-inch skillet cook mushrooms, celery, and onion in hot butter over medium heat for 5 minutes. Remove from heat; stir in basil and pepper. In a very large bowl combine mushroom mixture and bread cubes. Drizzle chicken broth over bread mixture to moisten, tossing gently. Transfer to a 3½- or 4-quart slow cooker.

2 Cover and cook on low-heat setting for 3½ to 4 hours. Just before serving, gently stir in pecans.

Nutrition Facts per serving: 234 cal., 13 g total fat (5 g sat. fat), 17 mg chol., 399 mg sodium, 24 g carbo., 2 g fiber, 6 g pro. **Daily Values:** 6% vit. A, 2% vit. C, 6% calcium, 10% iron

PREP:
30 minutes
COOK:
3½ to 4 hours (low)
MAKES:
12 servings

DRY BREAD CUBES
To make dry bread cubes for stuffing, cut fresh bread into ½-inch cubes. (You'll need 18 to 21 slices of bread to make 12 cups of dry cubes.) Spread cubes in a large shallow roasting pan. Bake, uncovered, in a 300°F oven for 10 to 15 minutes or until bread cubes are dry, stirring twice; cool. (Bread will continue to dry and crisp as it cools.)

This holiday-special stuffing features sausage and apples.

SAUSAGE & APPLE STUFFING

PREP:

30 minutes

COOK:

*4¹/₂ to 5 hours (low) or
2¹/₄ to 2¹/₂ hours (high)*

MAKES:

10 servings

Nonstick cooking spray

12	ounces bulk pork sausage
10	cups dry bread cubes
2	tart cooking apples, cored and coarsely chopped
¹/₂	cup sliced green onions
¹/₃	cup butter or margarine, melted
1	teaspoon poultry seasoning
¹/₄	teaspoon salt
¹/₄	teaspoon black pepper
1	to 1¹/₂ cups chicken broth

1 Lightly coat a 3¹/₂- to 4¹/₂-quart slow cooker with cooking spray. Set aside. In a large skillet cook sausage until meat is brown. Drain off fat. In a very large bowl combine sausage, bread cubes, apples, and green onions.

2 Drizzle melted butter over bread mixture. Sprinkle with poultry seasoning, salt, and pepper. Drizzle enough of the chicken broth over bread mixture to moisten, tossing gently. Transfer to prepared cooker.

3 Cover and cook on low-heat setting for 4¹/₂ to 5 hours or on high-heat setting for 2¹/₄ to 2¹/₂ hours.

Nutrition Facts per serving: 292 cal., 18 g total fat (8 g sat. fat), 37 mg chol., 596 mg sodium, 23 g carbo., 2 g fiber, 7 g pro. Daily Values: 6% vit. A, 4% vit. C, 5% calcium, 8% iron

DRY BREAD CUBES

To make dry bread cubes for stuffing, cut fresh bread into ¹/₂-inch cubes. (You'll need 15 to 18 slices of bread to make 10 cups of dry cubes.) Spread cubes in a large shallow roasting pan. Bake, uncovered, in a 300°F oven for 10 to 15 minutes or until bread cubes are dry, stirring twice; cool. (Bread will continue to dry and crisp as it cools.)

Bits of dried apricot are sun-flavored jewels in this pretty, earthy side dish.
Pair it with roast chicken or broiled salmon and steamed broccoli for an easy, colorful meal.

CREAMY WILD RICE PILAF

1	10¾-ounce can condensed cream of mushroom with roasted garlic or golden mushroom soup
1	cup uncooked wild rice, rinsed and drained
1	cup uncooked regular brown rice
1	cup shredded carrots
1	cup sliced fresh mushrooms
½	cup thinly sliced celery
⅓	cup chopped onion
¼	cup snipped dried apricots
1	teaspoon dried thyme, crushed
1	teaspoon poultry seasoning
¾	teaspoon salt
½	teaspoon black pepper
5½	cups water
½	cup dairy sour cream

PREP:

20 minutes

COOK:

*7 to 8 hours (low)
or 3½ to 4 hours (high)*

MAKES:

12 servings

1 In a 3½- or 4-quart slow cooker combine mushroom soup, wild rice, brown rice, carrots, mushrooms, celery, onion, dried apricots, thyme, poultry seasoning, salt, and pepper. Stir in water.

2 Cover and cook on low-heat setting for 7 to 8 hours or on high-heat setting for 3½ to 4 hours. Stir in sour cream.

Nutrition Facts per serving: 165 cal., 4 g total fat (2 g sat. fat), 4 mg chol., 339 mg sodium, 28 g carbo., 2 g fiber, 4 g pro. **Daily Values:** 52% vit. A, 3% vit. C, 4% calcium, 6% iron

Serve this sweet, pretty sauce with pork or poultry.

PEAR-CRANBERRY SAUCE

PREP:

15 minutes

COOK:

4 to 5 hours

CHILL:

2 hours

MAKES:

6 servings

1	medium orange
1	cup coarsely chopped cranberries (thawed, if frozen)
1	medium pear, cored and chopped
¾	cup sugar

1 Finely shred 1 teaspoon peel from orange; set aside. Peel and section orange, discarding seeds.

2 In a 1½-quart slow cooker stir together orange peel, orange sections, cranberries, pear, and sugar. Cover and cook for 4 to 5 hours.

3 Using a potato masher, crush fruit slightly. Cover and chill for at least 2 hours before serving.

Nutrition Facts per serving: 129 cal., 0 g total fat (0 g sat. fat), 0 mg chol., 0 mg sodium, 33 g carbo., 2 g fiber, 0 g pro. **Daily Values:** 1% vit. A, 26% vit. C, 1% calcium, 1% iron

*Note: Some 1½-quart slow cookers include variable heat settings; others offer only one standard (low) setting. The 1½-quart slow cooker recipes in this book were only tested on the low-heat setting, if one was present.

MEATY
MAIN
DISHES

4

An irresistible combination of molasses, rosemary, garlic, and roasted red peppers ushers an old-fashioned pot roast into a new, delicious millennium.

ROSEMARY BEEF ROAST

PREP:

30 minutes

COOK:

10 to 11 hours (low) or 5 to 5$\frac{1}{2}$ hours (high)

MAKES:

6 servings

1   2- to 2$\frac{1}{2}$-pound boneless beef chuck roast

2   cups fresh mushrooms, halved

1   medium onion, thinly sliced

$\frac{1}{2}$ cup bottled roasted red sweet peppers, drained and thinly sliced

1   14$\frac{1}{2}$-ounce can diced tomatoes, undrained

1   6-ounce can tomato paste

$\frac{1}{2}$ cup dry red wine or water

2   tablespoons quick-cooking tapioca

2   tablespoons mild-flavored molasses

1   teaspoon dried rosemary, crushed

$\frac{1}{2}$ teaspoon salt

$\frac{1}{2}$ teaspoon cracked black pepper

2   cloves garlic, minced

3   cups hot cooked couscous

1 Trim fat from meat. If necessary, cut meat to fit into a 3$\frac{1}{2}$- or 4-quart slow cooker. Place meat in cooker. Add mushrooms, onion, and roasted sweet peppers.

2 For sauce, in a medium bowl combine tomatoes, tomato paste, red wine, tapioca, molasses, rosemary, salt, black pepper, and garlic. Pour over mixture in cooker.

3 Cover and cook on low-heat setting for 10 to 11 hours or on high-heat setting for 5 to 5$\frac{1}{2}$ hours.

4 Remove meat and vegetables from cooker. Skim fat from sauce. Serve meat, vegetables, and sauce with hot cooked couscous.

Nutrition Facts per serving: 382 cal., 6 g total fat (2 g sat. fat), 89 mg chol., 434 mg sodium, 38 g carbo., 3 g fiber, 39 g pro. **Daily Values:** 81% vit. C, 7% calcium, 32% iron

Maque choux is a Cajun dish of corn smothered with green pepper, onions, and tomatoes. As you might expect, most versions bring a hot Cajun kick to the mix, and this recipe is no exception.

CAJUN POT ROAST WITH MAQUE CHOUX

1	2- to 2½-pound boneless beef chuck roast
1	tablespoon Cajun seasoning
1	10-ounce package frozen whole kernel corn
1	cup chopped green sweet pepper
½	cup chopped onion
1	teaspoon sugar
½	teaspoon bottled hot pepper sauce
⅛	teaspoon black pepper
1	14½-ounce can diced tomatoes, undrained

PREP:

20 minutes

COOK:

8 to 10 hours (low) or 4 to 5 hours (high)

MAKES:

6 servings

1 Trim fat from meat. Sprinkle Cajun seasoning evenly over meat; rub in with your fingers. If necessary, cut meat to fit into a 3½- to 4½-quart slow cooker. Place meat in cooker.

2 Add frozen corn, sweet pepper, onion, sugar, hot pepper sauce, and black pepper. Pour tomatoes over mixture in cooker.

3 Cover and cook on low-heat setting for 8 to 10 hours or on high-heat setting for 4 to 5 hours.

4 Remove meat from cooker. Drain vegetables, discarding cooking liquid. Serve meat with vegetables.

Nutrition Facts per serving: 255 cal., 5 g total fat (2 g sat. fat), 90 mg chol., 311 mg sodium, 17 g carbo., 2 g fiber, 34 g pro. **Daily Values:** 4% vit. A, 52% vit. C, 5% calcium, 26% iron

The savory appeal of this loaf comes from herbes de Provence, a melange of herbs common in the South of France. The mix usually includes basil, fennel, lavender, marjoram, rosemary, sage, savory, and thyme.

MEDITERRANEAN-STYLE POT ROAST

PREP:

20 minutes

COOK:

*8 to 10 hours (low)
or 4 to 5 hours (high)*

MAKES:

6 servings

1   2- to 3-pound boneless beef chuck pot roast
1   tablespoon cooking oil
1   medium onion, sliced
1   14½-ounce can diced tomatoes with basil, oregano, and garlic, undrained
¼   cup sliced pitted ripe olives
1   tablespoon Worcestershire sauce
2   teaspoons dried herbes de Provence, crushed
1   teaspoon coarsely ground black pepper
½   cup crumbled feta cheese (2 ounces)

1 Trim fat from meat. If necessary, cut meat to fit into a 3½- or 4-quart slow cooker. In a large skillet brown meat on all sides in hot oil. Drain off fat. Set aside.

2 In cooker place onion. Add meat. In a medium bowl stir together tomatoes, olives, Worcestershire sauce, herbes de Provence, and pepper. Pour over mixture in cooker.

3 Cover and cook on low-heat setting for 8 to 10 hours or on high-heat setting for 4 to 5 hours.

4 Remove meat from cooker. Cut meat into 6 serving-size pieces. Arrange meat on a serving platter. Using a slotted spoon, transfer vegetables to serving platter, reserving juices. Spoon enough of the juices over meat and vegetables to moisten. Sprinkle with feta cheese.

Nutrition Facts per serving: 274 cal., 10 g total fat (4 g sat. fat), 98 mg chol., 641 mg sodium, 9 g carbo., 1 g fiber, 35 g pro. **Daily Values:** 10% vit. A, 10% vit. C, 11% calcium, 30% iron

FRIENDS FOR DINNER
Looking for an easy dinner to share with friends after attending a ball game or other activity away from home? For such occasions, pull out the slow cooker and make recipes that include both meat and vegetables, such as pot roasts, thick soups, or hearty stews. Before leaving for the event, clean the greens and cut up vegetables for a salad to toss together when you return. To keep dessert simple, stock your refrigerator with ice cream and cookies.

Luscious mushroom sauce transforms a budget beef roast into a silver-spoon standout.

MUSHROOM-SAUCED POT ROAST

1	1½-pound boneless beef chuck eye roast, eye round roast, or round rump roast
4	medium potatoes (about 1½ pounds), quartered
1	16-ounce package frozen tiny whole carrots
1	4-ounce can mushroom stems and pieces, drained
½	teaspoon dried tarragon or basil, crushed
¼	teaspoon salt
1	10¾-ounce can condensed golden mushroom soup

1 Trim fat from meat. If necessary, cut meat to fit into a 3½- to 4½-quart slow cooker. Set aside.

2 In cooker combine potatoes, frozen carrots, mushrooms, tarragon, and salt. Add meat. Pour mushroom soup over mixture in cooker.

3 Cover and cook on low-heat setting for 10 to 12 hours or on high-heat setting for 5 to 6 hours.

Nutrition Facts per serving: 338 cal., 8 g total fat (3 g sat. fat), 62 mg chol., 817 mg sodium, 31 g carbo., 5 g fiber, 35 g pro. **Daily Values:** 355% vit. A, 26% vit. C, 4% calcium, 20% iron

PREP:

20 minutes

COOK:

10 to 12 hours (low) or 5 to 6 hours (high)

MAKES:

5 or 6 servings

Translated from German, sauerbraten means sour roast, but it's actually the sweet-sour mixture of ingredients that makes this roast so tasty and tender.

SAUERBRATEN

PREP:

25 minutes

COOK:

*10 to 12 hours (low)
or 5 to 6 hours (high)*

MAKES:

8 servings

1	3- to 3½-pound boneless beef chuck pot roast
10	medium carrots, cut into 1-inch pieces
5	stalks celery, cut into ½-inch pieces
3	small onions, sliced
½	cup raisins (optional)
1	cup water
¾	cup red wine vinegar
2	tablespoons brown sugar
1	teaspoon salt
¼	teaspoon black pepper
½	cup crushed gingersnaps

1 Trim fat from meat. If necessary, cut meat to fit into a 5- to 6-quart slow cooker. Set aside. In cooker place carrots, celery, onions, and, if desired, raisins. Add meat.

2 In a small bowl combine water, vinegar, brown sugar, salt, and pepper. Pour over mixture in cooker.

3 Cover and cook on low-heat setting for 10 to 12 hours or on high-heat setting for 5 to 6 hours.

4 Transfer meat and vegetables to a serving platter, reserving juices. Cover meat and vegetables and keep warm.

5 For gravy, pour juices into a glass measuring cup; skim off fat. Measure 3 cups juices. Pour juices into a medium saucepan; stir in gingersnaps. Cook and stir over medium heat until thickened and bubbly. Serve meat and vegetables with gravy.

Nutrition Facts per serving: 295 cal., 7 g total fat (2 g sat. fat), 101 mg chol., 499 mg sodium, 19 g carbo., 3 g fiber, 38 g pro. **Daily Values:** 387% vit. A, 13% vit. C, 5% calcium, 29% iron

The kick from this dish comes from the lively combo of flavors—hot-style tomato juice, Worcestershire sauce, garlic, and horseradish.

BLOODY MARY POT ROAST

1	3- to 3½-pound boneless beef chuck pot roast
2	tablespoons cooking oil (optional)
¾	cup hot-style tomato juice
¼	cup water
1	teaspoon Worcestershire sauce
2	cloves garlic, minced
2	tablespoons cold water
4	teaspoons cornstarch
1	tablespoon prepared horseradish

PREP:
20 minutes

COOK:
10 to 12 hours (low)
or 5 to 6 hours (high)

MAKES:
10 servings

1 Trim fat from meat. If necessary, cut meat to fit into a 3½- or 4-quart slow cooker. If desired, in a large skillet brown meat on all sides in hot oil. Drain off fat. Transfer meat to cooker.

2 In a small bowl combine tomato juice, the ¼ cup water, the Worcestershire sauce, and garlic. Pour over meat in cooker.

3 Cover and cook on low-heat setting for 10 to 12 hours or on high-heat setting for 5 to 6 hours.

4 Transfer meat to a serving platter, reserving juices. Cover meat and keep warm.

5 For gravy, pour juices into a glass measuring cup; skim off fat. Measure 1½ cups juices. In a small saucepan combine the 2 tablespoons cold water and the cornstarch; stir in juices. Cook and stir over medium heat until thickened and bubbly. Cook and stir for 2 minutes more. Stir in horseradish. Season gravy to taste with salt and black pepper. Serve meat with gravy.

Nutrition Facts per serving: 180 cal., 5 g total fat (2 g sat. fat), 81 mg chol., 255 mg sodium, 2 g carbo., 0 g fiber, 29 g pro. **Daily Values:** 2% vit. A, 5% vit. C, 1% calcium, 19% iron

KEEPING MEAT WARM
Few things are more satisfying than a piping-hot meal. To ensure the meat and vegetables stay warm while thickening the gravy or making a sauce, warm the platter or serving dish by running it under hot water and drying it quickly with a towel. Arrange the meat and vegetables on the platter and cover it with foil while making the sauce.

The snipped fresh cilantro and corn chips are optional, but they do a lot to bring the south-of-the-border appeal home, so it's worth the effort to use them. Serve with a yellow rice mix for something different.

MEXICAN-STYLE POT ROAST

PREP:

20 minutes

COOK:

*9 to 10 hours (low)
or 4 1/2 to 5 hours (high)*

MAKES:

6 to 8 servings

1   2 1/2- to 3-pound boneless beef chuck pot roast
    or pork shoulder roast

1   15-ounce can black beans, rinsed and drained

1   cup frozen whole kernel corn

1   medium onion, cut into wedges

1   cup bottled salsa

1/2   cup water

2   tablespoons quick-cooking tapioca

2   teaspoons chili powder

3   cups hot cooked rice

    Snipped fresh cilantro (optional)

    Crushed corn chips (optional)

1 Trim fat from meat. If necessary, cut meat to fit into a 3 1/2- or 4-quart slow cooker. Set aside. In cooker place black beans, frozen corn, and onion. Add meat.

2 For sauce, in a small bowl combine salsa, water, tapioca, and chili powder. Pour over mixture in cooker.

3 Cover and cook on low-heat setting for 9 to 10 hours or on high-heat setting for 4 1/2 to 5 hours.

4 Remove meat and vegetables from cooker. Skim fat from sauce. Serve meat, vegetables, and sauce with hot cooked rice. If desired, sprinkle with cilantro and corn chips.

Nutrition Facts per serving: 432 cal., 8 g total fat (2 g sat. fat), 112 mg chol., 405 mg sodium, 44 g carbo., 5 g fiber, 48 g pro. **Daily Values:** 9% vit. A, 10% vit. C, 6% calcium, 38% iron

Sure to become a seasonal tradition, this recipe highlights some of the produce you'll find at farmers' markets in the autumn of the year.

BEEF ROAST WITH TOMATO-WINE GRAVY

1	2- to 2½-pound boneless beef chuck pot roast
1	tablespoon cooking oil
2	medium turnips, peeled and cut into 1-inch pieces (2 cups)
1	15-ounce can tomato sauce
3	medium carrots, cut into ½-inch pieces
¼	cup dry red wine or beef broth
3	tablespoons quick-cooking tapioca
¼	teaspoon salt
⅛	teaspoon ground allspice
⅛	teaspoon black pepper
1	pound winter squash, peeled, seeded, and cut into thin wedges or 1½- to 2-inch pieces (2 cups)

PREP:
30 minutes
COOK:
10 to 12 hours (low) or 5 to 6 hours (high)
MAKES:
6 servings

1 Trim fat from meat. If necessary, cut meat to fit into a 3½- to 6-quart slow cooker. In a large skillet brown meat on all sides in hot oil. Drain off fat. Set aside.

2 In cooker combine turnips, tomato sauce, carrots, red wine, tapioca, salt, allspice, and pepper. Add meat and squash.

3 Cover and cook on low-heat setting for 10 to 12 hours or on high-heat setting for 5 to 6 hours.

4 Transfer meat and vegetables to a serving platter. Skim fat from tomato mixture. Serve meat and vegetables with tomato mixture.

Nutrition Facts per serving: 404 cal., 24 g total fat (9 g sat. fat), 87 mg chol., 537 mg sodium, 17 g carbo., 3 g fiber, 26 g pro. **Daily Values:** 183% vit. A, 20% vit. C, 4% calcium, 20% iron

A beef brisket jazzed up with sherry, garlic, ginger, and hoisin sauce is definitely Asian-inspired.

GINGERED BRISKET

PREP:

20 minutes

COOK:

*10 to 12 hours (low)
or 5 to 6 hours (high)*

MAKES:

6 to 8 servings

1	2½- to 3-pound fresh beef brisket
2	4½-ounce jars whole mushrooms, drained
2	tablespoons quick-cooking tapioca
¼	cup bottled hoisin sauce
¼	cup water
2	tablespoons reduced-sodium soy sauce
2	tablespoons dry sherry or water
1	tablespoon grated fresh ginger
½	teaspoon garlic powder
¼	to ½ teaspoon crushed red pepper
½	cup bias-sliced green onions
3	to 4 cups hot cooked rice

1 Trim fat from meat. If necessary, cut meat to fit into a 3½- or 4-quart slow cooker. Place meat in cooker. Add mushrooms and tapioca.

2 For sauce, in a small bowl combine hoisin sauce, water, soy sauce, dry sherry, ginger, garlic powder, and crushed red pepper. Pour over mixture in cooker.

3 Cover and cook on low-heat setting for 10 to 12 hours or on high-heat setting for 5 to 6 hours.

4 Transfer meat and mushrooms to a serving platter. If necessary, skim fat from sauce. Spoon some of the sauce over meat and mushrooms and sprinkle with bias-sliced green onions. Serve with hot cooked rice. Pass remaining sauce.

Nutrition Facts per serving: 418 cal., 10 g total fat (3 g sat. fat), 109 mg chol., 592 mg sodium, 33 g carbo., 2 g fiber, 44 g pro. **Daily Values:** 2% vit. A, 4% vit. C, 4% calcium, 29% iron

The longer a brisket cooks, the more tender it becomes, so if your crockery cooker has a high or low option, choose the low one.

TANGY BARBECUE BEEF SANDWICHES

2 tablespoons chili powder

1 teaspoon celery seeds

½ teaspoon salt

½ teaspoon black pepper

1 3-pound fresh beef brisket

2 medium onions, thinly sliced

1 cup bottled smoke-flavored barbecue sauce

½ cup beer or ginger ale

8 kaiser or Portuguese rolls, split and toasted

Bottled hot pepper sauce (optional)

Mango slices

PREP:
25 minutes
COOK:
10 to 12 hours (low)
STAND:
15 minutes
MAKES:
8 sandwiches

1 In a small bowl combine chili powder, celery seeds, salt, and pepper. Trim fat from meat. Sprinkle chili mixture evenly over meat; rub in with your fingers. If necessary, cut meat to fit into a 3½- to 6-quart slow cooker. Set aside.

2 In cooker place half of the sliced onions. Add meat and remaining sliced onions. In a small bowl stir together barbecue sauce and beer. Pour over mixture in cooker.

3 Cover and cook on low-heat setting for 10 to 12 hours. Remove meat from cooker; let stand for 15 minutes. Using two forks, pull meat apart into shreds. Return meat to cooker; heat through.

4 To serve, using a slotted spoon, place meat mixture on bottoms of rolls. If desired, season to taste with hot pepper sauce. Top with mango slices; replace tops of rolls.

Nutrition Facts per serving: 442 cal., 11 g total fat (3 g sat. fat), 98 mg chol., 971 mg sodium, 41 g carbo., 3 g fiber, 41 g pro. **Daily Values:** 36% vit. A, 16% vit. C, 9% calcium, 28% iron

Why wait for St. Patrick's Day to enjoy corned beef? This fruit-studded recipe feels right anytime from early fall to late spring. Rosemary-Buttered Potatoes (page 354) naturally make a suitable accompaniment.

ORANGE CORNED BEEF & DRIED FRUIT

PREP:

15 minutes

COOK:

*8 to 10 hours (low)
or 4 to 5 hours (high)*

MAKES:

6 servings

1   2½- to 3-pound corned beef brisket

1   7-ounce package mixed dried fruit

½   cup dried cranberries

2   tablespoons quick-cooking tapioca

½   cup orange juice

½   cup water

1   tablespoon mild-flavored molasses

¼   teaspoon ground cinnamon

⅛   teaspoon ground nutmeg

1 Trim fat from meat. If necessary, cut meat to fit into a 3½- or 4-quart slow cooker. If present, discard seasoning packet. Place meat in cooker.

2 Cut any large pieces of mixed dried fruit into quarters. Sprinkle mixed dried fruit, dried cranberries, and tapioca over meat in cooker. In a small bowl combine orange juice, water, molasses, cinnamon, and nutmeg. Pour over mixture in cooker.

3 Cover and cook on low-heat setting for 8 to 10 hours or on high-heat setting for 4 to 5 hours.

4 Remove meat from cooker. Thinly slice meat across the grain. Arrange meat slices on a serving platter. Spoon fruit mixture over meat.

Nutrition Facts per serving: 617 cal., 36 g total fat (12 g sat. fat), 185 mg chol., 2,151 mg sodium, 38 g carbo., 2 g fiber, 35 g pro. **Daily Values:** 1% vit. A, 19% vit. C, 4% calcium, 26% iron

On a chilly day, this slow-cooker version of the traditional meal warms you through and through.

NEW ENGLAND BOILED DINNER

1	3- to 3½-pound corned beef brisket
6	medium potatoes (about 2 pounds), peeled and quartered
6	medium carrots, cut into 2-inch pieces
1	large onion, quartered
3	cloves garlic, minced
2	teaspoons dill seeds
1	teaspoon dried rosemary, crushed
½	teaspoon salt
2	14-ounce cans beef broth
1	small head cabbage, cut into 8 wedges
1	recipe Horseradish Mustard Sauce (optional)

PREP:

25 minutes

COOK:

*11 to 12 hours (low)
or 5½ to 6 hours (high),
plus 30 minutes (high)*

MAKES:

8 servings

1. Trim fat from meat. If necessary, cut meat to fit into a 5- to 6-quart slow cooker. If present, discard seasoning packet. Set meat aside.

2. In cooker combine potatoes, carrots, onion, and garlic. Add meat; sprinkle with dill seeds, rosemary, and salt. Pour beef broth over mixture in cooker.

3. Cover and cook on low-heat setting for 11 to 12 hours or on high-heat setting for 5½ to 6 hours.

4. If using low-heat setting, turn to high-heat setting. Add cabbage wedges, pushing them down into liquid. Cover and cook for 30 to 60 minutes more or until cabbage is tender.

5. Remove meat from cooker. Thinly slice meat across the grain. Arrange meat slices on a serving platter. Using a slotted spoon, transfer vegetables to serving platter; discard cooking liquid. If desired, serve meat and vegetables with Horseradish Mustard Sauce.

Nutrition Facts per serving: 411 cal., 21 g total fat (6 g sat. fat), 86 mg chol., 648 mg sodium, 26 g carbo., 5 g fiber, 29 g pro. **Daily Values:** 233% vit. A, 110% vit. C, 7% calcium, 24% iron

**HORSERADISH
MUSTARD SAUCE**
In a small bowl stir together ½ cup mayonnaise, ½ cup dairy sour cream, 2 tablespoons horseradish mustard, and 2 teaspoons snipped fresh chives. Cover and chill for 5 to 24 hours.

When the cold wind blows, you can't have too many recipes for beef stew. Here fennel and parsnips offer a tantalizing change of pace from celery and carrots, and fresh spinach adds a dark green touch.

COUNTRY ITALIAN BEEF

PREP:

25 minutes

COOK:

8 to 10 hours (low) or 4 to 5 hours (high)

MAKES:

6 servings

2   pounds boneless beef chuck

3   medium parsnips, cut into 1-inch pieces

2   cups chopped onions

1   medium fennel bulb, trimmed and coarsely chopped (1 cup)

1   teaspoon dried rosemary, crushed

1   cup dry red wine or beef broth

1   6-ounce can tomato paste

¾   cup beef broth

2   tablespoons quick-cooking tapioca

1   teaspoon sugar

1   teaspoon salt

1   teaspoon finely shredded orange peel

½   teaspoon black pepper

4   cloves garlic, minced

3   cups torn fresh spinach

Hot mashed potatoes (optional)

1 Trim fat from meat. Cut meat into 2-inch pieces. Set aside.

2 In a 3½- or 4-quart slow cooker place parsnips, onions, and fennel. Add meat; sprinkle with rosemary.

3 In a small bowl combine wine, tomato paste, beef broth, tapioca, sugar, salt, orange peel, pepper, and garlic. Pour over mixture in cooker.

4 Cover and cook on low-heat setting for 8 to 10 hours or on high-heat setting for 4 to 5 hours. Just before serving, stir in spinach. If desired, serve meat mixture with hot mashed potatoes.

Nutrition Facts per serving: 336 cal., 6 g total fat (2 g sat. fat), 89 mg chol., 647 mg sodium, 28 g carbo., 10 g fiber, 36 g pro. **Daily Values:** 17% vit. A, 40% vit. C, 7% calcium, 35% iron

This hearty stew is the perfect way to use a small amount of leftover red wine. If you don't have any leftover wine and need to buy a new bottle, choose one of the same quality you would drink.

BEEF IN RED WINE GRAVY

1½	pounds lean beef stew meat
1	cup coarsely chopped onion
2	beef bouillon cubes or one 1-ounce envelope onion soup mix
3	tablespoons cornstarch
	Dash salt
	Dash black pepper
1½	cups dry red wine
	Hot cooked noodles (optional)

1 Cut meat into 1-inch pieces. In a 3½- or 4-quart slow cooker place meat and onion. Add bouillon cubes. Sprinkle with cornstarch, salt, and pepper. Pour red wine over mixture in cooker.

2 Cover and cook on low-heat setting for 10 to 12 hours or on high-heat setting for 5 to 6 hours. If desired, serve over hot cooked noodles.

Nutrition Facts per serving: 215 cal., 4 g total fat (1 g sat. fat), 64 mg chol., 405 mg sodium, 7 g carbo., 1 g fiber, 26 g pro. **Daily Values:** 2% vit. C, 2% calcium, 16% iron

PREP:

15 minutes

COOK:

*10 to 12 hours (low)
or 5 to 6 hours (high)*

MAKES:

6 servings

Thanks to ready-made stir-fry sauce and your slow cooker, this classic Chinese dish has never been easier to toss together.

SLOW COOKER BEEF LO MEIN

PREP:

25 minutes

COOK:

7 to 9 hours (low) or 3¹/₂ to 4¹/₂ hours (high), plus 30 minutes (high)

MAKES:

8 servings

2   pounds boneless beef sirloin steak, cut 1 inch thick

1   tablespoon cooking oil

1   large onion, sliced

1   8-ounce can sliced water chestnuts, drained

1   4¹/₂-ounce jar whole mushrooms, drained

1   12.1-ounce jar stir-fry sauce

1   tablespoon quick-cooking tapioca

1   16-ounce package loose-pack frozen broccoli, cauliflower, and carrots

¹/₃   cup cashews

12   ounces dried lo mein noodles

1 Trim fat from meat. Cut meat into 1-inch pieces. In a large skillet brown meat, half at a time, in hot oil. Drain off fat. Set aside.

2 In a 3¹/₂- or 4-quart slow cooker place onion. Add meat, water chestnuts, and mushrooms. In a small bowl stir together stir-fry sauce and tapioca. Pour over mixture in cooker.

3 Cover and cook on low-heat setting for 7 to 9 hours or on high-heat setting for 3¹/₂ to 4¹/₂ hours.

4 If using low-heat setting, turn to high-heat setting. Stir in frozen vegetables. Cover and cook for 30 to 40 minutes more or until vegetables are crisp-tender. Stir in cashews. Meanwhile, cook noodles according to package directions; drain. Serve meat mixture over noodles.

Nutrition Facts per serving: 447 cal., 11 g total fat (2 g sat. fat), 95 mg chol., 995 mg sodium, 52 g carbo., 4 g fiber, 35 g pro. **Daily Values:** 24% vit. A, 29% vit. C, 14% calcium, 25% iron

Paprikash (PAH-pree-kash) is a Hungarian dish that's often made with meat, onions, and as its name implies, paprika. This long-braising old-world stew is a natural for the slow cooker.

EASY HUNGARIAN PAPRIKASH

2	pounds lean beef stew meat
2	medium onions, sliced
1	cup chopped red or green sweet pepper
1	4½-ounce jar sliced mushrooms, drained
1	14½-ounce can diced tomatoes, drained
1	10¾-ounce can condensed cream of mushroom soup
1	tablespoon paprika
1	teaspoon dried thyme, crushed
¼	teaspoon coarsely ground black pepper
8	cups hot cooked noodles
½	cup dairy sour cream

PREP:

20 minutes

COOK:

*8 to 10 hours (low)
or 4 to 5 hours (high)*

MAKES:

8 servings

1 Cut meat into 1-inch pieces. Set aside. In a 3½- or 4-quart slow cooker place onions and sweet pepper. Add meat and mushrooms.

2 In a medium bowl stir together tomatoes, mushroom soup, paprika, thyme, and black pepper. Pour over mixture in cooker.

3 Cover and cook on low-heat setting for 8 to 10 hours or on high-heat setting for 4 to 5 hours. Serve meat mixture over hot cooked noodles. Top each serving with sour cream.

Nutrition Facts per serving: 452 cal., 12 g total fat (4 g sat. fat), 126 mg chol., 503 mg sodium, 50 g carbo., 4 g fiber, 34 g pro. Daily Values: 31% vit. A, 64% vit. C, 8% calcium, 35% iron

If you have a 5- or 6-quart slow cooker, you can super-size this recipe by doubling the ingredients (use the same cooking times). Then you'll have enough to please a hungry crowd.

ITALIAN BUFFET DINNER

PREP:

15 minutes

COOK:

*9 to 10 hours (low)
or 4½ to 5 hours (high),
plus 15 minutes (high)*

MAKES:

6 to 8 servings

2½	pounds boneless beef chuck
2	medium onions, cut into 1-inch pieces
1	large red sweet pepper, cut into ¾-inch pieces
1	14-ounce jar spaghetti sauce
½	teaspoon salt
½	teaspoon dried oregano, crushed
¼	teaspoon black pepper
2	cloves garlic, minced
2	medium zucchini, cut into ¾-inch pieces
4½	cups hot cooked spaghetti, mashed potatoes, or polenta
	Grated Parmesan cheese (optional)

1 Trim fat from meat. Cut meat into 1-inch pieces. In a 3½- or 4-quart slow cooker place meat, onions, and sweet pepper. In a medium bowl combine spaghetti sauce, salt, oregano, black pepper, and garlic. Pour over mixture in cooker.

2 Cover and cook on low-heat setting for 9 to 10 hours or on high-heat setting for 4½ to 5 hours.

3 If using low-heat setting, turn to high-heat setting. Stir in zucchini. Cover and cook about 15 minutes more or until zucchini is crisp-tender. Season to taste with additional salt and black pepper.

4 Serve meat mixture over hot cooked spaghetti. If desired, sprinkle each serving with Parmesan cheese.

Nutrition Facts per serving: 502 cal., 14 g total fat (4 g sat. fat), 89 mg chol., 900 mg sodium, 46 g carbo., 7 g fiber, 50 g pro. **Daily Values:** 30% vit. A, 96% vit. C, 7% calcium, 38% iron

Brimming with the taste of a traditional stir-fry, the sauce for this ever-so-easy beef and veggie dish surprisingly begins with an envelope of gravy mix.

ORIENTAL BEEF & BROCCOLI

1½	pounds boneless beef round steak
6	medium carrots, cut into 1-inch pieces
2	medium onions, cut into wedges
1	tablespoon grated fresh ginger
2	cloves garlic, minced
½	cup water
2	tablespoons reduced-sodium soy sauce
1	¾-ounce envelope beef gravy mix
4	cups broccoli florets
3	cups hot cooked rice

PREP:

20 minutes

COOK:

8 to 10 hours (low) or 4 to 5 hours (high), plus 15 minutes (high)

MAKES:

6 servings

1 Trim fat from meat. Cut meat across the grain into ½-inch strips. Set aside. In a 3½- or 4-quart slow cooker place carrots and onions. Add meat, ginger, and garlic. In a small bowl stir together water, soy sauce, and beef gravy mix. Pour over mixture in cooker.

2 Cover and cook on low-heat setting for 8 to 10 hours or on high-heat setting for 4 to 5 hours.

3 If using low-heat setting, turn to high-heat setting. Stir in broccoli. Cover and cook about 15 minutes more or until broccoli is crisp-tender. Serve meat mixture over hot cooked rice.

Nutrition Facts per serving: 327 cal., 6 g total fat (2 g sat. fat), 54 mg chol., 476 mg sodium, 37 g carbo., 4 g fiber, 31 g pro. **Daily Values:** 163% vit. A, 88% vit. C, 8% calcium, 22% iron

The classic Philadelphia cheese steak sandwich is made up of sliced beef, melted American cheese, and sautéed onions piled onto a roll. Ever since it was invented in the '30s, variations on the theme have been endless. This one folds herbs, garlic, peppers, and slow-cooker ease into the mix.

HERBED PHILLY STEAK SANDWICHES

PREP:

20 minutes

COOK:

*10 to 12 hours (low)
or 5 to 6 hours (high)*

MAKES:

8 sandwiches

1 tablespoon herb-pepper seasoning

4 cloves garlic, minced

2 to 2½ pounds fresh beef brisket or flank steak

2 medium red, yellow, and/or green sweet peppers, cut into bite-size strips

1 large onion, cut into thin wedges

1 10¾-ounce can condensed beefy mushroom soup

½ cup water

8 slices American cheese (8 ounces)

8 hoagie rolls, split and toasted

1 In a small bowl combine herb-pepper seasoning and garlic. Trim fat from meat. Sprinkle garlic mixture evenly over meat; rub in with your fingers. If necessary, cut meat to fit into a 3½- or 4-quart slow cooker. Place meat in cooker. Add sweet peppers and onion. In a small bowl combine mushroom soup and water. Pour over mixture in cooker.

2 Cover and cook on low-heat setting for 10 to 12 hours or on high-heat setting for 5 to 6 hours. Remove meat from cooker. Thinly slice meat across the grain.

3 To serve, arrange cheese slices on bottoms of rolls; add meat. Using a slotted spoon, spoon vegetables over meat. Drizzle with enough juices to moisten; replace tops of rolls.

Nutrition Facts per serving: 702 cal., 24 g total fat (9 g sat. fat), 95 mg chol., 1,492 mg sodium, 90 g carbo., 5 g fiber, 44 g pro. **Daily Values:** 39% vit. A, 83% vit. C, 29% calcium, 36% iron

Serve open-face steak sandwiches with this clever bistro-like twist. Focaccia bread is available at many bakeries and large supermarkets.

STEAK SANDWICHES WITH RATATOUILLE

1½	pounds beef flank steak
1	teaspoon dried Italian seasoning, crushed
⅛	teaspoon salt
⅛	teaspoon black pepper
1½	cups sliced fresh mushrooms
1	medium onion, finely chopped
2	cloves garlic, minced
1	14½-ounce can tomatoes, undrained and cut up
2	tablespoons red wine vinegar
1	medium yellow summer squash or zucchini, halved lengthwise and sliced ¼ inch thick
1	cup green, red, and/or yellow sweet pepper strips
1	9-inch Italian flatbread (focaccia)
1	6-ounce jar marinated artichoke hearts, drained and halved
⅓	cup finely shredded Asiago or Parmesan cheese

PREP:

20 minutes

COOK:

7 to 9 hours (low) or 3½ to 4½ hours (high), plus 30 minutes (high)

MAKES:

6 to 8 servings

1 Trim fat from meat. Sprinkle both sides of meat with Italian seasoning, salt, and pepper. If necessary, cut meat to fit into a 3½- or 4-quart slow cooker. Set aside.

2 In cooker place mushrooms, onion, and garlic. Add meat. Pour tomatoes and vinegar over mixture in cooker.

3 Cover and cook on low-heat setting for 7 to 9 hours or on high-heat setting for 3½ to 4½ hours.

4 If using low-heat setting, turn to high-heat setting. Add squash and sweet pepper. Cover and cook about 30 minutes more or until vegetables are crisp-tender.

5 Remove meat from cooker. Thinly slice meat across the grain. Arrange meat on flatbread. Stir artichoke hearts into vegetable mixture. Using a slotted spoon, spoon vegetable mixture over meat. Drizzle with enough of the cooking liquid to moisten; sprinkle with cheese. Cut into wedges.

Nutrition Facts per serving: 440 cal., 15 g total fat (5 g sat. fat), 58 mg chol., 369 mg sodium, 46 g carbo., 4 g fiber, 34 g pro. **Daily Values:** 8% vit. A, 52% vit. C, 14% calcium, 25% iron

When cooks want to bring some smoke with their fire, they use chipotle chile peppers, which are actually smoked jalapeños. Find them at the supermarket next to the canned chile peppers.

BEEF & CHIPOTLE BURRITOS

PREP:

20 minutes

COOK:

*8 to 10 hours (low)
or 4 to 5 hours (high)*

MAKES:

6 servings

1½ pounds boneless beef round steak, cut ¾ inch thick

1 14½-ounce can diced tomatoes, undrained

⅓ cup chopped onion

1 to 2 canned chipotle chile peppers in adobo sauce, chopped

1 teaspoon dried oregano, crushed

¼ teaspoon ground cumin

1 clove garlic, minced

6 9- to 10-inch tomato or plain flour tortillas, warmed

¾ cup shredded sharp cheddar cheese (3 ounces)

1 recipe Pico de Gallo Salsa

Shredded jicama or radishes (optional)

Dairy sour cream (optional)

1 Trim fat from meat. If necessary, cut meat to fit into a 3½- or 4-quart slow cooker. Place meat in cooker. Add tomatoes, onion, chipotle peppers, oregano, cumin, and garlic.

2 Cover and cook on low-heat setting for 8 to 10 hours or on high-heat setting for 4 to 5 hours.

3 Remove meat from cooker, reserving cooking liquid. Using two forks, pull meat apart into shreds. Stir enough of the liquid into meat to moisten.

4 To serve, spoon meat just below centers of tortillas. Top with cheese, Pico de Gallo Salsa, and, if desired, jicama and sour cream. Roll up tortillas.

Nutrition Facts per serving: 361 cal., 13 g total fat (5 g sat. fat), 71 mg chol., 433 mg sodium, 29 g carbo., 2 g fiber, 30 g pro. Daily Values: 11% vit. A, 30% vit. C, 19% calcium, 26% iron

**PICO DE GALLO
SALSA**

In a small bowl combine 2 medium tomatoes, finely chopped; 2 tablespoons finely chopped onion; 2 tablespoons snipped fresh cilantro; 1 fresh serrano chile pepper, seeded and finely chopped; and dash sugar. Cover and chill for several hours.

The combination of tender roast beef, a little beer, mustard, onions, and seasonings comes together for the sort of interesting and irresistible sandwich you find on brew-pub menus.

ONION & ROAST BEEF SANDWICHES

1	2½- to 3-pound boneless beef round tip roast
1	tablespoon cooking oil
4	medium onions, sliced
1	teaspoon dried oregano, crushed
½	teaspoon salt
¼	teaspoon black pepper
1½	cups beef broth
¾	cup dark beer or beef broth
3	tablespoons brown mustard
2	tablespoons brown sugar
1	tablespoon cider vinegar
2	cloves garlic, minced
8	hoagie rolls, split and toasted

PREP:

25 minutes

COOK:

*8 to 10 hours (low)
or 4 to 5 hours (high)*

MAKES:

8 servings

1 Trim fat from meat. If necessary, cut meat to fit into a 4- to 6-quart slow cooker. In a large skillet brown meat on all sides in hot oil. Drain off fat. Set aside.

2 In cooker place onions. Add meat; sprinkle with oregano, salt, and pepper. In a medium bowl stir together beef broth, beer, mustard, brown sugar, vinegar, and garlic. Pour over mixture in cooker.

3 Cover and cook on low-heat setting for 8 to 10 hours or on high-heat setting for 4 to 5 hours.

4 Remove meat and onions from cooker, reserving juices. Using two forks, pull meat apart into shreds. Skim fat from juices.

5 To serve, place meat and onions on bottoms of rolls. Drizzle with enough of the juices to moisten; replace tops of rolls. Pass remaining juices.

Nutrition Facts per serving: 656 cal., 17 g total fat (4 g sat. fat), 67 mg chol., 1,167 mg sodium, 81 g carbo., 5 g fiber, 44 g pro. **Daily Values:** 4% vit. C, 13% calcium, 40% iron

The well-seasoned meat is fall-apart tender, so don't attempt to slice it.
Instead use two forks to pull it into bite-size pieces.

ITALIAN BEEF SANDWICHES

PREP:

20 minutes

COOK:

10 to 12 hours (low)
or 5 to 6 hours (high)

MAKES:

10 to 12 sandwiches

1   4-pound boneless beef sirloin or round rump roast

1   cup water

1   0.7-ounce envelope Italian dry salad dressing mix

2   teaspoons dried Italian seasoning, crushed

½   to 1 teaspoon crushed red pepper

½   teaspoon garlic powder

10   to 12 kaiser or French-style rolls, split

Bottled roasted red sweet peppers, drained and
cut into strips (optional)

1 Trim fat from meat. Cut meat into 2- to 3-inch pieces. In a 3½- to 5-quart slow cooker place meat. In a small bowl combine water, salad dressing mix, Italian seasoning, crushed red pepper, and garlic powder. Pour over meat in cooker.

2 Cover and cook on low-heat setting for 10 to 12 hours or on high-heat setting for 5 to 6 hours.

3 Remove meat from cooker, reserving juices. Using two forks, pull meat apart into shreds.

4 To serve, place meat on bottoms of rolls. Drizzle with enough of the juices to moisten. If desired, top with roasted sweet pepper strips. Replace tops of rolls.

Nutrition Facts per serving: 396 cal., 10 g total fat (3 g sat. fat), 104 mg chol., 642 mg sodium, 31 g carbo., 1 g fiber, 41 g pro. **Daily Values:** 7% calcium, 33% iron

To trim preparation time, substitute an 18-ounce package of frozen cooked meatballs (about 32 meatballs) for the homemade ones. Stir the frozen meatballs into the sauce to coat, then cook as directed.

MEATBALL SANDWICHES

1	slightly beaten egg
²/₃	cup finely chopped onion
¹/₃	cup fine dry bread crumbs
¹/₂	teaspoon salt
¹/₂	teaspoon dried oregano, crushed
¹/₂	teaspoon black pepper
1¹/₂	pounds lean ground beef
1	15-ounce can tomato sauce
¹/₂	cup chopped green sweet pepper
2	tablespoons brown sugar
1	tablespoon prepared mustard
1	teaspoon chili powder
¹/₄	teaspoon garlic salt
¹/₈	teaspoon bottled hot pepper sauce
8	hoagie buns, split and toasted
8	slices provolone cheese

PREP:
30 minutes

BAKE:
20 minutes

COOK:
*3 to 4 hours (low)
or 1¹/₂ to 2 hours (high)*

OVEN:
350°F

MAKES:
8 sandwiches

1 For meatballs, in a large bowl combine egg, ¹/₃ cup of the onion, the bread crumbs, salt, oregano, and ¹/₄ teaspoon of the black pepper. Add ground beef; mix well. Shape into 32 meatballs. In a 15×10×1-inch baking pan arrange meatballs in a single layer. Bake, uncovered, in a 350° oven for 20 minutes. Drain well.

2 For sauce, in a 3¹/₂- or 4-quart slow cooker combine remaining ¹/₃ cup onion, remaining ¹/₄ teaspoon black pepper, the tomato sauce, sweet pepper, brown sugar, mustard, chili powder, garlic salt, and hot pepper sauce. Gently stir in meatballs.

3 Cover and cook on low-heat setting for 3 to 4 hours or on high-heat setting for 1¹/₂ to 2 hours.

4 To serve, place meatballs on bottoms of buns. Top with sauce and cheese slices; replace tops of buns.

Nutrition Facts per serving: 717 cal., 28 g total fat (11 g sat. fat), 98 mg chol., 1,516 mg sodium, 82 g carbo., 5 g fiber, 35 g pro. **Daily Values:** 9% vit. A, 13% vit. C, 34% calcium, 34% iron

French food isn't always fancy. Hailing from the southwest of France, a cassoulet is a rustic, rib-sticking stew that's made with white beans and a variety of meats. This version is 100-percent family fare!

MEATBALL CASSOULET

PREP:

25 minutes

COOK:

*8 to 9 hours (low)
or 4 to 4¹/₂ hours (high)*

MAKES:

4 or 5 servings

2   15-ounce cans Great Northern beans, rinsed and drained

2   cups tomato juice

1   12-ounce package frozen cooked Italian meatballs, thawed

8   ounces cooked smoked turkey sausage or Polish sausage, halved lengthwise and sliced

1   cup finely chopped carrots

1   cup chopped celery

1   cup chopped onion

1   tablespoon Worcestershire sauce

¹/₂   teaspoon dried basil, crushed

¹/₂   teaspoon dried oregano, crushed

¹/₂   teaspoon paprika

1 In a 3¹/₂- or 4-quart slow cooker combine Great Northern beans, tomato juice, meatballs, sausage, carrots, celery, onion, Worcestershire sauce, basil, oregano, and paprika.

2 Cover and cook on low-heat setting for 8 to 9 hours or on high-heat setting for 4 to 4¹/₂ hours.

Nutrition Facts per serving: 657 cal., 25 g total fat (11 g sat. fat), 93 mg chol., 1,655 mg sodium, 68 g carbo., 17 g fiber, 42 g pro. **Daily Values:** 171% vit. A, 53% vit. C, 21% calcium, 43% iron

Meatballs are time-consuming to make, so it's a convenience to buy them frozen. The sumptuous sauce here relies on mushroom soup for its base.

MEATBALLS IN DRIED TOMATO GRAVY

1	10¾-ounce can condensed cream of mushroom with roasted garlic soup
1	cup water
1	4½-ounce jar sliced mushrooms, drained
½	cup snipped dried tomatoes (not oil-packed)
½	cup chopped onion
½	teaspoon dried basil, crushed
½	teaspoon dried oregano, crushed
⅛	teaspoon black pepper
2	16-ounce packages frozen cooked Italian meatballs, thawed
1	recipe Polenta or 4 cups hot cooked noodles

PREP:
35 minutes
COOK:
*5 to 6 hours (low)
or 2½ to 3 hours (high)*
MAKES:
8 servings

1 In a 3½- or 4-quart slow cooker combine soup, water, mushrooms, dried tomatoes, onion, basil, oregano, and pepper. Stir in meatballs.

2 Cover and cook on low-heat setting for 5 to 6 hours or on high-heat setting for 2½ to 3 hours. Serve meatball mixture over Polenta.

Nutrition Facts per serving: 525 cal., 33 g total fat (16 g sat. fat), 89 mg chol., 1,599 mg sodium, 31 g carbo., 7 g fiber, 25 g pro. **Daily Values:** 8% vit. A, 6% vit. C, 19% calcium, 19% iron

POLENTA

In a large saucepan bring 3 cups milk just to simmering over medium heat. In a medium bowl combine 1 cup cornmeal, 1 cup water, and 1 teaspoon salt. Stir cornmeal mixture slowly into hot milk. Cook and stir until mixture comes to boiling; reduce heat to low. Cook, uncovered, for 10 to 15 minutes or until mixture is thick, stirring occasionally. (If mixture is thicker than you like, stir in additional milk.) Stir in 2 tablespoons butter or margarine until melted.

Aside from a streamlined prep time (thanks to some easy convenience products), this is a traditional take on the classic. True fans wouldn't want it any other way.

SWEDISH MEATBALLS

PREP:

20 minutes

COOK:

*5 to 6 hours (low)
or 2^1/$_2$ to 3 hours (high)*

MAKES:

10 servings

2   12-ounce jars beef gravy

3   4^1/$_2$-ounce jars sliced mushrooms, drained

1   large onion, cut into wedges

1   tablespoon Worcestershire sauce

^{1}/$_4$ teaspoon ground allspice

2   16-ounce packages frozen cooked plain meatballs, thawed

1   8-ounce carton dairy sour cream

6   cups hot cooked wide curly noodles

    Snipped fresh parsley (optional)

1 For gravy, in a 4^1/$_2$- or 5-quart slow cooker combine beef gravy, mushrooms, onion, Worcestershire sauce, and allspice. Stir in meatballs.

2 Cover and cook on low-heat setting for 5 to 6 hours or on high-heat setting for 2^1/$_2$ to 3 hours.

3 Gradually stir about ^{1}/$_2$ cup of the hot gravy into sour cream. Add sour cream mixture to cooker, stirring gently until combined. Serve meatball mixture over hot cooked noodles. If desired, sprinkle with parsley.

Nutrition Facts per serving: 503 cal., 31 g total fat (14 g sat. fat), 76 mg chol., 1,240 mg sodium, 37 g carbo., 4 g fiber, 20 g pro. **Daily Values:** 4% vit. A, 2% vit. C, 9% calcium, 17% iron

This recipe was developed with pizza lovers in mind. They'll find all the makings of pizza here—except for the dough.

MUSHROOM-PEPPERONI PASTA SAUCE

1	16-ounce package frozen cooked plain meatballs, thawed
1	15-ounce can pizza sauce
1	14½-ounce can diced tomatoes with basil, oregano, and garlic, undrained
1	14-ounce can reduced-sodium chicken broth
¾	cup chopped onion
1	6-ounce can tomato paste
1	4½-ounce jar sliced mushrooms, drained
⅛	teaspoon cayenne pepper
4	cloves garlic, minced
2	ounces chopped pepperoni
	Hot cooked pasta
	Shredded mozzarella cheese (optional)

PREP:
20 minutes

COOK:
8 to 10 hours (low) or 4 to 5 hours (high)

MAKES:
8 servings

1 In a 3½- or 4-quart slow cooker combine meatballs, pizza sauce, tomatoes, chicken broth, onion, tomato paste, mushrooms, cayenne pepper, and garlic.

2 Cover and cook on low-heat setting for 8 to 10 hours or on high-heat setting for 4 to 5 hours. Stir in pepperoni.

3 Serve meat mixture over hot cooked pasta. If desired, sprinkle each serving with mozzarella cheese.

Nutrition Facts per serving: 286 cal., 17 g total fat (7 g sat. fat), 42 mg chol., 1,255 mg sodium, 18 g carbo., 4 g fiber, 15 g pro. **Daily Values:** 6% vit. A, 20% vit. C, 7% calcium, 16% iron

Meatballs often win popularity contests conducted at the dinner table, and frozen meatballs are tops with the cook. Here the convenient bites fold into a creamy Alfredo sauce along with a spectrum of colorful vegetables.

EASY ALFREDO MEATBALLS

PREP:

15 minutes

COOK:

5 to 7 hours (low)
or 2½ to 3½ hours (high)

MAKES:

4 to 6 servings

1 16-ounce package frozen cooked plain or Italian meatballs, thawed

1 16-ounce package loose-pack frozen broccoli, corn, and red peppers, or broccoli, cauliflower, and red peppers

1 16-ounce jar Alfredo pasta sauce

½ cup water

1 teaspoon finely shredded lemon peel (optional)

⅛ teaspoon black pepper

Hot cooked noodles (optional)

1 In a 3½- or 4-quart slow cooker combine meatballs, frozen vegetables, pasta sauce, water, lemon peel (if desired), and black pepper.

2 Cover and cook on low-heat setting for 5 to 7 hours or on high-heat setting for 2½ to 3½ hours. If desired, serve meatball mixture over hot cooked noodles.

Nutrition Facts per serving: 632 cal., 48 g total fat (21 g sat. fat), 133 mg chol., 1,800 mg sodium, 28 g carbo., 5 g fiber, 21 g pro. **Daily Values:** 18% vit. A, 60% vit. C, 16% calcium, 8% iron

The salsa that's mixed into this saucy steak turns the flavor dial way up.
It's still as family-pleasing (and easy) as ever.

SALSA SWISS STEAK

2	pounds boneless beef round steak, cut ¾ inch thick
1	large green sweet pepper, cut into bite-size strips
1	medium onion, sliced
1	10¾-ounce can condensed cream of mushroom soup
1	cup bottled salsa
2	tablespoons all-purpose flour
1	teaspoon dry mustard
3	cups hot cooked rice

PREP:

15 minutes

COOK:

9 to 10 hours (low)
or 4½ to 5 hours (high)

MAKES:

6 servings

① Trim fat from meat. Cut meat into 6 serving-size pieces. In a 3½- or 4-quart slow cooker place meat, sweet pepper, and onion.

② In a medium bowl combine mushroom soup, salsa, flour, and dry mustard. Pour over mixture in cooker.

③ Cover and cook on low-heat setting for 9 to 10 hours or on high-heat setting for 4½ to 5 hours. Serve with hot cooked rice.

Nutrition Facts per serving: 410 cal., 12 g total fat (4 g sat. fat), 66 mg chol., 533 mg sodium, 32 g carbo., 2 g fiber, 41 g pro. **Daily Values:** 6% vit. A, 38% vit. C, 4% calcium, 23% iron

CUTTING VEGETABLES TO SIZE
Vegetables intended for slow cookers are cut into bite-size pieces not only for the convenience in eating but also for better cooking. Some vegetables take longer to cook than the meat in slow cookers. By cutting the vegetables into smaller pieces, you can be sure they will be tender and ready to eat when the meat is done.

Are you in the mood for Mexican, Cajun, or Italian tonight? All you have to do to change things is vary the canned seasoned tomatoes. The result is robust flavor that usually comes only from a long list of seasonings.

SO-EASY PEPPER STEAK

PREP:

15 minutes

COOK:

*10 to 12 hours (low)
or 5 to 6 hours (high)*

MAKES:

8 servings

2 pounds boneless beef round steak, cut ¾ to 1 inch thick

1 14½-ounce can Cajun-, Mexican-, or Italian-style stewed tomatoes, undrained

⅓ cup Italian-style tomato paste

½ teaspoon bottled hot pepper sauce

1 16-ounce package frozen pepper stir-fry vegetables (yellow, green, and red peppers and onion)

4 cups hot cooked noodles or hot mashed potatoes

1 Trim fat from meat. Cut meat into 8 serving-size pieces. Lightly sprinkle with salt and black pepper. In a 3½- or 4-quart slow cooker place meat. In a medium bowl combine tomatoes, tomato paste, and hot pepper sauce. Pour over meat in cooker. Add frozen vegetables.

2 Cover and cook on low-heat setting for 10 to 12 hours or on high-heat setting for 5 to 6 hours. Serve over hot cooked noodles.

Nutrition Facts per serving: 303 cal., 6 g total fat (2 g sat. fat), 80 mg chol., 416 mg sodium, 29 g carbo., 2 g fiber, 30 g pro. **Daily Values:** 7% vit. A, 47% vit. C, 2% calcium, 22% iron

For a deeper, richer flavor, stir a couple of tablespoons of red wine into the beef mixture just before serving.

MUSHROOM-SAUCED ROUND STEAK

2   pounds boneless beef round steak, cut ¾ inch thick

1   tablespoon cooking oil

2   medium onions, sliced

3   cups sliced fresh mushrooms

1   12-ounce jar beef gravy

1   1.1-ounce envelope mushroom gravy mix

Hot cooked noodles (optional)

PREP:

20 minutes

COOK:

8 to 10 hours (low)
or 4 to 5 hours (high)

MAKES:

8 servings

1 Trim fat from meat. Cut meat into 8 serving-size pieces. In a large skillet brown meat, half at a time, in hot oil. Drain off fat. Set aside.

2 In a 3½- or 4-quart slow cooker place onions. Add meat and mushrooms. In a small bowl stir together beef gravy and mushroom gravy mix. Pour over mixture in cooker.

3 Cover and cook on low-heat setting for 8 to 10 hours or on high-heat setting for 4 to 5 hours. If desired, serve over hot cooked noodles.

Nutrition Facts per serving: 194 cal., 7 g total fat (2 g sat. fat), 57 mg chol., 479 mg sodium, 7 g carbo., 1 g fiber, 24 g pro. **Daily Values:** 2% vit. C, 1% calcium, 16% iron

Pepper steak is a classic French dish that starts with cracked black pepper pressed into the meat and finishes with a topping of easy-to-make sauce. This simple slow cooker version sticks to that basic plan.

DIJON-PEPPER STEAK

PREP:

20 minutes

COOK:

*8 to 10 hours (low)
or 4 to 5 hours (high)*

MAKES:

6 servings

2   pounds boneless beef sirloin steak, cut 1 inch thick

1½ teaspoons cracked black pepper

1   tablespoon cooking oil

2   cups packaged peeled baby carrots

1   medium onion, sliced

1   10¾-ounce can condensed cream of celery soup

¼   cup Dijon-style mustard

   Hot cooked noodles or hot mashed potatoes (optional)

1 Trim fat from meat. Cut meat into 6 serving-size pieces. Sprinkle pepper evenly over meat; press in with your fingers. In a large skillet brown meat, half at a time, in hot oil. Drain off fat. Set aside.

2 In a 3½- or 4-quart slow cooker place carrots and onion. Add meat. In a medium bowl stir together celery soup and Dijon mustard. Pour over mixture in cooker.

3 Cover and cook on low-heat setting for 8 to 10 hours or on high-heat setting for 4 to 5 hours. If desired, serve over hot cooked noodles.

Nutrition Facts per serving: 266 cal., 9 g total fat (2 g sat. fat), 96 mg chol., 716 mg sodium, 9 g carbo., 2 g fiber, 33 g pro. **Daily Values:** 194% vit. A, 6% vit. C, 4% calcium, 26% iron

If you prefer spicy foods, go with the spicy bratwurst and bring a new flavor dimension to this American classic.

BEEF & BRATS

1   pound boneless beef round steak, cut 1 inch thick

4   ounces uncooked spicy bratwurst or other sausage, cut into ¾-inch slices

1   tablespoon cooking oil

1   small onion, sliced and separated into rings

2   tablespoons quick-cooking tapioca

1   teaspoon dried thyme, crushed

¼   teaspoon salt

¼   teaspoon black pepper

1   14-ounce can chunky tomatoes with garlic and spices, undrained

2   cups hot cooked noodles or rice

PREP:
15 minutes
COOK:
10 to 12 hours (low)
MAKES:
4 servings

1 Trim fat from meat. Cut meat into 4 serving-size pieces. In a large skillet brown meat and bratwurst on both sides in hot oil. Drain off fat. Set aside.

2 In a 3½- or 4-quart slow cooker place onion. Sprinkle with tapioca, thyme, salt, and pepper. Pour tomatoes over mixture in cooker. Add meat and bratwurst.

3 Cover and cook on low-heat setting for 10 to 12 hours. Serve with hot cooked noodles.

Nutrition Facts per serving: 429 cal., 18 g total fat (5 g sat. fat), 99 mg chol., 883 mg sodium, 35 g carbo., 3 g fiber, 32 g pro. **Daily Values:** 10% vit. A, 14% vit. C, 5% calcium, 26% iron

Short ribs are a prime candidate for the slow cooker if ever there was one! The extended cook time makes them melt-in-your-mouth tender.

SHORT RIBS WITH HORSERADISH SAUCE

PREP:

25 minutes

COOK:

9 to 10 hours (low) or 4¹/₂ to 5 hours (high)

MAKES:

6 servings

3	pounds boneless beef short ribs
3	large carrots, cut into 1-inch pieces
2	medium onions, cut into wedges
¹/₂	cup dry red wine or beef broth
¹/₄	cup beef broth
2	tablespoons Dijon-style mustard
1	bay leaf
¹/₂	teaspoon salt
¹/₂	teaspoon dried thyme, crushed
¹/₄	teaspoon black pepper
6	cloves garlic, minced
1	recipe Horseradish Sauce

1 Trim fat from meat. Cut meat into 2-inch pieces. Set aside. In a 4- to 5-quart slow cooker place carrots and onions. Add meat. In a small bowl stir together wine, beef broth, Dijon mustard, bay leaf, salt, thyme, pepper, and garlic. Pour over mixture in cooker.

2 Cover and cook on low-heat setting for 9 to 10 hours or on high-heat setting for 4¹/₂ to 5 hours.

3 Using a slotted spoon, transfer meat and vegetables to a serving dish, reserving cooking liquid. Discard bay leaf. Skim fat from liquid. Spoon enough of the liquid over meat and vegetables to moisten. Serve with Horseradish Sauce.

HORSERADISH SAUCE
In a small bowl combine one 8-ounce carton dairy sour cream, 2 to 3 tablespoons prepared horseradish, and ¹/₈ teaspoon salt. Cover and chill until ready to serve.

Nutrition Facts per serving: 491 cal., 27 g total fat (13 g sat. fat), 120 mg chol., 616 mg sodium, 10 g carbo., 2 g fiber, 47 g pro. **Daily Values:** 211% vit. A, 11% vit. C, 10% calcium, 25% iron

Beef short ribs are popping up on bistro menus everywhere, and it's no wonder; they're a great, full-flavored cut of meat that fits right into the down-to-earth feel of these informal-yet-gourmet venues. Here the ribs get five-star treatment with five-spice powder and other Asian flavorings.

GINGER-ORANGE GLAZED SHORT RIBS

3	pounds beef short ribs
1	large red onion, cut into wedges
1	cup orange marmalade
⅓	cup water
2	tablespoons rice vinegar
1	tablespoon soy sauce
2	teaspoons five-spice powder
2	teaspoons grated fresh ginger
½	to 1½ teaspoons chile oil
2	cloves garlic, minced

PREP:

20 minutes

COOK:

*11 to 12 hours (low)
or 5½ to 6 hours (high)*

MAKES:

4 to 6 servings

1 Trim fat from meat. Set aside. In a 3½- to 5-quart slow cooker place red onion. Add meat. In a medium bowl combine orange marmalade, water, rice vinegar, soy sauce, five-spice powder, ginger, chile oil, and garlic. Reserve ⅔ cup of the marmalade mixture for sauce; cover and chill. Pour remaining marmalade mixture over mixture in cooker.

2 Cover and cook on low-heat setting for 11 to 12 hours or on high-heat setting for 5½ to 6 hours.

3 For sauce, in a small saucepan bring reserved marmalade mixture to boiling; reduce heat. Boil gently, uncovered, for 5 minutes. Remove meat and onion from cooker; discard cooking liquid. Serve meat and onion with sauce.

Nutrition Facts per serving: 452 cal., 12 g total fat (5 g sat. fat), 64 mg chol., 385 mg sodium, 58 g carbo., 1 g fiber, 29 g pro. Daily Values: 1% vit. A, 11% vit. C, 8% calcium, 17% iron

The flavors of Eastern Europe's beloved borscht—a beet soup—readily transform into a hearty one-dish meal.

BORSCHT-STYLE SHORT RIBS

PREP:

25 minutes

COOK:

*7 to 8 hours (low)
or 3½ to 4 hours (high),
plus 1 hour (high)*

MAKES:

4 servings

2   pounds boneless beef short ribs

2   medium carrots, cut into ½-inch slices

1   medium beet, peeled and cut into strips (1 cup)

1   small turnip, peeled and cut into strips

1   stalk celery, sliced

1   medium onion, sliced

2   cups water

½   of a 6-ounce can (⅓ cup) tomato paste

1   tablespoon vinegar

1½   teaspoons sugar

1   teaspoon salt

¼   teaspoon black pepper

½   of a small head cabbage, cut into 4 wedges

¼   cup dairy sour cream

1 Trim fat from meat. Set aside. In a 4- to 5-quart slow cooker combine carrots, beet, turnip, celery, and onion. Add meat. In a medium bowl combine water, tomato paste, vinegar, sugar, salt, and pepper. Pour over mixture in cooker.

2 Cover and cook on low-heat setting for 7 to 8 hours or on high-heat setting for 3½ to 4 hours.

3 If using low-heat setting, turn to high-heat setting. Add cabbage wedges, pushing them down into liquid. Cover and cook about 1 hour more or just until cabbage is tender. Top each serving with sour cream.

Nutrition Facts per serving: 472 cal., 21 g total fat (9 g sat. fat), 109 mg chol., 850 mg sodium, 20 g carbo., 5 g fiber, 49 g pro. **Daily Values:** 158% vit. A, 60% vit. C, 11% calcium, 29% iron

Pronounced CHAW-lent, this dish of central European Jewish origin traditionally simmers on the stove top or bakes for many hours. The more controlled heat of your slow cooker gives similarly flavorful results.

CHOLENT

³/₄ cup dry Great Northern beans

2½ pounds beef short ribs

1 tablespoon cooking oil

5 medium carrots, cut into 1-inch pieces

2 medium red-skinned potatoes, cut into 1½-inch cubes

2 medium onions, cut into ¼-inch slices

½ cup regular barley

½ teaspoon salt

½ teaspoon black pepper

¼ teaspoon paprika

4 cloves garlic, minced

2½ cups beef broth

   Snipped fresh parsley

PREP:
40 minutes
STAND:
1 hour
COOK:
11 to 12 hours (low)
or 5½ to 6 hours (high)
MAKES:
6 to 8 servings

1 Rinse beans. In a large saucepan combine beans and 6 cups water. Bring to boiling; reduce heat. Simmer, uncovered, for 10 minutes. Remove from heat. Cover and let stand for 1 hour. Drain and rinse beans; set aside.

2 Trim fat from meat. Cut meat into 6 to 8 serving-size pieces. Sprinkle with a little salt and black pepper. In a 4-quart Dutch oven brown meat, half at a time, in hot oil. Drain off fat. Set aside.

3 In a 5- to 6-quart slow cooker combine beans, carrots, potatoes, onions, barley, the ½ teaspoon salt, the ½ teaspoon pepper, the paprika, and garlic. Add meat. Pour beef broth over mixture in cooker.

4 Cover and cook on low-heat setting for 11 to 12 hours or on high-heat setting for 5½ to 6 hours. Sprinkle each serving with parsley.

Nutrition Facts per serving: 371 cal., 9 g total fat (3 g sat. fat), 35 mg chol., 577 mg sodium, 46 g carbo., 11 g fiber, 27 g pro. Daily Values: 259% vit. A, 22% vit. C, 7% calcium, 24% iron

The pungent flavors of the Mediterranean—feta, oregano, and sun-dried tomatoes—infuse this otherwise all-American meatloaf. Consider serving it with orzo, an almond-shape pasta that cooks up quickly.

MEDITERRANEAN MEAT LOAF

PREP:

20 minutes

COOK:

*7 to 8 hours (low)
or 3 1/2 to 4 hours (high)*

MAKES:

4 to 6 servings

1	slightly beaten egg
2	tablespoons milk
1/2	cup fine dry bread crumbs
1/2	teaspoon salt
1/2	teaspoon dried oregano, crushed
1/4	teaspoon black pepper
2	cloves garlic, minced
1 1/2	pounds lean ground beef
1/2	cup crumbled feta cheese (2 ounces)
1/4	cup oil-packed dried tomatoes, drained and snipped
3	tablespoons bottled pizza or pasta sauce

1 In a medium bowl combine egg and milk. Stir in bread crumbs, salt, oregano, pepper, and garlic. Add ground beef, feta cheese, and dried tomatoes; mix well. Shape meat mixture into a 5-inch round loaf.

2 Tear off an 18-inch square piece of heavy foil. Cut into thirds. Fold each piece into thirds lengthwise. Crisscross strips and place meat loaf in center of foil strips. Bringing up strips, transfer loaf and foil to a 3 1/2- or 4-quart slow cooker (leave strips under loaf). Press loaf away from side of cooker. Fold strips down, leaving loaf exposed. Spread pizza sauce over loaf.

3 Cover and cook on low-heat setting for 7 to 8 hours or on high-heat setting for 3 1/2 to 4 hours. Using foil strips, carefully lift meat loaf from cooker. Discard foil strips.

Nutrition Facts per serving: 396 cal., 22 g total fat (9 g sat. fat), 173 mg chol., 873 mg sodium, 12 g carbo., 1 g fiber, 36 g pro. **Daily Values:** 5% vit. A, 17% vit. C, 13% calcium, 23% iron

The spoonful of pesto or tapenade—an olive paste that's becoming more and more widely available—separates the everyday beef ragout from the gourmet.

POLENTA WITH GROUND BEEF RAGOUT

1	pound lean ground beef
1	14½-ounce can Italian-style stewed tomatoes, undrained
3	medium carrots, cut into ½-inch slices
2	medium onions, cut into thin wedges
1	large red sweet pepper, cut into 1-inch pieces
½	cup beef broth
¼	teaspoon salt
¼	teaspoon black pepper
6	cloves garlic, minced
1	medium zucchini, halved lengthwise and cut into ¼-inch slices
1	16-ounce tube refrigerated cooked polenta
6	tablespoons purchased pesto or olive tapenade

PREP:
25 minutes

COOK:
7 to 9 hours (low) or 3½ to 4½ hours (high), plus 30 minutes (high)

MAKES:
6 servings

1 In a large skillet cook ground beef until meat is brown. Drain off fat. Transfer meat to a 3½- or 4-quart slow cooker. Stir in tomatoes, carrots, onions, sweet pepper, beef broth, salt, black pepper, and garlic.

2 Cover and cook on low-heat setting for 7 to 9 hours or on high-heat setting for 3½ to 4½ hours.

3 If using low-heat setting, turn to high-heat setting. Stir in zucchini. Cover and cook about 30 minutes more or until zucchini is crisp-tender.

4 Meanwhile, prepare polenta according to package directions. Serve meat mixture over polenta. Top each serving with pesto.

Nutrition Facts per serving: 388 cal., 20 g total fat (4 g sat. fat), 50 mg chol., 773 mg sodium, 30 g carbo., 5 g fiber, 20 g pro. **Daily Values:** 182% vit. A, 79% vit. C, 5% calcium, 12% iron

Put together a smorgasbord of nacho toppings—sour cream, salsa, sliced green onions, and shredded cheddar cheese—to accent each serving of this Tex-Mex main dish.

NACHO-STYLE BEEF & POTATOES

PREP:

15 minutes

COOK:

7 to 8 hours (low)
or 3¹/₂ to 4 hours (high)

MAKES:

4 servings

1   pound lean ground beef

1   cup chopped onion

1   11-ounce can condensed fiesta nacho cheese soup

1   cup milk

1   4-ounce can diced green chile peppers, undrained

6   medium potatoes (about 2 pounds), cut into wedges

¹/₄   teaspoon garlic salt

     Assorted toppings (such as dairy sour cream, bottled salsa, sliced green onions, and/or shredded cheddar cheese) (optional)

1   In a large skillet cook ground beef and onion until meat is brown. Drain off fat. Stir in cheese soup, milk, and green chile peppers.

2   In a 3¹/₂- or 4-quart slow cooker place potato wedges. Sprinkle with garlic salt. Pour meat mixture over potatoes in cooker.

3   Cover and cook on low-heat setting for 7 to 8 hours or on high-heat setting for 3¹/₂ to 4 hours.

4   Stir gently before serving. If desired, serve with toppings.

Nutrition Facts per serving: 550 cal., 23 g total fat (10 g sat. fat), 90 mg chol., 809 mg sodium, 52 g carbo., 6 g fiber, 32 g pro. **Daily Values:** 19% vit. A, 70% vit. C, 19% calcium, 32% iron

This classic Better Homes and Gardens® recipe has been a favorite for decades. Originally a simmer-on-the-stove affair, it was only a matter of time before the Test Kitchen perfected the recipe for the crockery cooker.

SPAGHETTI SAUCE ITALIANO

1	pound lean ground beef
8	ounces bulk Italian sausage
1	28-ounce can diced tomatoes, undrained
2	6-ounce cans tomato paste
2	4½-ounce jars sliced mushrooms, drained
1	cup chopped onion
¾	cup chopped green sweet pepper
½	cup dry red wine or water
⅓	cup water
1	2¼-ounce can sliced pitted ripe olives, drained
2	teaspoons sugar
1½	teaspoons Worcestershire sauce
½	teaspoon salt
½	teaspoon chili powder
⅛	teaspoon black pepper
2	cloves garlic, minced
8	cups hot cooked spaghetti (1 pound)
½	cup finely shredded Parmesan cheese

PREP:
25 minutes

COOK:
9 to 10 hours (low) or 4½ to 5 hours (high)

MAKES:
8 servings

1 In a large skillet cook ground beef and Italian sausage until meat is brown. Drain off fat.

2 Transfer meat mixture to a 3½- to 4½-quart slow cooker. Stir in tomatoes, tomato paste, mushrooms, onion, sweet pepper, wine, water, ripe olives, sugar, Worcestershire sauce, salt, chili powder, black pepper, and garlic.

3 Cover and cook on low-heat setting for 9 to 10 hours or on high-heat setting for 4½ to 5 hours.

4 Serve meat mixture over hot cooked spaghetti. Sprinkle each serving with Parmesan cheese.

Nutrition Facts per serving: 637 cal., 24 g total fat (11 g sat. fat), 79 mg chol., 1,359 mg sodium, 60 g carbo., 6 g fiber, 38 g pro. **Daily Values:** 8% vit. A, 54% vit. C, 49% calcium, 32% iron

This recipe won honors in the Better Homes and Gardens® Prize Tested Recipe contest. As its name suggests, it's a shoo-in for healthy appetites.

HEARTY HODGEPODGE

PREP:

20 minutes

COOK:

7 to 8 hours (low) or 3 1/2 to 4 hours (high)

MAKES:

8 servings

1 1/2	pounds lean ground beef
2	10 3/4-ounce cans condensed minestrone soup
1	21-ounce can pork and beans in tomato sauce
1	12-ounce can tomato juice
1	cup sliced celery
1	cup chopped onion
1	cup water
2	teaspoons Worcestershire sauce
1	teaspoon dried oregano, crushed
1/4	teaspoon black pepper
1	clove garlic, minced

1 In a large skillet cook ground beef until meat is brown. Drain off fat.

2 Transfer meat to a 3 1/2- or 4-quart slow cooker. Stir in minestrone soup, pork and beans, tomato juice, celery, onion, water, Worcestershire sauce, oregano, pepper, and garlic.

3 Cover and cook on low-heat setting for 7 to 8 hours or on high-heat setting for 3 1/2 to 4 hours.

Nutrition Facts per serving: 287 cal., 10 g total fat (4 g sat. fat), 62 mg chol., 1,116 mg sodium, 28 g carbo., 7 g fiber, 22 g pro. **Daily Values:** 29% vit. A, 21% vit. C, 9% calcium, 29% iron

Make their mouths water with fruit-studded stuffing topped with a peach-glazed roast. A salad and your favorite vegetables round out this sweet home-style dinner.

PORK ROAST WITH CORN BREAD STUFFING

Nonstick cooking spray

1   2- to 2½-pound boneless pork top loin roast (single loin)

1   tablespoon cooking oil

4   cups corn bread stuffing mix

¾   cup reduced-sodium chicken broth

½   cup mixed dried fruit bits

¼   cup chopped onion

½   cup peach spreadable fruit

1   teaspoon finely shredded lemon peel

¼   teaspoon ground cinnamon

PREP:
25 minutes

COOK:
5 to 6 hours (low) or 2½ to 3 hours (high)

MAKES:
8 servings

1. Lightly coat a 3½- or 4-quart slow cooker with cooking spray. Trim fat from meat. If necessary, cut meat to fit into cooker. Sprinkle meat with salt and black pepper. In a large skillet brown meat on all sides in hot oil. Drain off fat. Set aside.

2. In a large bowl toss together stuffing mix, chicken broth, dried fruit, and onion. In prepared cooker place stuffing mixture. Add meat. In a small bowl stir together peach spreadable fruit, lemon peel, and cinnamon. Spread over meat in cooker.

3. Cover and cook on low-heat setting for 5 to 6 hours or on high-heat setting for 2½ to 3 hours. Remove meat from cooker. Cut meat into slices. Stir stuffing; serve with meat.

Nutrition Facts per serving: 408 cal., 9 g total fat (2 g sat. fat), 67 mg chol., 639 mg sodium, 52 g carbo., 0 g fiber, 29 g pro. **Daily Values:** 2% vit. C, 3% calcium, 14% iron

Thanks to the slow cooker, gathering the family around the table for a roast doesn't have to be a weekends-only affair. This roast is special enough for Sunday, but you can look forward to coming home to it any day of the week.

ORANGE-APPLE PORK ROAST

PREP:

25 minutes

COOK:

8 to 10 hours (low)
or 4 to 5 hours (high)

MAKES:

6 to 8 servings

1	2- to 2½-pound boneless pork shoulder roast
½	teaspoon salt
½	teaspoon black pepper
2	tablespoons cooking oil
1	16-ounce package peeled baby carrots
1½	cups applesauce
¼	cup frozen orange juice concentrate, thawed
¼	cup water
2	tablespoons quick-cooking tapioca
1½	teaspoons dried thyme, crushed

1 Trim fat from meat. If necessary, cut meat to fit into a 3½- or 4-quart slow cooker. Sprinkle meat with salt and pepper. In a large skillet brown meat on all sides in hot oil. Drain off fat. Transfer meat to cooker. Add baby carrots.

2 In a medium bowl combine applesauce, orange juice concentrate, water, tapioca, and thyme. Pour over mixture in cooker.

3 Cover and cook on low-heat setting for 8 to 10 hours or on high-heat setting for 4 to 5 hours.

4 Using a slotted spoon, transfer meat and baby carrots to a serving platter. Spoon some of the cooking juices over meat and carrots. Pass remaining juices.

Nutrition Facts per serving: 388 cal., 16 g total fat (5 g sat. fat), 102 mg chol., 329 mg sodium, 28 g carbo., 3 g fiber, 31 g pro. **Daily Values:** 385% vit. A, 40% vit. C, 7% calcium, 16% iron

Noodles or brown rice complements the fragrant apple-spice sauce and super-tender meat. Complete the menu with coleslaw and a fruit crisp or pie for dessert.

PORK ROAST & HARVEST VEGETABLES

1	1½- to 2-pound boneless pork shoulder roast
1	tablespoon cooking oil
3	medium parsnips, cut into ½-inch slices
3	medium carrots, cut into ½-inch slices
1	large green sweet pepper, cut into wedges
2	stalks celery, cut into ½-inch slices
3	tablespoons quick-cooking tapioca
1	6-ounce can apple juice concentrate, thawed
¼	cup water
1	teaspoon instant beef bouillon granules
¼	teaspoon ground cinnamon
¼	teaspoon black pepper

PREP:

30 minutes

COOK:

10 to 12 hours (low) or 5 to 6 hours (high)

MAKES:

6 servings

1 Trim fat from meat. If necessary, cut meat to fit into a 3½- to 5-quart slow cooker. In a large skillet brown meat on all sides in hot oil. Drain off fat. Set aside.

2 In cooker combine parsnips, carrots, sweet pepper, and celery. Sprinkle with tapioca. In a small bowl combine apple juice concentrate, water, bouillon granules, cinnamon, and black pepper. Pour over vegetables in cooker. Add meat.

3 Cover and cook on low-heat setting for 10 to 12 hours or on high-heat setting for 5 to 6 hours.

4 Transfer meat and vegetables to a serving platter. Strain cooking juices; skim off fat. Drizzle some of the juices over meat and vegetables. Pass remaining juices.

Nutrition Facts per serving: 309 cal., 9 g total fat (3 g sat. fat), 73 mg chol., 272 mg sodium, 32 g carbo., 4 g fiber, 24 g pro. **Daily Values:** 157% vit. A, 50% vit. C, 5% calcium, 13% iron

It seems almost magical that so few ingredients can produce such great dimensions in flavor.

PORK ROAST WITH PLUM SAUCE

PREP:

20 minutes

COOK:

8 to 10 hours (low)
or 4 to 5 hours (high)

MAKES:

6 to 8 servings

1	3½- to 4-pound boneless pork shoulder roast
1	large onion, sliced
1	1-ounce envelope onion soup mix
1	18-ounce jar plum preserves
¼	cup chicken broth
2	tablespoons Dijon-style mustard
1	tablespoon quick-cooking tapioca
3	to 4 cups hot cooked rice

1 Trim fat from meat. If necessary, cut meat to fit into a 3½- or 4-quart slow cooker. Set aside. In cooker place onion. Add meat; sprinkle with onion soup mix.

2 For sauce, in a medium bowl combine plum preserves, chicken broth, Dijon mustard, and tapioca. Pour over mixture in cooker.

3 Cover and cook on low-heat setting for 8 to 10 hours or on high-heat setting for 4 to 5 hours.

4 Transfer meat and onion to a serving platter. Skim fat from sauce. Spoon some of the sauce over meat and onion. Serve with hot cooked rice. Pass remaining sauce.

Nutrition Facts per serving: 733 cal., 16 g total fat (5 g sat. fat), 171 mg chol., 563 mg sodium, 86 g carbo., 2 g fiber, 55 g pro. Daily Values: 18% vit. C, 5% calcium, 25% iron

TRIMMING AND SKIMMING FAT

Thanks to low, moist heat, slow cooking requires little fat. For low-fat meals, choose lean cuts of meat and trim away as much fat as possible. Remove poultry skin before cooking. If you want to brown the meat, use a nonstick skillet coated with nonstick cooking spray. Before serving the meal, use a slotted spoon to transfer the meat and vegetables to a serving platter. Pour the cooking liquid into a glass measuring cup and let it stand for 1 to 2 minutes. Once the fat rises to the top, skim off any visible fat with a metal spoon.

Combine Asian flavors and an American cut of meat, and you get a best-of-the-East-and-West delight!

ASIAN PORK POT ROAST

1   2½- to 3-pound boneless pork shoulder roast
1   16-ounce package frozen stir-fry vegetables
¾   cup bottled sweet-and-sour sauce
2   tablespoons quick-cooking tapioca
1   teaspoon five-spice powder
3   cups hot cooked rice or rice noodles
    Crushed red pepper

PREP:
15 minutes
COOK:
9 to 10 hours (low)
or 4½ to 5 hours (high)
MAKES:
6 to 8 servings

1 Trim fat from meat. If necessary, cut meat to fit into a 4- to 5-quart slow cooker. Set aside. In cooker place frozen vegetables. Add meat.

2 For sauce, in a small bowl combine sweet-and-sour sauce, tapioca, and five-spice powder. Pour over mixture in cooker.

3 Cover and cook on low-heat setting for 9 to 10 hours or on high-heat setting for 4½ to 5 hours.

4 Remove meat and vegetables from cooker. Skim fat from sauce. Season to taste with salt. Serve meat, vegetables, and sauce with hot cooked rice. Sprinkle with crushed red pepper.

Nutrition Facts per serving: 419 cal., 14 g total fat (5 g sat. fat), 126 mg chol., 281 mg sodium, 38 g carbo., 2 g fiber, 41 g pro. **Daily Values:** 14% vit. A, 20% vit. C, 6% calcium, 21% iron

For a swift and colorful side dish that helps bring out the best of this delightful, fennel-infused roast, consider serving Broccoli & Peppers (page 348).

ITALIAN PORK WITH MASHED SWEET POTATOES

PREP:

20 minutes

COOK:

*8 to 10 hours (low)
or 4 to 5 hours (high)*

MAKES:

4 servings

1 teaspoon fennel seeds, crushed

½ teaspoon dried oregano, crushed

½ teaspoon garlic powder

½ teaspoon paprika

¼ teaspoon salt

¼ teaspoon black pepper

1 1½- to 2-pound boneless pork shoulder roast

1 pound sweet potatoes, peeled and cut into 1-inch pieces

1 cup chicken broth

1 In a small bowl combine fennel seeds, oregano, garlic powder, paprika, salt, and pepper. Trim fat from meat. Sprinkle fennel mixture evenly over meat; rub in with your fingers. If necessary, cut meat to fit into a 3½- or 4-quart slow cooker. Set aside.

2 In cooker place sweet potatoes. Add meat. Pour chicken broth over mixture in cooker.

3 Cover and cook on low-heat setting for 8 to 10 hours or on high-heat setting for 4 to 5 hours.

4 Remove meat from cooker. Cut meat into slices. Using a slotted spoon, transfer sweet potatoes to a medium bowl. Using a potato masher, mash sweet potatoes, adding enough of the liquid, if necessary, to moisten. Serve meat with mashed sweet potatoes.

Nutrition Facts per serving: 356 cal., 14 g total fat (5 g sat. fat), 115 mg chol., 525 mg sodium, 21 g carbo., 3 g fiber, 35 g pro. **Daily Values:** 299% vit. A, 23% vit. C, 6% calcium, 16% iron

Onion soup mix has long been a favorite ingredient for time-pressed cooks. Combined with cranberry-orange relish and Dijon mustard, this pork roast is endowed with a windfall of flavor.

CRANBERRY-MUSTARD PORK ROAST

1   2½- to 3-pound boneless pork sirloin or shoulder roast

1   tablespoon cooking oil

1   10- to 12-ounce package frozen cranberry-orange relish, thawed

1   1-ounce envelope onion soup mix

2   tablespoons Dijon-style mustard

2   tablespoons water

PREP:

20 minutes

COOK:

5 to 6 hours (low)
or 2½ to 3 hours (high)

MAKES:

8 servings

1   Trim fat from meat. In a large skillet brown meat on all sides in hot oil. Drain off fat. Transfer meat to a 3½- or 4-quart slow cooker. In a medium bowl combine cranberry-orange relish, soup mix, Dijon mustard, and water. Pour over meat in cooker.

2   Cover and cook on low-heat setting for 5 to 6 hours or on high-heat setting for 2½ to 3 hours.

3   Remove meat from cooker, reserving juices. If present, remove string or netting from meat. Cut meat into slices. Skim any fat from juices. Serve meat with juices.

Nutrition Facts per serving: 264 cal., 9 g total fat (3 g sat. fat), 89 mg chol., 279 mg sodium, 12 g carbo., 1 g fiber, 30 g pro. **Daily Values:** 1% vit. A, 8% vit. C, 2% calcium, 7% iron

Here's a great idea for leftovers: Toast rye bread slices and spread one side with a creamy mustard blend. Top with drained sauerkraut, shredded pork roast, and shredded Swiss cheese. Broil 3 to 4 inches from the heat for 2 to 3 minutes or until cheese melts.

SAUERKRAUT & PORK SHOULDER ROAST

PREP:

15 minutes

COOK:

*8 to 10 hours (low)
or 4 to 5 hours (high)*

MAKES:

8 servings

1   2½-pound boneless pork shoulder or sirloin roast

2   tablespoons creamy Dijon-style mustard blend

1   14½-ounce can sauerkraut with caraway seeds, rinsed and drained

1   cup regular or nonalcoholic beer

1 Trim fat from meat. If necessary, cut meat to fit into a 3½- or 4-quart slow cooker. Lightly sprinkle meat with salt and black pepper. Spread mustard over meat. Set aside.

2 In cooker place rinsed and drained sauerkraut. Add meat. Pour beer over mixture in cooker.

3 Cover and cook on low-heat setting for 8 to 10 hours or on high-heat setting for 4 to 5 hours. Remove meat from cooker. If present, remove string or netting from meat. Cut meat into slices. Serve meat with sauerkraut.

Nutrition Facts per serving: 230 cal., 10 g total fat (3 g sat. fat), 92 mg chol., 546 mg sodium, 4 g carbo., 1 g fiber, 29 g pro. **Daily Values:** 15% vit. A, 83% vit. C, 3% calcium, 14% iron

Dried Japanese somen noodles have a very fine texture similar to that of vermicelli. Look for them, wrapped in bundles, wherever Asian foods are sold. In a pinch, substitute dried vermicelli.

PORK LO MEIN

1½	pounds boneless pork shoulder
2	cups frozen sliced carrots
1	12-ounce jar teriyaki glaze
2	medium onions, cut into wedges
1	cup thinly bias-sliced celery
1	8-ounce can sliced water chestnuts, drained
1	5-ounce can sliced bamboo shoots, drained
1	teaspoon grated fresh ginger
1	6-ounce package frozen pea pods
1	cup broccoli florets
9	ounces dried somen noodles
½	cup cashews

1 Trim fat from meat. Cut meat into ¾-inch pieces. In a 3½- or 4-quart slow cooker combine meat, frozen carrots, teriyaki glaze, onions, celery, water chestnuts, bamboo shoots, and ginger.

2 Cover and cook on low-heat setting for 6½ to 7 hours or on high-heat setting for 3½ to 4 hours.

3 If using low-heat setting, turn to high-heat setting. Stir in frozen pea pods and broccoli. Cover and cook for 10 to 15 minutes more or until pea pods are crisp-tender.

4 Meanwhile, cook noodles according to package directions; drain. Serve meat mixture over noodles. Sprinkle each serving with cashews.

Nutrition Facts per serving: 509 cal., 12 g total fat (3 g sat. fat), 73 mg chol., 2,274 mg sodium, 66 g carbo., 6 g fiber, 33 g pro. **Daily Values:** 187% vit. A, 35% vit. C, 13% calcium, 23% iron

PREP:

20 minutes

COOK:

6½ to 7 hours (low) or 3½ to 4 hours (high), plus 10 minutes (high)

MAKES:

6 servings

Scented with delectable fresh basil and shallots, this one-dish dinner is fancy enough to entertain with any night of the week, plus it frees the cook to visit with guests.

LEMONY PORK & VEGETABLES

PREP:

30 minutes

COOK:

*7 to 8 hours (low)
or 3¹/₂ to 4 hours (high),
plus 5 minutes (high)*

MAKES:

6 servings

2	pounds boneless pork shoulder
¹/₄	cup all-purpose flour
¹/₂	teaspoon black pepper
2	tablespoons cooking oil
1	16-ounce package peeled baby carrots
8	ounces parsnips, cut into ¹/₂-inch slices
2	medium shallots, sliced
1	medium lemon, quartered
¹/₄	cup finely shredded fresh basil
1	14-ounce can chicken broth
1¹/₃	cups quick-cooking couscous

1 Trim fat from meat. Cut meat into 1-inch pieces. In a plastic bag combine flour and pepper. Add meat pieces, a few pieces at a time, shaking to coat. In a large skillet cook meat, half at a time, in hot oil until brown. Drain off fat. Set aside.

2 In a 3¹/₂- to 6-quart slow cooker place carrots, parsnips, shallots, lemon, and basil. Add meat. Pour chicken broth over mixture in cooker.

3 Cover and cook on low-heat setting for 7 to 8 hours or on high-heat setting for 3¹/₂ to 4 hours. Remove lemon pieces.

4 Transfer meat and vegetables to a serving dish, reserving juices. Cover meat and vegetables and keep warm. Measure 1³/₄ cups juices; return to cooker. If using low-heat setting, turn to high-heat setting. Stir couscous into juices. Cover and cook for 5 minutes more. Fluff couscous with a fork. Serve meat and vegetables with couscous.

Nutrition Facts per serving: 511 cal., 16 g total fat (4 g sat. fat), 101 mg chol., 368 mg sodium, 53 g carbo., 7 g fiber, 38 g pro. **Daily Values:** 193% vit. A, 44% vit. C, 8% calcium, 20% iron

BROWNING MEAT

At one time, browning the meat was the first step in any slow-cooker recipe. But after testing hundreds of slow-cooker recipes, the Better Homes and Gardens® Home Economists have found that browning is more a matter of preference than necessity. Brown the meat if you like the bit of color and flavor it may add, or save some time and skip that step. The exception: Ground meat and ground poultry always should be browned to prevent clumping, add appetizing color, and reduce the amount of fat.

The deep, aromatic flavors in this dish call for a sprightly accompaniment.
A crisp salad tossed with a tart, garlicky vinaigrette definitely does the trick.

CUMIN & CORIANDER PORK

2	cups fresh mushrooms, quartered
1	large onion, cut into wedges
2½	to 3 pounds boneless pork shoulder
1	tablespoon cooking oil
1	cup apple juice
2	tablespoons cider vinegar
1	tablespoon brown sugar
1	teaspoon coriander seeds, crushed
1	teaspoon cumin seeds, crushed
¾	teaspoon salt
½	teaspoon black pepper
1	8-ounce carton dairy sour cream
2	tablespoons all-purpose flour
	Hot mashed potatoes or hot cooked noodles (optional)

PREP:
30 minutes

COOK:
8 to 10 hours (low)
or 4 to 5 hours (high),
plus 10 minutes (high)

MAKES:
6 servings

1 In a 3½- or 4-quart slow cooker place mushrooms and onion. Trim fat from meat. Cut meat into ¾-inch pieces. In a large skillet brown meat, half at a time, in hot oil. Transfer meat to cooker.

2 Carefully add apple juice to drippings in skillet. Bring to a gentle boil, stirring to loosen browned bits from bottom of skillet. Remove from heat. Stir in vinegar, brown sugar, coriander seeds, cumin seeds, salt, and pepper. Pour over mixture in cooker.

3 Cover and cook on low-heat setting for 8 to 10 hours or on high-heat setting for 4 to 5 hours.

4 If using low-heat setting, turn to high-heat setting. In a small bowl combine sour cream and flour. Gradually stir about ½ cup of the hot cooking liquid into sour cream mixture. Add sour cream mixture to cooker, stirring gently until combined. Cover and cook for 10 to 15 minutes more or until thickened.

5 If desired, serve meat mixture over hot mashed potatoes.

Nutrition Facts per serving: 594 cal., 43 g total fat (17 g sat. fat), 149 mg chol., 439 mg sodium, 15 g carbo., 1 g fiber, 35 g pro. Daily Values: 6% vit. A, 6% vit. C, 9% calcium, 16% iron

*Marengo refers to the battle Napoleon won against Austria in 1800.
To celebrate the victory, Napoleon's chef invented a dish similar to this one.*

PORK & MUSHROOM MARENGO

PREP:

25 minutes

COOK:

*8 to 10 hours (low)
or 4 to 5 hours (high),
plus 15 minutes (high)*

MAKES:

4 servings

1½   pounds boneless pork shoulder

1   tablespoon cooking oil

8   ounces fresh mushrooms, sliced

1   medium onion, chopped

1   14½-ounce can tomatoes, undrained and cut up

1   cup water

1   tablespoon snipped fresh marjoram or 1 teaspoon dried marjoram, crushed

1½   teaspoons snipped fresh thyme or ½ teaspoon dried thyme, crushed

1   teaspoon instant chicken bouillon granules

¼   teaspoon salt

  Dash black pepper

⅓   cup cold water

3   tablespoons all-purpose flour

2   cups hot cooked rice

1   Trim fat from meat. Cut meat into 1-inch pieces. In a large skillet brown meat, half at a time, in hot oil. Drain off fat. Set aside.

2   In a 3½- to 5-quart slow cooker place mushrooms and onion. Add meat. In a medium bowl combine tomatoes, the 1 cup water, the dried marjoram and thyme (if using), bouillon granules, salt, and pepper. Pour over mixture in cooker.

3   Cover and cook on low-heat setting for 8 to 10 hours or on high-heat setting for 4 to 5 hours.

4   If using low-heat setting, turn to high-heat setting. In a small bowl stir together the ⅓ cup cold water and the flour. Stir into mixture in cooker. Cover and cook for 15 to 20 minutes more or until thickened. If using, stir in fresh marjoram and thyme. Serve meat mixture over hot cooked rice.

Nutrition Facts per serving: 481 cal., 22 g total fat (7 g sat. fat), 112 mg chol., 610 mg sodium, 36 g carbo., 2 g fiber, 35 g pro. **Daily Values:** 6% vit. A, 32% vit. C, 5% calcium, 32% iron

Hosting a house full of guests? Set up this easygoing three-course spread: Start with a tray of cheeses, olives, and raw vegetables; continue with these delicious pork sandwiches and macaroni or potato salad; and end with a selection of cookies.

CRANBERRY BBQ PORK SANDWICHES

3½	to 4 pounds boneless pork shoulder
1	tablespoon cooking oil
1½	cups chopped red onions
1	16-ounce can whole cranberry sauce
⅔	cup bottled barbecue sauce
¼	cup spicy brown mustard
2	tablespoons quick-cooking tapioca
12	kaiser rolls, split and toasted

PREP:

30 minutes

COOK:

*6 to 8 hours (low)
or 3 to 4 hours (high)*

MAKES:

12 sandwiches

1 Trim fat from meat. Cut meat into ¾-inch pieces. In a large skillet brown meat, one-third at a time, in hot oil. Drain off fat.

2 Transfer meat to a 3½- or 4-quart slow cooker. Add red onions. In a medium bowl stir together cranberry sauce, barbecue sauce, mustard, and tapioca. Pour over mixture in cooker.

3 Cover and cook on low-heat setting for 6 to 8 hours or on high-heat setting for 3 to 4 hours.

4 Remove meat from cooker, reserving juices. Using two forks, pull meat apart into shreds. Skim fat from juices. Stir enough of the juices into meat to moisten. Serve meat on toasted rolls.

Nutrition Facts per serving: 393 cal., 9 g total fat (2 g sat. fat), 59 mg chol., 561 mg sodium, 50 g carbo., 2 g fiber, 27 g pro. **Daily Values:** 3% vit. A, 6% vit. C, 8% calcium, 17% iron

In eastern North Carolina, home of vinegar-sauced barbecued pork, coleslaw is a must-have accompaniment to these famous sandwiches. Spoon some slaw onto the bun with the meat or serve it on the side.

PORK & SLAW BARBECUE ROLLS

PREP:

20 minutes

COOK:

*10 to 12 hours (low)
or 5 to 6 hours (high)*

MAKES:

16 sandwiches

1	4- to 5-pound pork shoulder roast
¾	cup cider vinegar
2	tablespoons brown sugar
½	teaspoon salt
½	teaspoon crushed red pepper
¼	teaspoon black pepper
16	kaiser rolls, split and toasted
	Deli coleslaw

1 Trim fat from meat. If necessary, cut meat to fit into a 4- to 6-quart slow cooker. Place meat in cooker. In a small bowl combine vinegar, brown sugar, salt, crushed red pepper, and black pepper. Pour over meat in cooker.

2 Cover and cook on low-heat setting for 10 to 12 hours or on high-heat setting for 5 to 6 hours.

3 Remove meat from cooker, reserving juices. When cool enough to handle, cut meat off bones and coarsely chop. Skim fat from juices. Stir enough of the juices into meat to moisten. Serve meat on toasted rolls. Top with coleslaw.

Nutrition Facts per serving: 272 cal., 6 g total fat (2 g sat. fat), 41 mg chol., 563 mg sodium, 34 g carbo., 1 g fiber, 18 g pro. **Daily Values:** 3% vit. A, 3% vit. C, 6% calcium, 16% iron

Shredded tender pork and onions stuff these tortilla wraps. Spoon on Pico de Gallo (see recipe, page 166) and avocado dip for an even greater Caribbean experience.

CUBAN PORK TORTILLA ROLL-UPS

½	cup lime juice
¼	cup grapefruit juice
¼	cup water
2	bay leaves
1	teaspoon dried oregano, crushed
½	teaspoon salt
½	teaspoon ground cumin
¼	teaspoon black pepper
3	cloves garlic, minced
1	3-pound boneless pork shoulder roast
1	large onion, sliced
	Shredded lettuce (optional)
	Chopped tomato (optional)
8	to 10 flour tortillas, warmed
	Purchased frozen avocado dip (guacamole), thawed (optional)

PREP:
25 minutes

MARINATE:
6 hours

COOK:
*10 to 12 hours (low)
or 5 to 6 hours (high)*

MAKES:
8 to 10 servings

1 For marinade, in a small bowl combine lime juice, grapefruit juice, water, bay leaves, oregano, salt, cumin, pepper, and garlic. Trim fat from meat. If necessary, cut meat to fit into a 3½- to 5-quart slow cooker. Using a large fork, pierce meat in several places. Place in a resealable plastic bag set in a shallow dish. Pour marinade over meat; seal bag. Marinate in the refrigerator for 6 to 24 hours, turning bag occasionally.

2 In cooker place onion. Add meat and marinade. Cover and cook on low-heat setting for 10 to 12 hours or on high-heat setting for 5 to 6 hours.

3 Remove meat and onion from cooker, reserving juices. Using two forks, pull meat apart into shreds. Remove bay leaves. Skim fat from juices.

4 Serve meat, onion, and, if desired, lettuce and tomato in tortillas with small bowls of the hot juices. If desired, pass avocado dip.

Nutrition Facts per serving: 398 cal., 19 g total fat (6 g sat. fat), 90 mg chol., 420 mg sodium, 27 g carbo., 1 g fiber, 29 g pro. **Daily Values:** 15% vit. C, 9% calcium, 18% iron

Napa cabbage, sometimes labeled Chinese cabbage, and bok choy are not the same vegetable but are kitchen cousins. Either one adequately provides these wraps with fresh crunch and color.

ASIAN PORK WRAPS

PREP:

25 minutes

COOK:

*8 to 10 hours (low)
or 4 to 5 hours (high)*

MAKES:

8 sandwiches

1	teaspoon ground ginger
½	teaspoon garlic powder
1	2½- to 3-pound boneless pork shoulder roast
1	16-ounce package frozen stir-fry vegetables
1	8½-ounce jar plum or hoisin sauce
½	cup chicken broth
8	10-inch flour tortillas, warmed
2	cups shredded or coarsely chopped Chinese (napa) cabbage or bok choy

1 In a small bowl combine ginger and garlic powder. Trim fat from meat. Sprinkle ginger mixture evenly over meat; rub in with your fingers. If necessary, cut meat to fit into a 3½- or 4-quart slow cooker. Place meat in cooker.

2 Add frozen vegetables and half of the plum sauce. (Cover and chill remaining plum sauce until needed.) Pour broth over mixture in cooker.

3 Cover and cook on low-heat setting for 8 to 10 hours or on high-heat setting for 4 to 5 hours.

4 Remove meat from cooker. Using two forks, pull meat apart into shreds. Transfer to a large bowl. Using a slotted spoon, transfer vegetables to the same bowl; discard juices. Stir remaining plum sauce into meat mixture.

5 To serve, arrange meat mixture just below centers of tortillas. Top with shredded cabbage. Fold bottom edge of each tortilla up and over filling. Fold in opposite sides; roll up from bottom. Secure with wooden toothpicks.

Nutrition Facts per serving: 435 cal., 15 g total fat (5 g sat. fat), 96 mg chol., 493 mg sodium, 41 g carbo., 3 g fiber, 32 g pro. **Daily Values:** 15% vit. A, 23% vit. C, 12% calcium, 22% iron

With a little cornstarch magic, hot-style vegetable juice, the convenient ingredient here. transforms into a tomatoey sauce with just the right hit of pepper. Hint: To better control the amount of heat that goes in, use regular vegetable juice and bottled hot pepper sauce to taste.

PORK CHOPS WITH A KICK

2	stalks celery, bias-sliced
1	large onion, chopped
8	boneless pork loin chops, cut ¾ inch thick
2	cups red and/or green sweet pepper strips
½	teaspoon cracked black pepper
2	cups hot-style vegetable juice
2	tablespoons cornstarch
2	tablespoons cold water

PREP:
25 minutes
COOK:
5 to 6 hours (low)
or 2½ to 3 hours (high)
MAKES:
8 servings

1 In a 3½- or 4-quart slow cooker place celery and onion. Trim fat from chops. Add chops to cooker in layers, sprinkling sweet pepper strips and black pepper between chops. Pour vegetable juice over mixture in cooker.

2 Cover and cook on low-heat setting for 5 to 6 hours or on high-heat setting for 2½ to 3 hours.

3 Transfer chops and vegetables to a serving platter, reserving juices. Cover chops and vegetables and keep warm.

4 For sauce, strain juices into a glass measuring cup; skim off fat. Measure 2 cups juices. Pour juices into a medium saucepan. Combine cornstarch and cold water; stir into juices in saucepan. Cook and stir over medium heat until thickened and bubbly. Cook and stir for 2 minutes more. Serve chops and vegetables with sauce.

Nutrition Facts per serving: 189 cal., 6 g total fat (2 g sat. fat), 54 mg chol., 254 mg sodium, 9 g carbo., 2 g fiber, 23 g pro. **Daily Values:** 51% vit. A, 119% vit. C, 2% calcium, 7% iron

THICKENING JUICES
Unlike the bottom heat of a saucepan, the heat in a slow cooker comes from coils that wrap around the sides of the pot. Therefore a cooker that is at least half full will cook more efficiently than one with less volume. When you remove the meat from the cooker, the juices likely will fill the cooker less than halfway. To thicken juices, you'll need to transfer them to a saucepan. Leaving them in the cooker won't bring about the results you desire.

The full-flavored sauce features a balance of sweetness and tang.
The brown rice accompaniment provides a nutty complement.

SWEET-SAUCED PORK CHOPS

PREP:

20 minutes

COOK:

6 to 7 hours (low)
or 3 to 3 1/2 hours (high)

MAKES:

6 servings

1	cup sliced celery
1/2	cup coarsely chopped onion
6	pork loin chops (with bone), cut 3/4 inch thick
1/2	teaspoon salt
1/4	teaspoon black pepper
1	7- to 8-ounce package mixed dried fruit
1	cup cranberry juice
1/2	cup apricot or peach preserves
1/4	cup packed brown sugar
1/4	cup spicy brown mustard
2	tablespoons quick-cooking tapioca
1	tablespoon freshly grated ginger or 1/4 teaspoon ground ginger
3	cups hot cooked brown rice

1 In a 3 1/2- or 4-quart slow cooker place celery and onion. Trim fat from chops. Sprinkle chops with salt and pepper. Cut up any large pieces of dried fruit. Add chops and dried fruit to cooker.

2 For sauce, in a medium bowl combine cranberry juice, apricot preserves, brown sugar, brown mustard, tapioca, and ginger. Pour over mixture in cooker.

3 Cover and cook on low-heat setting for 6 to 7 hours or on high-heat setting for 3 to 3 1/2 hours. Serve over hot cooked rice.

Nutrition Facts per serving: 505 cal., 8 g total fat (2 g sat. fat), 62 mg chol., 445 mg sodium, 83 g carbo., 3 g fiber, 27 g pro. **Daily Values:** 1% vit. A, 35% vit. C, 8% calcium, 16% iron

This Tuscan-inspired dish goes well with—what else?—a side of pasta.
Toss your favorite with a little olive oil and herbs and dinner's set.

TOMATO-SAUCED PORK CHOPS

6   boneless pork loin chops, cut ¾ inch thick

1   tablespoon cooking oil

1   1-ounce envelope onion soup mix

1   15-ounce can Great Northern or small white beans,
    rinsed and drained

1   14½-ounce can diced tomatoes with basil, oregano,
    and garlic, undrained

2   tablespoons dry red wine or water

PREP:

15 minutes

COOK:

7 to 8 hours (low)
or 3½ to 4 hours (high)

MAKES:

6 servings

1 Trim fat from chops. In a 12-inch skillet brown chops on both sides in hot oil. Drain off fat. Transfer chops to a 3½- or 4-quart slow cooker. Sprinkle chops with onion soup mix. Pour Great Northern beans and tomatoes over chops in cooker.

2 Cover and cook on low-heat setting for 7 to 8 hours or on high-heat setting for 3½ to 4 hours.

3 Transfer chops to a serving platter. Stir wine into bean mixture. Using a slotted spoon, spoon beans and tomatoes over chops; discard cooking liquid.

Nutrition Facts per serving: 381 cal., 11 g total fat (3 g sat. fat), 93 mg chol., 594 mg sodium, 24 g carbo., 4 g fiber, 44 g pro. **Daily Values:** 8% vit. A, 10% vit. C, 12% calcium, 20% iron

If you like those filling skillet dinners served at popular chain restaurants, chances are you'll like this even more.

PORK CHOPS O'BRIEN

PREP:

20 minutes

COOK:

*7 to 9 hours (low)
or 3^1/$_2$ to 4^1/$_2$ hours (high)*

MAKES:

4 servings

Nonstick cooking spray

5   cups loose-pack frozen diced hash brown potatoes with onion and peppers, thawed

1   10^3/$_4$-ounce can reduced-fat and reduced-sodium condensed cream of mushroom soup

^{1}/$_2$ cup roasted red sweet peppers, drained and chopped

^{1}/$_2$ cup dairy sour cream

^{1}/$_2$ cup shredded Colby Jack cheese (2 ounces)

^{1}/$_4$ teaspoon black pepper

4   pork loin chops (with bone), cut ^{3}/$_4$ inch thick

1   tablespoon cooking oil

1   2.8-ounce can french-fried onions

1 Lightly coat a 3^1/$_2$- or 4-quart slow cooker with cooking spray; set aside. In a large bowl combine hash brown potatoes, mushroom soup, roasted sweet peppers, sour cream, Colby Jack cheese, and black pepper. Transfer potato mixture to prepared cooker.

2 Trim fat from chops. In a large skillet brown chops on both sides in hot oil. Drain off fat. Place chops on top of mixture in cooker.

3 Cover and cook on low-heat setting for 7 to 9 hours or on high-heat setting for 3^1/$_2$ to 4^1/$_2$ hours. Before serving, sprinkle with fried onions.

Nutrition Facts per serving: 670 cal., 29 g total fat (9 g sat. fat), 92 mg chol., 639 mg sodium, 64 g carbo., 4 g fiber, 37 g pro. **Daily Values:** 7% vit. A, 122% vit. C, 24% calcium, 21% iron

A glistening orange marmalade and mustard sauce tops these chops and winter squash slices. Steam green beans or asparagus to serve on the side.

ORANGE-MUSTARD PORK CHOPS

2	small or medium acorn squash (1½ to 2 pounds)
1	large onion, halved lengthwise and sliced
6	pork chops (with bone), cut ¾ inch thick
½	cup chicken broth
⅓	cup orange marmalade
1	tablespoon honey mustard or Dijon-style mustard
1	teaspoon dried marjoram or thyme, crushed
¼	teaspoon black pepper
2	tablespoons cornstarch
2	tablespoons cold water

PREP:

25 minutes

COOK:

5 to 6 hours (low) or 2½ to 3 hours (high)

MAKES:

6 servings

1. Cut squash in half lengthwise. Remove seeds and membranes. Cut each half into 3 wedges. In a 5- to 6-quart slow cooker place squash and onion. Trim fat from chops. Place chops on top of squash and onion.

2. In a small bowl stir together chicken broth, orange marmalade, mustard, marjoram, and pepper. Pour over mixture in cooker.

3. Cover and cook on low-heat setting for 5 to 6 hours or on high-heat setting for 2½ to 3 hours. Transfer chops and vegetables to a serving platter, reserving juices. Cover meat and vegetables and keep warm.

4. For sauce, strain juices into a glass measuring cup; skim off fat. Measure 1¾ cups juices, adding water, if necessary. Pour juices into a medium saucepan. Combine cornstarch and the cold water; stir into juices in saucepan. Cook and stir over medium heat until thickened and bubbly. Cook and stir for 2 minutes more. Serve chops and vegetables with sauce.

Nutrition Facts per serving: 265 cal., 8 g total fat (3 g sat. fat), 65 mg chol., 168 mg sodium, 27 g carbo., 3 g fiber, 21 g pro. **Daily Values:** 3% vit. A, 20% vit. C, 7% calcium, 10% iron

Seasoned chili beans and bottled salsa are true timesavers. When incorporated in a recipe, you don't have to round up or measure out little bits of this and that to get a full-flavored dish.

SOUTHWEST PORK CHOPS

PREP:

15 minutes

COOK:

*5 hours (low)
or 2 1/2 hours (high),
plus 30 minutes (high)*

MAKES:

6 servings

6   pork rib chops (with bone), cut 3/4 inch thick

1   15 1/2-ounce can Mexican-style chili beans

1 1/4   cups bottled salsa

1   cup fresh or frozen whole kernel corn

2   cups hot cooked rice

  Snipped fresh cilantro (optional)

1   Trim fat from chops. In a 3 1/2- or 4-quart slow cooker place chops. Add chili beans and salsa.

2   Cover and cook on low-heat setting for 5 hours or on high-heat setting for 2 1/2 hours.

3   If using low-heat setting, turn to high-heat setting. Stir in corn. Cover and cook for 30 minutes more. Serve over hot cooked rice. If desired, sprinkle with cilantro.

Nutrition Facts per serving: 334 cal., 7 g total fat (2 g sat. fat), 77 mg chol., 716 mg sodium, 34 g carbo., 4 g fiber, 33 g pro. **Daily Values:** 5% vit. A, 13% vit. C, 6% calcium, 19% iron

MICROWAVING LEFTOVER RICE

Next time you cook rice, cook extra to refrigerate in an airtight container for up to 1 week. To reheat the chilled cooked rice, place rice in a microwave-safe container and cover with vented plastic wrap. For 2 cups chilled rice, add 1 tablespoon water and microwave on 100-percent power (high) for 2 to 3 minutes or until heated through, stirring once. After the rice is heated, fluff gently with a fork.

The sauce resembles chunky spiced applesauce, but it's really a combination of apple butter, tapioca, and quartered apples.

APPLE BUTTER-SAUCED PORK CHOPS

6	boneless cooked smoked pork chops
1	cup apple butter
1	teaspoon quick-cooking tapioca
½	teaspoon dried sage, crushed
2	large red apples
3	cups hot cooked couscous

PREP:

10 minutes

COOK:

*6 to 7 hours (low)
or 3 to 3½ hours (high)*

MAKES:

6 servings

1 In a 3½- or 4-quart slow cooker place chops. For sauce, in a small bowl combine apple butter, tapioca, and sage. Pour over chops in cooker. If desired, peel apples. Core and cut apples into quarters. Place apples on top of mixture in cooker.

2 Cover and cook on low-heat setting for 6 to 7 hours or on high-heat setting for 3 to 3½ hours. Serve over hot cooked couscous.

Nutrition Facts per serving: 518 cal., 12 g total fat (4 g sat. fat), 40 mg chol., 641 mg sodium, 87 g carbo., 5 g fiber, 16 g pro. **Daily Values:** 4% vit. A, 5% vit. C, 3% calcium, 6% iron

Here the fresh and bold spices are a fitting match for the big, meaty appeal of country-style ribs.

PLUM-SAUCED PORK RIBS

PREP:

15 minutes

COOK:

*8 to 10 hours (low)
or 4 to 5 hours (high)*

MAKES:

4 to 6 servings

2½   to 3 pounds pork country-style ribs

1   cup orange juice

⅓   cup bottled plum sauce

⅓   cup bottled hoisin sauce

4   teaspoons quick-cooking tapioca

2   teaspoons grated fresh ginger

¼   teaspoon five-spice powder or ⅛ teaspoon ground cloves and ⅛ teaspoon anise seeds, crushed

¼   teaspoon black pepper

1 If necessary, cut ribs to fit into a 3½- or 4-quart slow cooker. Place ribs in cooker. For sauce, in a medium bowl stir together orange juice, plum sauce, hoisin sauce, tapioca, ginger, five-spice powder, and pepper. Pour over ribs in cooker.

2 Cover and cook on low-heat setting for 8 to 10 hours or on high-heat setting for 4 to 5 hours.

3 Transfer ribs to a serving platter. Skim fat from sauce. Serve ribs with sauce.

Nutrition Facts per serving: 377 cal., 14 g total fat (5 g sat. fat), 101 mg chol., 446 mg sodium, 29 g carbo., 0 g fiber, 32 g pro. **Daily Values:** 5% vit. A, 54% vit. C, 6% calcium, 14% iron

Use some of the peach preserves mixture to moisten and flavor the meat as it cooks; reserve the rest for a succulent sauce to spoon over the finished ribs.

COUNTRY-STYLE PEACH RIBS

3	pounds pork country-style ribs
1	medium onion, sliced and separated into rings
1	18-ounce jar peach or apricot preserves
½	cup orange juice or water
2	tablespoons bottled teriyaki sauce
¼	to ½ teaspoon crushed red pepper
3	cloves garlic, minced

PREP:
20 minutes

COOK:
8 to 10 hours (low) or 4 to 5 hours (high)

MAKES:
4 to 6 servings

1 If necessary, cut ribs to fit into a 5- to 6-quart slow cooker. Set aside. In cooker place onion. Add ribs. In a medium bowl combine peach preserves, orange juice, teriyaki sauce, crushed red pepper, and garlic. Reserve 1 cup of the peach mixture for sauce; cover and chill until needed. Pour remaining peach mixture over ribs in cooker.

2 Cover and cook on low-heat setting for 8 to 10 hours or on high-heat setting for 4 to 5 hours.

3 For sauce, in a small saucepan bring reserved peach mixture to boiling; reduce heat. Simmer, uncovered, for 5 minutes. Remove ribs and sliced onion from cooker; discard cooking liquid. Serve ribs and onion with sauce.

Nutrition Facts per serving: 680 cal., 15 g total fat (5 g sat. fat), 121 mg chol., 513 mg sodium, 95 g carbo., 2 g fiber, 38 g pro. **Daily Values:** 2% vit. A, 50% vit. C, 8% calcium, 16% iron

Grab extra napkins. These boneless pork ribs cooked in a spicy barbecue sauce guarantee messy faces and fingers.

BARBECUE-SAUCED PORK RIBS

PREP:

15 minutes

COOK:

8 to 10 hours (low) or 4 to 5 hours (high)

MAKES:

6 servings

1½	cups bottled barbecue sauce
1	cup chopped celery
¾	cup chopped green sweet pepper
½	cup chopped onion
½	cup beef broth
2	tablespoons quick-cooking tapioca
1	canned chipotle chile pepper in adobo sauce, finely chopped (optional)
2	teaspoons brown sugar
½	teaspoon salt
¼	teaspoon black pepper
1	clove garlic, minced
2	pounds boneless pork country-style ribs
3	cups hot cooked noodles

1 For sauce, in a 3½- to 5-quart slow cooker combine barbecue sauce, celery, sweet pepper, onion, beef broth, tapioca, chipotle pepper (if desired), brown sugar, salt, black pepper, and garlic. Add ribs, stirring to coat with sauce.

2 Cover and cook on low-heat setting for 8 to 10 hours or on high-heat setting for 4 to 5 hours.

3 Transfer ribs to a serving platter. Skim fat from sauce. Spoon some of the sauce over ribs. Serve with hot cooked noodles. Pass remaining sauce.

Nutrition Facts per serving: 452 cal., 13 g total fat (4 g sat. fat), 122 mg chol., 1,203 mg sodium, 45 g carbo., 2 g fiber, 34 g pro. **Daily Values:** 7% vit. A, 29% vit. C, 6% calcium, 17% iron

The spicy name befits this spicy dish. Three kinds of pepper—hot pepper sauce, cayenne pepper, and black pepper—provide the kick to these Asian-style ribs.

PEPPERY ASIAN RIBS

3½	pounds pork country-style ribs
6	green onions, chopped
¼	cup reduced-sodium soy sauce
¼	cup molasses
2	tablespoons brown sugar
2	tablespoons bottled hoisin sauce
2	tablespoons white wine vinegar
2	teaspoons toasted sesame oil
2	teaspoons lemon juice
½	teaspoon ground ginger
½	teaspoon garlic powder
½	teaspoon chili powder
½	teaspoon bottled hot pepper sauce
¼	teaspoon cayenne pepper
¼	teaspoon black pepper
2	cups hot cooked rice

1 If necessary, cut ribs to fit into a 3½- or 4-quart slow cooker. Place ribs in cooker.

2 For sauce, in a small bowl combine green onions, soy sauce, molasses, brown sugar, hoisin sauce, vinegar, toasted sesame oil, lemon juice, ginger, garlic powder, chili powder, hot pepper sauce, cayenne pepper, and black pepper. Pour over ribs in cooker, turning ribs to coat with sauce.

3 Cover and cook on low-heat setting for 8 to 10 hours or on high-heat setting for 4 to 5 hours.

4 Transfer ribs to a serving platter. Strain sauce; skim off fat. Serve sauce over ribs and hot cooked rice.

Nutrition Facts per serving: 532 cal., 31 g total fat (11 g sat. fat), 69 mg chol., 511 mg sodium, 32 g carbo., 0 g fiber, 30 g pro. **Daily Values:** 3% vit. A, 6% vit. C, 3% calcium, 18% iron

PREP:

15 minutes

COOK:

8 to 10 hours (low) or 4 to 5 hours (high)

MAKES:

6 servings

SWEET 'N' PEPPERY RIB SANDWICHES
Prepare Peppery Asian Ribs as directed, except omit the hot cooked rice. Remove cooked meat from bones. Using two forks, pull meat apart into shreds. To serve, place meat on split and toasted large sesame buns or kaiser rolls. Pass sauce. Makes 8 to 10 sandwiches.

Expect this new way to do ham to become an old favorite in no time.

HAM WITH CARROTS & PARSNIPS

PREP:

10 minutes

COOK:

8 to 9 hours (low)
or 4 to 4½ hours (high)

STAND:

10 minutes

MAKES:

8 servings

1   16-ounce package peeled baby carrots

1   pound parsnips, cut into ½-inch slices

1   2- to 2½-pound cooked boneless ham portion

1   cup apple juice

¼   cup packed brown sugar

¼   cup honey mustard

⅛   teaspoon ground cloves

1 In a 5- to 6-quart slow cooker place carrots and parsnips.

2 If desired, score ham by making diagonal cuts in a diamond pattern. Place ham on top of carrots and parsnips. In a small bowl combine apple juice, brown sugar, mustard, and cloves. Pour over mixture in cooker.

3 Cover and cook on low-heat setting for 8 to 9 hours or on high-heat setting for 4 to 4½ hours.

4 Remove ham from cooker; cover and let stand for 10 minutes. Meanwhile, using a slotted spoon, transfer vegetables to a large bowl. If desired, using a potato masher, mash vegetables, adding enough of the liquid, if necessary, to moisten. Slice ham and serve with vegetables.

Nutrition Facts per serving: 315 cal., 12 g total fat (4 g sat. fat), 65 mg chol., 1,581 mg sodium, 30 g carbo., 4 g fiber, 21 g pro. **Daily Values:** 287% vit. A, 17% vit. C, 5% calcium, 11% iron

Stuffed baked potatoes are a popular pub food in England. Serve these with glasses of English beer the next time you have your "mates" over for an informal get-together.

HAM & BROCCOLI POTATOES

2 cups shredded smoked Gouda cheese (8 ounces)

1 10¾-ounce can condensed cream of celery or cream of chicken soup

1 10-ounce package frozen chopped broccoli, thawed

8 ounces diced cooked ham

6 medium potatoes, baked and split

1 tablespoon snipped fresh chives

PREP:
15 minutes

COOK:
1½ to 2½ hours

MAKES:
6 servings

1 In a 1½-quart slow cooker combine Gouda cheese, celery soup, broccoli, and ham.

2 Cover and cook for 1½ to 2½ hours. Stir before serving. Spoon ham mixture over baked potatoes. Sprinkle with chives.

Nutrition Facts per serving: 352 cal., 16 g total fat (9 g sat. fat), 53 mg chol., 1,487 mg sodium, 34 g carbo., 4 g fiber, 19 g pro. **Daily Values:** 22% vit. A, 78% vit. C, 29% calcium, 17% iron

*Note: Some 1½-quart slow cookers include variable heat settings; others offer only one standard (low) setting. The 1½-quart slow cooker recipes in this book were only tested on the low-heat setting, if one was present.

BAKING POTATOES

To bake potatoes, first scrub them and pat dry. Then prick with a fork. (If desired, for soft skins, rub potatoes with shortening or wrap each potato in foil.) Bake potatoes in a 425°F oven for 40 to 60 minutes or until tender. Roll each potato gently under your hand. Using a knife, cut an X in each top. Press in and up on ends of each potato.

It's amazing how much richness a touch of cream brings to this zesty sauce. In fact it's the creaminess that takes the dish from everyday fare to company-special status.

PASTA WITH TOMATO-CREAM SAUCE

PREP:

20 minutes

COOK:

6 to 8 hours (low)
or 3 to 4 hours (high)

MAKES:

8 servings

1	pound bulk hot Italian sausage
2	cups chopped onions
4	cloves garlic, minced
2	14½-ounce cans diced tomatoes, undrained
1	15-ounce can tomato sauce
3	tablespoons quick-cooking tapioca
2	teaspoons dried Italian seasoning, crushed
¼	teaspoon salt
¼	teaspoon black pepper
½	cup whipping cream
8	cups hot cooked spaghetti (1 pound)
	Finely shredded or grated Parmesan cheese (optional)
	Snipped fresh parsley (optional)

1 In a large skillet cook Italian sausage, onions, and garlic until meat is brown and onions are tender. Drain off fat.

2 Transfer meat mixture to a 3½- or 4-quart slow cooker. Stir in tomatoes, tomato sauce, tapioca, Italian seasoning, salt, and pepper.

3 Cover and cook on low-heat setting for 6 to 8 hours or on high-heat setting for 3 to 4 hours.

4 Just before serving, stir in cream. Serve meat mixture over hot cooked spaghetti. If desired, sprinkle each serving with cheese and parsley.

Nutrition Facts per serving: 517 cal., 24 g total fat (10 g sat. fat), 64 mg chol., 908 mg sodium, 56 g carbo., 4 g fiber, 17 g pro. **Daily Values:** 4% vit. A, 28% vit. C, 9% calcium, 21% iron

Artichoke hearts fit right in to a terrifically traditional Italian pasta sauce.

PASTA ALLA ITALIANO

1	pound bulk Italian sausage
1	large onion, chopped
6	cloves garlic, minced
1	28-ounce can crushed tomatoes, undrained
2	4½-ounce jars sliced mushrooms, drained
1	8- or 9-ounce package frozen artichoke hearts, thawed and cut up
1	cup tomato juice
½	cup dry red wine or water
1	tablespoon quick-cooking tapioca
½	teaspoon salt
½	teaspoon dried rosemary, crushed
¼	teaspoon black pepper
	Several dashes bottled hot pepper sauce
12	ounces dried rigatoni or spaghetti, cooked and drained
	Grated Parmesan cheese (optional)

PREP:
20 minutes
COOK:
8 to 10 hours (low) or 4 to 5 hours (high)
MAKES:
6 servings

1 In a large skillet cook Italian sausage, onion, and garlic until meat is brown and onion is tender. Drain off fat.

2 Transfer meat mixture to a 3½- or 4-quart slow cooker. Stir in tomatoes, mushrooms, artichoke hearts, tomato juice, wine, tapioca, salt, rosemary, black pepper, and hot pepper sauce.

3 Cover and cook on low-heat setting for 8 to 10 hours or on high-heat setting for 4 to 5 hours. Serve meat mixture over hot cooked rigatoni. If desired, sprinkle each serving with Parmesan cheese.

Nutrition Facts per serving: 542 cal., 18 g total fat (7 g sat. fat), 51 mg chol., 1,101 mg sodium, 64 g carbo., 7 g fiber, 23 g pro. **Daily Values:** 24% vit. A, 42% vit. C, 10% calcium, 30% iron

American cooks have taken Italian pizza in a dozen delicious directions, but here's one they haven't tried yet: as a saucy mixture spooned over toasted slices of French bread.

PIZZA IN A POT

PREP:

15 minutes

COOK:

6 to 8 hours (low)
or 3 to 4 hours (high)

MAKES:

10 servings

1½ pounds bulk Italian sausage or lean ground beef

1 medium onion, cut into thin wedges

1 15-ounce can pizza sauce with cheese

1 14½-ounce can Italian-style stewed tomatoes, undrained

1 4½-ounce jar sliced mushrooms or one 2¼-ounce can sliced pitted ripe olives, drained

1 16-ounce loaf Italian bread

1 8-ounce package shredded pizza cheese

1 In a large skillet cook Italian sausage and onion until meat is brown and onion is tender. Drain off fat.

2 Transfer meat mixture to a 3½- or 4-quart slow cooker. Stir in pizza sauce, tomatoes, and mushrooms.

3 Cover and cook on low-heat setting for 6 to 8 hours or on high-heat setting for 3 to 4 hours.

4 Preheat broiler. Bias-slice bread into 1-inch slices. Arrange bread on a large baking sheet. Broil 3 to 4 inches from the heat for 1 to 2 minutes or until golden. Spoon meat mixture on top of bread slices. Sprinkle with pizza cheese.

Nutrition Facts per serving: 465 cal., 27 g total fat (10 g sat. fat), 69 mg chol., 1,379 mg sodium, 32 g carbo., 3 g fiber, 19 g pro. **Daily Values:** 8% vit. A, 12% vit. C, 24% calcium, 16% iron

All you need are some crusty bread and a selection of your favorite mustards, and you have a robust German meal at your fingertips.

POTATOES, KRAUT & SAUSAGE SUPPER

1	20-ounce package refrigerated diced potatoes with onions
1	cup chopped green sweet pepper
1	cup chopped carrots
1½	pounds cooked smoked Polish sausage, halved lengthwise and bias-sliced
⅔	cup apple cider or apple juice
1	tablespoon cider vinegar
½	teaspoon caraway seeds
¼	teaspoon salt
¼	teaspoon black pepper
1	14- to 16-ounce can sauerkraut, drained
2	tablespoons snipped fresh parsley

PREP:

15 minutes

COOK:

5 to 6 hours (low) or 2½ to 3 hours (high), plus 30 minutes (high)

MAKES:

8 servings

1 In a 4½- to 5½-quart slow cooker combine potatoes, sweet pepper, and carrots. Add sausage.

2 In a small bowl stir together apple cider, vinegar, caraway seeds, salt, and black pepper. Pour over mixture in cooker.

3 Cover and cook on low-heat setting for 5 to 6 hours or on high-heat setting for 2½ to 3 hours. If using low-heat setting, turn to high-heat setting. Stir in sauerkraut. Cover and cook for 30 minutes more.

4 To serve, transfer sausage mixture to a serving dish. Sprinkle with fresh parsley.

Nutrition Facts per serving: 374 cal., 25 g total fat (9 g sat. fat), 60 mg chol., 1,291 mg sodium, 24 g carbo., 4 g fiber, 14 g pro. **Daily Values:** 80% vit. A, 54% vit. C, 4% calcium, 14% iron

Introduce your kids to the simple joys of beenie-weenies with this nearly homemade version of the classic.

BEANS & FRANKS

PREP:

10 minutes

COOK:

*6 to 8 hours (low)
or 3 to 4 hours (high)*

MAKES:

6 servings

3 16-ounce cans pork and beans in tomato sauce
1 16-ounce package frankfurters, cut into 1-inch pieces
½ cup catsup
¼ cup chopped onion
¼ cup molasses
1 tablespoon prepared mustard
4 slices bacon, crisp-cooked, drained, and crumbled
¼ cup sliced green onions (optional)

1 In a 3½- or 4-quart slow cooker combine pork and beans, frankfurters, catsup, onion, molasses, and mustard.

2 Cover and cook on low-heat setting for 6 to 8 hours or on high-heat setting for 3 to 4 hours. Sprinkle with crumbled bacon and, if desired, green onions.

Nutrition Facts per serving: 549 cal., 26 g total fat (10 g sat. fat), 57 mg chol., 2,182 mg sodium, 61 g carbo., 11 g fiber, 22 g pro. **Daily Values:** 10% vit. A, 17% vit. C, 17% calcium, 51% iron

The golden gravy spooned over this tender lamb and roasted vegetables imparts a mustard-lemon heaven.

LEMON-MUSTARD LAMB ROAST

½	teaspoon lemon-pepper seasoning
½	teaspoon dry mustard
1	2- to 2½-pound boneless lamb shoulder roast
1	tablespoon cooking oil
4	medium potatoes (about 1½ pounds), quartered
1½	cups tiny whole carrots
1	cup chicken broth
¼	cup Dijon-style mustard
2	tablespoons quick-cooking tapioca
1	tablespoon lemon juice
½	teaspoon dried rosemary, crushed
¼	teaspoon finely shredded lemon peel
¼	teaspoon black pepper
2	cloves garlic, minced
1	8- or 9-ounce package frozen artichoke hearts, thawed

PREP:

25 minutes

COOK:

*8 to 10 hours (low)
or 4 to 5 hours (high),
plus 30 minutes (high)*

MAKES:

4 servings

1 In a small bowl combine lemon-pepper seasoning and dry mustard. Trim fat from meat. Sprinkle mustard mixture evenly over meat; rub in with your fingers. If necessary, cut meat to fit into a 3½- or 4-quart slow cooker. In a large skillet brown meat on all sides in hot oil. Drain off fat. Set aside.

2 In cooker place potatoes and carrots. Add meat. For gravy, in a small bowl combine chicken broth, Dijon mustard, tapioca, lemon juice, rosemary, lemon peel, pepper, and garlic. Pour over mixture in cooker.

3 Cover and cook on low-heat setting for 8 to 10 hours or on high-heat setting for 4 to 5 hours. If using low-heat setting, turn to high-heat setting. Stir in artichoke hearts. Cover and cook for 30 minutes more.

4 Remove meat and vegetables from cooker. If present, remove string or netting from meat. Skim fat from gravy. Serve meat and vegetables with gravy.

Nutrition Facts per serving: 539 cal., 19 g total fat (5 g sat. fat), 148 mg chol., 694 mg sodium, 40 g carbo., 8 g fiber, 51 g pro. **Daily Values:** 232% vit. A, 45% vit. C, 12% calcium, 32% iron

Enjoy tender lamb, tiny new potatoes, and colorful carrots draped in a creamy dill sauce.

BRAISED LAMB WITH DILL SAUCE

PREP:

20 minutes

COOK:

*8 to 10 hours (low)
or 4 to 5 hours (high)*

MAKES:

6 servings

1½   pounds tiny new potatoes

5   medium carrots, cut into 1-inch pieces

2   pounds lean boneless lamb

1¼   cups water

1   tablespoon snipped fresh dill or 1 teaspoon dried dill

½   teaspoon salt

¼   teaspoon black pepper

½   cup plain yogurt

2   tablespoons all-purpose flour

1 Remove a narrow strip of peel from center of each new potato. In a 3½- or 4-quart slow cooker place potatoes and carrots. Trim fat from meat. Cut meat into 1-inch pieces. Add meat and water to cooker. Sprinkle with 2 teaspoons of the fresh dill or ½ teaspoon of the dried dill, the salt, and pepper.

2 Cover and cook on low-heat setting for 8 to 10 hours or on high-heat setting for 4 to 5 hours. Remove meat and vegetables from cooker, reserving juices. Cover meat and vegetables and keep warm.

3 For sauce, pour juices into a glass measuring cup; skim off fat. Measure 1 cup juices. In a small saucepan stir together yogurt and flour. Stir in juices and remaining 1 teaspoon fresh or ½ teaspoon dried dill. Cook and stir over medium heat until thickened and bubbly. Cook and stir for 1 minute more. Season to taste with additional salt and black pepper. Serve meat and vegetables with sauce.

Nutrition Facts per serving: 303 cal., 5 g total fat (2 g sat. fat), 96 mg chol., 327 mg sodium, 27 g carbo., 3 g fiber, 35 g pro. **Daily Values:** 256% vit. A, 34% vit. C, 8% calcium, 26% iron

Chutney, a condiment often used in Indian cooking, is made of chopped fresh fruit (mango is a classic), vegetables, and spices, and often enlivened with hot peppers, fresh ginger, or vinegar. Look for it in the gourmet section or the condiment aisle.

CHUTNEY-SAUCED LAMB

1½	pounds lean lamb stew meat
1	tablespoon cooking oil
1	20-ounce can pineapple chunks, drained
2	cups frozen small whole onions
1	9-ounce jar fruit chutney
½	cup mixed dried fruit bits
1	tablespoon quick-cooking tapioca
1	tablespoon balsamic vinegar
1	teaspoon finely shredded lemon peel
3	cups hot cooked couscous or rice

PREP:

20 minutes

COOK:

*6 to 8 hours (low)
or 3 to 4 hours (high)*

MAKES:

6 servings

1 Cut meat into 1-inch pieces. In a large skillet brown meat, half at a time, in hot oil. Drain off fat.

2 Transfer meat to a 3½- or 4-quart slow cooker. Stir in pineapple chunks, onions, chutney, dried fruit, tapioca, vinegar, and lemon peel.

3 Cover and cook on low-heat setting for 6 to 8 hours or on high-heat setting for 3 to 4 hours. Serve meat mixture with hot cooked couscous.

Nutrition Facts per serving: 413 cal., 6 g total fat (2 g sat. fat), 72 mg chol., 118 mg sodium, 63 g carbo., 4 g fiber, 27 g pro. **Daily Values:** 18% vit. A, 35% vit. C, 9% calcium, 16% iron

As this dish cooks, the kitchen fills with the exotic aromas of a North African spice market. For even more flavor, add ¼ to ½ teaspoon ground turmeric to the slow cooker along with the couscous.

MOROCCAN-STYLE LAMB

PREP:

20 minutes

COOK:

*9 to 10 hours (low)
or 4¹/₂ to 5¹/₂ hours (high),
plus 5 minutes (high)*

MAKES:

6 servings

2	pounds lean boneless lamb
3	medium tomatoes, chopped
2	large onions, cut into wedges
2	cups chicken broth
2	medium carrots, cut into 1-inch pieces
1½	teaspoons ground cumin
½	teaspoon ground turmeric
¼	teaspoon crushed red pepper (optional)
1	10-ounce package quick-cooking couscous
¼	cup dried currants or raisins

1 Trim fat from meat. Cut meat into ¾-inch pieces. In a 3½- or 4-quart slow cooker combine meat, tomatoes, onions, chicken broth, carrots, cumin, turmeric, and, if desired, crushed red pepper.

2 Cover and cook on low-heat setting for 9 to 10 hours or on high-heat setting for 4½ to 5½ hours.

3 Using a slotted spoon, transfer meat and vegetables to a serving dish, reserving juices. Cover meat and vegetables and keep warm. Skim fat from juices. If using low-heat setting, turn to high-heat setting. Stir couscous and currants into juices. Cover and cook for 5 minutes more.

4 Fluff couscous with a fork. Serve meat and vegetables over couscous.

Nutrition Facts per serving: 440 cal., 7 g total fat (2 g sat. fat), 98 mg chol., 452 mg sodium, 52 g carbo., 5 g fiber, 39 g pro. **Daily Values:** 111% vit. A, 27% vit. C, 5% calcium, 22% iron

STORING LEFTOVERS

For safety reasons, do not leave food in slow cookers to cool after cooking. Also don't use slow cookers as storage containers or place them in the refrigerator. To properly store cooked food, remove food from the cooker. (If the food is very hot, transfer it to a large shallow container to cool.) After it has sufficiently cooled (hold for no longer than 2 hours at room temperature), transfer the food to refrigerator (or freezer) storage containers. Cover tightly; label and date the containers.

Lamb shanks are an underused and wonderfully flavorful cut of lamb, ideal for the slow cooke, The lamb literally falls off the bone when cooked through. Infused with orange and spices, it is the perfect supper to warm up chilly March days.

SPICY LAMB SHANKS

2	large oranges
5	medium carrots, cut into 2-inch pieces
1½	cups frozen small whole onions
4	large cloves garlic, thinly sliced
4	meaty lamb shanks (about 4 pounds), cut into 3- to 4-inch pieces
6	inches stick cinnamon, broken into 1-inch pieces
1¼	cups beef broth
1½	teaspoons ground cardamom
1	teaspoon ground cumin
½	teaspoon salt
½	teaspoon ground turmeric
½	teaspoon black pepper
2	tablespoons cold water
4	teaspoons cornstarch
⅓	cup pitted kalamata or other black olives, halved (if desired)
1	tablespoon snipped fresh cilantro

PREP:
25 minutes
COOK:
8 to 9 hours (low)
MAKES:
4 to 6 servings

1 Using a vegetable peeler, remove orange part of peel from 1 of the oranges. Cut peel into thin strips (should have about ¼ cup). Squeeze juice from both oranges to make about ⅔ cup. Set aside.

2 In a 5- to 6-quart slow cooker place carrots, onions, and garlic. Add orange peel strips, meat, and stick cinnamon. In a small bowl stir together orange juice, beef broth, cardamom, cumin, salt, turmeric, and pepper. Pour over mixture in cooker. Cover and cook on low-heat setting for 8 to 9 hours.

3 Using a slotted spoon, transfer meat and vegetables to a serving dish, reserving juices. Cover meat and vegetables and keep warm. Remove stick cinnamon. For sauce, pour juices into a glass measuring cup; skim off fat. Measure 1½ cups juices. Pour juices into a small saucepan. Combine cold water and cornstarch; stir into juices in saucepan. Cook and stir over medium heat until thickened and bubbly. Cook and stir for 2 minutes more.

4 Serve meat and vegetables with sauce. Sprinkle with kalamata olives and cilantro.

Nutrition Facts per serving: 461 cal., 21 g total fat (8 g sat. fat), 150 mg chol., 760 mg sodium, 22 g carbo., 6 g fiber, 44 g pro. Daily Values: 538% vit. A, 38% vit. C, 9% calcium, 24% iron

Make sure the lamb shanks you buy for this Greek-inspired dinner will fit into your slow cooker. If they're too large, have the butcher saw them in half crosswise.

MEDITERRANEAN LAMB SHANKS

PREP:

25 minutes

COOK:

7 to 9 hours (low) or 3 1/2 to 4 1/2 hours (high)

MAKES:

4 servings

1	tablespoon dried oregano, crushed
1/4	teaspoon salt
4	cloves garlic, minced
4	meaty lamb shanks (about 4 pounds), cut into 3- to 4-inch pieces
1	15-ounce can garbanzo beans (chickpeas), rinsed and drained
1	14 1/2-ounce can diced tomatoes, undrained
1/2	cup chopped onion
2	tablespoons lemon juice
1/2	teaspoon ground allspice
1/2	teaspoon black pepper
7	cups coarsely chopped fresh spinach
1/2	cup plain yogurt
1/4	cup chopped cucumber
1	tablespoon snipped fresh mint

1 In a small bowl combine oregano, salt, and garlic. Sprinkle oregano mixture evenly over meat; rub in with your fingers. Set aside.

2 In a 4 1/2- to 6-quart slow cooker combine garbanzo beans, tomatoes, onion, lemon juice, allspice, and pepper. Add meat.

3 Cover and cook on low-heat setting for 7 to 9 hours or on high-heat setting for 3 1/2 to 4 1/2 hours.

4 Remove meat from cooker; cover and keep warm. Stir spinach into mixture in cooker. In a small bowl combine yogurt, cucumber, and mint.

5 To serve, divide spinach mixture among shallow bowls; add meat. Top each serving with yogurt mixture.

Nutrition Facts per serving: 455 cal., 20 g total fat (8 g sat. fat), 117 mg chol., 850 mg sodium, 28 g carbo., 9 g fiber, 40 g pro. **Daily Values:** 94% vit. A, 51% vit. C, 21% calcium, 38% iron

Lamb lovers will try to get home early when you make these flavorful—and colorful—lamb sandwiches.

SWEET & SPICY LAMB WRAPS

1	2½- to 3-pound boneless lamb shoulder roast
1	large onion, cut into wedges
½	cup chutney
½	cup chicken broth
1	tablespoon cider vinegar
1	teaspoon crushed red pepper
¼	cup mayonnaise or salad dressing
¼	cup plain yogurt
2	tablespoons chutney, large pieces snipped
½	teaspoon curry powder
8	pita bread rounds
3	cups shredded lettuce
1	medium tomato, seeded and chopped

PREP:

25 minutes

COOK:

*10 to 12 hours (low)
or 5 to 6 hours (high)*

MAKES:

8 sandwiches

1 Trim fat from meat. If necessary, cut meat to fit into a 3½- or 4-quart slow cooker. Set aside. In cooker place onion. Add meat.

2 In a small bowl stir together the ½ cup chutney, the chicken broth, vinegar, and crushed red pepper. Pour over mixture in cooker.

3 Cover and cook on low-heat setting for 10 to 12 hours or on high-heat setting for 5 to 6 hours. Remove meat and onion from cooker, reserving cooking liquid.

4 Using two forks, pull meat apart into shreds. If desired, stir enough of the liquid into meat to moisten. For sauce, in a small bowl stir together mayonnaise, yogurt, the 2 tablespoons chutney, and the curry powder.

5 To serve, place meat mixture along centers of pita rounds. Top with lettuce and tomato; drizzle with sauce. Fold both sides of each pita up around filling.

Nutrition Facts per serving: 619 cal., 30 g total fat (11 g sat. fat), 100 mg chol., 541 mg sodium, 54 g carbo., 3 g fiber, 31 g pro. **Daily Values:** 31% vit. A, 32% vit. C, 11% calcium, 24% iron

What to do with that venison the hunter in your family brought home?
Cook it up in this meaty and satisfying braise.

BRAISED VENISON WITH GRAVY

PREP:

25 minutes

COOK:

*10 to 12 hours (low)
or 5 to 6 hours (high)*

MAKES:

6 to 8 servings

1   2- to 3-pound boneless venison shoulder or rump roast

1   tablespoon cooking oil

1   medium onion, finely chopped

1   medium carrot, finely chopped

1   6-ounce can (¾ cup) tomato juice

1   teaspoon instant beef bouillon granules

½   cup dairy sour cream

3   tablespoons all-purpose flour

     Hot cooked noodles or hot mashed potatoes (optional)

1 Trim fat from meat. If necessary, cut meat to fit into a 3½- or 4-quart slow cooker. In a large skillet brown meat on all sides in hot oil. Drain off fat. Set aside.

2 In cooker place onion and carrot. Add meat. In a small bowl combine tomato juice and bouillon granules. Pour over mixture in cooker.

3 Cover and cook on low-heat setting for 10 to 12 hours or on high-heat setting for 5 to 6 hours. Transfer meat to a serving platter, reserving cooking liquid. Cover meat and keep warm.

4 For gravy, pour liquid into a glass measuring cup; skim off fat. Measure 2 cups liquid, adding water, if necessary. Pour liquid into a small saucepan. In a small bowl stir together sour cream and flour; stir into liquid in saucepan. Cook and stir over medium heat until thickened and bubbly. Cook and stir for 1 minute more. If desired, season to taste with salt and black pepper.

5 Serve gravy over meat and, if desired, hot cooked noodles.

Nutrition Facts per serving: 211 cal., 8 g total fat (3 g sat. fat), 98 mg chol., 463 mg sodium, 7 g carbo., 1 g fiber, 26 g pro. **Daily Values:** 57% vit. A, 11% vit. C, 3% calcium, 23% iron

POULTRY ENTRÉES

5

If you have extra chipotle chile peppers, pack them covered with the sauce from the can in a freezer container. Seal, label, and freeze for up to 2 months, and thaw in the refrigerator when needed.

SWEET & SMOKY CHICKEN

PREP:

15 minutes

COOK: .

*6 to 7 hours (low)
or 3 to 3¹/₂ hours (high)*

MAKES:

4 to 6 servings

2¹/₂ to 3 pounds meaty chicken pieces (breast halves, thighs, and drumsticks), skinned

¹/₄ teaspoon salt

¹/₈ teaspoon black pepper

1 cup chicken broth

¹/₂ cup seedless raspberry jam

¹/₂ cup snipped dried apricots

1 to 2 canned chipotle chile peppers in adobo sauce, chopped, plus 1 tablespoon adobo sauce

1 tablespoon quick-cooking tapioca, finely ground

1 In a 3¹/₂- or 4-quart slow cooker place chicken pieces. Sprinkle with salt and black pepper. For sauce, in a small bowl stir together chicken broth, raspberry jam, dried apricots, chipotle peppers and adobo sauce, and tapioca. Pour over chicken in cooker.

2 Cover and cook on low-heat setting for 6 to 7 hours or on high-heat setting for 3 to 3¹/₂ hours. Transfer chicken to a serving platter. Serve sauce over chicken.

Nutrition Facts per serving: 412 cal., 10 g total fat (3 g sat. fat), 115 mg chol., 549 mg sodium, 41 g carbo., 2 g fiber, 38 g pro. **Daily Values:** 25% vit. A, 7% vit. C, 3% calcium, 14% iron

A luscious recipe if there ever was one: The already-creamy Alfredo sauce garners extra richness from cubes of cream cheese.

BASIL-CREAM CHICKEN THIGHS

2½	pounds chicken thighs, skinned
¼	teaspoon black pepper
1	3-ounce package cream cheese, cubed
1	10-ounce container refrigerated Alfredo sauce
¼	cup water
1	teaspoon dried basil, crushed
1	16-ounce package loose-pack frozen broccoli, cauliflower, and carrots
3	cups hot cooked fettuccine

1 In a 3½- or 4-quart slow cooker place chicken thighs. Sprinkle with pepper. Add cream cheese. In a small bowl stir together Alfredo sauce, water, and basil. Pour over mixture in cooker. Top with frozen vegetables.

2 Cover and cook on low-heat setting for 6 to 7 hours or on high-heat setting for 3 to 3½ hours. Transfer chicken to a serving platter. Stir vegetable mixture. Serve over chicken and hot cooked fettuccine.

Nutrition Facts per serving: 456 cal., 24 g total fat (12 g sat. fat), 136 mg chol., 415 mg sodium, 27 g carbo., 4 g fiber, 30 g pro. **Daily Values:** 37% vit. A, 36% vit. C, 12% calcium, 14% iron

PREP:

15 minutes

COOK:

*6 to 7 hours (low)
or 3 to 3½ hours (high)*

MAKES:

6 servings

Lemon, pineapple, and orange provide both sweetness and tang, while the spices add a dash of intrigue. If you like, substitute aromatic basmati rice for the couscous.

SPICY CITRUS CHICKEN

PREP:

20 minutes

COOK:

*8 to 9 hours (low)
or 4 to 4 1/2 hours (high)*

MAKES:

4 servings

1	6-ounce can frozen pineapple-orange juice concentrate, thawed
1/2	cup catsup
2	tablespoons lemon juice
1/4	teaspoon cayenne pepper
2	tablespoons quick-cooking tapioca
2	inches stick cinnamon
8	whole allspice
4	whole cloves
2 1/2	to 3 pounds meaty chicken pieces (breast halves, thighs, and drumsticks), skinned
	Hot cooked couscous

1 For sauce, in a small bowl combine juice concentrate, catsup, lemon juice, and cayenne pepper. In a 3 1/2- or 4-quart slow cooker place about half of the sauce. Stir in tapioca.

2 For spice bag, cut a double thickness of 100-percent-cotton cheesecloth into a 4-inch square. Place stick cinnamon, allspice, and cloves in center of cloth. Bring corners together and tie with a clean string. Place bag in cooker. Add chicken pieces. Pour remaining sauce over mixture in cooker.

3 Cover and cook on low-heat setting for 8 to 9 hours or on high-heat setting for 4 to 4 1/2 hours. Transfer chicken to a serving platter. Remove spice bag. Strain sauce; skim off fat. Serve sauce over chicken and hot cooked couscous.

Nutrition Facts per serving: 471 cal., 9 g total fat (3 g sat. fat), 115 mg chol., 479 mg sodium, 54 g carbo., 2 g fiber, 41 g pro. **Daily Values:** 7% vit. A, 164% vit. C, 4% calcium, 11% iron

Remember this recipe for one of those hectic days when there's too much to do. All you need are three ingredients and your cooker, and you can be on your way.

ITALIAN CHICKEN & VEGETABLES

4   small chicken legs (thigh-drumstick piece)
    (2½ to 3 pounds total), skinned

1   26-ounce jar roasted garlic pasta sauce

1   16-ounce package frozen pepper stir-fry vegetables

3   cups hot cooked noodles

⅓   cup shredded mozzarella cheese or finely
    shredded Parmesan cheese

PREP:

15 minutes

COOK:

*6 to 7 hours (low)
or 3 to 3½ hours (high)*

MAKES:

4 servings

1 In a 3½- or 4-quart slow cooker place chicken legs. Add pasta sauce and frozen vegetables.

2 Cover and cook on low-heat setting for 6 to 7 hours or on high-heat setting for 3 to 3½ hours.

3 Serve chicken and vegetable mixture with hot cooked noodles. Sprinkle with mozzarella cheese.

Nutrition Facts per serving: 500 cal., 12 g total fat (3 g sat. fat), 174 mg chol., 796 mg sodium, 52 g carbo., 6 g fiber, 45 g pro. **Daily Values:** 29% vit. A, 89% vit. C, 22% calcium, 28% iron

Thanks to this easy recipe, there's no need to wait for the holidays to serve the ever-favorite poultry-and-stuffing combo! For the stuffing, be sure to use a hard-crusted, dense sourdough loaf. It takes a brawny bread to render the best texture.

CHICKEN WITH SOURDOUGH STUFFING

PREP:

20 minutes

COOK:

*6 to 6¹/₂ hours (low)
or 3 to 3¹/₂ hours (high)*

MAKES:

6 servings

6	cups crusty, rustic-style, open-textured sourdough bread cut into 1-inch cubes
1¹/₃	cups chopped tomatoes
1	cup finely chopped carrots
¹/₂	cup chicken broth
1¹/₂	teaspoons dried thyme, crushed
¹/₄	teaspoon coarsely ground black pepper
6	small chicken legs (thigh-drumstick piece) (3³/₄ to 4¹/₂ pounds total)
¹/₃	cup thinly sliced leek or chopped onion

1 For stuffing, in a large bowl combine bread cubes, tomatoes, and carrots. In a small bowl combine chicken broth, thyme, and pepper. Drizzle broth mixture over bread mixture, tossing gently. (Stuffing will not be completely moistened.)

2 In a 4- to 5-quart slow cooker place chicken legs and leek. Lightly pack stuffing on top of chicken. Cover and cook on low-heat setting for 6 to 6¹/₂ hours or on high-heat setting for 3 to 3¹/₂ hours.

3 Using a slotted spoon, transfer stuffing, chicken, and leek to a serving platter; discard juices.

Nutrition Facts per serving: 412 cal., 17 g total fat (5 g sat. fat), 105 mg chol., 409 mg sodium, 28 g carbo., 1 g fiber, 35 g pro. **Daily Values:** 85% vit. A, 17% vit. C, 3% calcium, 19% iron

Here the southern Italian spirit shines through by way of capers and olives. If you prefer, substitute your favorite pasta for the almond-shape orzo.

PUTTANESCA CHICKEN

2½   to 3 pounds meaty chicken pieces (breast halves, thighs, and drumsticks), skinned

¼   teaspoon salt

⅛   teaspoon black pepper

1   26-ounce jar pasta sauce with olives

2   tablespoons drained capers

1   teaspoon finely shredded lemon peel

3   cups hot cooked orzo pasta (rosamarina)

1 In a 3½- or 4-quart slow cooker place chicken pieces. Sprinkle with salt and pepper. For sauce, in a medium bowl stir together pasta sauce, capers, and lemon peel. Pour over chicken in cooker.

2 Cover and cook on low-heat setting for 6 to 7 hours or on high-heat setting for 3 to 3½ hours. Serve chicken and sauce over hot cooked orzo.

Nutrition Facts per serving: 315 cal., 8 g total fat (2 g sat. fat), 77 mg chol., 678 mg sodium, 30 g carbo., 3 g fiber, 30 g pro. **Daily Values:** 10% vit. A, 11% vit. C, 8% calcium, 16% iron

PREP:

20 minutes

COOK:

*6 to 7 hours (low)
or 3 to 3½ hours (high)*

MAKES:

6 servings

To ensure proper doneness, place ingredients in the slow cooker in the order given in the recipe. Generally vegetables are added first, and the meat is last.

CHICKEN & MUSHROOMS IN WINE SAUCE

PREP:

25 minutes

COOK:

*7 to 8 hours (low)
or 3^1/$_2$ to 4 hours (high)*

MAKES:

4 to 6 servings

**FIX IT AHEAD
AND FREEZE**

With a large-capacity slow cooker, you can cook once and have enough leftovers for two or three more dinners. Immediately after the meal, transfer the leftover food to freezer-safe containers. Label and freeze for up to 6 months. When ready to serve, thaw the food in the refrigerator. Transfer to a saucepan; cook and stir over low heat until heated through. Or place the food in a microwave-safe dish and heat, stirring several times.

3	cups sliced fresh mushrooms
1	large onion, chopped
2	cloves garlic, minced
2^1/$_2$	to 3 pounds meaty chicken pieces (breast halves, thighs, and drumsticks), skinned
^{3}/$_4$	cup chicken broth
1	6-ounce can tomato paste
^{1}/$_4$	cup dry red wine or chicken broth
2	tablespoons quick-cooking tapioca
2	tablespoons snipped fresh basil or 1^1/$_2$ teaspoons dried basil, crushed
2	teaspoons sugar
^{1}/$_4$	teaspoon salt
^{1}/$_4$	teaspoon black pepper
2	cups hot cooked noodles
2	tablespoons finely shredded Parmesan cheese

1️⃣ In a 3^1/$_2$- to 5-quart slow cooker place mushrooms, onion, and garlic. Add chicken pieces. In a medium bowl combine chicken broth, tomato paste, wine, tapioca, dried basil (if using), sugar, salt, and pepper. Pour over mixture in cooker.

2️⃣ Cover and cook on low-heat setting for 7 to 8 hours or on high-heat setting for 3^1/$_2$ to 4 hours. If using, stir in fresh basil.

3️⃣ Serve chicken and mushroom mixture over hot cooked noodles. Sprinkle with Parmesan cheese.

Nutrition Facts per serving: 469 cal., 12 g total fat (3 g sat. fat), 144 mg chol., 468 mg sodium, 41 g carbo., 5 g fiber, 46 g pro. **Daily Values:** 13% vit. A, 37% vit. C, 7% calcium, 35% iron

Why stop for takeout when you can head directly home where this Asian favorite is ready and waiting in your slow cooker?

MOO SHU-STYLE CHICKEN

2½	to 3 pounds meaty chicken pieces (breast halves, thighs, and drumsticks), skinned
¼	teaspoon salt
⅛	teaspoon black pepper
½	cup water
¼	cup soy sauce
2	teaspoons toasted sesame oil
¾	teaspoon ground ginger
8	7- to 8-inch flour tortillas
½	cup bottled hoisin sauce
2	cups packaged shredded broccoli (broccoli slaw mix) or packaged shredded cabbage with carrot (coleslaw mix)

PREP:

20 minutes

COOK:

6 to 7 hours (low) or 3 to 3½ hours (high)

MAKES:

4 servings

1 In a 3½- or 4-quart slow cooker place chicken pieces. Sprinkle with salt and pepper. In a small bowl stir together water, soy sauce, sesame oil, and ginger. Pour over chicken in cooker.

2 Cover and cook on low-heat setting for 6 to 7 hours or on high-heat setting for 3 to 3½ hours.

3 Remove chicken from cooker, reserving cooking liquid. When cool enough to handle, remove chicken from bones. Using two forks, pull chicken apart into shreds. Return chicken to cooker; heat through.

4 To serve, spread each tortilla with 1 tablespoon of the hoisin sauce. Using a slotted spoon, spoon shredded chicken just below centers of tortillas. Top with shredded broccoli. Fold bottom edge of each tortilla up and over filling. Fold in opposite sides; roll up from bottom.

Nutrition Facts per serving: 520 cal., 18 g total fat (4 g sat. fat), 115 mg chol., 1,315 mg sodium, 44 g carbo., 3 g fiber, 44 g pro. **Daily Values:** 17% vit. A, 69% vit. C, 12% calcium, 23% iron

Put away your juicer. The citrusy tang in this recipe comes from lemonade concentrate. As for the other ingredients you need, you are likely to have them on your shelf already.

SAUCY SWEET & SOUR CHICKEN

PREP:

15 minutes

COOK:

6 to 7 hours (low) or 3 to 3½ hours (high)

MAKES:

4 to 6 servings

2½ to 3 pounds meaty chicken pieces (breast halves, thighs, and drumsticks), skinned

¼ teaspoon salt

½ of a 12-ounce can (about ¾ cup) frozen lemonade concentrate, thawed

3 tablespoons brown sugar

3 tablespoons catsup

1 tablespoon vinegar

2 tablespoons cornstarch

2 tablespoons cold water

2 to 3 cups hot cooked rice

1 In a 3½- or 4-quart slow cooker place chicken pieces. Sprinkle with salt. In a medium bowl combine lemonade concentrate, brown sugar, catsup, and vinegar. Pour over chicken in cooker.

2 Cover and cook on low-heat setting for 6 to 7 hours or on high-heat setting for 3 to 3½ hours. Transfer chicken to a serving platter; cover and keep warm.

3 For sauce, pour cooking liquid into a medium saucepan. Skim off fat. Combine cornstarch and cold water; stir into liquid in saucepan. Cook and stir over medium heat until thickened and bubbly. Cook and stir for 2 minutes more. Spoon sauce over chicken. Serve with hot cooked rice.

Nutrition Facts per serving: 489 cal., 9 g total fat (3 g sat. fat), 115 mg chol., 390 mg sodium, 60 g carbo., 1 g fiber, 39 g pro. **Daily Values:** 3% vit. A, 15% vit. C, 4% calcium, 17% iron

Some say there are as many versions of mole (MO-lay), a sauce traditionally made with chiles and chocolate, as there are great home cooks in Mexico. Declare this slow-simmering version your own house specialty. Hint: For a more traditional garnish, sprinkle with toasted pepitas (pumpkin seeds) instead of almonds.

MOLE WITH CHICKEN & RICE

1	14½-ounce can diced tomatoes, undrained
½	cup chopped onion
¼	cup slivered almonds, toasted
2	canned jalapeño chile peppers, drained
3	tablespoons unsweetened cocoa powder
3	tablespoons raisins
1	tablespoon sesame seeds
1	teaspoon sugar
¼	teaspoon salt
¼	teaspoon ground cinnamon
⅛	teaspoon ground nutmeg
⅛	teaspoon ground coriander
3	cloves garlic, quartered
2	tablespoons quick-cooking tapioca
1	2½- to 3-pound broiler-fryer chicken, cut up and skinned
2	tablespoons slivered almonds, toasted
	Hot cooked rice

PREP:

25 minutes

COOK:

9 to 11 hours (low) or 4½ to 5½ hours (high)

MAKES:

4 to 6 servings

1 For sauce, in a blender container or food processor bowl combine tomatoes, onion, the ¼ cup almonds, the jalapeño peppers, cocoa powder, raisins, sesame seeds, sugar, salt, cinnamon, nutmeg, coriander, and garlic. Cover and blend or process until mixture resembles a coarse puree.

2 In a 3½- or 4-quart slow cooker place tapioca. Add chicken pieces and sauce. Cover and cook on low-heat setting for 9 to 11 hours or on high-heat setting for 4½ to 5½ hours.

3 Transfer chicken to a serving platter. Stir sauce; pour over chicken. Sprinkle with the 2 tablespoons almonds. Serve with hot cooked rice.

Nutrition Facts per serving: 448 cal., 23 g total fat (5 g sat. fat), 99 mg chol., 586 mg sodium, 24 g carbo., 4 g fiber, 36 g pro. **Daily Values:** 3% vit. A, 17% vit. C, 12% calcium, 18% iron

If you think chutney is one of those high-end, elusive ingredients that you have to drive all over town to find, think again. These days the condiment is widely available at supermarkets.

BARBECUE-CHUTNEY CHICKEN

PREP:

15 minutes

COOK:

6 to 7 hours (low)
or 3 to 3½ hours (high)

MAKES:

4 to 6 servings

1 medium onion, cut into wedges

3 pounds meaty chicken pieces (breast halves, thighs, and drumsticks), skinned

¼ teaspoon salt

⅛ teaspoon black pepper

½ cup mango chutney

⅔ cup bottled barbecue sauce

1 teaspoon curry powder

2 to 3 cups hot cooked rice

1 In a 3½- or 4-quart slow cooker place onion. Add chicken pieces; sprinkle with salt and pepper. Snip any large pieces of chutney. In a small bowl stir together chutney, barbecue sauce, and curry powder. Pour over mixture in cooker.

2 Cover and cook on low-heat setting for 6 to 7 hours or on high-heat setting for 3 to 3½ hours. Serve chicken and chutney mixture with hot cooked rice.

Nutrition Facts per serving: 538 cal., 12 g total fat (3 g sat. fat), 138 mg chol., 647 mg sodium, 57 g carbo., 2 g fiber, 48 g pro. **Daily Values:** 35% vit. A, 33% vit. C, 5% calcium, 20% iron

For some comfort-food aficionados, only one way to serve chicken and noodles is acceptable—over a heaping scoop of mashed potatoes. If you're in that camp, you might want to opt for the convenience of refrigerated mashed potatoes.

SLOW COOKER CHICKEN & NOODLES

2	cups sliced carrots
1½	cups chopped onions
1	cup sliced celery
2	tablespoons snipped fresh parsley
1	bay leaf
3	medium chicken legs (thigh-drumstick piece) (about 2 pounds total), skinned
2	10¾-ounce cans reduced-fat and reduced-sodium condensed cream of chicken soup
½	cup water
1	teaspoon dried thyme, crushed
¼	teaspoon black pepper
10	ounces dried wide noodles (about 5 cups)
1	cup frozen peas

PREP:

25 minutes

COOK:

8 to 9 hours (low)
or 4 to 4½ hours (high)

MAKES:

6 servings

1 In a 3½- or 4-quart slow cooker place carrots, onions, celery, parsley, and bay leaf. Add chicken legs. In a medium bowl stir together chicken soup, water, thyme, and pepper. Pour over mixture in cooker.

2 Cover and cook on low-heat setting for 8 to 9 hours or on high-heat setting for 4 to 4½ hours. Remove chicken from cooker. Remove bay leaf.

3 Meanwhile, cook noodles according to package directions; drain. When chicken is cool enough to handle, remove chicken from bones. Cut chicken into bite-size pieces. Stir chicken and frozen peas into mixture in cooker.

4 Gently stir cooked noodles into chicken mixture. Season to taste with salt and additional pepper.

Nutrition Facts per serving: 406 cal., 7 g total fat (2 g sat. fat), 122 mg chol., 532 mg sodium, 56 g carbo., 5 g fiber, 28 g pro. **Daily Values:** 127% vit. A, 60% vit. C, 6% calcium, 19% iron

Pepperoni certainly isn't for pizza alone. Here its bold flavor enlivens a zesty pasta topper. Save the extra pepperoni to fold into an omelet or toss into a salad.

PEPPERONI CHICKEN

PREP:

15 minutes

COOK:

*6 to 7 hours (low)
or 3 to 3½ hours (high)*

MAKES:

4 to 6 servings

2½ to 3 pounds meaty chicken pieces (breast halves, thighs, and drumsticks), skinned

⅛ teaspoon black pepper

1 15-ounce container refrigerated marinara sauce or 2 cups desired pasta sauce

½ of a 3-ounce package sliced pepperoni, halved

½ cup pitted kalamata or ripe olives, halved

8 ounces dried mostaccioli pasta

1 In a 3½- or 4-quart slow cooker place chicken pieces. Sprinkle with pepper. For sauce, in a medium bowl stir together marinara sauce, pepperoni, and olives. Pour over chicken in cooker.

2 Cover and cook on low-heat setting for 6 to 7 hours or on high-heat setting for 3 to 3½ hours.

3 Meanwhile, cook pasta according to package directions; drain. Serve chicken and sauce over hot cooked pasta.

Nutrition Facts per serving: 595 cal., 20 g total fat (5 g sat. fat), 124 mg chol., 1,041 mg sodium, 52 g carbo., 4 g fiber, 48 g pro. **Daily Values:** 9% vit. A, 9% vit. C, 4% calcium, 21% iron

The rice cooks right in this one-dish winner. Simply stir it into the chicken mixture.

EASY CHICKEN & RICE

2	cups sliced fresh mushrooms
1	cup sliced celery
½	cup chopped onion
1½	teaspoons dried dill
¼	teaspoon black pepper
2	pounds chicken thighs, skinned
1	10¾-ounce can condensed cream of mushroom or cream of chicken soup
¾	cup chicken broth
1½	cups uncooked instant rice

PREP:

15 minutes

COOK:

5 to 6 hours (low) or 2½ to 3 hours (high), plus 10 minutes (high)

MAKES:

4 servings

1 In a 3½- or 4-quart slow cooker combine mushrooms, celery, onion, dill, and pepper. Add chicken thighs. In a small bowl combine mushroom soup and chicken broth. Pour over mixture in cooker.

2 Cover and cook on low-heat setting for 5 to 6 hours or on high-heat setting for 2½ to 3 hours.

3 If using low-heat setting, turn to high-heat setting. Stir in rice. Cover and cook about 10 minutes more or until rice is tender.

Nutrition Facts per serving: 516 cal., 12 g total fat (3 g sat. fat), 108 mg chol., 840 mg sodium, 66 g carbo., 3 g fiber, 34 g pro. Daily Values: 4% vit. A, 12% vit. C, 7% calcium, 29% iron

This recipe is called Angel Chicken both because it's heavenly and because it's served over angel hair pasta. Angel hair especially makes sense when you're in a hurry, as it cooks up quickly.

ANGEL CHICKEN

PREP:

15 minutes

COOK:

4 to 5 hours (low)

MAKES:

6 servings

6   skinless, boneless chicken breast halves (about 2 pounds total)

$^{1}/_{4}$ cup butter or margarine

1   0.7-ounce envelope Italian dry salad dressing mix

1   10$^{3}/_{4}$-ounce can condensed golden mushroom soup

$^{1}/_{2}$ of an 8-ounce tub cream cheese with chives and onion

$^{1}/_{2}$ cup dry white wine or water

3   cups hot cooked angel-hair pasta

    Snipped fresh chives (optional)

1 In a 3$^{1}/_{2}$- or 4-quart slow cooker place chicken pieces. For sauce, in a medium saucepan melt butter. Stir in salad dressing mix. Stir in mushroom soup, cream cheese, and wine. Pour over chicken in cooker.

2 Cover and cook on low-heat setting for 4 to 5 hours. Serve chicken and sauce over hot cooked pasta. If desired, sprinkle with chives.

Nutrition Facts per serving: 451 cal., 18 g total fat (9 g sat. fat), 132 mg chol., 1,065 mg sodium, 26 g carbo., 2 g fiber, 41 g pro. **Daily Values:** 13% vit. A, 3% vit. C, 3% calcium, 12% iron

Here's a sauce that's sweet and pretty. Use orange sections or slices for an equally pretty garnish. Serve with hot cooked brown rice, which is rich in fiber.

TERIYAKI CHICKEN WITH ORANGE SAUCE

1	16-ounce package loose-pack frozen broccoli, baby carrots, and water chestnuts
2	tablespoons quick-cooking tapioca
1	pound skinless, boneless chicken breast halves or thighs, cut into 1-inch pieces
¾	cup chicken broth
3	tablespoons orange marmalade
2	tablespoons bottled teriyaki sauce
1	teaspoon dry mustard
½	teaspoon ground ginger
2	cups hot cooked rice

1 In a 3½- or 4-quart slow cooker combine frozen vegetables and tapioca. Add chicken pieces.

2 In a small bowl combine chicken broth, orange marmalade, teriyaki sauce, dry mustard, and ginger. Pour over mixture in cooker.

3 Cover and cook on low-heat setting for 4 to 5 hours or on high-heat setting for 2 to 2½ hours. Serve chicken mixture with hot cooked rice.

Nutrition Facts per serving: 375 cal., 4 g total fat (1 g sat. fat), 79 mg chol., 790 mg sodium, 52 g carbo., 4 g fiber, 30 g pro. **Daily Values:** 40% vit. A, 16% vit. C, 3% calcium, 17% iron

PREP:

15 minutes

COOK:

4 to 5 hours (low) or 2 to 2½ hours (high)

MAKES:

4 servings

PUT COOKING ON HOLD

Are there times when you worry that your slow cooker dinner will finish cooking long before you arrive home? Here's a remedy: Use an automatic timer to start the cooker 1 to 2 hours (no longer) after you leave the house. When using a timer, be sure all ingredients are well chilled when you place them in the cooker. Note: To ensure food safety, never use this method with frozen poultry or fish.

Americans only recently have discovered the creamy richness white kidney beans bring to cooking, but Italians have been savoring the legumes for ages. This recipe gives you a chance to see firsthand what they can do. Serve it in shallow bowls with crusty bread.

ITALIAN CHICKEN WITH WHITE BEANS

PREP:

20 minutes

COOK:

6 to 7 hours (low)
or 3 to 3¹/₂ hours (high)

STAND:

10 minutes

MAKES:

6 to 8 servings

1	cup chopped onion
1	cup chopped carrots
¹/₂	cup thinly sliced celery
3	cloves garlic, minced
2	pounds skinless, boneless chicken thighs
¹/₄	teaspoon salt
¹/₈	teaspoon black pepper
1	14¹/₂-ounce can diced tomatoes, undrained
¹/₂	cup chicken broth
¹/₂	cup dry white wine or chicken broth
1¹/₂	teaspoons dried Italian seasoning, crushed
1	15- or 19-ounce can white kidney (cannellini) beans, rinsed and drained
	Grated Parmesan cheese

1 In a 3¹/₂- or 4-quart slow cooker combine onion, carrots, celery, and garlic. Add chicken thighs; sprinkle with salt and pepper. In a medium bowl stir together tomatoes, chicken broth, wine, and Italian seasoning. Pour over mixture in cooker.

2 Cover and cook on low-heat setting for 6 to 7 hours or on high-heat setting for 3 to 3¹/₂ hours. Remove liner from cooker, if possible, or turn off cooker. Stir kidney beans into mixture in cooker. Cover and let stand for 10 minutes.

3 Using a slotted spoon, transfer chicken and vegetables to a serving dish, reserving cooking liquid. Drizzle chicken and vegetables with enough of the liquid to moisten. Sprinkle each serving with cheese.

Nutrition Facts per serving: 296 cal., 7 g total fat (2 g sat. fat), 123 mg chol., 577 mg sodium, 19 g carbo., 5 g fiber, 37 g pro. **Daily Values:** 105% vit. A, 27% vit. C, 13% calcium, 17% iron

Fennel looks like a pot-bellied cousin to celery and has a mild licorice-like flavor that pairs well with the fruit in this dish.

FENNEL & PEAR CHICKEN THIGHS

1	medium fennel bulb, trimmed and sliced (1¼ cups)
2	6- or 7-ounce jars sliced mushrooms, drained
½	cup coarsely snipped dried pears
2	tablespoons quick-cooking tapioca, finely ground
2½	pounds skinless, boneless chicken thighs
¾	teaspoon salt
½	teaspoon dried thyme, crushed
½	teaspoon cracked black pepper
1	cup pear nectar or apple juice
3	cups hot cooked couscous or rice
	Snipped fennel tops (optional)

PREP:

15 minutes

COOK:

*7 to 8 hours (low)
or 3½ to 4 hours (high)*

MAKES:

6 servings

1 In a 3½- or 4-quart slow cooker place sliced fennel, mushrooms, and dried pears. Sprinkle with tapioca. Add chicken thighs; sprinkle with salt, thyme, and pepper. Pour pear nectar over mixture in cooker.

2 Cover and cook on low-heat setting for 7 to 8 hours or on high-heat setting for 3½ to 4 hours.

3 Serve chicken mixture over hot cooked couscous. If desired, sprinkle with snipped fennel tops.

Nutrition Facts per serving: 407 cal., 7 g total fat (2 g sat. fat), 157 mg chol., 657 mg sodium, 41 g carbo., 4 g fiber, 42 g pro. **Daily Values:** 3% vit. A, 14% vit. C, 4% calcium, 16% iron

A good one for families with big appetites, this South American-style one-dish meal features rice and two kinds of beans. The contrast of sweet cranberry and hot chipotle chile pepper is a popular one indeed.

CRANBERRY-CHIPOTLE CHICKEN

PREP:

30 minutes

COOK:

6 to 7 hours (low) or 3 to 3 1/2 hours (high)

MAKES:

6 servings

8   ounces bacon, cut into 1-inch pieces

1   cup chopped onion

1   15-ounce can black beans, rinsed and drained

1   15-ounce can white kidney (cannellini) beans, rinsed and drained

1   cup chopped roma tomatoes

1/2   cup uncooked long grain rice

1/2   cup chicken broth

1/2   teaspoon salt

1/2   teaspoon ground cumin

1/4   teaspoon ground cinnamon

3   cloves garlic, minced

1   pound skinless, boneless chicken thighs

1   16-ounce can whole cranberry sauce

1   canned chipotle chile pepper in adobo sauce, finely chopped

1   tablespoon lime juice

1/4   teaspoon salt

1 In a large skillet cook bacon and onion over medium heat until bacon is crisp. Drain off fat.

2 Transfer bacon mixture to a 3 1/2- or 4-quart slow cooker. Stir in black beans, kidney beans, tomatoes, rice, chicken broth, the 1/2 teaspoon salt, the cumin, cinnamon, and garlic. Add chicken thighs.

3 In a small bowl combine cranberry sauce, chipotle pepper, lime juice, and the 1/4 teaspoon salt. Pour over mixture in cooker.

4 Cover and cook on low-heat setting for 6 to 7 hours or on high-heat setting for 3 to 3 1/2 hours.

Nutrition Facts per serving: 517 cal., 14 g total fat (3 g sat. fat), 72 mg chol., 1,137 mg sodium, 71 g carbo., 11 g fiber, 28 g pro. **Daily Values:** 9% vit. A, 24% vit. C, 8% calcium, 22% iron

Mashed potatoes and their required peeling, boiling, and mashing certainly don't qualify as hassle-free fare, but their premashed, refrigerated counterparts do. Use the convenient kind as a satisfying topper for this casserole-style dish.

POTATO-TOPPED CHICKEN & VEGETABLES

1	16-ounce package peeled baby carrots
1	medium onion, cut into wedges
2	pounds skinless, boneless chicken thighs
1	10¾-ounce can condensed cream of chicken or cream of mushroom soup
1	teaspoon dried basil, crushed
¼	teaspoon black pepper
1	20-ounce package refrigerated mashed potatoes
½	cup shredded cheddar cheese (2 ounces)
4	cloves garlic, minced

PREP:

20 minutes

COOK:

7 to 8 hours (low)
or 3½ to 4 hours (high),
plus 30 minutes (low)

MAKES:

6 servings

1 In a 3½- to 4½-quart slow cooker combine carrots and onion. Add chicken thighs. In a medium bowl combine chicken soup, basil, and pepper. Spoon over mixture in cooker.

2 Cover and cook on low-heat setting for 7 to 8 hours or on high-heat setting for 3½ to 4 hours.

3 If using high-heat setting, turn to low-heat setting. In a large bowl stir together mashed potatoes, cheddar cheese, and garlic. Spoon over chicken mixture. Cover and cook about 30 minutes more or until potatoes are heated through. (Do not overcook or potatoes will become too soft.)

Nutrition Facts per serving: 393 cal., 14 g total fat (5 g sat. fat), 135 mg chol., 707 mg sodium, 27 g carbo., 4 g fiber, 37 g pro. **Daily Values:** 391% vit. A, 44% vit. C, 13% calcium, 14% iron

In India, the people grind fresh curry powder each day, combining as many as 16 to 20 spices. You can shortcut that step with your favorite ready-to-use blend, but don't skimp on the toppings: Raisins and peanuts balance the spicy mixture with a hint of sweetness.

CHICKEN CURRY

PREP:

30 minutes

COOK:

*6 to 8 hours (low) or
3 to 4 hours (high),
plus 30 minutes (high)*

MAKES:

8 servings

3	tablespoons all-purpose flour
3	tablespoons curry powder
1½	teaspoons ground cumin
1	teaspoon salt
1½	pounds skinless, boneless chicken breast halves or thighs, cut into 1-inch pieces
2	cups peeled and chopped potatoes
1½	cups bias-sliced carrots
1	cup coarsely chopped cooking apple
¾	cup chopped onion
1	fresh jalapeño chile pepper*, seeded and finely chopped
1	teaspoon instant chicken bouillon granules
2	cloves garlic, minced
½	cup water
1	13½-ounce can unsweetened coconut milk
4	cups hot cooked rice
¼	cup raisins
¼	cup chopped peanuts

1 In a plastic bag combine flour, curry powder, cumin, and salt. Add chicken pieces, a few at a time, shaking to coat. Set aside.

2 In a 3½- or 4-quart slow cooker combine potatoes, carrots, apple, onion, jalapeño pepper, bouillon granules, and garlic. Add chicken. Pour water over mixture in cooker.

3 Cover and cook on low-heat setting for 6 to 8 hours or on high-heat setting for 3 to 4 hours.

4 If using low-heat setting, turn to high-heat setting. Stir in coconut milk. Cover and cook for 30 minutes more.

5 Serve chicken mixture over hot cooked rice. Sprinkle with raisins and chopped peanuts.

Nutrition Facts per serving: 409 cal., 14 g total fat (10 g sat. fat), 49 mg chol., 513 mg sodium, 45 g carbo., 4 g fiber, 26 g pro. **Daily Values:** 129% vit. A, 20% vit. C, 6% calcium, 25% iron

*See note, page 52.

The sweet licorice flavor of the anise seeds blended with the fruitiness of plums and oranges renders a hint of exotic Asian fare. The orange couscous is a snap to prepare—stir it into marmalade-infused boiling water about 5 minutes before the chicken is done.

CHICKEN WITH ORANGE COUSCOUS

2½	to 2¾ pounds skinless, boneless chicken thighs
¾	cup bottled plum sauce
⅓	cup orange juice
¼	cup orange marmalade
2	tablespoons quick-cooking tapioca
¼	teaspoon anise seeds, crushed
2¼	cups water
1	tablespoon orange marmalade
1	10-ounce package quick-cooking couscous
¼	teaspoon salt
	Orange slices (optional)

PREP:

20 minutes

COOK:

*5 to 6 hours (low)
or 2½ to 3 hours (high)*

MAKES:

6 servings

1 In a 3½- or 4-quart slow cooker place chicken thighs. For sauce, in a small bowl combine plum sauce, orange juice, the ¼ cup orange marmalade, the tapioca, and anise seeds. Pour over chicken in cooker.

2 Cover and cook on low-heat setting for 5 to 6 hours or on high-heat setting for 2½ to 3 hours. Remove chicken; cover and keep warm. Skim fat from sauce.

3 In a medium saucepan bring water and the 1 tablespoon orange marmalade to boiling; remove from heat. Stir in couscous and salt. Cover and let stand for 5 minutes. Fluff couscous with a fork.

4 Serve chicken and sauce with couscous. If desired, garnish with orange slices.

Nutrition Facts per serving: 534 cal., 8 g total fat (2 g sat. fat), 157 mg chol., 404 mg sodium, 70 g carbo., 3 g fiber, 44 g pro. **Daily Values:** 21% vit. A, 13% vit. C, 5 % calcium, 16% iron

You can adapt a surprising number of classic international favorites to the slow cooker. This version of tasty Chinese takeout is yet another case in point.

CASHEW CHICKEN

PREP:

15 minutes

COOK:

*6 to 8 hours (low)
or 3 to 4 hours (high)*

MAKES:

6 servings

1	10¾-ounce can condensed golden mushroom soup
2	tablespoons soy sauce
½	teaspoon ground ginger
1½	pounds chicken breast tenderloins
1	cup sliced fresh mushrooms or one 4½-ounce jar sliced mushrooms, drained
1	cup sliced celery
1	cup packaged shredded carrots
1	8-ounce can sliced water chestnuts, drained
½	cup cashews
3	cups hot cooked rice

1 In a 3½- or 4-quart slow cooker combine mushroom soup, soy sauce, and ginger. Stir in chicken tenderloins, mushrooms, celery, carrots, and water chestnuts.

2 Cover and cook on low-heat setting for 6 to 8 hours or on high-heat setting for 3 to 4 hours.

3 Just before serving, stir in cashews. Serve chicken mixture over hot cooked rice.

Nutrition Facts per serving: 364 cal., 9 g total fat (2 g sat. fat), 68 mg chol., 789 mg sodium, 38 g carbo., 3 g fiber, 33 g pro. **Daily Values:** 100% vit. A, 7% vit. C, 4% calcium, 17% iron

CAN I USE A DIFFERENT SIZE COOKER?

The recipes in this book give a range of cooker sizes (such as 4½- to 6-quart). It's important not to use a cooker that's larger or smaller than the specified range. A slow cooker works most efficiently when it's one-half to two-thirds full. This is because the heat comes from coils around the sides of the pot, rather than from the bottom as in conventional cooking.

Follow two secrets to success when making dumplings: First, be sure the stew is bubbling hot before dropping in the dough. Second, don't open the cooker until the minimum cooking time has passed; otherwise the dumplings may deflate.

CHICKEN & DUMPLINGS

2	cups chopped carrots
2	cups chopped potatoes
1½	cups chopped parsnips
2	bay leaves
1	teaspoon dried sage, crushed
¼	teaspoon black pepper
1	clove garlic, minced
2	pounds skinless, boneless chicken thighs, cut into 1-inch pieces
1	14-ounce can chicken broth
1	10¾-ounce can condensed cream of chicken soup
1	tablespoon cornstarch
½	cup all-purpose flour
½	cup shredded cheddar cheese (2 ounces)
⅓	cup cornmeal
1	teaspoon baking powder
1	slightly beaten egg
2	tablespoons milk
2	tablespoons butter or margarine, melted

PREP:

25 minutes

COOK:

8 to 10 hours (low) or 4 to 5 hours (high), plus 25 minutes (high)

MAKES:

8 servings

1 In a 4- or 5-quart slow cooker combine carrots, potatoes, parsnips, bay leaves, sage, pepper, and garlic, and ½ teaspoon *salt*. Add chicken. In a medium bowl gradually whisk chicken broth into chicken soup. Pour over mixture in cooker.

2 Cover and cook on low-heat setting for 8 to 10 hours or on high-heat setting for 4 to 5 hours. If using low-heat setting, turn to high-heat setting. Using a wooden spoon, stir chicken mixture. Remove bay leaves. Combine cornstarch and 2 tablespoons *cold water;* stir into chicken mixture.

3 For dumplings, in a medium bowl stir together flour, cheddar cheese, cornmeal, baking powder, and ¼ teaspoon *salt.* In a small bowl combine egg, milk, and melted butter. Add egg mixture to flour mixture; stir just until moistened. Spoon batter into 8 mounds on top of chicken mixture. Cover and cook for 25 to 30 minutes more or until a wooden toothpick inserted into a dumpling comes out clean. (Do not lift cover during cooking.)

Nutrition Facts per serving: 361 cal., 14 g total fat (6 g sat. fat), 140 mg chol., 948 mg sodium, 29 g carbo., 4 g fiber, 29 g pro. Daily Values: 163% vit. A, 22% vit. C, 13% calcium, 15% iron

When it comes to eating, kids love options, so set out a variety of colored tortillas—green, orange, and white—to choose from. (You needn't tell them the green ones have anything to do with spinach!)

SPICY CHICKEN BURRITOS

PREP:

25 minutes

COOK:

6 to 7 hours (low)
or 3 to 3 1/2 hours (high)

STAND:

5 minutes

MAKES:

6 to 8 servings

1   medium zucchini, halved lengthwise and sliced 3/4 inch thick

1   large green sweet pepper, cut into 1-inch pieces

1   medium onion, coarsely chopped

1   stalk celery, coarsely chopped

1 1/2   pounds skinless, boneless chicken breast halves, cut into 1/2-inch strips

1   8-ounce jar green taco sauce

1   teaspoon instant chicken bouillon granules

1/2   teaspoon ground cumin

1   cup uncooked instant rice

6   to 8 nine- to ten-inch spinach, chile, or plain flour tortillas, warmed

3/4   cup shredded Monterey Jack cheese with jalapeño peppers (3 ounces)

2   small tomatoes, chopped

2   green onions, sliced

1 In a 3 1/2- or 4-quart slow cooker combine zucchini, sweet pepper, onion, and celery. Add chicken strips. In a small bowl combine taco sauce, bouillon granules, and cumin. Pour over mixture in cooker.

2 Cover and cook on low-heat setting for 6 to 7 hours or on high-heat setting for 3 to 3 1/2 hours. Turn off cooker. Stir in rice. Cover and let stand for 5 minutes.

3 To serve, arrange chicken mixture just below centers of tortillas. Top with Monterey Jack cheese, tomatoes, and green onions. Fold bottom edge of each tortilla up and over filling. Fold in opposite sides; roll up from bottom. If necessary, secure with wooden toothpicks.

Nutrition Facts per serving: 408 cal., 10 g total fat (4 g sat. fat), 81 mg chol., 735 mg sodium, 43 g carbo., 3 g fiber, 35 g pro. **Daily Values:** 25% vit. A, 58% vit. C, 18% calcium, 19% iron

For something out of the ordinary, serve this classic chicken dish over polenta.

EASY CHICKEN CACCIATORE

3 cups frozen small whole onions

2 large red sweet peppers, cut into 1-inch pieces

1½ pounds skinless, boneless chicken thighs, cut into 1-inch pieces

1½ cups fire-roasted tomato and garlic pasta sauce

⅓ cup dry white wine or water

½ teaspoon salt

¼ teaspoon black pepper

1⅓ cups quick-cooking polenta mix

Snipped fresh parsley (optional)

PREP:

20 minutes

COOK:

*4 to 5 hours (low)
or 2½ to 3 hours (high)*

MAKES:

6 servings

1 In a 3½- or 4-quart slow cooker place onions and sweet peppers. Add chicken pieces. In a small bowl combine pasta sauce, wine, salt, and pepper. Pour over mixture in cooker.

2 Cover and cook on low-heat setting for 4 to 5 hours or on high-heat setting for 2½ to 3 hours.

3 Meanwhile, in a large saucepan bring 4 cups lightly *salted water* to boiling. Gradually stir in polenta mix. Return to boiling, stirring constantly; reduce heat to low. Cook, uncovered, about 5 minutes or until very thick.

4 Divide polenta among shallow serving bowls; top with chicken mixture. If desired, sprinkle each serving with parsley.

Nutrition Facts per serving: 370 cal., 8 g total fat (2 g sat. fat), 93 mg chol., 813 mg sodium, 43 g carbo., 6 g fiber, 29 g pro. **Daily Values:** 72% vit. A, 167% vit. C, 19% calcium, 21% iron

A wonderful blend of tangy cranberry and sweet lemonade makes a winning sauce for chicken and wild rice. To save time, leave the apple wedges unpeeled; they'll retain their shape better too.

CRANBERRY CHICKEN

PREP:

15 minutes

COOK:

6 to 7 hours (low)
or 3 to 3½ hours (high)

MAKES:

6 servings

2 medium apples, cored and cut into wedges

1 medium onion, thinly sliced

6 skinless, boneless chicken breast halves (about 2 pounds total)

1 16-ounce can whole cranberry sauce

¼ cup frozen lemonade concentrate, thawed

2 tablespoons quick-cooking tapioca

2 tablespoons honey

¼ teaspoon salt

2 6-ounce packages long grain and wild rice mix

1 In a 3½- or 4-quart slow cooker combine apples and onion. Add chicken pieces. In a medium bowl combine cranberry sauce, lemonade concentrate, tapioca, honey, and salt. Pour over mixture in cooker.

2 Cover and cook on low-heat setting for 6 to 7 hours or on high-heat setting for 3 to 3½ hours.

3 Meanwhile, in a large saucepan prepare rice mixes (including seasoning packets) according to package directions. Serve chicken and apple mixture over hot cooked rice.

Nutrition Facts per serving: 565 cal., 2 g total fat (1 g sat. fat), 88 mg chol., 993 mg sodium, 96 g carbo., 4 g fiber, 40 g pro. **Daily Values:** 4% vit. A, 14% vit. C, 5% calcium, 12% iron

Although a dozen garlic cloves seem likely to overpower, they're the secret to this recipe. The garlic mellows as it cooks, infusing the chicken with irresistible flavor.

CHICKEN WITH GARLIC, PEPPERS & ARTICHOKES

1	medium onion, chopped
12	cloves garlic, minced
1	tablespoon olive oil or cooking oil
1	8- or 9-ounce package frozen artichoke hearts
1	medium red sweet pepper, cut into strips
1/2	cup chicken broth
1	tablespoon quick-cooking tapioca
2	teaspoons dried rosemary, crushed
1	teaspoon finely shredded lemon peel
1/2	teaspoon black pepper
1 1/2	pounds skinless, boneless chicken breast halves or thighs
4	cups hot cooked brown rice

PREP:

20 minutes

COOK:

*6 to 7 hours (low)
or 3 to 3 1/2 hours (high)*

MAKES:

6 servings

1 In a small skillet cook onion and garlic in hot oil over medium heat about 5 minutes or until tender, stirring occasionally.

2 Transfer onion mixture to a 3 1/2- or 4-quart slow cooker. Stir in frozen artichoke hearts, sweet pepper, chicken broth, tapioca, rosemary, lemon peel, and black pepper. Add chicken pieces, spooning some of the artichoke mixture over chicken.

3 Cover and cook on low-heat setting for 6 to 7 hours or on high-heat setting for 3 to 3 1/2 hours. Serve chicken and artichoke mixture with hot cooked rice.

Nutrition Facts per serving: 341 cal., 6 g total fat (1 g sat. fat), 66 mg chol., 159 mg sodium, 39 g carbo., 6 g fiber, 32 g pro. **Daily Values:** 11% vit. A, 62% vit. C, 7% calcium, 10% iron

These chicken sandwich wedges, like those served at fancy bistros. make you feel like you're dining out even when you eat them at home. Focaccia is available at many bakeries and large supermarkets.

CHICKEN PESTO SANDWICH

PREP:

20 minutes

COOK:

*5 to 6 hours (low)
or 2¹/₂ to 3 hours (high),
plus 30 minutes (high)*

MAKES:

6 to 8 servings

1	teaspoon dried Italian seasoning, crushed
¹/₄	teaspoon salt
¹/₄	teaspoon black pepper
1	pound skinless, boneless chicken breast halves
2	cups sliced fresh mushrooms
¹/₂	cup sliced onion
2	cloves garlic, minced
1	14¹/₂-ounce can tomatoes, undrained and cut up
2	tablespoons red wine vinegar
1	medium yellow summer squash or zucchini, halved lengthwise and sliced ¹/₄ inch thick
1	cup green, red, and/or yellow sweet pepper strips
¹/₃	cup mayonnaise or salad dressing
2	tablespoons purchased basil pesto
1	9-inch Italian flatbread (focaccia), cut in half horizontally
¹/₃	cup finely shredded Parmesan cheese

1 In a small bowl combine Italian seasoning, salt, and black pepper. Sprinkle seasoning mixture evenly over chicken pieces; rub in with your fingers. Set aside.

2 In a 3¹/₂- or 4-quart slow cooker combine mushrooms, onion, and garlic. Add chicken. Pour tomatoes and vinegar over mixture in cooker.

3 Cover and cook on low-heat setting for 5 to 6 hours or on high-heat setting for 2¹/₂ to 3 hours.

4 If using low-heat setting, turn to high-heat setting. Add squash and sweet pepper. Cover and cook for 30 minutes more.

5 Meanwhile, in a small bowl combine mayonnaise and pesto. Spread evenly over cut sides of flatbread. Transfer chicken to a cutting board. Thinly slice chicken. Arrange chicken on bottom half of bread. Using a slotted spoon, spoon vegetable mixture over chicken. Sprinkle with Parmesan cheese. Add top half of bread. Cut into wedges.

Nutrition Facts per serving: 450 cal., 19 g total fat (4 g sat. fat), 54 mg chol., 424 mg sodium, 41 g carbo., 5 g fiber, 29 g pro. **Daily Values:** 14% vit. A, 56% vit. C, 17% calcium, 11% iron

Mediterranean can mean many things, but it always means you're in for a treat!
Here cinnamon and feta give this dish an intriguing Greek angle.

MEDITERRANEAN CHICKEN & PASTA

1	pound uncooked ground chicken or turkey
1	14½-ounce can diced tomatoes with basil, oregano, and garlic, undrained
1½	cups tomato juice
1½	cups water
2	medium carrots, very thinly sliced
1	medium onion, cut into wedges
1	stalk celery, finely chopped
1	teaspoon dried Italian seasoning, crushed
½	teaspoon salt
½	teaspoon ground cinnamon
1	cup medium shell pasta
1	cup crumbled feta cheese (4 ounces)

1 In a large skillet cook ground chicken until brown. Drain off fat.

2 Transfer chicken to a 3½- or 4-quart slow cooker. Stir in tomatoes, tomato juice, water, carrots, onion wedges, celery, Italian seasoning, salt, and cinnamon.

3 Cover and cook on low-heat setting for 4½ to 5½ hours or on high-heat setting for 2¼ to 2¾ hours.

4 If using low-heat setting, turn to high-heat setting. Stir in pasta. Cover and cook for 30 to 45 minutes more or until pasta is tender. Sprinkle each serving with feta cheese.

Nutrition Facts per serving: 437 cal., 18 g total fat (6 g sat. fat), 33 mg chol., 1,650 mg sodium, 39 g carbo., 4 g fiber, 31 g pro. **Daily Values:** 181% vit. A, 47% vit. C, 31% calcium, 27% iron

PREP:

25 minutes

COOK:

4½ to 5½ hours (low) or 2¼ to 2¾ hours (high), plus 30 minutes (high)

MAKES:

4 to 6 servings

GETTING A HEAD START ON DINNER
Your slow cooker makes entertaining easy, and you can make it even easier by doing some preparation ahead of time. If the recipe calls for cooked poultry or meat, cook it the night before. You also can brown ground poultry, ground beef, or ground sausage and store in the refrigerator. (Wait until morning to brown poultry pieces, meat cubes, and roasts.) Clean and cut up vegetables and store in separate containers in the refrigerator. In the morning, place the ingredients in the slow cooker, turn it on, and go on your way.

This major league spaghetti sauce is lower in calories and fat than most sauces made with ground beef. If 8 cups of sauce is more than your family eats at one meal, freeze the leftovers for another time.

CHICKEN SPAGHETTI SAUCE

PREP:

25 minutes

COOK:

8 to 9 hours (low)
or 4 to 4¹/₂ hours (high)

MAKES:

8 to 10 servings

1	pound uncooked ground chicken or turkey
6	cloves garlic, minced
3	14¹/₂-ounce cans stewed tomatoes, undrained
2	6-ounce cans tomato paste
¹/₂	cup chopped green sweet pepper
1¹/₂	teaspoons dried Italian seasoning, crushed
1	bay leaf
¹/₂	teaspoon salt
¹/₈	teaspoon bottled hot pepper sauce (optional)
8	cups hot cooked pasta
	Grated Parmesan cheese (optional)

1 In a large skillet cook ground chicken and garlic until chicken is brown. Drain off fat.

2 Transfer chicken mixture to a 3¹/₂- or 4-quart slow cooker. Stir in tomatoes, tomato paste, sweet pepper, Italian seasoning, bay leaf, salt, and, if desired, hot pepper sauce.

3 Cover and cook on low-heat setting for 8 to 9 hours or on high-heat setting for 4 to 4¹/₂ hours. Remove bay leaf.

4 Serve chicken mixture over hot cooked pasta. If desired, sprinkle each serving with Parmesan cheese.

Nutrition Facts per serving: 387 cal., 7 g total fat (1 g sat. fat), 45 mg chol., 801 mg sodium, 61 g carbo., 6 g fiber, 20 g pro. **Daily Values:** 22% vit. A, 48% vit. C, 8% calcium, 25% iron

Only the grapes grown in and around the village of Chablis, France, produce true Chablis wines. But did you know that the grape used in these wines is Chardonnay? If you want a similar, yet less expensive variety, use a reliable California Chardonnay to make this recipe. Or try your favorite dry white wine.

TURKEY CHABLIS

¾ cup dry white wine

½ cup chopped onion

1 bay leaf

1 clove garlic, minced

1 3½- to 4-pound frozen boneless turkey, thawed

1 teaspoon dried rosemary, crushed

¼ teaspoon black pepper

⅓ cup half-and-half, light cream, or milk

2 tablespoons cornstarch

PREP:

15 minutes

COOK:

*9 to 10 hours (low)
or 4½ to 5 hours (high)*

MAKES:

6 to 8 servings

1 In a 3½- to 6-quart slow cooker combine wine, onion, bay leaf, and garlic. If turkey is wrapped in netting, remove netting. If present, remove gravy packet and chill for another use. In a small bowl combine rosemary and pepper. Sprinkle rosemary mixture evenly over turkey; rub in with your fingers. Place turkey in cooker.

2 Cover and cook on low-heat setting for 9 to 10 hours or on high-heat setting for 4½ to 5 hours. Remove turkey from cooker, reserving juices. Cover turkey and keep warm.

3 For gravy, strain juices into a glass measuring cup; skim off fat. Measure 1⅓ cups juices. Pour juices into a small saucepan. Combine half-and-half and cornstarch; stir into juices in saucepan. Cook and stir over medium heat until thickened and bubbly. Cook and stir for 2 minutes more.

4 Slice turkey; arrange on a serving platter. Spoon some of the gravy over turkey. Pass remaining gravy.

Nutrition Facts per serving: 365 cal., 9 g total fat (3 g sat. fat), 176 mg chol., 193 mg sodium, 5 g carbo., 0 g fiber, 58 g pro. **Daily Values:** 1% vit. A, 2% vit. C, 6% calcium, 23% iron

If you have yet to discover the meaty pleasures of black-eyed peas, this is your chance.
This Southwestern angle on the Southern favorite will make you a fan for sure.

TEXAS TURKEY BONANZA

PREP:

20 minutes

COOK:

8 to 10 hours (low)
or 4 to 5 hours (high),
plus 30 minutes (high)

MAKES:

6 servings

2	cups dry black-eyed peas
1	to 3 fresh jalapeño chile peppers*, seeded and quartered lengthwise
1½	teaspoons dried sage, crushed
1	teaspoon salt
1	pound turkey breast tenderloins or pork tenderloin, cut into 1½-inch pieces
2	medium yellow summer squash, cut into wedges
½	cup finely chopped red onion
	Snipped fresh cilantro
1	recipe Lime Sour Cream (optional)

LIME SOUR CREAM
In a small bowl combine ½ cup dairy sour cream, ½ teaspoon finely shredded lime peel, and 1 tablespoon lime juice. Cover and chill until ready to serve.

1 Rinse black-eyed peas. In a large saucepan combine peas and 5 cups water. Bring to boiling; reduce heat. Simmer, uncovered, for 10 minutes. Drain and rinse peas.

2 In a 4- or 4½-quart slow cooker combine peas, jalapeño peppers, sage, and salt. Stir in 3 cups *fresh water*. Add turkey tenderloins.

3 Cover and cook on low-heat setting for 8 to 10 hours or on high-heat setting for 4 to 5 hours.

4 If using low-heat setting, turn to high-heat setting. Stir in squash. Cover and cook about 30 minutes more or until squash is crisp-tender.

5 Sprinkle each serving with onion and cilantro. If desired, top with Lime Sour Cream and additional finely chopped fresh jalapeño chile peppers.

Nutrition Facts per serving: 144 cal., 1 g total fat (0 g sat. fat), 47 mg chol., 423 mg sodium, 13 g carbo., 4 g fiber, 21 g pro. **Daily Values:** 11% vit. A, 14% vit. C, 8% calcium, 8% iron

*See note, page 52.

Hard to believe this rich-tasting gravy starts with a mix. If you are really pressed for time, take advantage of fully cooked frozen turkey meatballs.

SLOW COOKED MEATBALLS WITH GRAVY

2	slightly beaten eggs
¾	cup seasoned fine dry bread crumbs
½	cup finely chopped onion
½	cup finely chopped celery
2	tablespoons snipped fresh parsley
¼	teaspoon black pepper
⅛	teaspoon garlic powder
2	pounds uncooked ground turkey or chicken
1½	teaspoons cooking oil
1	10½-ounce can reduced-sodium condensed cream of mushroom soup
1	cup water
1	0.9-ounce envelope turkey gravy mix
1	bay leaf
½	teaspoon finely shredded lemon peel
½	teaspoon dried thyme, crushed
	Hot cooked mashed potatoes or noodles

PREP:

30 minutes

COOK:

6 to 8 hours (low) or 3 to 4 hours (high)

MAKES:

8 servings

1 In a large bowl combine eggs, bread crumbs, onion, celery, parsley, pepper, and garlic powder. Add ground turkey; mix well. Shape into 1½-inch meatballs.

2 In a large skillet brown meatballs, half at a time, in hot oil. (If necessary, add more oil during cooking.) Drain off fat. Transfer meatballs to a 3½- or 4-quart slow cooker.

3 For gravy, in a medium bowl combine mushroom soup, water, gravy mix, bay leaf, lemon peel, and thyme. Pour over meatballs in cooker.

4 Cover and cook on low-heat setting for 6 to 8 hours or on high-heat setting for 3 to 4 hours. Remove bay leaf.

5 Serve meatballs and gravy with hot cooked mashed potatoes. Sprinkle with additional snipped fresh parsley.

Nutrition Facts per serving: 289 cal., 14 g total fat (4 g sat. fat), 144 mg chol., 852 mg sodium, 14 g carbo., 1 g fiber, 24 g pro. **Daily Values:** 3% vit. A, 4% vit. C, 5% calcium, 11% iron

For a less spicy pasta sauce, use ground turkey in place of the hot Italian turkey sausage. Freeze any leftover sauce for another night.

TURKEY SAUSAGE WITH PEPPER SAUCE

PREP:

25 minutes

COOK:

8 to 10 hours (low) or 4 to 5 hours (high)

MAKES:

6 to 8 servings

1½ pounds uncooked turkey Italian sausage (remove casings, if present)

4 cups chopped peeled tomatoes (6 large) or two 14½-ounce cans tomatoes, undrained and cut up

2 medium green and/or yellow sweet peppers, cut into strips

2 cups sliced fresh mushrooms

2 6-ounce cans Italian-style tomato paste

1 large onion, chopped

1 teaspoon sugar

1 bay leaf

½ teaspoon black pepper

2 cloves garlic, minced

12 to 16 ounces dried penne, rigatoni, or other pasta

Finely shredded Parmesan cheese (optional)

1 In a large skillet cook turkey sausage until brown. Drain off fat. Transfer cooked sausage to a 3½- to 5-quart slow cooker. Stir in tomatoes, sweet peppers, mushrooms, tomato paste, onion, sugar, bay leaf, pepper, and garlic.

2 Cover and cook on low-heat setting for 8 to 10 hours or on high-heat setting for 4 to 5 hours. Remove bay leaf.

3 Meanwhile, cook pasta according to package directions; drain. Serve sausage mixture over hot cooked pasta. If desired, sprinkle each serving with Parmesan cheese.

Nutrition Facts per serving: 517 cal., 14 g total fat (4 g sat. fat), 60 mg chol., 1,394 mg sodium, 69 g carbo., 6 g fiber, 30 g pro. **Daily Values:** 18% vit. A, 106% vit. C, 6% calcium, 37% iron

MEATLESS MAIN DISHES

6

For easy serve-alongs, simply pick up a fruit salad from the deli and a package of Mexican-style rice mix.

MEATLESS BURRITOS

PREP:

20 minutes

COOK:

6 to 8 hours (low)
or 3 to 4 hours (high)

MAKES:

16 servings

WARMING TORTILLAS
Stack tortillas and wrap tightly in foil. Heat in a 350°F oven about 10 minutes or until softened and heated through.

3	15-ounce cans red kidney and/or black beans, rinsed and drained
1	14½-ounce can diced tomatoes, undrained
1½	cups bottled salsa or picante sauce
1	11-ounce can whole kernel corn with sweet peppers, drained
1	fresh jalapeño chile pepper*, seeded and finely chopped (optional)
2	teaspoons chili powder
2	cloves garlic, minced
16	8- to 10-inch flour tortillas, warmed
2	cups shredded lettuce
1	cup shredded taco cheese or cheddar cheese (4 ounces)
	Sliced green onions and/or dairy sour cream (optional)

1 In a 3½- or 4-quart slow cooker combine beans, tomatoes, salsa, corn, jalapeño pepper (if desired), chili powder, and garlic.

2 Cover and cook on low-heat setting for 6 to 8 hours or on high-heat setting for 3 to 4 hours.

3 To serve, spoon bean mixture just below centers of tortillas. Top with lettuce and taco cheese. If desired, top with green onions and/or sour cream. Fold bottom edge of each tortilla up and over filling. Fold in opposite sides; roll up from bottom.

Nutrition Facts per serving: 205 cal., 3 g total fat (2 g sat. fat), 7 mg chol., 471 mg sodium, 34 g carbo., 6 g fiber, 8 g pro. **Daily Values:** 10% vit. A, 14% vit. C, 12% calcium, 13% iron

*See note, page 52.

Fix this mélange of vegetables and barley in late summer when zucchini and tomatoes are at their best. A slow cooker prepares the meal without heating up the kitchen— a major plus during the dog days of summer.

VEGETABLE MEDLEY WITH BARLEY

1	15-ounce can black beans, rinsed and drained
1	14-ounce can vegetable or chicken broth
1	10-ounce package frozen whole kernel corn
1	large onion, chopped
1	medium green sweet pepper, chopped
1	medium carrot, thinly sliced
½	cup regular barley
2	tablespoons snipped fresh parsley
1	teaspoon dried basil or oregano, crushed
½	teaspoon salt
¼	teaspoon black pepper
2	cloves garlic, minced
2	medium tomatoes, coarsely chopped
1	medium zucchini, halved lengthwise and thinly sliced (1¼ cups)
1	tablespoon lemon juice

PREP:
20 minutes

COOK:
7 to 8 hours (low) or 3½ to 4 hours (high), plus 30 minutes (high)

MAKES:
4 servings

1 In a 3½- to 5-quart slow cooker combine black beans, vegetable broth, frozen corn, onion, sweet pepper, carrot, barley, parsley, basil, salt, black pepper, and garlic.

2 Cover and cook on low-heat setting for 7 to 8 hours or on high-heat setting for 3½ to 4 hours.

3 If using low-heat setting, turn to high-heat setting. Stir in tomatoes, zucchini, and lemon juice. Cover and cook about 30 minutes more or until zucchini is crisp-tender.

Nutrition Facts per serving: 278 cal., 2 g total fat (0 g sat. fat), 0 mg chol., 1,001 mg sodium, 62 g carbo., 13 g fiber, 14 g pro. **Daily Values:** 48% vit. A, 80% vit. C, 8% calcium, 17% iron

Who could miss the meat when such a thick, rich mixture tops the pasta?

PESTO BEANS & PASTA

PREP:

20 minutes

COOK:

7 to 9 hours (low)
or 3¹/₂ to 4¹/₂ hours (high)

MAKES:

6 to 8 servings

2   19-ounce cans white kidney (cannellini) beans, rinsed and drained

1   14¹/₂-ounce can Italian-style stewed tomatoes, undrained

1   medium green sweet pepper, chopped

1   medium red sweet pepper, chopped

1   medium onion, cut into thin wedges

2   teaspoons dried Italian seasoning, crushed

¹/₂   teaspoon cracked black pepper

4   cloves garlic, minced

¹/₂   cup vegetable broth

¹/₂   cup dry white wine or vegetable broth

1   7-ounce container basil pesto

12   ounces dried penne pasta

¹/₂   cup finely shredded Parmesan or Romano cheese

1 In a 3¹/₂- or 4-quart slow cooker combine kidney beans, tomatoes, sweet peppers, onion, Italian seasoning, black pepper, and garlic. Pour vegetable broth and wine over mixture in cooker.

2 Cover and cook on low-heat setting for 7 to 9 hours or on high-heat setting for 3¹/₂ to 4¹/₂ hours. Using a slotted spoon, transfer bean mixture to a very large serving bowl, reserving cooking liquid. Stir basil pesto into bean mixture.

3 Meanwhile, cook pasta according to package directions; drain. Add pasta to bean mixture; toss gently to combine, adding enough of the liquid to make mixture of desired consistency. Sprinkle each serving with Parmesan cheese.

Nutrition Facts per serving: 580 cal., 20 g total fat (2 g sat. fat), 10 mg chol., 843 mg sodium, 80 g carbo., 11 g fiber, 25 g pro. **Daily Values:** 25% vit. A, 82% vit. C, 21% calcium, 25% iron

Got fiber? This flavorful dish comes with 14 healthful grams per serving.

FRUITED COUSCOUS & BEANS

2   15-ounce cans Great Northern or pinto beans,
    rinsed and drained

1   large onion, finely chopped

1   cup golden raisins

1   cup mixed dried fruit bits

2   teaspoons grated fresh ginger

¾   teaspoon salt

¼   teaspoon crushed red pepper

1   14-ounce can vegetable or chicken broth

1¾ cups unsweetened pineapple juice

1   10-ounce package quick-cooking couscous

1   tablespoon olive oil

½   cup sliced almonds, toasted

    Sliced green onions (optional)

PREP:

20 minutes

COOK:

*6 to 7 hours (low)
or 3 to 3½ hours (high)*

STAND:

5 minutes

MAKES:

6 servings

1 In a 3½- or 4-quart slow cooker combine Great Northern beans, onion, raisins, dried fruit bits, ginger, salt, and crushed red pepper. Pour vegetable broth and pineapple juice over mixture in cooker.

2 Cover and cook on low-heat setting for 6 to 7 hours or on high-heat setting for 3 to 3½ hours. Turn off cooker.

3 Stir in couscous and oil. Cover and let stand for 5 to 10 minutes or until couscous is tender. Fluff with a fork. Sprinkle each serving with toasted almonds and, if desired, green onions.

Nutrition Facts per serving: 623 cal., 9 g total fat (1 g sat. fat), 0 mg chol., 596 mg sodium, 120 g carbo., 14 g fiber, 22 g pro. Daily Values: 37% vit. C, 16% calcium, 25% iron

Typically a ragout is a stew of meat and vegetables that's thick, rich, and well-seasoned. This ragout mixes together earthy mushrooms, crunchy fennel, and beans to produce a meatless dish that's 100-percent deserving of its name.

MUSHROOM & FENNEL RAGOUT

PREP:

20 minutes

COOK:

*8 to 9 hours (low)
or 4 to 4½ hours (high)*

MAKES:

4 servings

8 ounces fresh mushrooms, quartered

8 roma tomatoes, coarsely chopped

1 19-ounce can fava beans, rinsed and drained

1 large fennel bulb, trimmed and coarsely chopped

¼ cup vegetable broth

1 tablespoon quick-cooking tapioca

1 teaspoon dried Italian seasoning, crushed

½ teaspoon salt

¼ teaspoon black pepper

6 ounces dried penne pasta

2 tablespoons pine nuts, toasted

① In a 3½- or 4-quart slow cooker combine mushrooms, roma tomatoes, fava beans, fennel, broth, tapioca, Italian seasoning, salt, and pepper.

② Cover and cook on low-heat setting for 8 to 9 hours or on high-heat setting for 4 to 4½ hours.

③ Meanwhile, cook pasta according to package directions; drain. Add pasta to bean mixture; toss gently to combine. Sprinkle each serving with toasted pine nuts.

Nutrition Facts per serving: 347 cal., 5 g total fat (1 g sat. fat), 0 mg chol., 811 mg sodium, 62 g carbo., 25 g fiber, 18 g pro. **Daily Values:** 20% vit. A, 66% vit. C, 9% calcium, 16% iron

Eggplant's spongy texture soaks up the flavors of any foods it's cooked with. Here eggplant chunks cook in a traditional spaghetti sauce made thick with olives and mushrooms.

PASTA WITH EGGPLANT SAUCE

1	medium eggplant
1	28-ounce can whole Italian-style tomatoes, cut up
1	6-ounce can Italian-style tomato paste
1	4½-ounce jar sliced mushrooms, drained
1	medium onion, chopped
¼	cup dry red wine or water
¼	cup water
1½	teaspoons dried oregano, crushed
2	cloves garlic, minced
½	cup pitted kalamata or ripe olives, sliced
2	tablespoons snipped fresh parsley
4	cups hot cooked penne pasta
⅓	cup grated or finely shredded Parmesan cheese
2	tablespoons pine nuts, toasted (optional)

PREP:

20 minutes

COOK:

*7 to 8 hours (low)
or 3½ to 4 hours (high)*

MAKES:

6 servings

1 If desired, peel eggplant. Cut eggplant into 1-inch cubes. In a 3½- to 5½-quart slow cooker combine eggplant, tomatoes, tomato paste, mushrooms, onion, wine, water, oregano, and garlic.

2 Cover and cook on low-heat setting for 7 to 8 hours or on high-heat setting for 3½ to 4 hours. Stir in olives and parsley. Season to taste with salt and black pepper.

3 Serve eggplant mixture over hot cooked pasta. Sprinkle each serving with Parmesan cheese and, if desired, toasted pine nuts.

Nutrition Facts per serving: 259 cal., 6 g total fat (1 g sat. fat), 4 mg chol., 804 mg sodium, 42 g carbo., 7 g fiber, 10 g pro. **Daily Values:** 18% vit. A, 37% vit. C, 13% calcium, 20% iron

This elegant dish is sure to impress company. Round out the menu with asparagus or sugar snap peas, a tossed salad, and French bread.

RAVIOLI WITH MUSHROOM-WINE SAUCE

PREP:

20 minutes

COOK:

*4 to 6 hours (low) or
2 to 3 hours (high),
plus 20 minutes (high)*

MAKES:

4 servings

4   cups sliced fresh button mushrooms

4   cups sliced fresh portobello, shiitake, and/or crimini mushrooms

2   14½-ounce cans diced tomatoes, undrained

½   cup water

⅓   cup dry red wine or water

½   teaspoon salt

¼   teaspoon dried rosemary, crushed

¼   teaspoon crushed red pepper

4   cloves garlic, minced

1   9-ounce package refrigerated cheese-filled ravioli

   Finely shredded Parmesan cheese

1 In a 4- to 5-quart slow cooker combine mushrooms, tomatoes, water, wine, salt, rosemary, crushed red pepper, and garlic.

2 Cover and cook on low-heat setting for 4 to 6 hours or on high-heat setting for 2 to 3 hours.

3 If using low-heat setting, turn to high-heat setting. Stir in ravioli. Cover and cook about 20 minutes more or until pasta is tender. Sprinkle each serving with Parmesan cheese.

Nutrition Facts per serving: 360 cal., 7 g total fat (3 g sat. fat), 32 mg chol., 1,068 mg sodium, 62 g carbo., 9 g fiber, 18 g pro. **Daily Values:** 2% vit. A, 27% vit. C, 18% calcium, 16% iron

For variety, purchase polenta with wild mushrooms or Italian-flavored polenta. Look for tubes of polenta in the produce section of your supermarket.

SWEET BEANS & LENTILS OVER POLENTA

1	14-ounce can vegetable broth
1	12-ounce package frozen green soybeans
1	cup brown lentils, rinsed and drained
1	medium red sweet pepper, chopped
½	cup water
1	teaspoon dried oregano, crushed
½	teaspoon salt
2	cloves garlic, minced
2	medium tomatoes, chopped
1	16-ounce tube refrigerated cooked polenta

1 In a 3½- or 4-quart slow cooker combine vegetable broth, soybeans, lentils, sweet pepper, water, oregano, salt, and garlic.

2 Cover and cook on low-heat setting for 7 to 8 hours or on high-heat setting for 3½ to 4 hours. Stir in tomatoes.

3 Meanwhile, prepare polenta according to package directions. Serve lentil mixture over polenta.

Nutrition Facts per serving: 280 cal., 5 g total fat (1 g sat. fat), 0 mg chol., 794 mg sodium, 43 g carbo., 15 g fiber, 19 g pro. **Daily Values:** 30% vit. A, 85% vit. C, 12% calcium, 26% iron

PREP:

20 minutes

COOK:

7 to 8 hours (low) or 3½ to 4 hours (high)

MAKES:

6 servings

BROTH OPTIONS

Canned broths and bouillon granules and cubes are handy alternatives to homemade chicken, beef, or vegetable broth. Canned chicken, beef, and vegetable broth are ready to use. Instant bouillon granules and cubes come in beef, chicken, vegetable, and onion flavors. Mixing 1 cube or 1 teaspoon of granules with 1 cup of boiling water is an easy way to make broth. If you're watching your sodium intake, use a lower-sodium broth and adjust the seasoning in the recipe to taste.

When you need a change, serve the vegetable mixture on tostada shells with shredded lettuce, chopped tomato, and shredded cheese for a taco-style salad.

SLOPPY VEGGIE SANDWICHES

PREP:

20 minutes

COOK:

3 to 3¹/₂ hours (high), plus 30 minutes (high)

MAKES:

8 sandwiches

1	cup chopped carrots
1	cup chopped celery
²/₃	cup brown lentils, rinsed and drained
²/₃	cup uncooked regular brown rice
¹/₂	cup chopped onion
2	tablespoons brown sugar
2	tablespoons prepared mustard
¹/₂	teaspoon salt
¹/₈	to ¹/₄ teaspoon cayenne pepper
1	clove garlic, minced
2	14-ounce cans vegetable or chicken broth
1	15-ounce can tomato sauce
2	tablespoons apple cider vinegar
8	whole wheat hamburger buns or French-style rolls, split and toasted

1 In a 3¹/₂- or 4-quart slow cooker combine carrots, celery, lentils, brown rice, onion, brown sugar, mustard, salt, cayenne pepper, and garlic. Stir in vegetable broth.

2 Cover and cook on high-heat setting for 3 to 3¹/₂ hours. Stir in tomato sauce and vinegar. Cover and cook for 30 minutes more.

3 Serve lentil mixture on toasted buns.

Nutrition Facts per serving: 261 cal., 4 g total fat (1 g sat. fat), 0 mg chol., 1,036 mg sodium, 50 g carbo., 8 g fiber, 11 g pro. **Daily Values:** 78% vit. A, 5% vit. C, 7% calcium, 21% iron

If you love taco salad, you'll welcome this easy version loaded with vegetables and plenty of zing.

LENTIL TACO SALAD

2	cups coarsely chopped red and/or green sweet peppers
1	cup brown lentils, rinsed and drained
1	cup chopped onion
½	cup uncooked regular brown rice
2	teaspoons chili powder
¼	teaspoon salt
3	cloves garlic, minced
2	14-ounce cans vegetable broth
1	medium yellow summer squash, quartered lengthwise and sliced ½ inch thick (1½ cups)
8	cups tortilla chips, broken
2	cups shredded lettuce
2	cups chopped tomatoes
½	cup dairy sour cream

PREP:

25 minutes

COOK:

*10 to 12 hours (low) or
5 to 6 hours (high),
plus 15 minutes (high)*

MAKES:

8 servings

1 In a 3½-quart slow cooker combine sweet peppers, lentils, onion, brown rice, chili powder, salt, and garlic. Pour vegetable broth over mixture in cooker.

2 Cover and cook on low-heat setting for 10 to 12 hours or on high-heat setting for 5 to 6 hours.

3 If using low-heat setting, turn to high-heat setting. Stir in squash. Cover and cook about 15 minutes more or until squash is crisp-tender.

4 Serve lentil mixture over tortilla chips. Top with lettuce, tomatoes, and sour cream.

Nutrition Facts per serving: 324 cal., 11 g total fat (3 g sat. fat), 5 mg chol., 669 mg sodium, 49 g carbo., 12 g fiber, 12 g pro. Daily Values: 163% vit. A, 130% vit. C, 9% calcium, 18% iron

For a perky complement to this hearty pilaf, try Asian Pea Pod Salad (page 339).

LENTIL & BULGUR PILAF WITH FETA

PREP:

15 minutes

COOK:

3 hours (high)

STAND:

10 minutes

MAKES:

6 servings

2	14-ounce cans vegetable or chicken broth
4	medium carrots, sliced
2	cups frozen whole kernel corn
1	cup bulgur
½	cup brown lentils, rinsed and drained
1	teaspoon dried oregano, crushed
1	teaspoon ground cumin
¼	teaspoon ground coriander
¼	teaspoon black pepper
4	cloves garlic, minced
2	cups chopped tomatoes
¾	cup crumbled feta cheese (3 ounces)

1 In a 3½- or 4-quart slow cooker combine vegetable broth, carrots, frozen corn, bulgur, lentils, oregano, cumin, coriander, pepper, and garlic. Cover and cook on high-heat setting for 3 hours.

2 Stir in tomatoes. Turn off cooker. Cover and let stand for 10 minutes. Sprinkle each serving with feta cheese.

Nutrition Facts per serving: 272 cal., 6 g total fat (3 g sat. fat), 16 mg chol., 822 mg sodium, 47 g carbo., 12 g fiber, 14 g pro. **Daily Values:** 218% vit. A, 28% vit. C, 13% calcium, 15% iron

Brightly colored vegetables plus a bright blend of seasonings and luscious coconut milk combine to make a meatless dinner that's anything but dull.

CURRIED VEGETABLE RICE

3 cups coarsely chopped red-skinned potatoes

2 cups peeled and coarsely chopped sweet potatoes

1 cup coarsely chopped carrots

½ cup chopped onion

2 teaspoons grated fresh ginger

1 teaspoon salt

1 teaspoon curry powder

½ teaspoon ground cumin

2 cloves garlic, minced

1 14-ounce can vegetable broth

1 13½-ounce can unsweetened coconut milk

1½ cups uncooked instant rice

1 cup frozen peas

½ cup dry roasted cashews

PREP:
25 minutes
COOK:
7 to 8 hours (low) or 3½ to 4 hours (high), plus 5 minutes
MAKES:
6 servings

1 In a 3½- or 4-quart slow cooker combine potatoes, sweet potatoes, carrots, onion, ginger, salt, curry powder, cumin, and garlic. Pour vegetable broth and coconut milk over mixture in cooker.

2 Cover and cook on low-heat setting for 7 to 8 hours or on high-heat setting for 3½ to 4 hours.

3 Stir in rice and frozen peas. Cover and cook for 5 minutes more. Sprinkle each serving with cashews.

Nutrition Facts per serving: 522 cal., 21 g total fat (15 g sat. fat), 0 mg chol., 805 mg sodium, 75 g carbo., 7 g fiber, 11 g pro. Daily Values: 267% vit. A, 42% vit. C, 6% calcium, 30% iron

Wild rice mix is a super-tasty ingredient, but precooking it for casseroles can be a time-consuming hassle. That's not a problem here—it cooks with everything else in your crockery cooker.

WILD RICE WITH PINTO BEANS

PREP:

15 minutes

COOK:

*7 to 8 hours (low)
or 3$\frac{1}{2}$ to 4 hours (high)*

MAKES:

6 servings

2   15-ounce cans pinto beans, rinsed and drained

1   14$\frac{1}{2}$-ounce can diced tomatoes with onion and garlic, undrained

1   6-ounce package long grain and wild rice mix

1   medium onion, chopped

1   stalk celery, sliced

$\frac{1}{4}$ teaspoon black pepper

2   14-ounce cans vegetable broth

1 In a 3$\frac{1}{2}$- or 4-quart slow cooker combine pinto beans, tomatoes, rice mix (including seasoning packet), onion, celery, and pepper. Pour vegetable broth over mixture in cooker.

2 Cover and cook on low-heat setting for 7 to 8 hours or on high-heat setting for 3$\frac{1}{2}$ to 4 hours.

Nutrition Facts per serving: 245 cal., 2 g total fat (0 g sat. fat), 0 mg chol., 1,683 mg sodium, 51 g carbo., 8 g fiber, 11 g pro. **Daily Values:** 2% vit. A, 14% vit. C, 9% calcium, 20% iron

BEANS ON CALL

Canned beans are rich in fiber and protein and easy to use, but they also contain a hefty dose of sodium. Home-cooked dried beans offer all the nutrients of canned without the large dose of sodium, and they are available in many more varieties. When you have time, cook dried beans and freeze them in 2-cup portions. Whenever a recipe calls for a 15-ounce can of beans, thaw a container of cooked beans to use instead.

Three kinds of grains make up this wholesome, filling, and infinitely interesting dish. Round out the meal with a selection from the "Swift Sides for Slow Cooked Suppers" chapter, such as Cranberry Coleslaw (page 340).

MULTIGRAIN PILAF

⅔ cup wheat berries

½ cup regular barley

½ cup uncooked wild rice

2 14-ounce cans vegetable or chicken broth

2 cups frozen green soybeans or baby lima beans

1 medium red sweet pepper, chopped

1 medium onion, finely chopped

1 tablespoon butter or margarine

¾ teaspoon dried sage, crushed

½ teaspoon salt

¼ teaspoon coarsely ground black pepper

4 cloves garlic, minced

Grated Parmesan cheese (optional)

PREP:

25 minutes

COOK:

6 to 8 hours (low)
or 3 to 4 hours (high)

MAKES:

6 servings

1 Rinse and drain wheat berries, barley, and wild rice. In a 3½- or 4-quart slow cooker combine wheat berries, barley, wild rice, vegetable broth, soybeans, sweet pepper, onion, butter, sage, salt, black pepper, and garlic.

2 Cover and cook on low-heat setting for 6 to 8 hours or on high-heat setting for 3 to 4 hours. Stir before serving. If desired, sprinkle each serving with Parmesan cheese.

Nutrition Facts per serving: 342 cal., 9 g total fat (2 g sat. fat), 5 mg chol., 814 mg sodium, 50 g carbo., 10 g fiber, 20 g pro. Daily Values: 28% vit. A, 83% vit. C, 17% calcium, 24% iron

If you have an oval 3½- or 4-quart slow cooker, you can use it for this particular recipe.

HOMINY & BLACK BEAN STUFFED PEPPERS

PREP:

15 minutes

COOK:

6 to 6½ hours (low)
or 3 to 3½ hours (high)

MAKES:

4 servings

2   cups bottled thick and chunky salsa

½   of a 6-ounce can (⅓ cup) tomato paste

½   teaspoon ground cumin

4   medium green and/or yellow sweet peppers

1   15-ounce can black beans, rinsed and drained

1   15-ounce can golden hominy, drained

1   cup shredded cheddar cheese (4 ounces)

1 In a medium bowl stir together salsa, tomato paste, and cumin. Set aside. Remove tops, seeds, and membranes from sweet peppers. In a medium bowl stir together ¾ cup of the salsa mixture, the black beans, hominy, and ½ cup of the cheese. Spoon into pepper shells.

2 In a 5- to 6-quart slow cooker place remaining salsa mixture. Place peppers, filled sides up, in cooker. Cover and cook on low-heat setting for 6 to 6½ hours or on high-heat setting for 3 to 3½ hours.

3 Transfer sweet peppers to dinner plates. Spoon salsa mixture over peppers and sprinkle with remaining ½ cup cheese.

Nutrition Facts per serving: 349 cal., 11 g total fat (6 g sat. fat), 30 mg chol., 1,752 mg sodium, 50 g carbo., 11 g fiber, 17 g pro. **Daily Values:** 41% vit. A, 166% vit. C, 27% calcium, 16% iron

This classic sauce also fares well over baked potatoes. Use the delayed-start feature on your oven to bake the potatoes while you're out of the house. Everything will be ready to put on the table when you walk through the door.

MARINARA SAUCE

1	28-ounce can whole Italian-style tomatoes, undrained and cut up
2	cups coarsely chopped carrots
1½	cups sliced celery
1	cup chopped onion
1	cup chopped green sweet pepper
1	6-ounce can tomato paste
½	cup water
2	teaspoons sugar
2	teaspoons dried Italian seasoning, crushed
1	bay leaf
1	teaspoon salt
¼	teaspoon black pepper
3	cloves garlic, minced
12	ounces dried pasta, cooked and drained
	Grated Romano cheese (optional)

1 In a 3½- or 4-quart slow cooker combine tomatoes, carrots, celery, onion, sweet pepper, tomato paste, water, sugar, Italian seasoning, bay leaf, salt, black pepper, and garlic.

2 Cover and cook on low-heat setting for 8 to 10 hours or on high-heat setting for 4 to 5 hours. Remove bay leaf.

3 Serve tomato mixture over hot cooked pasta. If desired, sprinkle each serving with Romano cheese.

Nutrition Facts per serving: 308 cal., 1 g total fat (0 g sat. fat), 0 mg chol., 636 mg sodium, 64 g carbo., 6 g fiber, 11 g pro. **Daily Values:** 224% vit. A, 82% vit. C, 9% calcium, 20% iron

PREP:

20 minutes

COOK:

8 to 10 hours (low) or 4 to 5 hours (high)

MAKES:

6 servings

Corn pudding—a favorite holiday side dish—rises to main-dish status when you enrich it with cream cheese. A crisp side salad and fresh bakery bread round out the meal.

SOUTHERN CORN PUDDING

PREP:

20 minutes

COOK:

2¹⁄₂ to 3 hours (high)

COOL:

15 minutes

MAKES:

6 to 8 servings

Nonstick cooking spray

1 8-ounce package cream cheese, softened

2 eggs

2¹⁄₂ cups frozen whole kernel corn

1 14³⁄₄-ounce can cream-style corn

¹⁄₃ cup finely chopped onion

1 teaspoon dried thyme, crushed

1 8¹⁄₂-ounce package corn muffin mix

1 cup evaporated milk

2 tablespoons butter or margarine, melted

1 cup chopped tomatoes

1 Lightly coat a 3¹⁄₂- or 4-quart slow cooker with cooking spray; set aside.

2 In a large mixing bowl beat cream cheese with an electric mixer on medium to high speed for 30 seconds. Add eggs; beat until nearly smooth. Stir in frozen corn, cream-style corn, onion, and thyme. Add muffin mix, milk, and butter; stir just until combined. Spoon into prepared cooker.

3 Cover and cook on high-heat setting for 2¹⁄₂ to 3 hours. Remove liner from cooker, if possible, or turn off cooker. Let stand, uncovered, for 15 minutes to cool slightly before serving. Sprinkle with tomatoes.

Nutrition Facts per serving: 532 cal., 27 g total fat (13 g sat. fat), 136 mg chol., 702 mg sodium, 63 g carbo., 3 g fiber, 14 g pro. **Daily Values:** 26% vit. A, 24% vit. C, 16% calcium, 13% iron

Spicy hot tomato juice lends its spunk to this meatless chili. For even more heat, use 2 teaspoons of chili powder. Set out bowls of sour cream and chopped green onion to add the finishing touch to this hearty chili.

VEGETABLE CHILI

2	15-ounce cans red kidney beans, rinsed and drained
3	cups hot-style tomato juice or vegetable juice
1	15¼-ounce can whole kernel corn, drained
1	14½-ounce can chunky chili-style tomatoes or Mexican-style stewed tomatoes, undrained
1	cup chopped onion
1	cup chopped green sweet pepper
1	cup chopped celery
1	to 2 teaspoons chili powder
¼	teaspoon salt
¼	teaspoon black pepper
1	clove garlic, minced

PREP:

15 minutes

COOK:

9 to 10 hours (low) or 4½ to 5 hours (high)

MAKES:

6 servings

1 In a 4- or 4½-quart slow cooker combine kidney beans, tomato juice, corn, tomatoes, onion, sweet pepper, celery, chili powder, salt, black pepper, and garlic.

2 Cover and cook on low-heat setting for 9 to 10 hours or on high-heat setting for 4½ to 5 hours.

Nutrition Facts per serving: 229 cal., 1 g total fat (0 g sat. fat), 0 mg chol., 1,271 mg sodium, 51 g carbo., 12 g fiber, 14 g pro. **Daily Values:** 22% vit. A, 92% vit. C, 8% calcium, 19% iron

Be sure to use converted rice for this dish. Long-grain and quick cooking rices lose their shape when cooked in soup for lengthy times.

SAVORY BEAN & SPINACH SOUP

PREP:

15 minutes

COOK:

*5 to 7 hours (low)
or 2$\frac{1}{2}$ to 3$\frac{1}{2}$ hours (high)*

MAKES:

6 servings

3	14-ounce cans vegetable broth
1	15-ounce can tomato puree
1	15-ounce can small white or Great Northern beans, rinsed and drained
$\frac{1}{2}$	cup uncooked converted rice
$\frac{1}{2}$	cup finely chopped onion
1	teaspoon dried basil, crushed
$\frac{1}{4}$	teaspoon salt
$\frac{1}{4}$	teaspoon black pepper
2	cloves garlic, minced
8	cups coarsely chopped fresh spinach or kale leaves
	Finely shredded Parmesan cheese

1 In a 3$\frac{1}{2}$- or 4-quart slow cooker combine vegetable broth, tomato puree, white beans, rice, onion, basil, salt, pepper, and garlic.

2 Cover and cook on low-heat setting for 5 to 7 hours or on high-heat setting for 2$\frac{1}{2}$ to 3$\frac{1}{2}$ hours.

3 Just before serving, stir in spinach. Sprinkle each serving with Parmesan cheese.

Nutrition Facts per serving: 150 cal., 3 g total fat (1 g sat. fat), 4 mg chol., 1,137 mg sodium, 31 g carbo., 8 g fiber, 9 g pro. **Daily Values:** 46% vit. A, 35% vit. C, 11% calcium, 27% iron

For a more substantial comfort meal, serve grilled cheese sandwiches and glasses of cold milk with this home-style soup.

VEGETABLE-BARLEY SOUP

3½	cups water
1	14½-ounce can diced tomatoes, undrained
1½	cups sliced zucchini
1	10-ounce package frozen mixed vegetables
1	8-ounce can tomato sauce
1	cup chopped celery
½	cup regular barley
½	cup chopped onion
2	large vegetable bouillon cubes (each cube makes 2 cups broth)
1½	teaspoons dried Italian seasoning, crushed

PREP:

15 minutes

COOK:

8 to 10 hours (low) or 4 to 5 hours (high)

MAKES:

3 servings

1 In a 3½- or 4-quart slow cooker combine water, tomatoes, zucchini, frozen mixed vegetables, tomato sauce, celery, barley, onion, bouillon cubes, and Italian seasoning.

2 Cover and cook on low-heat setting for 8 to 10 hours or on high-heat setting for 4 to 5 hours.

Nutrition Facts per serving: 254 cal., 2 g total fat (0 g sat. fat), 0 mg chol., 1,430 mg sodium, 54 g carbo., 12 g fiber, 10 g pro. **Daily Values:** 110% vit. A, 74% vit. C, 12% calcium, 22% iron

This vegetable soup holds its own. A mix of garbanzo beans and potatoes sport enough heft to stand in for a full meal.

CREAM OF VEGETABLE SOUP

PREP:

20 minutes

COOK:

*7 to 9 hours (low)
or 3¹/₂ to 4¹/₂ hours (high),
plus 15 minutes (high)*

MAKES:

6 to 8 servings

1	16-ounce package frozen small whole onions
2	cups cubed potatoes
2	cups sliced carrots
1	15-ounce can garbanzo beans (chickpeas) or navy beans, rinsed and drained
1	10-ounce package frozen whole kernel corn
1	cup sliced celery
¹/₂	teaspoon salt
¹/₂	teaspoon paprika
¹/₂	teaspoon black pepper
2	14-ounce cans vegetable or chicken broth
1¹/₂	cups half-and-half or light cream
¹/₄	cup all-purpose flour

1 In a 4¹/₂- to 5¹/₂-quart slow cooker combine onions, potatoes, carrots, garbanzo beans, frozen corn, celery, salt, paprika, and pepper. Pour vegetable broth over mixture in cooker.

2 Cover and cook on low-heat setting for 7 to 9 hours or on high-heat setting for 3¹/₂ to 4¹/₂ hours. If using low-heat setting, turn to high-heat setting.

3 In a medium bowl stir half-and-half into flour. Stir into mixture in cooker. Cover and cook for 15 minutes more. Season to taste with salt and black pepper.

Nutrition Facts per serving: 282 cal., 9 g total fat (4 g sat. fat), 22 mg chol., 1,079 mg sodium, 48 g carbo., 8 g fiber, 9 g pro. **Daily Values:** 211% vit. A, 30% vit. C, 19% calcium, 13% iron

PERFECT FOR POTLUCKS

BONUS CHAPTER

Simple Slow Cooker Recipes

BONUS CHAPTER

What's the secret to the zip in these zippy meatballs? Italian sausage, Italian salad dressing, green chile peppers, and chili sauce all play a part.

ZIPPY ITALIAN MINI MEATBALLS

PREP:

30 minutes

BAKE:

20 minutes

COOK:

3 to 4 hours (low)
or 1 1/2 to 2 hours (high)

OVEN:

350°F

MAKES:

48 appetizers

1   slightly beaten egg

1/3   cup fine dry bread crumbs

1   0.7-ounce envelope Italian dry salad dressing mix

1/2   teaspoon crushed red pepper

2   cloves garlic, minced

1   pound lean ground beef

8   ounces bulk Italian sausage

1/4   cup canned crushed pineapple, well drained

1/4   cup canned diced green chile peppers, well drained

1/4   cup shredded mozzarella cheese (1 ounce)

1/2   cup bottled Italian salad dressing

1/2   cup pineapple or plum preserves

1/2   cup bottled chili sauce

1 For meatballs, in a large bowl combine egg, bread crumbs, dry salad dressing mix, crushed red pepper, and garlic. Add ground beef, Italian sausage, pineapple, green chile peppers, and mozzarella cheese; mix well. Shape into 48 meatballs.

2 In a 15×10×1-inch baking pan arrange meatballs in a single layer. Bake, uncovered, in a 350° oven for 20 minutes. Drain well. Transfer meatballs to a 3 1/2- or 4-quart slow cooker.

SHAPING MEATBALLS
Here's an easy way to make uniformly shaped meatballs. Pat the meat mixture into an 8×6-inch rectangle on a piece of waxed paper. Cut the meat into 1-inch cubes, then use your hands to roll each cube into a ball.

3 For sauce, in a medium bowl combine bottled salad dressing, pineapple preserves, and chili sauce. Pour over meatballs in cooker. Cover and cook on low-heat setting for 3 to 4 hours or on high-heat setting for 1 1/2 to 2 hours.

4 Stir gently before serving. Serve meatballs with wooden toothpicks.

Nutrition Facts per serving: 62 cal., 4 g total fat (1 g sat. fat), 14 mg chol., 165 mg sodium, 4 g carbo., 0 g fiber, 3 g pro. **Daily Values:** 1% vit. A, 2% vit. C, 1% calcium, 2% iron

Bowl game parties (and the like) are all about big food, and this big, bold dish definitely fits the bill!

VEGETABLE CHILI CON QUESO

1	15-ounce can pinto beans, rinsed and drained
1	15-ounce can black beans, rinsed and drained
1	15-ounce can chili beans with chili gravy
1	10-ounce can chopped tomatoes and green chile peppers, undrained
1	medium zucchini, chopped
1	medium yellow summer squash, chopped
1	large onion, chopped
¼	cup tomato paste
2	to 3 teaspoons chili powder
4	cloves garlic, minced
3	cups shredded Colby Jack cheese (12 ounces)
	Tortilla or corn chips

PREP:

20 minutes

COOK:

*6 to 7 hours (low)
or 3 to 3 1/2 hours (high)*

MAKES:

32 (1/4-cup) servings

1 In a 3 1/2- or 4-quart slow cooker combine pinto beans, black beans, chili beans, tomatoes, zucchini, yellow squash, onion, tomato paste, chili powder, and garlic.

2 Cover and cook on low-heat setting for 6 to 7 hours or on high-heat setting for 3 to 3 1/2 hours. Stir in Colby Jack cheese until melted. Serve immediately or keep warm on low-heat setting for up to 1 hour. Serve dip with chips.

Nutrition Facts per serving: 81 cal., 4 g total fat (2 g sat. fat), 9 mg chol., 231 mg sodium, 8 g carbo., 2 g fiber, 5 g pro. **Daily Values:** 6% vit. A, 5% vit. C, 10% calcium, 3% iron

BONUS CHAPTER
Simple
Slow Cooker
Recipes
BONUS CHAPTER

This is the kind of dip your friends will long remember and often request.

SPICY CHICKEN-BEAN DIP

PREP:

15 minutes

COOK:

2¹/₂ to 3 hours (low)

MAKES:

26 (¹/₄-cup) servings

2	8-ounce tubs cream cheese with chive and onion
1	10-ounce can chopped tomatoes and green chile peppers, undrained
¹/₄	cup milk
1	teaspoon ground cumin
¹/₂	teaspoon fajita seasoning
2	cups finely chopped cooked chicken
2	cups shredded American cheese (8 ounces)
2	cups shredded Monterey Jack cheese (8 ounces)
1	15-ounce can white kidney (cannellini) or small white beans, rinsed and drained
2	tablespoons snipped fresh cilantro
	Pita wedges, toasted, and/or tortilla chips

1 In a 3¹/₂- or 4-quart slow cooker combine cream cheese, tomatoes, milk, cumin, and fajita seasoning. Stir in chicken, American cheese, Monterey Jack cheese, and kidney beans.

2 Cover and cook on low-heat setting for 2¹/₂ to 3 hours. Serve immediately or keep warm on low-heat setting for up to 2 hours.

3 Just before serving, stir in cilantro. Serve dip with toasted pita wedges and/or chips.

Nutrition Facts per serving: 153 cal., 11 g total fat (7 g sat. fat), 39 mg chol., 323 mg sodium, 5 g carbo., 1 g fiber, 8 g pro. **Daily Values:** 9% vit. A, 2% vit. C, 15% calcium, 2% iron

Here's a sandwich that's perfect for tailgate picnics and other chilly-weather get-togethers.
Tote the spicy filling to the game right in the slow cooker and assemble the sandwiches on the spot.

SOUTHWESTERN SHREDDED BEEF SANDWICHES

1	tablespoon ground cumin
1	tablespoon chili powder
1/4	teaspoon salt
1/8	teaspoon black pepper
1	3- to 3 1/2-pound boneless beef chuck roast
1	14 1/2-ounce can stewed tomatoes, undrained
1	cup coarsely chopped onion
2	4-ounce cans diced green chile peppers, undrained
2	tablespoons chopped pickled jalapeño chile peppers (optional)
1/4	cup snipped fresh cilantro
2	cups shredded cheddar or Monterey Jack cheese (8 ounces)
16	onion buns or kaiser rolls, split and toasted
	Lettuce leaves

PREP:

25 minutes

COOK:

10 to 12 hours (low)
or 5 to 6 hours (high)

MAKES:

16 sandwiches

1 In a small bowl combine cumin, chili powder, salt, and black pepper. Trim fat from meat. Sprinkle cumin mixture evenly over meat; rub in with your fingers. If necessary, cut meat to fit into a 4- or 4 1/2-quart slow cooker. Place meat in cooker. Add tomatoes, onion, green chile peppers, and, if desired, jalapeño peppers.

2 Cover and cook on low-heat setting for 10 to 12 hours or on high-heat setting for 5 to 6 hours. Remove meat from cooker, reserving juices. Using two forks, pull meat apart into shreds. Return meat to cooker; heat through. Stir in cilantro.

3 To serve, sprinkle cheddar cheese on bottoms of buns. Using a slotted spoon, spoon about 1/2 cup of the meat mixture on each bun bottom. Add lettuce; replace tops of buns.

Nutrition Facts per serving: 359 cal., 12 g total fat (5 g sat. fat), 69 mg chol., 573 mg sodium, 34 g carbo., 2 g fiber, 28 g pro. **Daily Values:** 12% vit. A, 14% vit. C, 19% calcium, 25% iron

Put together three of the all-time favorite Italian convenience products—spaghetti sauce, frozen ravioli, and frozen Italian meatballs—and you have a super-speedy dish that promises to please.

SAUCY RAVIOLI WITH MEATBALLS

PREP:

20 minutes

COOK:

4$\frac{1}{2}$ to 5 hours (low) or 2$\frac{1}{2}$ to 3 hours (high)

STAND:

15 minutes

MAKES:

10 to 12 servings

Nonstick cooking spray

2 26-ounce jars spaghetti sauce with mushrooms and onions

2 24-ounce packages frozen ravioli

1 12-ounce package frozen cooked Italian meatballs, thawed

2 cups shredded mozzarella cheese (8 ounces)

$\frac{1}{2}$ cup finely shredded Parmesan cheese

1 Lightly coat a 5$\frac{1}{2}$- or 6-quart slow cooker with cooking spray. Add 1 cup of the spaghetti sauce. Add one package of the frozen ravioli and the meatballs. Sprinkle with 1 cup of the mozzarella cheese. Top with remaining spaghetti sauce from first jar. Add remaining package of ravioli and remaining 1 cup mozzarella cheese. Pour spaghetti sauce from second jar over mixture in cooker.

2 Cover and cook on low-heat setting for 4$\frac{1}{2}$ to 5 hours or on high-heat setting for 2 $\frac{1}{2}$ to 3 hours. Turn off cooker. Sprinkle with Parmesan cheese. Cover and let stand for 15 minutes before serving.

Nutrition Facts per serving: 510 cal., 18 g total fat (8 g sat. fat), 78 mg chol., 1,551 mg sodium, 67 g carbo., 5 g fiber, 26 g pro. **Daily Values:** 28% vit. A, 18% vit. C, 41% calcium, 16% iron

In Cincinnati chili parlors, chili is often served over spaghetti. Great for potluck dinners, this version—with ziti (thick tube shapes) or gemelli (short twists)—has the consistency of a casserole.

CINCINNATI-STYLE CHILI CASSEROLE

2	pounds lean ground beef
2	cups chopped onions
1	26-ounce jar garlic pasta sauce
1	15-ounce can red kidney beans, rinsed and drained
1/2	cup water
2	tablespoons chili powder
2	tablespoons semisweet chocolate pieces
1	tablespoon vinegar
1	teaspoon ground cinnamon
1	teaspoon instant beef bouillon granules
1/4	teaspoon cayenne pepper
1/4	teaspoon ground allspice
1	pound dried cut ziti or gemelli pasta
	Shredded cheddar cheese (optional)

PREP:

25 minutes

COOK:

*8 to 10 hours (low)
or 4 to 5 hours (high)*

MAKES:

16 servings

1 In a 12-inch skillet cook ground beef and onions until meat is brown. Drain off fat. Transfer meat mixture to a 4- to 5-quart slow cooker. Stir in pasta sauce, kidney beans, water, chili powder, chocolate pieces, vinegar, cinnamon, bouillon granules, cayenne pepper, and allspice.

2 Cover and cook on low-heat setting for 8 to 10 hours or on high-heat setting for 4 to 5 hours.

3 Before serving, cook pasta according to package directions; drain well. Add pasta to meat mixture in cooker; toss gently to combine. If desired, sprinkle with cheddar cheese and additional chopped onion.

Nutrition Facts per serving: 257 cal., 7 g total fat (2 g sat. fat), 36 mg chol., 277 mg sodium, 33 g carbo., 4 g fiber, 17 g pro. **Daily Values:** 10% vit. A, 7% vit. C, 5% calcium, 16% iron

BONUS CHAPTER
Simple Slow Cooker Recipes
BONUS CHAPTER

Here's another good recipe to serve if you know kids will be at the party. Mac and cheese with taco flavorings combines two of their favorite foods into one yummy dish.

MEXICALI MAC & CHEESE

PREP:

20 minutes

COOK:

5$\frac{1}{2}$ to 6 hours (low)

MAKES:

10 servings

2 pounds lean ground beef

1 cup chopped onion

3 cups shredded Mexican blend cheese (12 ounces)

1 16-ounce jar salsa

1 15-ounce jar cheese dip

1 4-ounce can diced green chile peppers, undrained

1 2$\frac{1}{4}$-ounce can sliced pitted ripe olives, drained

12 ounces dried elbow macaroni

1 In a large skillet cook ground beef and onion until meat is brown and onion is tender. Drain off fat. Transfer meat mixture to a very large bowl. Stir in Mexican blend cheese, salsa, cheese dip, green chile peppers, and olives. Transfer mixture to a 4$\frac{1}{2}$- to 6-quart slow cooker.

2 Cover and cook on low-heat setting for 5$\frac{1}{2}$ to 6 hours. Before serving, cook macaroni according to package directions; drain. Stir macaroni into mixture in cooker.

Nutrition Facts per serving: 577 cal., 32 g total fat (17 g sat. fat), 113 mg chol., 1,337 mg sodium, 36 g carbo., 2 g fiber, 35 g pro. **Daily Values:** 14% vit. A, 19% vit. C, 36% calcium, 19% iron

TIPS FOR TOTING

Foods prepared in slow cookers travel easily to parties. After the food is completely cooked, wrap the slow cooker in heavy foil, several layers of newspaper, or a thick towel. Then place the slow cooker in an insulated container. The food should stay hot for as long as 2 hours—don't hold the food for longer than 2 hours before serving. If electricity is available at your party site, take along a heavy extension cord and plug in the slow cooker. The food will stay warm for several hours on the low-heat setting.

Party-goers will enjoy this on top of a mound of shredded lettuce. The crushed tortillas add the fun, crunchy texture that hard-shell tacos are all about.

TACO CASSEROLE

Nonstick cooking spray
- 1½ pounds lean ground beef
- 1 cup chopped onion
- 1 1¼-ounce envelope taco seasoning mix
- 1 26- to 28-ounce jar meatless spaghetti sauce
- 1 15-ounce can red kidney beans, rinsed and drained
- 1 4-ounce can diced green chile peppers, drained
- 1 cup shredded taco cheese (4 ounces)
- ½ cup coarsely crushed corn chips
- 4 cups shredded lettuce
Dairy sour cream (optional)

1 Lightly coat a 3½- to 4½-quart slow cooker with cooking spray; set aside. In a 12-inch skillet cook ground beef and onion until meat is brown and onion is tender. Drain off fat. Stir taco seasoning mix into meat mixture. Transfer meat mixture to prepared cooker. Stir in spaghetti sauce, kidney beans, and green chile peppers.

2 Cover and cook on low-heat setting for 4 to 5 hours or on high-heat setting for 2 to 2½ hours.

3 Just before serving, sprinkle with taco cheese and corn chips. Serve meat mixture over lettuce. If desired, top each serving with sour cream.

Nutrition Facts per serving: 407 cal., 20 g total fat (8 g sat. fat), 84 mg chol., 1,214 mg sodium, 29 g carbo., 7 g fiber, 31 g pro. Daily Values: 31% vit. A, 36% vit. C, 17% calcium, 24% iron

PREP:
25 minutes

COOK:
*4 to 5 hours (low)
or 2 to 2½ hours (high)*

MAKES:
8 servings

These perfectly seasoned sloppy joe-style sandwiches are just the right consistency, thanks to a can of tomato soup.

SAUCY CHEESEBURGER SANDWICHES

PREP:

20 minutes

COOK:

6 to 8 hours (low) or 3 to 4 hours (high), plus 5 minutes (low)

MAKES:

12 to 15 servings

2½   pounds lean ground beef

1   10¾-ounce can condensed tomato soup

1   cup finely chopped onion

¼   cup water

2   tablespoons tomato paste

1   tablespoon Worcestershire sauce

1   tablespoon prepared mustard

2   teaspoons dried Italian seasoning, crushed

¼   teaspoon black pepper

2   cloves garlic, minced

6   ounces American cheese, cut into cubes

12   to 15 hamburger buns, split and toasted

1 In a 12-inch skillet cook ground beef until brown. Drain off fat. Transfer meat to a 3½- or 4-quart slow cooker. Stir in tomato soup, onion, water, tomato paste, Worcestershire sauce, mustard, Italian seasoning, pepper, and garlic.

2 Cover and cook on low-heat setting for 6 to 8 hours or on high-heat setting for 3 to 4 hours.

3 If using high-heat setting, turn to low-heat setting. Stir in American cheese. Cover and cook for 5 to 10 minutes more or until cheese is melted. Serve meat mixture on hamburger buns.

Nutrition Facts per serving: 357 cal., 16 g total fat (7 g sat. fat), 73 mg chol., 664 mg sodium, 28 g carbo., 2 g fiber, 25 g pro. **Daily Values:** 6% vit. A, 3% vit. C, 16% calcium, 20% iron

A rarebit burger is an ordinary hamburger that has been draped in rarebit sauce (a cheesy English concoction also known as Welsh rabbit). The slow cooker mixes it all up, and you simply spoon it onto a bun.

RAREBIT BURGERS

2½   pounds lean ground beef

1½   cups chopped onions

  4   cloves garlic, minced

  1   15- to16-ounce can nacho cheese sauce

  8   roma tomatoes, seeded and chopped

  2   teaspoons Worcestershire sauce

  1   teaspoon dry mustard

16   to 20 kaiser rolls or hamburger buns, split and toasted

1 In a 12-inch skillet cook ground beef, onions, and garlic until meat is brown and onions are tender. Drain off fat.

2 Transfer meat mixture to a 4- to 5-quart slow cooker. Stir in cheese sauce, tomatoes, Worcestershire sauce, and dry mustard.

3 Cover and cook on low-heat setting for 6 to 8 hours or on high-heat setting for 3 to 4 hours. Season to taste with salt and black pepper. Serve meat mixture on kaiser rolls.

Nutrition Facts per serving: 336 cal., 12 g total fat (4 g sat. fat), 49 mg chol., 584 mg sodium, 36 g carbo., 2 g fiber, 20 g pro. **Daily Values:** 4% vit. A, 11% vit. C, 10% calcium, 20% iron

PREP:

20 minutes

COOK:

*6 to 8 hours (low)
or 3 to 4 hours (high)*

MAKES:

16 to 20 servings

Bound to stand out on the potluck table, this ravioli dish with sun-dried tomato pasta sauce both delights and enthralls. Everyone will ask for your secret.

ITALIAN RAVIOLI CASSEROLE

PREP:

20 minutes

COOK:

*4 to 5 hours (low)
or 2¹/₂ to 3 hours (high)*

STAND:

15 minutes

MAKES:

10 servings

Nonstick cooking spray

1 pound bulk Italian sausage

1 pound lean ground beef

1 cup chopped onion

2 cloves garlic, minced

2 26- to 28-ounce jars sun-dried tomato pasta sauce

1 15-ounce can tomato sauce

1 teaspoon dried Italian seasoning, crushed

2 25-ounce packages frozen cheese-filled ravioli

2¹/₂ cups shredded Italian blend cheese (10 ounces)

1 Lightly coat a 5¹/₂- or 6-quart slow cooker with cooking spray; set aside.

2 For sauce, in a 12-inch skillet cook sausage, ground beef, onion, and garlic until meat is brown and onion is tender. Drain off fat. Stir in pasta sauce, tomato sauce, and Italian seasoning.

3 Place 1 cup of the meat mixture in prepared cooker. Add one package of the frozen ravioli and sprinkle with 1 cup of the Italian blend cheese. Top with half of the remaining meat mixture. Add remaining package of ravioli and 1 cup of the remaining cheese. Top with remaining meat mixture. (Wrap and chill remaining cheese until needed.)

4 Cover and cook on low-heat setting for 4 to 5 hours or on high-heat setting for 2¹/₂ to 3 hours. Turn off cooker. Sprinkle with remaining cheese. Cover and let stand for 15 minutes before serving.

Nutrition Facts per serving: 716 cal., 35 g total fat (13 g sat. fat), 125 mg chol., 1,597 mg sodium, 63 g carbo., 4 g fiber, 36 g pro. **Daily Values:** 18% vit. A, 15% vit. C, 39% calcium, 17% iron

This savory baked bean dish is a real filler-upper! In fact, served with coleslaw and corn bread, it's a hassle-free supper for a housefull of kids.

MEATY BAKED BEANS

8	ounces lean ground beef
8	ounces bulk pork sausage
1	cup chopped onion
2	cloves garlic, minced
2	16-ounce cans pork and beans in tomato sauce
2	15-ounce cans red kidney or pinto beans, rinsed and drained
2	15-ounce cans butter or black beans, rinsed and drained
1	cup bottled barbecue sauce
½	cup packed brown sugar or granulated sugar
¼	cup water
4	slices bacon, crisp-cooked, drained, and crumbled
2	tablespoons lime juice
2	tablespoons prepared mustard
1	teaspoon chili powder
¼	teaspoon black pepper

PREP:

25 minutes

COOK:

*5 to 6 hours (low)
or 2½ to 3 hours (high)*

MAKES:

12 to 16 servings

1 In a large skillet cook ground beef, sausage, onion, and garlic until meat is brown. Drain off fat.

2 Transfer meat mixture to a 4½- to 6-quart slow cooker. Stir in pork and beans, kidney beans, butter beans, barbecue sauce, sugar, water, bacon, lime juice, mustard, chili powder, and pepper.

3 Cover and cook on low-heat setting for 5 to 6 hours or on high-heat setting for 2½ to 3 hours.

Nutrition Facts per serving: 379 cal., 11 g total fat (4 g sat. fat), 31 mg chol., 1,279 mg sodium, 52 g carbo., 11 g fiber, 17 g pro. **Daily Values:** 5% vit. A, 9% vit. C, 10% calcium, 27% iron

BONUS CHAPTER
Simple Slow Cooker Recipes
BONUS CHAPTER

For a youngster's birthday party, keep the focus on the fun! That means fun foods such as chips, veggies, and dips, plus a slow cooker of saucy franks.

CHILI-SAUCED BEEF & FRANKS

PREP:

25 minutes

COOK:

*4 to 6 hours (low)
or 2 to 3 hours (high)*

MAKES:

16 servings

1   pound lean ground beef

1   cup chopped onion

1   16-ounce package frankfurters, cut into ½-inch slices

1   15-ounce can small red beans, rinsed and drained

1   15-ounce can chili without beans

1   10-ounce can chopped tomatoes and green chile peppers, undrained

1   teaspoon chili powder

¼   teaspoon ground cumin

16   frankfurter buns, split

Shredded cheddar cheese (optional)

1 In a large skillet cook ground beef and onion until meat is brown and onion is tender. Drain off fat.

2 Transfer meat mixture to a 3½- or 4-quart slow cooker. Stir in frankfurters, red beans, chili without beans, tomatoes and chile peppers, chili powder, and cumin.

3 Cover and cook on low-heat setting for 4 to 6 hours or on high-heat setting for 2 to 3 hours.

4 Serve frankfurter mixture on buns. If desired, sprinkle with cheddar cheese and additional chopped onion.

Nutrition Facts per serving: 483 cal., 32 g total fat (12 g sat. fat), 66 mg chol., 1,395 mg sodium, 27 g carbo., 3 g fiber, 22 g pro. **Daily Values:** 3% vit. A, 2% vit. C, 9% calcium, 18% iron

For something a little different, consider serving a flavored mayonnaise with these sandwiches. One sparked with chipotle peppers or minced garlic really stirs things up.

TAILGATE SHREDDED PORK SANDWICHES

1½	teaspoons black pepper
1	teaspoon garlic powder
1	teaspoon onion powder
1	teaspoon celery salt
½	teaspoon salt
1	2½- to 3-pound boneless pork shoulder roast
1	medium onion, cut into thin wedges
½	cup chicken broth
8	kaiser or French-style rolls, split and toasted
½	cup mayonnaise or salad dressing
8	tomato slices
8	lettuce leaves

PREP:

20 minutes

COOK:

*8 to 10 hours (low)
or 4 to 5 hours (high)*

MAKES:

8 sandwiches

1 In a small bowl stir together pepper, garlic powder, onion powder, celery salt, and salt. Trim fat from meat. Sprinkle pepper mixture evenly over meat; rub in with your fingers. If necessary, cut meat to fit into a 3½- or 4-quart slow cooker.

2 In cooker place onion. Add meat. Pour broth over mixture in cooker.

3 Cover and cook on low-heat setting for 8 to 10 hours or on high-heat setting for 4 to 5 hours. Remove meat from cooker; discard cooking liquid. Using two forks, pull meat apart into shreds.

4 To serve, spread cut sides of rolls with mayonnaise. Place meat on bottoms of buns. Using a slotted spoon, spoon onion wedges on top of meat. Add tomato slices and lettuce leaves; replace tops of rolls.

Nutrition Facts per serving: 497 cal., 24 g total fat (6 g sat. fat), 104 mg chol., 897 mg sodium, 33 g carbo., 2 g fiber, 34 g pro. **Daily Values:** 7% vit. A, 12% vit. C, 11% calcium, 23% iron

BONUS CHAPTER
Simple Slow Cooker Recipes
BONUS CHAPTER

If you're a fan of scalloped ham and potatoes, you'll appreciate this simple slow cooker method for achieving a similar dish.

NEW POTATOES & HAM

PREP:

20 minutes

COOK:

*6 to 8 hours (low)
or 3 to 4 hours (high),
plus 20 minutes (high)*

MAKES:

6 servings

2	pounds tiny new potatoes, halved
4½	cups cubed cooked ham (1½ pounds)
1	teaspoon dried dill
¼	teaspoon black pepper
1	10¾-ounce can condensed French onion soup
1	cup water
1	8-ounce carton dairy sour cream
¼	cup all-purpose flour

1 In a 3½- or 4-quart slow cooker place potatoes and ham; sprinkle with dill and pepper. Pour onion soup and water over mixture in cooker.

2 Cover and cook on low-heat setting for 6 to 8 hours or on high-heat setting for 3 to 4 hours.

3 In a small bowl stir together sour cream and flour. Gradually stir about 1 cup of the hot cooking liquid into sour cream mixture. Add sour cream mixture to cooker, stirring gently until combined.

4 If using low-heat setting, turn to high-heat setting. Cover and cook for 20 to 30 minutes more or until slightly thickened and bubbly around edge.

Nutrition Facts per serving: 447 cal., 21 g total fat (9 g sat. fat), 82 mg chol., 1,940 mg sodium, 38 g carbo., 3 g fiber, 26 g pro. **Daily Values:** 6% vit. A, 40% vit. C, 8% calcium, 20% iron

This spicy-sweet recipe gets a lot of flavor from just a little ham and andouille (ahn-DOO-ee) sausage—a bold, spicy sausage used often in Cajun cooking. If you can't find andouille, you can substitute smoked sausage, but the dish won't reach quite the same level of smokiness.

SMOKY BEANS WITH HAM & SAUSAGE

2	16-ounce cans pork and beans in tomato sauce
2	15-ounce cans small red beans, rinsed and drained
2	15-ounce cans black beans, rinsed and drained
2	12-ounce bottles chili sauce
1½	cups cubed cooked ham
8	ounces cooked andouille sausage, halved lengthwise and cut into ½-inch slices
1	cup chopped onion
1	cup chopped green sweet pepper
¼	cup packed brown sugar
1	tablespoon chili powder
1	tablespoon drained and finely chopped canned chipotle chile peppers in adobo sauce
1	teaspoon dry mustard
½	teaspoon black pepper
2	cloves garlic, minced

PREP:

25 minutes

COOK:

5 to 6 hours (low) or 2½ to 3 hours (high)

MAKES:

14 to 16 servings

1 In a 5- to 6-quart slow cooker combine pork and beans, red beans, black beans, chili sauce, ham, sausage, onion, sweet pepper, brown sugar, chili powder, chipotle chile peppers, dry mustard, black pepper, and garlic.

2 Cover and cook on low-heat setting for 5 to 6 hours or on high-heat setting for 2½ to 3 hours.

Nutrition Facts per serving: 316 cal., 8 g total fat (3 g sat. fat), 24 mg chol., 1,631 mg sodium, 50 g carbo., 13 g fiber, 19 g pro. **Daily Values:** 13% vit. A, 32% vit. C, 10% calcium, 25% iron

BONUS CHAPTER
Simple Slow Cooker Recipes
BONUS CHAPTER

The ever-favorite combo of robust sausage, tender tortellini, tangy pasta sauce, and creamy mozzarella cheese makes a big splash at any party!

TORTELLINI CASSEROLE

PREP:

20 minutes

COOK:

*6 to 8 hours (low)
or 3 to 4 hours (high),
plus 15 minutes (low)*

MAKES:

6 servings

Nonstick cooking spray

12 ounces bulk Italian sausage

8 ounces lean ground beef

1 26-ounce jar marinara pasta sauce

1 14½-ounce can diced tomatoes with onion and garlic, undrained

½ cup chopped red or yellow sweet pepper

1 teaspoon dried Italian seasoning, crushed

1 9-ounce package refrigerated cheese tortellini

1 cup shredded mozzarella cheese (4 ounces)

1 Lightly coat a 3½- or 4-quart slow cooker with cooking spray; set aside. In a large skillet cook Italian sausage and ground beef until meat is brown. Drain off fat.

2 Transfer meat to prepared cooker. Stir in pasta sauce, tomatoes, sweet pepper, and Italian seasoning.

3 Cover and cook on low-heat setting for 6 to 8 hours or on high-heat setting for 3 to 4 hours.

4 If using high-heat setting, turn to low-heat setting. Add tortellini, stirring to coat with tomato mixture. Cover and cook for 15 to 20 minutes more or until tortellini is tender. Sprinkle with mozzarella cheese.

Nutrition Facts per serving: 542 cal., 31 g total fat (12 g sat. fat), 100 mg chol., 1,525 mg sodium, 36 g carbo., 4 g fiber, 29 g pro. **Daily Values:** 25% vit. A, 60% vit. C, 25% calcium, 23% iron

Take this one to gatherings where you know the folks are going to be really hungry, such as after a sporting event.

FOUR-CHEESE SAUSAGE & POTATOES

1   pound bulk Italian sausage

1   28-ounce package loose-pack frozen diced hash brown potatoes with onion and peppers, thawed

1   14- to 16-ounce jar cheddar cheese pasta sauce

1   8-ounce package cream cheese, cut into cubes

1   cup finely shredded Monterey Jack cheese (4 ounces)

1   cup shredded American cheese (4 ounces)

¼   teaspoon black pepper

1 In a large skillet cook Italian sausage until meat is brown. Drain off fat.

2 Transfer sausage to a very large bowl. Stir in hash brown potatoes, pasta sauce, cream cheese, Monterey Jack cheese, American cheese, and pepper. Transfer sausage mixture to a 3½- or 4-quart slow cooker.

3 Cover and cook on low-heat setting for 5 to 6 hours. Stir before serving.

Nutrition Facts per serving: 521 cal., 38 g total fat (20 g sat. fat), 115 mg chol., 1,085 mg sodium, 21 g carbo., 2 g fiber, 20 g pro. **Daily Values:** 20% vit. A, 20% vit. C, 30% calcium, 11% iron

PREP:

20 minutes

COOK:

5 to 6 hours (low)

MAKES:

6 servings

THAWING HASH BROWN POTATOES
Place frozen potatoes in a colander. Rinse with cool water, stirring until thawed. Drain well.

In every group of friends, there's a cook who's known for his or her outstanding baked beans recipe. With this dish, that person could be you!

SAUCY BAKED BEANS WITH SAUSAGE

PREP:

15 minutes

COOK:

*5 to 6 hours (low)
or 2¹/₂ to 3 hours (high)*

MAKES:

10 servings

2	15-ounce cans Great Northern beans, rinsed and drained
2	15-ounce cans small red beans, rinsed and drained
12	ounces cooked smoked sausage, cut into ¹/₂-inch slices
1¹/₄	cups catsup
1	medium red onion, finely chopped
¹/₂	cup pure maple syrup or maple-flavored syrup
¹/₄	cup packed brown sugar
2	tablespoons prepared mustard
¹/₄	teaspoon black pepper

1 In a 3¹/₂- or 4-quart slow cooker combine Great Northern beans, red beans, sausage, catsup, red onion, maple syrup, brown sugar, mustard, and pepper.

2 Cover and cook on low-heat setting for 5 to 6 hours or on high-heat setting for 2¹/₂ to 3 hours.

Nutrition Facts per serving: 372 cal., 12 g total fat (4 g sat. fat), 23 mg chol., 1,261 mg sodium, 54 g carbo., 10 g fiber, 18 g pro. **Daily Values:** 6% vit. A, 10% vit. C, 12% calcium, 18% iron

Nearly everyone loves Italian Sausage Sandwiches, but why wait for a party to make them? Mix up a batch of the sandwich filling for your family tonight, then divide and freeze the leftovers for up to 1 month. They make simple suppers for busy days.

ITALIAN SAUSAGE SANDWICHES

1½	pounds bulk Italian sausage
1½	pounds uncooked ground turkey
1½	cups meatless spaghetti sauce
1	cup chopped onion or green sweet pepper
1	6-ounce can tomato paste
¼	teaspoon crushed red pepper
12	hoagie buns, split and toasted
1	cup shredded mozzarella cheese (4 ounces)

PREP:
20 minutes

COOK:
*6 to 8 hours (low)
or 3 to 4 hours (high)*

MAKES:
12 sandwiches

1 In a large skillet cook half of the Italian sausage and half of the ground turkey until meat is brown. Drain off fat. Transfer meat to a 3½- or 4-quart slow cooker. Repeat with remaining sausage and remaining turkey.

2 Stir spaghetti sauce, onion, tomato paste, and crushed red pepper into meat in cooker.

3 Cover and cook on low-heat setting for 6 to 8 hours or on high-heat setting for 3 to 4 hours. Serve meat mixture on hoagie buns. Top with mozzarella cheese.

Nutrition Facts per serving: 559 cal., 22 g total fat (8 g sat. fat), 79 mg chol., 1,154 mg sodium, 57 g carbo., 4 g fiber, 31 g pro. **Daily Values:** 12% vit. A, 16% vit. C, 19% calcium, 19% iron

French, Spanish, and African cuisines are the foundations of Creole cooking. With such wide and varied origins, it's no wonder the cooking style appeals to such a wide range of people.

CREOLE CHICKEN

PREP:

25 minutes

COOK:

5 to 6 hours (low)
or 2½ to 3 hours (high)

STAND:

10 minutes

MAKES:

6 servings

1	pound skinless, boneless chicken thighs, cut into ¾-inch pieces
1	14½-ounce can diced tomatoes, undrained
1	14-ounce can chicken broth
8	ounces cooked smoked Polish sausage, coarsely chopped
1	cup diced cooked ham
¾	cup chopped onion
1	6-ounce can tomato paste
½	cup water
1½	teaspoons Cajun seasoning
	Several dashes bottled hot pepper sauce
2	cups uncooked instant rice
1	cup chopped green sweet pepper

1 In a 3½- or 4-quart slow cooker combine chicken, tomatoes, chicken broth, sausage, ham, onion, tomato paste, water, Cajun seasoning, and hot pepper sauce.

2 Cover and cook on low-heat setting for 5 to 6 hours or on high-heat setting for 2½ to 3 hours.

3 Turn off cooker. Stir in rice and sweet pepper. Cover and let stand for 10 to 15 minutes or until rice is tender and most of the liquid is absorbed. Pass additional hot pepper sauce.

Nutrition Facts per serving: 439 cal., 18 g total fat (6 g sat. fat), 99 mg chol., 1,362 mg sodium, 41 g carbo., 2 g fiber, 28 g pro. **Daily Values:** 18% vit. A, 73% vit. C, 6% calcium, 21% iron

*Legend has it that Chicken Tetrazzini was created for a famous opera singer,
but you don't have to love opera to enjoy it.*

EASY CHICKEN TETRAZZINI

2½	pounds skinless, boneless chicken breast halves and/or thighs, cut into 1-inch pieces
2	4½-ounce jars sliced mushrooms, drained
1	16-ounce jar Alfredo pasta sauce
¼	cup chicken broth or water
2	tablespoons dry sherry (optional)
¼	teaspoon black pepper
¼	teaspoon ground nutmeg
10	ounces broken dried spaghetti or linguine, cooked and drained
¾	cup thinly sliced green onions
⅔	cup grated Parmesan cheese

PREP:

20 minutes

COOK:

*5 to 6 hours (low)
or 2½ to 3 hours (high)*

MAKES:

8 servings

1 In a 3½- or 4-quart slow cooker combine chicken and mushrooms.

2 In a medium bowl stir together Alfredo sauce, chicken broth, sherry (if desired), pepper, and nutmeg. Pour over mixture in cooker.

3 Cover and cook on low-heat setting for 5 to 6 hours or on high-heat setting for 2½ to 3 hours.

4 Stir in hot cooked spaghetti, green onions, and ½ cup of the Parmesan cheese. Sprinkle with remaining Parmesan cheese.

Nutrition Facts per serving: 433 cal., 14 g total fat (7 g sat. fat), 120 mg chol., 701 mg sodium, 31 g carbo., 2 g fiber, 43 g pro. **Daily Values:** 8% vit. A, 6% vit. C, 16% calcium, 13% iron

This dish is patterned after a popular oven casserole. The spoonable bite-size pieces are just right for a potluck spread.

ONE-DISH CHICKEN, BROCCOLI & RICE

PREP:

20 minutes

COOK:

4 to 5 hours (low) or 2 to 2¹/₂ hours (high), plus 30 minutes (high)

MAKES:

8 servings

2	pounds skinless, boneless chicken breast halves and/or thighs, cut into bite-size pieces
³/₄	cup chopped onion
2	10³/₄-ounce cans condensed cream of mushroom soup
1	14-ounce can chicken broth
1	8-ounce package shredded process cheese food
¹/₂	teaspoon black pepper
1	16-ounce package frozen cut broccoli, thawed and well drained
2¹/₄	cups uncooked instant white rice

1 In a 4- to 5-quart slow cooker combine chicken and onion. In a medium bowl stir together mushroom soup, chicken broth, cheese food, and pepper. Pour over mixture in cooker.

2 Cover and cook on low-heat setting for 4 to 5 hours or on high-heat setting for 2 to 2¹/₂ hours.

3 If using low-heat setting, turn to high-heat setting. Stir in broccoli and rice. Cover and cook for 30 minutes more.

Nutrition Facts per serving: 428 cal., 15 g total fat (7 g sat. fat), 85 mg chol., 1,149 mg sodium, 34 g carbo., 3 g fiber, 37 g pro. **Daily Values:** 28% vit. A, 50% vit. C, 24% calcium, 16% iron

Mexican-inspired food always brings color and excitement to the table. With this layered casserole, diners can indulge in a portion or two without having to load up their plates with the whole enchilada.

CHICKEN ENCHILADA CASSEROLE

Nonstick cooking spray

9   6-inch corn tortillas

1   11-ounce can whole kernel corn with sweet peppers, drained

1   6-ounce package refrigerated cooked Southwestern-flavor chicken breast strips, cut up

1   4-ounce can diced green chile peppers, undrained

2   cups shredded Mexican blend cheese (8 ounces)

1   19-ounce can enchilada sauce

1   15-ounce can black beans, rinsed and drained

1   6-ounce carton frozen avocado dip (guacamole), thawed

½   cup dairy sour cream

PREP:

15 minutes

COOK:

*5 hours (low)
or 2½ hours (high)*

STAND:

15 minutes

MAKES:

8 servings

1 Lightly coat a 3½- or 4-quart slow cooker with cooking spray. Place 3 of the tortillas in bottom of prepared cooker, overlapping as necessary. Top with corn, half of the chicken, and half of the green chile peppers; sprinkle with ½ cup of the cheese. Pour about ¾ cup of the enchilada sauce over mixture in cooker.

2 Repeat with 3 more tortillas, the black beans, remaining chicken, and remaining green chile peppers; sprinkle with another ½ cup of the cheese. Pour another ¾ cup of the enchilada sauce over mixture. Top with remaining 3 tortillas, remaining 1 cup cheese, and remaining enchilada sauce.

3 Cover and cook on low-heat setting for 5 hours or on high-heat setting for 2½ hours. Remove liner from cooker, if possible, or turn off cooker. Cover and let stand for 15 minutes. Serve with avocado dip and sour cream.

Nutrition Facts per serving: 368 cal., 18 g total fat (7 g sat. fat), 44 mg chol., 1,031 mg sodium, 39 g carbo., 6 g fiber, 18 g pro. **Daily Values:** 17% vit. A, 14% vit. C, 25% calcium, 15% iron

If you're going to a bring-a-dish gathering with people you don't know, don't worry! Chicken and stuffing always satisfies.

CHICKEN & STUFFING CASSEROLE

PREP:

30 minutes

COOK:

4¹/₂ to 5 hours (low)

MAKES:

16 to 20 servings

COOKED CHICKEN

For 2¹/₂ cups cubed cooked chicken, poach 3 or 4 skinless, boneless chicken breast halves in boiling water or chicken broth, covered, about 12 minutes or until no longer pink. Drain, cool slightly, and chop. Or look for frozen chopped, cooked chicken in your supermarket.

¹/₂   cup butter or margarine

1   cup thinly sliced celery

³/₄   cup chopped onion

    Nonstick cooking spray

1   6-ounce package long grain and wild rice mix

1   14-ounce package herb-seasoned stuffing croutons

4   cups cubed cooked chicken

1   8-ounce can sliced mushrooms, drained

¹/₄   cup snipped fresh parsley

1¹/₂   teaspoons poultry seasoning

¹/₄   teaspoon black pepper

2   slightly beaten eggs

2   14-ounce cans reduced-sodium chicken broth

1   10³/₄-ounce can reduced-fat and reduced-sodium condensed cream of chicken or cream of mushroom soup

1   In a large skillet heat butter over medium heat until melted. Add celery and onion; cook about 5 minutes or until vegetables are tender. Set aside.

2   Lightly coat a 5¹/₂- or 6-quart slow cooker with cooking spray. Add rice mix (reserve seasoning packet). Using a slotted spoon, transfer celery and onion to cooker, reserving butter. Stir to combine.

3   Place croutons in a very large bowl. Stir in butter from cooking vegetables, chicken, mushrooms, parsley, poultry seasoning, pepper, and seasoning packet from rice mix.

4   In a medium bowl combine eggs, broth, and chicken soup. Pour over crouton mixture, tossing gently to moisten. Transfer mixture to cooker.

5   Cover and cook on low-heat setting for 4¹/₂ to 5 hours. Stir gently before serving.

Nutrition Facts per serving: 287 cal., 11 g total fat (5 g sat. fat), 76 mg chol., 903 mg sodium, 31 g carbo., 3 g fiber, 16 g pro. **Daily Values:** 8% vit. A, 4% vit. C, 5% calcium, 12% iron

You might assume this dish has Asian roots, but it actually originated in the United States. Evaporated milk makes for a creamy, mouthwatering sauce.

CHICKEN À LA KING

4   cups chopped cooked chicken or turkey

2   10¾-ounce cans condensed cream of chicken soup

2   4½-ounce jars sliced mushrooms, drained

¾   cup chopped green sweet pepper

¾   cup chopped celery

1   5-ounce can (⅔ cup) evaporated milk

½   of a 7-ounce jar roasted red sweet peppers, drained and coarsely chopped (½ cup)

½   cup chopped onion

3   tablespoons dry sherry, dry white wine, or milk

1   teaspoon dried basil, crushed

½   teaspoon black pepper

1   10-ounce package frozen peas

4   or 5 English muffins, split and toasted; 8 to 10 baked potatoes; or 4 to 5 cups hot cooked rice

PREP:
20 minutes

COOK:
*6 to 7 hours (low)
or 3 to 3½ hours (high)*

STAND:
10 minutes

MAKES:
8 to 10 servings

1 In a 4- to 5-quart slow cooker combine chicken, chicken soup, mushrooms, green sweet pepper, celery, evaporated milk, roasted sweet peppers, onion, sherry, basil, and black pepper.

2 Cover and cook on low-heat setting for 6 to 7 hours or on high-heat setting for 3 to 3½ hours. Turn off cooker. Stir in frozen peas. Cover and let stand for 10 minutes.

3 Serve chicken mixture over English muffin halves, baked potatoes, or hot cooked rice.

Nutrition Facts per serving: 357 cal., 12 g total fat (4 g sat. fat), 74 mg chol., 940 mg sodium, 31 g carbo., 5 g fiber, 28 g pro. **Daily Values:** 15% vit. A, 74% vit. C, 14% calcium, 16% iron

A can of cola moistens and slightly sweetens this sandwich filling. Slather on the mustard and serve these sandwiches with forks just in case some of the filling escapes the bun.

CHICKEN SLOPPY JOES

PREP:

20 minutes

COOK:

*6 to 7 hours (low)
or 3 to 3½ hours (high)*

MAKES:

10 to 12 sandwiches

2	pounds uncooked ground chicken or turkey
1½	cups finely chopped celery
1	cup finely chopped onion
1	12-ounce can cola
2	teaspoons dry mustard
½	teaspoon salt
½	teaspoon black pepper
¼	teaspoon cayenne pepper (optional)
	Prepared mustard
10	to 12 hamburger buns, split and toasted
	Dill pickle slices

1 In a large skillet cook ground chicken, celery, and onion until chicken is brown. Drain off fat. Transfer chicken mixture to a 3½- or 4-quart slow cooker.

2 In a small bowl combine cola, dry mustard, salt, black pepper, and, if desired, cayenne pepper. Stir into mixture in cooker.

3 Cover and cook on low-heat setting for 6 to 7 hours or on high-heat setting for 3 to 3½ hours.

4 To serve, spread mustard on bottoms of buns. Using a slotted spoon, place chicken mixture on bun bottoms. Top with pickle slices and additional chopped onion; replace tops of buns.

Nutrition Facts per serving: 284 cal., 10 g total fat (1 g sat. fat), 0 mg chol., 415 mg sodium, 28 g carbo., 2 g fiber, 20 g pro.

Cook and shred the turkey before heading out so these spicy sandwiches are party-ready when you arrive. If smaller portions are desired for an hors d'oeuvre-style spread, purchase mini buns from the bakery.

HOT & PEPPERY TURKEY SANDWICHES

3	pounds turkey thighs, skinned
1/2	cup packed brown sugar
1/4	cup prepared mustard
2	tablespoons catsup
2	tablespoons cider vinegar
1	tablespoon quick-cooking tapioca
2	teaspoons liquid smoke
1	teaspoon salt
1	teaspoon coarsely ground black pepper
1	teaspoon crushed red pepper
8	hamburger buns, split and toasted
1	cup deli coleslaw

PREP:

30 minutes

COOK:

10 to 12 hours (low) or 5 to 6 hours (high), plus 15 minutes (low)

MAKES:

8 sandwiches

1 In a 3 1/2- or 4-quart slow cooker place turkey thighs. In a small bowl combine brown sugar, mustard, catsup, vinegar, tapioca, liquid smoke, salt, black pepper, and crushed red pepper. Pour over turkey in cooker.

2 Cover and cook on low-heat setting for 10 to 12 hours or on high-heat setting for 5 to 6 hours.

3 Remove turkey from cooker, reserving juices. Using two forks, pull turkey apart into shreds. Skim fat from juices. Return turkey to cooker. If using high-heat setting, turn to low-heat setting. Cover and cook for 15 to 30 minutes more or until heated through.

4 Serve turkey mixture on hamburger buns. Top with coleslaw.

Nutrition Facts per serving: 339 cal., 7 g total fat (2 g sat. fat), 76 mg chol., 728 mg sodium, 41 g carbo., 2 g fiber, 26 g pro. **Daily Values:** 3% vit. A, 10% vit. C, 10% calcium, 21% iron

An elegant entrée with a fancy French name becomes a crowd-pleasing potluck casserole.

TURKEY & WILD RICE AMANDINE

PREP:

20 minutes

COOK:

6 to 7 hours (low)
or 3 to 3¹/₂ hours (high)

MAKES:

10 servings

1   15-ounce jar whole straw mushrooms, drained
1   10³/₄-ounce can condensed cream of mushroom with roasted garlic soup
1   8-ounce can sliced water chestnuts, drained
1   cup uncooked wild rice, rinsed and drained
1   cup uncooked regular brown rice
¹/₂   cup chopped onion
¹/₄   teaspoon black pepper
3   14-ounce cans reduced-sodium chicken broth
¹/₂   cup water
3   cups chopped cooked turkey or chicken
¹/₂   cup dairy sour cream
¹/₂   cup sliced almonds, toasted

1 In a 4- to 5-quart slow cooker combine mushrooms, mushroom soup, water chestnuts, wild rice, brown rice, onion, and pepper. Stir in chicken broth and water.

2 Cover and cook on low-heat setting for 6 to 7 hours or on high-heat setting for 3 to 3¹/₂ hours. Stir in turkey and sour cream. Sprinkle with toasted almonds.

Nutrition Facts per serving: 316 cal., 11 g total fat (3 g sat. fat), 36 mg chol., 721 mg sodium, 34 g carbo., 4 g fiber, 22 g pro. **Daily Values:** 2% vit. A, 2% vit. C, 6% calcium, 14% iron

If you have visitors during the Thanksgiving holiday, you'll likely treat them to turkey and all the trimmings. Afterwards you can take a day off from cooking and make this simple supper from the leftovers.

EASY TURKEY DIVAN

	Nonstick cooking spray
1	10¾-ounce can condensed golden mushroom soup
⅓	cup mayonnaise or salad dressing
¼	cup milk
1	tablespoon prepared mustard
¼	teaspoon black pepper
4½	cups chopped cooked turkey or chicken (1½ pounds)
1	16-ounce package frozen cut broccoli
2	4½-ounce jars sliced mushrooms, drained
1	cup shredded American cheese (4 ounces)
⅓	cup sliced almonds, toasted

PREP:

20 minutes

COOK:

*4 to 5 hours (low)
or 2 to 2½ hours (high),
plus 30 minutes*

MAKES:

6 servings

1 Lightly coat a 3½- or 4-quart slow cooker with cooking spray. In prepared cooker combine mushroom soup, mayonnaise, milk, mustard, and pepper. Stir in turkey, broccoli, and mushrooms.

2 Cover and cook on low-heat setting for 4 to 5 hours or on high-heat setting for 2 to 2½ hours. Stir in American cheese. Cover and cook for 30 minutes more. Sprinkle with toasted almonds.

Nutrition Facts per serving: 450 cal., 26 g total fat (8 g sat. fat), 105 mg chol., 1,015 mg sodium, 12 g carbo., 5 g fiber, 41 g pro. **Daily Values:** 43% vit. A, 72% vit. C, 22% calcium, 19% iron

Because all of the flavors in this chunky casserole are somewhat mild, they meld into a satisfying dish that pleases many tastes.

TURKEY-VEGETABLE GOULASH

PREP:

15 minutes

COOK:

*6 to 8 hours (low) or
3 to 4 hours (high),
plus 20 minutes (high)*

MAKES:

6 servings

1	pound uncooked ground turkey
1	14½-ounce can diced tomatoes with basil, oregano, and garlic, undrained
1	10-ounce package frozen mixed vegetables
1½	cups water
1	8-ounce can tomato sauce
2	stalks celery, sliced
1	small onion, chopped
1	0.9-ounce envelope turkey gravy mix
1	cup dried fine egg noodles
⅓	cup shredded sharp cheddar, Monterey Jack, or Parmesan cheese

1 In a large skillet cook ground turkey until brown. Drain off fat. Transfer turkey to a 3½- or 4-quart slow cooker. Stir in tomatoes, frozen vegetables, water, tomato sauce, celery, onion, and gravy mix.

2 Cover and cook on low-heat setting for 6 to 8 hours or on high-heat setting for 3 to 4 hours.

3 If using low-heat setting, turn to high-heat setting. Stir in noodles. Cover and cook for 20 to 30 minutes more or until noodles are tender. Sprinkle with cheddar cheese.

Nutrition Facts per serving: 251 cal., 9 g total fat (3 g sat. fat), 73 mg chol., 918 mg sodium, 22 g carbo., 3 g fiber, 19 g pro. **Daily Values:** 58% vit. A, 18% vit. C, 13% calcium, 16% iron

BUYING GROUND POULTRY

Many people assume that ground turkey and ground chicken are always leaner alternatives to ground beef, but they're not. Some products contain dark meat and/or skin, which are less lean than breast meat. When a recipe calls for ground turkey or chicken, look for the leanest meat you can find. If you can't find packages that are specifically labeled as breast meat only, ask the butcher to skin, bone, and grind turkey or chicken breasts for you, or grind it yourself using a coarse blade in a food grinder.

Baked bean combos are always appreciated at potlucks. Here sausage joins the merry mix of beans, making a main dish out of the popular side.

FOUR-BEAN & SAUSAGE DINNER

1	pound cooked smoked turkey sausage, halved lengthwise and cut into ½-inch pieces
1	15-ounce can red kidney beans, rinsed and drained
1	15-ounce can black beans, rinsed and drained
1	15-ounce can Great Northern beans, rinsed and drained
1	15-ounce can butter beans, rinsed and drained
1	8-ounce can tomato sauce
1	medium green sweet pepper, chopped
½	cup chopped onion
½	cup catsup
¼	cup packed brown sugar
2	teaspoons Worcestershire sauce
1	teaspoon dry mustard
½	teaspoon bottled hot pepper sauce

PREP:

15 minutes

COOK:

8 to 10 hours (low) or 4 to 5 hours (high)

MAKES:

8 servings

1 In a 3½- or 4-quart slow cooker combine sausage, kidney beans, black beans, Great Northern beans, butter beans, tomato sauce, sweet pepper, onion, catsup, brown sugar, Worcestershire sauce, dry mustard, and hot pepper sauce.

2 Cover and cook on low-heat setting for 8 to 10 hours or on high-heat setting for 4 to 5 hours.

Nutrition Facts per serving: 324 cal., 5 g total fat (1 g sat. fat), 38 mg chol., 1,243 mg sodium, 50 g carbo., 11 g fiber, 24 g pro. **Daily Values:** 5% vit. A, 24% vit. C, 10% calcium, 22% iron

The fun of potlucks is sampling a spoonful of this and that on a buffet—but don't be surprised if some party-goers sneak an extra helping of this chock-full shrimp concoction.

CAJUN SHRIMP & RICE

PREP:

20 minutes

COOK:

*5 to 6 hours (low)
or 3 to 3½ hours (high),
plus 15 minutes (high)*

MAKES:

6 servings

1   28-ounce can tomatoes, undrained and cut up

1   14-ounce can chicken broth

1   cup chopped onion

1   cup chopped green sweet pepper

1   6-ounce package long grain and wild rice mix

¼   cup water

½   teaspoon Cajun seasoning

2   cloves garlic, minced

1   pound cooked, peeled, and deveined shrimp
     Bottled hot pepper sauce (optional)

1 In a 3½- or 4-quart slow cooker combine tomatoes, chicken broth, onion, sweet pepper, rice mix (including seasoning packet), water, Cajun seasoning, and garlic.

2 Cover and cook on low-heat setting for 5 to 6 hours or on high-heat setting for 3 to 3½ hours.

3 If using low-heat setting, turn to high-heat setting. Stir in shrimp. Cover and cook for 15 minutes more. If desired, pass hot pepper sauce.

Nutrition Facts per serving: 223 cal., 2 g total fat (0 g sat. fat), 147 mg chol., 1,063 mg sodium, 32 g carbo., 3 g fiber, 21 g pro. **Daily Values:** 23% vit. A, 71% vit. C, 9% calcium, 21% iron

Even the kids at the party will dig into the vegetables when they're served up in an irresistibly cheesy sauce.

CHEESY VEGETABLE CASSEROLE

1 16-ounce jar cheddar cheese pasta sauce

1 8-ounce tub cream cheese with chive and onion

¼ cup hot water

½ teaspoon black pepper

3 16-ounce packages loose-pack frozen broccoli, cauliflower, and carrots

Milk

½ cup ranch-flavor or regular sliced almonds, toasted

PREP:

15 minutes

COOK:

6 to 7 hours (low)
or 3 to 3½ hours (high)

MAKES:

12 side-dish servings

1 In a 4½- to 6-quart slow cooker whisk together pasta sauce, cream cheese, hot water, and pepper (mixture may appear curdled). Add frozen vegetables, stirring to coat with cheese mixture.

2 Cover and cook on low-heat setting for 6 to 7 hours or on high-heat setting for 3 to 3½ hours. Stir gently. If necessary, stir in enough milk to make mixture of desired consistency. Sprinkle with almonds.

Nutrition Facts per serving: 188 cal., 13 g total fat (6 g sat. fat), 33 mg chol., 575 mg sodium, 10 g carbo., 4 g fiber, 5 g pro. **Daily Values:** 54% vit. A, 47% vit. C, 11% calcium, 2% iron

Like the pioneers, this dish forges new territory. Featuring not two but three kinds of beans, it's a must at picnics, potlucks, and backyard barbecues.

PIONEER BEANS

PREP:

25 minutes

COOK:

5 to 6 hours (low) or 2¹/₂ to 3 hours (high)

MAKES:

24 side-dish servings

8	ounces sliced bacon, chopped
1¹/₂	cups chopped green sweet peppers
1	cup chopped onion
1	31-ounce can pork and beans in tomato sauce
2	15-ounce cans red kidney beans, rinsed and drained
2	15-ounce cans butter beans, rinsed and drained
1	24-ounce bottle (2 cups) catsup
¹/₂	cup packed brown sugar
¹/₂	cup molasses
2	tablespoons vinegar
2	tablespoons prepared mustard

1 In a large skillet cook bacon, sweet peppers, and onion until vegetables are tender. Drain off fat.

2 Transfer bacon mixture to a 4¹/₂- to 6-quart slow cooker. Stir in pork and beans, kidney beans, butter beans, catsup, brown sugar, molasses, vinegar, and mustard.

3 Cover and cook on low-heat setting for 5 to 6 hours or on high-heat setting for 2¹/₂ to 3 hours.

Nutrition Facts per serving: 196 cal., 3 g total fat (2 g sat. fat), 6 mg chol., 767 mg sodium, 36 g carbo., 6 g fiber, 8 g pro. **Daily Values:** 8% vit. A, 21% vit. C, 7% calcium, 15% iron

Every potluck table needs a good vegetable side dish. The trick is to keep it hot and appetizing.

CREAMY BROCCOLI & CAULIFLOWER

1   10¾-ounce can condensed cream of chicken soup

1   8-ounce tub cream cheese with chive and onion

¼   cup milk

1   teaspoon finely shredded lemon peel

1   16-ounce package frozen cauliflower

1   16-ounce package frozen cut broccoli

1   cup crushed rich round crackers

2   tablespoons butter or margarine, melted

PREP:

15 minutes

COOK:

*6 to 8 hours (low)
or 3 to 4 hours (high)*

MAKES:

10 side-dish servings

1 In a 3½- or 4-quart slow cooker combine chicken soup, cream cheese, milk, and lemon peel. Add frozen cauliflower and broccoli, stirring to coat with cheese mixture.

2 Cover and cook on low-heat setting for 6 to 8 hours or on high-heat setting for 3 to 4 hours. Stir gently. If necessary, stir in enough additional milk to make mixture of desired consistency.

3 Before serving, in a small bowl combine crushed crackers and melted butter. Sprinkle over vegetable mixture.

Nutrition Facts per serving: 203 cal., 14 g total fat (8 g sat. fat), 32 mg chol., 456 mg sodium, 14 g carbo., 3 g fiber, 5 g pro. **Daily Values:** 29% vit. A, 68% vit. C, 9% calcium, 6% iron

Call on these rich potatoes when you're going to a potluck or hosting a large dinner party. They'll make a hassle-free, impressive side dish to a succulent roast.

PARTY POTATOES WITH BACON

PREP:

20 minutes

COOK:

5¹/₂ to 6 hours (low)

MAKES:

8 to 10 side-dish servings

1	16-ounce jar Alfredo pasta sauce
2	tablespoons milk
³/₄	cup chopped onion
³/₄	cup chopped red and/or green sweet pepper
¹/₂	teaspoon black pepper
2	cloves garlic, minced
6	large potatoes, peeled (if desired) and cut into ¹/₄-inch slices (about 8 cups)
1	3-ounce package cooked bacon slices, chopped
1	4¹/₂-ounce can sliced pitted ripe olives, drained
¹/₄	cup thinly sliced green onions

1 In a medium bowl stir together Alfredo sauce and milk. Stir in onion, sweet pepper, black pepper, and garlic. Set aside.

2 In a 5- to 6-quart slow cooker layer one-third of the potatoes and one-third of the bacon. Spread one-third of the sauce mixture over mixture in cooker. Repeat. Top with remaining potatoes and remaining sauce mixture. (Wrap and chill remaining bacon until ready to serve.)

3 Cover and cook on low-heat setting for 5¹/₂ to 6 hours. Before serving, sprinkle with olives, green onions, and remaining bacon.

Nutrition Facts per serving: 269 cal., 12 g total fat (5 g sat. fat), 35 mg chol., 578 mg sodium, 35 g carbo., 4 g fiber, 7 g pro. **Daily Values:** 22% vit. A, 83% vit. C, 9% calcium, 16% iron

TIMESAVING PASTA SAUCES

Prepared pasta sauces in jars, cans, and refrigerated containers provide a boon to time-pressed cooks. Because most have a long shelf life, you can stock for last-minute meal preparation. Dress them up with these ingredients:

• Add cooked ham pieces and frozen peas to light alfredo sauce and heat through. Serve over rotini or other pasta.

• Toss grilled vegetables and prepared pesto sauce with bow tie pasta.

• Add cooked Italian sausage and grilled red sweet peppers to chunky marinara sauce and serve over linguine. Sprinkle with snipped fresh basil.

This recipe is a surefire potluck pleaser, but remember it at the holidays, too, when you're short on stove and oven space. It's a great way to serve potatoes—no one will miss the gravy.

COMPANY-SPECIAL SCALLOPED POTATOES

Nonstick cooking spray

1½ pounds Yukon gold potatoes

1½ pounds sweet potatoes

1 7-ounce round smoked Gouda cheese or 8 ounces American cheese, shredded

1 10¾-ounce can condensed cream of celery soup

1 8-ounce carton dairy sour cream

½ cup chicken broth

1 large onion, sliced

PREP:
25 minutes

COOK:
6 to 8 hours (low)
or 3 to 4 hours (high)

MAKES:
10 side-dish servings

1 Lightly coat a 4½- or 5-quart slow cooker with cooking spray; set aside.

2 Thinly slice Yukon gold potatoes (do not peel). Peel and cut sweet potatoes into ¼-inch slices. Set aside.

3 In a medium bowl combine cheese, celery soup, sour cream, and chicken broth. In prepared cooker layer half of the potatoes and half of the onion. Spread half of the soup mixture over mixture in cooker. Repeat.

4 Cover and cook on low-heat setting for 6 to 8 hours or on high-heat setting for 3 to 4 hours.

Nutrition Facts per serving: 265 cal., 12 g total fat (7 g sat. fat), 26 mg chol., 612 mg sodium, 33 g carbo., 4 g fiber, 8 g pro. **Daily Values:** 264% vit. A, 39% vit. C, 18% calcium, 8% iron

The sweet potato goes from humble to highly rated when mingled with the sweetness and tang of orange juice and apricots.

MAPLE-ORANGE SWEET POTATOES

PREP:

20 minutes

COOK:

*8 to 9 hours (low)
or 4 to 4¹/₂ hours (high)*

MAKES:

10 side-dish servings

Nonstick cooking spray

1 16-ounce package peeled baby carrots

2 pounds sweet potatoes, peeled and cut into 1¹/₂-inch pieces

1 cup snipped dried apricots

¹/₂ cup pure maple syrup or maple-flavored syrup

¹/₄ cup frozen orange juice concentrate, thawed

¹/₄ cup water

2 tablespoons butter or margarine, melted

¹/₂ teaspoon salt

¹/₄ teaspoon white pepper

¹/₄ teaspoon ground cinnamon

1 Lightly coat a 3¹/₂- or 4-quart slow cooker with cooking spray. Add carrots. Top with sweet potatoes and dried apricots.

2 In a small bowl combine maple syrup, orange juice concentrate, water, butter, salt, white pepper, and cinnamon. Pour over mixture in cooker.

3 Cover and cook on low-heat setting for 8 to 9 hours or on high-heat setting for 4 to 4¹/₂ hours. Serve with a slotted spoon.

Nutrition Facts per serving: 194 cal., 3 g total fat (2 g sat. fat), 7 mg chol., 168 mg sodium, 42 g carbo., 5 g fiber, 2 g pro. **Daily Values:** 487% vit. A, 41% vit. C, 5% calcium, 8% iron

Potluck-style entertaining during the holidays makes perfect sense: No one gets stuck with the stress, and everyone can partake in the fun. Here's your contribution to the table.

HOLIDAY SWEET POTATOES & CRANBERRIES

Nonstick cooking spray

1/2	cup pure maple syrup or maple-flavored syrup
3	tablespoons butter or margarine, melted
2	tablespoons Dijon-style mustard
1/2	teaspoon salt
1/4	teaspoon black pepper
3 1/2	pounds sweet potatoes, peeled and cut into 1-inch pieces
2/3	cup dried cranberries

1 Lightly coat a 3 1/2- or 4-quart slow cooker with cooking spray. In prepared cooker combine maple syrup, melted butter, mustard, salt, and pepper. Stir in sweet potatoes and dried cranberries.

2 Cover and cook on low-heat setting for 6 1/2 to 7 1/2 hours or on high-heat setting for 2 1/2 to 3 hours.

Nutrition Facts per serving: 224 cal., 4 g total fat (2 g sat. fat), 10 mg chol., 186 mg sodium, 46 g carbo., 4 g fiber, 2 g pro. Daily Values: 416% vit. A, 30% vit. C, 4% calcium, 5% iron

PREP:
30 minutes

COOK:
*6 1/2 to 7 1/2 hours (low)
or 2 1/2 to 3 hours (high)*

MAKES:
10 side-dish servings

If a friend of yours is having a "turkey and all the trimmings" dinner and wisely asks for each guest's help in bringing the trimmings, volunteer this unique dish.

WILD RICE WITH PECANS & CHERRIES

PREP:

20 minutes

COOK:

5 to 6 hours (low)

STAND:

10 minutes

MAKES:

15 side-dish servings

3	14-ounce cans chicken broth
2½	cups uncooked wild rice, rinsed and drained
1	cup coarsely shredded carrots
1	4½-ounce jar sliced mushrooms, drained
2	tablespoons butter or margarine, melted
2	teaspoons dried marjoram, crushed
¼	teaspoon salt
¼	teaspoon black pepper
⅔	cup dried tart cherries
⅔	cup sliced green onions
½	cup coarsely chopped pecans, toasted

1 In a 3½- or 4-quart slow cooker combine chicken broth, wild rice, carrots, mushrooms, melted butter, marjoram, salt, and pepper.

2 Cover and cook on low-heat setting for 5 to 6 hours. Turn off cooker. Stir in dried cherries and green onions. Cover and let stand for 10 minutes.

3 Just before serving, sprinkle with pecans. Serve with a slotted spoon.

Nutrition Facts per serving: 169 cal., 5 g total fat (1 g sat. fat), 4 mg chol., 423 mg sodium, 27 g carbo., 3 g fiber, 5 g pro. **Daily Values:** 43% vit. A, 3% vit. C, 2% calcium, 5% iron

Ever show up at a potluck with the same side dish five other people brought?
With this creative, colorful bread pudding, the likelihood of that happening is next to nil.

VEGETABLE BREAD PUDDING

2	slightly beaten eggs
1/2	cup shredded Swiss or Gruyère cheese (2 ounces)
1/2	teaspoon dried basil, crushed
1/4	teaspoon salt
1/4	teaspoon dried sage, crushed
1/8	teaspoon black pepper
1 1/2	cups whole milk, half-and-half, or light cream
3	cups dry sourdough bread cubes
1/3	cup frozen whole kernel corn
1/3	cup bottled roasted red sweet peppers, drained and chopped
1/3	cup chopped zucchini

1 In a large bowl combine eggs, Swiss cheese, basil, salt, sage, and black pepper. Whisk in milk. Gently stir in bread cubes, corn, roasted sweet peppers, and zucchini. Pour into a 1-quart soufflé dish (dish will be full). Cover dish tightly with foil.

2 In a 4- to 5-quart slow cooker place 1 cup warm water. Tear off an 18×12-inch piece of heavy foil. Cut in half lengthwise. Fold each piece into thirds lengthwise. Crisscross strips and place soufflé dish in center of foil strips. Bringing up strips, transfer dish and foil to cooker (leave strips under dish).

3 Cover and cook on low-heat setting for 5 hours or on high-heat setting for 2 1/2 hours. Using foil strips, carefully lift dish from cooker. Discard foil strips. Serve pudding warm.

Nutrition Facts per serving: 177 cal., 7 g total fat (4 g sat. fat), 88 mg chol., 325 mg sodium, 19 g carbo., 1 g fiber, 9 g pro. **Daily Values:** 6% vit. A, 40% vit. C, 19% calcium, 6% iron

PREP:

25 minutes

COOK:

*5 hours (low) or
2 1/2 hours (high)*

MAKES:

6 side-dish servings

DRY BREAD CUBES

To make dry bread, cut fresh bread into 1/2-inch cubes. (You'll need about 3 3/4 cups fresh bread cubes to make 3 cups of dry cubes.) Spread cubes in a shallow baking pan. Bake, uncovered, in a 300°F oven for 10 to 15 minutes or until bread cubes are dry, stirring twice; cool. Or let bread stand, loosely covered, at room temperature for 8 to 12 hours.

BONUS CHAPTER
Simple Slow Cooker Recipes
BONUS CHAPTER

If you're on the list to bring a dessert for a fall or winter gathering, consider this sweet-and-saucy way to serve apples.

SWEET VANILLA APPLES

PREP:

20 minutes

COOK:

*6 to 8 hours (low)
or 3 to 4 hours (high)*

MAKES:

8 servings

	Nonstick cooking spray
8	cups peeled and sliced cooking apples
½	cup dried cranberries or cherries
½	cup golden raisins
1	4-serving-size package instant vanilla or French vanilla pudding mix
½	cup packed brown sugar
2	teaspoons finely shredded lemon peel
1	teaspoon apple pie spice
1¼	cups half-and-half or light cream
1½	teaspoons vanilla
8	slices purchased pound cake or angel food cake

1 Lightly coat a 3½- or 4-quart slow cooker with cooking spray. Add sliced apples, dried cranberries, and raisins. In a medium bowl combine pudding mix, brown sugar, lemon peel, and apple pie spice. Stir in half-and-half and vanilla. Pour over mixture in cooker.

2 Cover and cook on low-heat setting for 6 to 8 hours or on high-heat setting for 3 to 4 hours.

3 Stir gently before serving. Serve apple mixture over cake slices.

Nutrition Facts per serving: 563 cal., 20 g total fat (11 g sat. fat), 180 mg chol., 497 mg sodium, 96 g carbo., 5 g fiber, 6 g pro. **Daily Values:** 13% vit. A, 10% vit. C, 10% calcium, 11% iron

SWIFT SIDES FOR SLOW COOKED SUPPERS

8

BONUS CHAPTER

Simple Slow Cooker Recipes

BONUS CHAPTER

Heading into a manic Monday? Prepare this salad and Coffee Angel Dessert (page 374) the night before and a slow cooker sandwich recipe in the morning. Monday night never looked so good.

PEPPERCORN RANCH PASTA & VEGGIE SALAD

START TO FINISH:

30 minutes

MAKES:

6 servings

8	ounces dried gemelli or penne pasta
2	cups loose-pack frozen broccoli, corn, and red peppers
⅔	cup grape tomatoes, halved
⅓	cup chopped red onion
¼	teaspoon black pepper
¾	cup bottled peppercorn ranch salad dressing
1	cup finely shredded cheddar cheese (4 ounces)

1 Cook pasta according to package directions, adding frozen vegetables the last 2 minutes of cooking; drain. Rinse with cold water; drain again. Transfer to a large bowl.

2 Stir in grape tomatoes, red onion, and pepper. Pour salad dressing over pasta mixture; toss gently to coat. Add cheese; toss gently to combine. Serve immediately or cover and chill for up to 24 hours. If necessary, stir in additional salad dressing or milk to make salad of desired consistency.

Nutrition Facts per serving: 395 cal., 23 g total fat (6 g sat. fat), 21 mg chol., 479 mg sodium, 36 g carbo., 2 g fiber, 11 g pro. **Daily Values:** 11% vit. A, 27% vit. C, 16% calcium, 9% iron

*Did you know that traditional Greek salads often don't include lettuce?
True to that tradition, this sprightly salad makes a great side dish when you're tired
of lettuce but still want something tangy, crunchy, and overflowing with vegetables.*

GREEK SALAD

3	medium tomatoes, cut into wedges
1	medium cucumber, halved lengthwise and thinly sliced
1	small red onion, cut into thin wedges
1	recipe Greek Vinaigrette
8	to 10 pitted kalamata olives
½	cup crumbled feta cheese (2 ounces)

1 In a medium bowl combine tomatoes, cucumber, and red onion.

2 Pour Greek Vinaigrette over tomato mixture; toss gently to coat. Sprinkle with olives and feta cheese.

Nutrition Facts per serving: 154 cal., 12 g total fat (4 g sat. fat), 17 mg chol., 369 mg sodium, 9 g carbo., 2 g fiber, 4 g pro. **Daily Values:** 17% vit. A, 43% vit. C, 12% calcium, 6% iron

START TO FINISH:
15 minutes
MAKES:
4 servings

GREEK VINAIGRETTE
In a screw-top jar combine 2 tablespoons olive oil or salad oil; 2 tablespoons lemon juice; 2 teaspoons snipped fresh oregano or ½ teaspoon dried oregano, crushed; ⅛ teaspoon salt; and ⅛ teaspoon black pepper. Cover and shake well.

You'll be surprised at how good peanuts and peas taste together, especially when they're draped in a sweet and tangy sour cream dressing.

PEA & PEANUT SALAD

1   10-ounce package frozen peas, thawed and drained

1   cup Spanish or honey-roasted peanuts

¼   cup dairy sour cream

2   tablespoons mayonnaise or salad dressing

½   teaspoon sugar

1 In a medium bowl combine peas and peanuts. For dressing, in a small bowl stir together sour cream, mayonnaise, and sugar.

2 Pour dressing over pea mixture; toss gently to coat.

Nutrition Facts per serving: 346 cal., 26 g total fat (5 g sat. fat), 9 mg chol., 131 mg sodium, 17 g carbo., 6 g fiber, 15 g pro. **Daily Values:** 12% vit. A, 12% vit. C, 5% calcium, 8% iron

You could serve this as a first course to a sit-down meal with friends. It also makes a substantial side for a soup or stew supper.

ROMA TOMATO SALAD

1	pound roma tomatoes, coarsely chopped
4	ounces mozzarella or provolone cheese, cubed
⅔	cup pimiento-stuffed green olives
¼	cup bottled Italian vinaigrette or Italian salad dressing

1 In a medium bowl combine tomatoes, mozzarella cheese, and olives. Pour vinaigrette over tomato mixture; toss gently to coat.

2 Let stand for 5 minutes before serving.

Nutrition Facts per serving: 126 cal., 10 g total fat (3 g sat. fat), 11 mg chol., 510 mg sodium, 5 g carbo., 1 g fiber, 5 g pro. **Daily Values:** 14% vit. A, 27% vit. C, 13% calcium, 4% iron

PREP:
10 minutes
STAND:
5 minutes
MAKES:
6 servings

This salad is a tantalizing explosion of flavors and textures, the perfect contrast to a hearty and rustic, long-simmered main dish.

MANGO-BROCCOLI SALAD

START TO FINISH:

20 minutes

MAKES:

8 servings

4   cups chopped broccoli

1   large ripe mango, seeded, peeled, and chopped

1   small red onion, cut into thin wedges

½   cup cashews

½   cup bottled buttermilk ranch salad dressing

2   tablespoons orange juice

1   tablespoon prepared horseradish

1   11-ounce can mandarin orange sections, drained

1 In a large bowl combine broccoli, mango, red onion, and cashews. For dressing, in small bowl stir together buttermilk ranch dressing, orange juice, and horseradish.

2 Pour dressing over broccoli mixture; toss gently to coat. Gently stir in mandarin oranges. Serve immediately or cover and chill for up to 2 hours.

Nutrition Facts per serving: 175 cal., 12 g total fat (2 g sat. fat), 1 mg chol., 195 mg sodium, 16 g carbo., 3 g fiber, 3 g pro. Daily Values: 46% vit. A, 109% vit. C, 4% calcium, 6% iron

Need a new idea for a tossed green side? With pea pods, hoisin sauce, and sesame seeds, this one brings Asian flair to the salad bowl.

ASIAN PEA POD SALAD

  6 cups torn romaine lettuce

  2 cups fresh pea pods, trimmed and halved crosswise

  ⅓ cup bottled Italian salad dressing

  1 tablespoon bottled hoisin sauce

  1 tablespoon sesame seeds, toasted

1 In a large salad bowl toss together romaine and pea pods. For dressing, in a small bowl combine Italian dressing and hoisin sauce.

2 Pour dressing over romaine mixture; toss gently to coat. Sprinkle with sesame seeds.

Nutrition Facts per serving: 98 cal., 7 g total fat (1 g sat. fat), 0 mg chol., 153 mg sodium, 6 g carbo., 2 g fiber, 2 g pro. **Daily Values:** 31% vit. A, 25% vit. C, 4% calcium, 6% iron

The cranberry's sweet-tart edge is a welcome addition to this creamy coleslaw. Try this with one of the slow cooked sandwiches in this book.

CRANBERRY COLESLAW

START TO FINISH:

15 minutes

MAKES:

6 servings

5	cups shredded cabbage (1 small head)
¼	cup mayonnaise or salad dressing
1	to 2 tablespoons honey
1	tablespoon vinegar
¼	cup chopped fresh cranberries or snipped dried cranberries

1 In a large bowl place cabbage. For dressing, in a small bowl stir together mayonnaise, honey, and vinegar. Stir in cranberries.

2 Pour dressing over cabbage; toss gently to coat. Serve immediately or cover and chill for up to 45 minutes.

Nutrition Facts per serving: 94 cal., 7 g total fat (1 g sat. fat), 5 mg chol., 63 mg sodium, 7 g carbo., 2 g fiber, 1 g pro. **Daily Values:** 2% vit. A, 32% vit. C, 3% calcium, 2% iron

Watercress's peppery notes enliven the classic fruit-and-spinach salad.

STRAWBERRY-SPINACH SALAD

4   cups torn spinach or 2 cups torn spinach and 2 cups torn mixed salad greens

1   cup watercress

1   cup sliced strawberries

½   of a small red onion, thinly sliced

½   cup bottled oil-and-vinegar salad dressing or poppy seed salad dressing

START TO FINISH:

20 minutes

MAKES:

4 servings

1 In a large salad bowl combine spinach, watercress, sliced strawberries, and sliced red onion.

2 Pour salad dressing over spinach mixture; toss gently to coat.

Nutrition Facts per serving: 168 cal., 16 g total fat (2 g sat. fat), 0 mg chol., 468 mg sodium, 8 g carbo., 2 g fiber, 2 g pro. **Daily Values:** 41% vit. A, 68% vit. C, 11% iron

Choose whichever fruits strike your fancy—and whichever are looking good at the market— for this easy fresh fruit fix-up.

BERRY-DRESSED FRESH FRUIT

START TO FINISH:

15 minutes

MAKES:

6 servings

⅓ cup bottled reduced-calorie raspberry vinaigrette

1 tablespoon honey

1½ teaspoons snipped fresh mint or ½ teaspoon snipped fresh marjoram

4 cups assorted fresh fruit (such as cut-up bananas, apples, kiwifruit, or pears and/or berries)

1 For dressing, in a medium bowl combine bottled raspberry vinaigrette, honey, and mint.

2 Add assorted fresh fruit; toss gently to coat.

Nutrition Facts per serving: 102 cal., 2 g total fat (0 g sat. fat), 0 mg chol., 121 mg sodium, 21 g carbo., 3 g fiber, 1 g pro. **Daily Values:** 2% vit. A, 77% vit. C, 2% calcium, 2% iron

If desired, increase seedless green grapes to ½ cup and omit the dried fruit.
Or substitute ¼ cup mixed dried fruit for the raisins.

WALDORF SALAD

2	cups chopped apples or pears
1½	teaspoons lemon juice
¼	cup chopped celery
¼	cup chopped walnuts or pecans, toasted
¼	cup raisins, snipped pitted whole dates, or dried tart cherries
¼	cup seedless green grapes, halved
⅓	cup vanilla, lemon, or orange low-fat yogurt
2	tablespoons mayonnaise or salad dressing

START TO FINISH:
15 minutes
MAKES:
4 servings

1 In a medium bowl toss apples with lemon juice. Stir in celery, walnuts, raisins, and grapes.

2 For dressing, in a small bowl stir together yogurt and mayonnaise. Pour dressing over apple mixture; toss gently to coat. Serve immediately or cover and chill for up to 8 hours.

Nutrition Facts per serving: 193 cal., 11 g total fat (1 g sat. fat), 3 mg chol., 57 mg sodium, 24 g carbo., 3 g fiber, 3 g pro. Daily Values: 1% vit. A, 11% vit. C, 5% calcium, 3% iron

This apple salad provides a cool, creamy contrast to a spicy chili.

CREAMY APPLE SALAD

3   cups chopped apples (about 3 medium)

1   8-ounce can pineapple tidbits (juice pack), drained

½   cup coarsely chopped walnuts

1   small stalk celery, finely chopped

½   of an 8-ounce container frozen whipped dessert topping, thawed

1 In a large bowl combine apples, pineapple, walnuts, and celery.

2 Fold whipped topping into apple mixture just until combined.

Nutrition Facts per serving: 173 cal., 13 g total fat (6 g sat. fat), 31 mg chol., 13 mg sodium, 14 g carbo., 2 g fiber, 2 g pro. **Daily Values:** 7% vit. A, 9% vit. C, 3% calcium, 2% iron

Hearty stews and meaty roasts often call for something fruity and light on the side. This is a great choice.

ORANGE DREAM FRUIT SALAD

1   cup chopped mango or papaya

1   cup seedless red and/or green grapes, halved

1   11-ounce can mandarin orange sections, drained

½   cup orange yogurt

¼   teaspoon poppy seeds

START TO FINISH:
15 minutes
MAKES:
4 to 6 servings

1 In a medium bowl combine mango, grapes, and mandarin oranges. For dressing, in a small bowl stir together yogurt and poppy seeds.

2 Pour dressing over mango mixture; toss gently to coat.

Nutrition Facts per serving: 136 cal., 1 g total fat (0 g sat. fat), 2 mg chol., 26 mg sodium, 32 g carbo., 2 g fiber, 2 g pro. **Daily Values:** 46% vit. A, 52% vit. C, 7% calcium, 3% iron

Roasting asparagus brings out a mellow flavor that blanching simply can't achieve. Try this gourmet dish with a long-braising meat, such as short ribs.

CITRUS-ROASTED ASPARAGUS

PREP:
15 minutes

BAKE:
11 minutes

OVEN:
475°F

MAKES:
6 servings

1/3	cup orange marmalade
2	tablespoons pure maple syrup or maple-flavored syrup
1	teaspoon snipped fresh thyme or 1/4 teaspoon dried thyme, crushed
1 1/2	pounds asparagus spears
1 1/2	cups thinly sliced sweet onions (such as Vidalia or Walla Walla)
2	tablespoons olive oil
3/4	teaspoon salt
1/2	teaspoon cracked black pepper

1 In a small bowl combine orange marmalade, maple syrup, and thyme; set aside.

2 Snap off and discard woody bases from asparagus. If desired, scrape off scales. Place asparagus spears in a single layer in a shallow roasting pan. Top with onions. Drizzle with olive oil; toss gently to coat. Sprinkle with salt and pepper.

3 Bake, uncovered, in a 475° oven for 10 to 12 minutes or just until tender. Spoon orange marmalade mixture over vegetables; toss gently to coat. Bake for 1 minute more.

Nutrition Facts per serving: 134 cal., 5 g total fat (1 g sat. fat), 0 mg chol., 312 mg sodium, 21 g carbo., 2 g fiber, 3 g pro. **Daily Values:** 2% vit. A, 32% vit. C, 3% calcium, 4% iron

Two key ingredients—feta cheese and walnuts—elevate green beans from everyday to gourmet.

GREEN BEANS WITH FETA & WALNUTS

12 ounces green beans, cut into 1-inch pieces (about 2¼ cups)

2 tablespoons water

⅓ cup chopped walnuts

2 tablespoons butter or margarine

½ cup crumbled feta cheese or cubed mozzarella cheese

1 In a microwave-safe baking dish or casserole combine green beans and water. Cover and microwave on 100-percent power (high) for 12 to 14 minutes or just until tender, stirring once after 6 minutes; drain. Cover and keep warm.

2 In a microwave-safe bowl combine walnuts and butter. Microwave, uncovered, on high for 1½ to 2½ minutes or until butter is bubbly and just starting to brown, stirring after 1 minute. Spoon walnut mixture over green beans. Add feta cheese; toss gently to combine.

Nutrition Facts per serving: 194 cal., 17 g total fat (7 g sat. fat), 33 mg chol., 277 mg sodium, 8 g carbo., 4 g fiber, 6 g pro. **Daily Values:** 17% vit. A, 20% vit. C, 14% calcium, 7% iron

PREP:
10 minutes

COOK:
14 minutes

MAKES:
4 servings

If it's something colorful you're after, choose a yellow or red sweet pepper to contrast the green broccoli. Drizzle the lemon mixture over the vegetables just before serving; if the dish stands for a while, the lemon causes the broccoli's color to fade.

BROCCOLI & PEPPERS

PREP:

10 minutes

COOK:

8 minutes

MAKES:

6 servings

1   pound broccoli, cut into florets

1   medium sweet pepper, cut into 1-inch pieces

2   tablespoons butter or margarine

1   teaspoon finely shredded lemon peel

1   tablespoon lemon juice

1 In a steamer basket over simmering water place broccoli and sweet pepper. Cover and steam for 8 to 12 minutes or until vegetables are crisp-tender. Arrange vegetables on a serving platter.

2 Meanwhile, in a small saucepan melt butter. Stir in lemon peel and lemon juice. Drizzle lemon mixture over vegetables.

Nutrition Facts per serving: 63 cal., 4 g total fat (3 g sat. fat), 11 mg chol., 62 mg sodium, 6 g carbo., 3 g fiber, 2 g pro. **Daily Values:** 47% vit. A, 156% vit. C, 4% calcium, 4% iron

Mango chutney is your ticket to making Brussels sprouts a popular side dish.

GLAZED BRUSSELS SPROUTS

1   10-ounce package frozen Brussels sprouts

2   tablespoons mango chutney

1   tablespoon butter or margarine

1 Cook Brussels sprouts according to package directions; drain Brussels sprouts, removing from pan. In the same saucepan heat chutney and butter over medium-low heat until melted.

2 Add Brussels sprouts to chutney mixture in saucepan; toss gently to coat. Season to taste with salt and black pepper.

Nutrition Facts per serving: 110 cal., 4 g total fat (3 g sat. fat), 11 mg chol., 159 mg sodium, 17 g carbo., 4 g fiber, 4 g pro. **Daily Values:** 26% vit. A, 97% vit. C, 3% calcium, 5% iron

START TO FINISH:

15 minutes

MAKES:

3 servings

STOCKING YOUR PANTRY
Keep your freezer and pantry stocked with standbys so last-minute meal preparations go more smoothly and extra trips to the grocery store prove unnecessary. In the freezer, store a variety of frozen vegetables (to serve on the side or add to recipes), frozen fruit, and brown-and-serve rolls. In the pantry, stock up on packaged rice and noodle mixes, salad dressings, and muffin mixes to round out your meals.

This crisp vegetable dish is good enough for company.

CRUNCHY CABBAGE

START TO FINISH:

15 minutes

MAKES:

6 servings

¼ cup water

1 teaspoon instant beef bouillon granules

6 cups packaged shredded cabbage with carrot (coleslaw mix)

½ cup sliced green onions

¼ teaspoon salt

¼ teaspoon black pepper

⅓ cup chopped pecans

2 tablespoons butter or margarine, melted

1 teaspoon prepared mustard

Dash paprika

1 In a large saucepan combine water and beef bouillon granules; heat until dissolved. Stir in coleslaw mix, green onions, salt, and pepper.

2 Cover and cook over medium-low heat about 5 minutes or until cabbage is crisp-tender, stirring once or twice. If necessary, drain. In a small bowl combine pecans, melted butter, and mustard. Pour over cabbage mixture; toss to coat. Sprinkle with paprika.

Nutrition Facts per serving: 104 cal., 9 g total fat (3 g sat. fat), 11 mg chol., 336 mg sodium, 7 g carbo., 3 g fiber, 2 g pro. **Daily Values:** 98% vit. A, 31% vit. C, 5% calcium, 4% iron

Two tablespoons of balsamic vinegar updates a classic side dish of glazed carrots.

SWEET-SOUR CARROT COINS

1½ pounds medium carrots and/or parsnips, peeled and
cut into ¼-inch slices

¼ cup packed brown sugar

2 tablespoons olive oil

2 tablespoons balsamic vinegar or white wine vinegar

1 teaspoon cornstarch

START TO FINISH:
20 minutes
MAKES:
8 servings

1 In a covered medium saucepan cook carrots in a small amount of boiling, lightly salted water for 7 to 9 minutes or until crisp-tender. Drain carrots, removing from pan.

2 In the same saucepan stir together brown sugar, oil, vinegar, and cornstarch. Cook and stir over medium heat until slightly thickened. Add carrots. Cook, uncovered, about 2 minutes more or until carrots are glazed, stirring frequently.

Nutrition Facts per serving: 91 cal., 4 g total fat (0 g sat. fat), 0 mg chol., 71 mg sodium, 15 g carbo., 3 g fiber, 1 g pro. **Daily Values:** 192% vit. A, 4% vit. C, 2% calcium, 5% iron

*When you're looking for a fresh substitute for carrots or potatoes, try parsnips.
Brown sugar and apples beautifully accent their nutty flavor.*

CIDER-GLAZED PARSNIPS & APPLES

1 pound medium parsnips, peeled and cut into ¼-inch slices

¾ cup apple cider or apple juice

2 tablespoons brown sugar

2 tablespoons butter or margarine

2 medium cooking apples, cored and thinly sliced

1 In a covered large skillet cook parsnips in simmering apple cider for 7 to 9 minutes or until crisp-tender. Remove parsnips and any liquid from skillet; set parsnips and liquid aside.

2 In the same skillet combine brown sugar and butter. Cook, uncovered, over medium-high heat about 1 minute or until mixture starts to thicken. Add apples, parsnips, and reserved liquid. Cook, uncovered, about 2 minutes more or until parsnips are glazed, stirring frequently.

Nutrition Facts per serving: 206 cal., 7 g total fat (4 g sat. fat), 16 mg chol., 74 mg sodium, 38 g carbo., 7 g fiber, 1 g pro. Daily Values: 5% vit. A, 26% vit. C, 5% calcium, 5% iron

You'll love the crunch and color this dish brings to a slow cooked supper.

SNOW PEAS & TOMATOES

6   cups fresh snow pea pods (about 1 pound)

1   large shallot, sliced

2   teaspoons peanut oil

¼   teaspoon toasted sesame oil

1   tablespoon bottled teriyaki sauce

½   cup grape, cherry, and/or pear-shape red and/or yellow tomatoes, halved

2   teaspoons sesame seeds, toasted

START TO FINISH:

15 minutes

MAKES:

6 servings

1 Remove strings and tips from pea pods; set aside. In a 12-inch skillet cook shallot in hot peanut and sesame oil over medium heat until tender.

2 Add pea pods and teriyaki sauce. Cook and stir for 2 to 3 minutes or until pea pods are crisp-tender. Stir in tomatoes; cook for 1 minute more. Sprinkle with sesame seeds.

Nutrition Facts per serving: 58 cal., 2 g total fat (0 g sat. fat), 0 mg chol., 120 mg sodium, 7 g carbo., 2 g fiber, 3 g pro. Daily Values: 5% vit. A, 66% vit. C, 3% calcium, 9% iron

Why eat plain boiled potatoes when you can have something really special with a few extra ingredients?

ROSEMARY-BUTTERED POTATOES

PREP:

15 minutes

COOK:

15 minutes

MAKES:

12 servings

12   small red-skinned potatoes (about 3 pounds)

¼   cup butter or margarine

1   tablespoon snipped fresh rosemary or 1 teaspoon dried rosemary, crushed

½   teaspoon salt

¼   teaspoon black pepper

1 Scrub potatoes; cut into quarters. In a 4-quart Dutch oven cook potatoes in a small amount of boiling, lightly salted water for 15 to 20 minutes or until tender; drain. Return potatoes to Dutch oven; cover and keep warm.

2 Meanwhile, in a small skillet heat butter over low heat until melted. Stir in rosemary, salt, and pepper. Cook and stir for 2 minutes. Pour butter mixture over potatoes; toss gently to coat.

Nutrition Facts per serving: 143 cal., 4 g total fat (2 g sat. fat), 10 mg chol., 36 mg sodium, 25 g carbo., 1 g fiber, 3 g pro. **Daily Values:** 3% vit. A, 24% vit. C, 1% calcium, 12% iron

American bistro chefs have turned the making of mashed potatoes into an art.
This smoky cheese and garlic recipe follows their lead.

SMOKED CHEDDAR MASHED POTATOES

¼   cup finely chopped onion or shallots

2   cloves garlic, minced (optional)

2   tablespoons butter or margarine

1⅓   cups milk

½   of a 22-ounce package frozen mashed potatoes (about 3 cups)

¾   cup shredded smoked cheddar cheese (3 ounces)

2   slices bacon, crisp-cooked, drained, and crumbled

START TO FINISH:

20 minutes

MAKES:

4 servings

1 In a medium saucepan cook onion and garlic (if desired) in hot butter over medium-high heat about 3 minutes or until tender. Stir in milk. Bring to simmering.

2 Stir in mashed potatoes. Reduce heat to medium. Cook and stir for 2 to 4 minutes or until potatoes are desired consistency and heated through. Remove from heat. Stir in cheddar cheese and crumbled bacon. Cover and let stand for 2 minutes.

Nutrition Facts per serving: 314 cal., 20 g total fat (11 g sat. fat), 53 mg chol., 491 mg sodium, 24 g carbo., 2 g fiber, 12 g pro. **Daily Values:** 12% vit. A, 2% vit. C, 26% calcium, 2% iron

Liven up roasts with this boldly flavored take on one of America's favorite side dishes. No boiling or peeling needed—the quick recipe relies on refrigerated mashed potatoes.

ZESTY MASHED POTATOES

START TO FINISH:

15 minutes

MAKES:

8 servings

½   cup chopped red onion and/or sliced green onions

1   tablespoon butter or margarine

1½   teaspoons Jamaican jerk seasoning

¼   teaspoon black pepper

2   20-ounce packages refrigerated mashed potatoes

1   8-ounce carton regular or light dairy sour cream

① In a large saucepan cook onion in hot butter over medium heat for 3 to 4 minutes or until tender. Stir in jerk seasoning and pepper.

② Stir in mashed potatoes and sour cream. Cook until heated through, stirring frequently.

Nutrition Facts per serving: 189 cal., 10 g total fat (5 g sat. fat), 17 mg chol., 300 mg sodium, 21 g carbo., 1 g fiber, 4 g pro. **Daily Values:** 6% vit. A, 42% vit. C, 5% calcium, 4% iron

No matter what the main dish, a side of yellow summer squash and green zucchini colors a slow cooked supper.

PARMESAN-TOSSED SQUASH

1   medium zucchini, cut into ¼-inch slices

1   medium yellow summer squash, cut into ¼-inch slices

2   tablespoons snipped fresh oregano or 2 teaspoons dried oregano, crushed

2   tablespoons olive oil or cooking oil

¼   cup finely shredded Parmesan cheese

START TO FINISH:

15 minutes

MAKES:

4 servings

1 In a microwave-safe 1½-quart casserole combine zucchini, yellow squash, oregano, and olive oil. Cover and microwave on 100-percent power (high) for 4 to 6 minutes or just until squash is tender, stirring once after 2 minutes.

2 Sprinkle with Parmesan cheese; toss gently to coat.

Nutrition Facts per serving: 101 cal., 9 g total fat (2 g sat. fat), 6 mg chol., 77 mg sodium, 3 g carbo., 1 g fiber, 3 g pro. **Daily Values:** 6% vit. A, 13% vit. C, 8% calcium, 2% iron

Even a small sprinkling of herbs takes the boredom out of plain old pasta.

MIXED PASTAS WITH FRESH HERBS

START TO FINISH:

20 minutes

MAKES:

8 servings

8   ounces assorted dried pastas (with similar cooking times)

2   tablespoons olive oil

2   tablespoons snipped mixed fresh herbs (such as sage, rosemary, and basil)

¼   teaspoon salt

¼   teaspoon coarsely ground black pepper

1 Cook assorted pastas according to package directions; drain. Return pasta to saucepan.

2 Add oil, fresh herbs, salt, and pepper; toss gently to coat.

Nutrition Facts per serving: 136 cal., 4 g total fat (0 g sat. fat), 0 mg chol., 74 mg sodium, 21 g carbo., 11 g fiber, 4 g pro. **Daily Values:** 1% calcium, 5% iron

Serve this sprightly side with any meat that braises or simmers a long time.
The lemon peel will add a jolt of freshness to the meal.

LIGHT & LEMONY FETTUCCINE

1	9-ounce package refrigerated plain or spinach fettuccine
2	tablespoons butter
½	teaspoon finely shredded lemon peel
¼	teaspoon salt
¼	teaspoon black pepper

START TO FINISH:
15 minutes
MAKES:
3 servings

1 Cook fettuccine according to package directions; drain. Return fettuccine to saucepan.

2 Add butter, lemon peel, salt, and pepper; toss gently to coat.

Nutrition Facts per serving: 164 cal., 6 g total fat (3 g sat. fat), 54 mg chol., 154 mg sodium, 23 g carbo., 1 g fiber, 5 g pro. **Daily Values:** 3% vit. A, 1% calcium, 8% iron

If your slow cooker recipe suggests serving a side of rice, but you want something more varied, try this zippy pilaf.

GINGERED RICE PILAF

START TO FINISH:

20 minutes

MAKES:

6 servings

2   cups cut-up fresh vegetables from salad bar (such as sugar snap peas, carrots, mushrooms, and/or onions)

1   tablespoon cooking oil

1   teaspoon grated fresh ginger

1   clove garlic, minced

1   14-ounce can reduced-sodium chicken broth

2   cups uncooked instant white rice

¼   teaspoon salt

¼   teaspoon black pepper

2   tablespoons rice vinegar

2   tablespoons chopped peanuts

1 If necessary, cut vegetables into small pieces. In a medium saucepan heat oil over medium-high heat. Add ginger and garlic; cook and stir for 30 seconds. Add vegetables; cook and stir for 2 minutes.

2 Carefully add chicken broth to saucepan. Bring to boiling. Stir in rice, salt, and pepper. Return to boiling; reduce heat. Cover and simmer for 5 minutes. Remove from heat.

3 Let stand, covered, for 5 minutes. Sprinkle with rice vinegar; gently fluff with a fork. Transfer to a serving bowl. Sprinkle with peanuts.

Nutrition Facts per serving: 185 cal., 4 g total fat (1 g sat. fat), 0 mg chol., 289 mg sodium, 32 g carbo., 2 g fiber, 5 g pro. **Daily Values:** 57% vit. A, 9% vit. C, 2% calcium, 10% iron

*When your family is ready to eat but dinner still needs to simmer awhile,
serve this bread with pizza sauce to stave off hunger.*

OLIVE BREAD

½   cup grated Parmesan cheese
1   2¼-ounce can sliced pitted ripe olives, drained
4   or 5 cloves garlic, minced
1   10-ounce package refrigerated pizza dough
    Bottled pizza sauce, warmed

PREP:
20 minutes
BAKE:
18 minutes
OVEN:
400°F
MAKES:
12 servings

1 Set aside 1 tablespoon of the Parmesan cheese. For filling, in a small bowl combine remaining Parmesan cheese, olives, and garlic. Lightly grease a baking sheet; set aside.

2 On a lightly floured surface, roll pizza dough into a 14×10-inch rectangle. Sprinkle ⅓ cup of the filling along a short side of the dough in a 2-inch band. Fold dough over filling, allowing about two-thirds of the dough to extend beyond filling. Sprinkle another ⅓ cup of the filling on top of filled layer, pressing lightly. Fold dough back over filling, making about a 3-inch pleat. Repeat filling and folding dough accordion-style once more with remaining filling.

3 Gently pat sides of loaf to form a 10½×3-inch rectangle; seal ends. Place on prepared baking sheet. Brush with a little water and sprinkle with reserved Parmesan cheese.

4 Bake in a 400° oven for 18 to 20 minutes or until golden. Serve warm with pizza sauce.

Nutrition Facts per serving: 83 cal., 3 g total fat (1 g sat. fat), 3 mg chol., 285 mg sodium, 11 g carbo., 1 g fiber, 3 g pro. **Daily Values:** 1% vit. A, 3% vit. C, 7% calcium, 5% iron

Try these terrific muffins with any Southern- or south-of-the-border inspired dish.

SOUTHERN CORN BREAD MINI MUFFINS

PREP:
15 minutes
BAKE:
10 minutes
COOL:
5 minutes
OVEN:
400°F
MAKES:
24 muffins

¼	cup butter or margarine, softened
1	tablespoon honey
	Dash cayenne pepper or several dashes bottled hot pepper sauce
2	tablespoons jalapeño pepper jelly
1	slightly beaten egg
¼	cup buttermilk
1	8½-ounce package corn muffin mix
½	cup frozen whole kernel corn, thawed
½	cup shredded taco cheese or cheddar cheese (2 ounces)

1 Grease bottoms and halfway up the sides of twenty-four 1¾-inch muffin cups; set aside.

2 For butter spread, in a small bowl combine butter, honey, and cayenne pepper; set aside.

3 In a microwave-safe medium bowl microwave jalapeño jelly on 100-percent power (high) for 20 to 40 seconds or until melted. Stir in egg and buttermilk. Add muffin mix; stir just until moistened. Stir in corn and taco cheese.

4 Spoon batter into prepared muffin cups, filling each two-thirds full. Bake in a 400° oven for 10 to 12 minutes or until golden and a wooden toothpick inserted in centers comes out clean.

5 Cool in muffin cups on a wire rack for 5 minutes. Remove from muffin cups; serve warm with butter spread.

Nutrition Facts per serving: 103 cal., 3 g total fat (3 g sat. fat), 22 mg chol., 157 mg sodium, 10 g carbo., 0 g fiber, 1 g pro. **Daily Values:** 4% vit. A, 6% calcium, 1% iron

BREAD IDEAS

One thing to love about slow cooker foods is that you need only bread and a salad or a fresh fruit or vegetable plate to complete a meal. Keep a supply of various baking mixes on hand so you can quickly bake a batch of muffins or biscuits to serve with dinner. For variety, stir canned diced green chile peppers into corn muffin batter or mix grated Parmesan cheese into biscuit mix.

These meat-studded muffins go great with creamy, veggie-packed soups.

BACON-CHEESE CORN MUFFINS

8	slices bacon
1	cup chopped onion
1¼	cups all-purpose flour
¾	cup cornmeal
⅓	cup sugar
1	tablespoon baking powder
½	teaspoon salt
2	slightly beaten eggs
1	cup milk
2	tablespoons butter or margarine, melted
1	cup shredded sharp cheddar cheese (4 ounces)

PREP:
25 minutes
BAKE:
15 minutes
COOL:
5 minutes
OVEN:
400°F
MAKES:
16 muffins

1 Grease bottoms and halfway up the sides of sixteen 2½-inch muffin cups or line with paper bake cups; set aside. In a 12-inch skillet cook bacon over medium heat until crisp. Drain bacon, reserving 2 tablespoons drippings in skillet. Crumble bacon; set aside. Add onion to reserved drippings in skillet; cook and stir until tender. Using a slotted spoon, remove onion; set aside.

2 In a large bowl combine flour, cornmeal, sugar, baking powder, and salt. Make a well in center of flour mixture. In a small bowl combine eggs, milk, and melted butter. Add to flour mixture all at once; stir just until moistened. Fold in bacon, onion, and cheddar cheese.

3 Spoon batter into prepared muffin cups, filling each two-thirds full. Bake in a 400° oven for 15 to 18 minutes or until golden and a wooden toothpick inserted in centers comes out clean.

4 Cool in muffin cups on a wire rack for 5 minutes. Remove from muffin cups; serve warm.

Nutrition Facts per serving: 169 cal., 8 g total fat (4 g sat. fat), 43 mg chol., 273 mg sodium, 18 g carbo., 1 g fiber, 6 g pro. **Daily Values:** 5% vit. A, 1% vit. C, 12% calcium, 5% iron

STAGGERING BATCHES OF MUFFINS
If you don't have 16 muffin cups, chill any remaining batter while the first batch of muffins bakes. Bake remaining batter as directed.

The traditional baking powder biscuit is hard to beat—except when you add a little dill and cheese to the mix. These add a homespun touch to any Sunday dinner.

CHEESE-HERB BISCUITS

PREP:

20 minutes

BAKE:

10 minutes

OVEN:

450°F

MAKES:

10 to 12 biscuits

2	cups all-purpose flour
4	teaspoons baking powder
¹/₂	teaspoon salt
¹/₄	cup shortening
³/₄	cup shredded Gruyère cheese (3 ounces)
2	tablespoons snipped fresh dill
²/₃	cup milk

1 In a medium bowl stir together flour, baking powder, and salt. Cut in shortening until mixture resembles coarse crumbs. Stir in Gruyère cheese and dill. Make a well in center of flour mixture. Add milk all at once; stir just until moistened.

2 On a lightly floured surface, knead dough by gently folding and pressing dough for 10 to 12 strokes or until nearly smooth. Pat dough to ¹/₂-inch thickness. Cut dough with a floured 2¹/₂-inch round cutter. Place biscuits on an ungreased baking sheet.

3 Bake in a 450° oven for 10 to 12 minutes or until golden. Serve warm.

Nutrition Facts per serving: 174 cal., 8 g total fat (3 g sat. fat), 10 mg chol., 311 mg sodium, 19 g carbo., 1 g fiber, 5 g pro. **Daily Values:** 3% vit. A, 14% calcium, 6% iron

This recipe, which features a clever topping, stands up as an appetizer or a side. Either way it will be memorable.

NUTTY HERBED FOCACCIA WEDGES

1	6½-ounce container semisoft cheese with garlic and herb
¼	cup pine nuts or chopped almonds, toasted
1	teaspoon bottled minced roasted garlic
¼	teaspoon black pepper
1	10-inch Italian flatbread (focaccia)

PREP:
10 minutes
BROIL:
2 minutes
MAKES:
12 servings

1 Preheat broiler. Line a baking sheet with foil; set aside.

2 In a small bowl combine cheese, nuts, roasted garlic, and pepper. Spread cheese mixture over flatbread. Place on prepared baking sheet.

3 Broil about 4 inches from the heat for 2 to 4 minutes or until cheese mixture is bubbly and starts to brown. Cut into wedges; serve warm.

Nutrition Facts per serving: 170 cal., 8 g total fat (4 g sat. fat), 14 mg chol., 0 mg sodium, 19 g carbo., 1 g fiber, 6 g pro. **Daily Values:** 5% calcium, 3% iron

If you're looking for a full-bodied bread to round out a meal of light soup, look no further.

TOMATO-PESTO TOAST

PREP:

15 minutes

BROIL:

3 minutes

MAKES:

12 to 16 servings

2　French-style rolls (about 6 inches long), cut into ½-inch slices

¾　cup purchased or homemade pesto

2　or 3 roma tomatoes, cut lengthwise into thin slices

⅓　cup crumbled feta cheese

　　Coarsely cracked black pepper

1 Preheat broiler. Arrange bread slices on the unheated rack of a broiler pan. Broil 4 to 5 inches from the heat about 2 minutes or until toasted, turning once halfway through broiling.

2 Spread a scant 1 tablespoon pesto on each slice of toasted bread; top each with a tomato slice. Sprinkle with feta cheese and pepper. Broil for 1 to 2 minutes more or until heated through, watching carefully.

Nutrition Facts per serving: 160 cal., 9 g total fat (2 g sat. fat), 8 mg chol., 289 mg sodium, 15 g carbo., 1 g fiber, 6 g pro. **Daily Values:** 2% vit. A, 5% vit. C, 11% calcium, 6% iron

The basic breadstick recipe here provides an easy serve-along with any soup or stew.
Try the variations for gourmet options.

FAST FLATBREAD STICKS

1	10-ounce package refrigerated pizza dough
2	tablespoons butter or margarine, melted
½	cup finely shredded Parmesan or Romano cheese
1	tablespoon snipped fresh basil, oregano, and/or thyme or 1 teaspoon dried basil, oregano, and/or thyme, crushed

1 Lightly grease a large baking sheet. Unroll pizza dough onto prepared baking sheet. Using your hands, press dough into a 12×9-inch rectangle. Brush with melted butter.

2 In a small bowl combine Parmesan cheese and basil; sprinkle over dough. Using a sharp knife or pizza cutter, cut dough into twelve 9×1-inch sticks.

3 Bake in a 425° oven for 10 to 13 minutes or until golden. Separate sticks; serve immediately.

Nutrition Facts per serving: 197 cal., 10 g total fat (5 g sat. fat), 21 mg chol., 532 mg sodium, 16 g carbo., 1 g fiber, 11 g pro. **Daily Values:** 5% vit. A, 28% calcium, 7% iron

PREP:
15 minutes
BAKE:
10 minutes
OVEN:
425°F
MAKES:
12 servings

TOMATO & HERB FLATBREAD STICKS
Prepare Fast Flatbread Sticks as directed, except thinly slice 3 roma tomatoes; pat dry with paper towels. Arrange tomato slices on top of butter-coated dough. Sprinkle with cheese mixture. Cut and bake as directed.

ONION, WALNUT, & SWISS FLATBREAD STICKS
Prepare Fast Flatbread Sticks as directed, except omit Parmesan or Romano cheese and herbs. In a small bowl combine ¾ cup shredded Swiss cheese (3 ounces), ⅓ cup finely chopped onion, and ¼ cup chopped walnuts; sprinkle over dough. Cut and bake as directed.

These cheese and herb breadsticks are great with cold-weather soups and stews, and pair up nicely with summer salads too.

CHEESE & HERB BREADSTICK TWISTS

PREP:

15 minutes

BAKE:

12 minutes

OVEN:

350°F

MAKES:

10 twists

¼ cup oil-packed dried tomatoes

¼ cup grated Romano cheese

2 teaspoons water

1½ teaspoons snipped fresh rosemary or ½ teaspoon dried rosemary, crushed

⅛ teaspoon cracked black pepper

1 10-ounce package refrigerated pizza dough

1 Drain dried tomatoes, reserving oil; finely snip tomatoes. For filling, in a small bowl combine dried tomatoes, 2 teaspoons of the reserved oil, the Romano cheese, water, rosemary, and pepper. Lightly grease a baking sheet; set aside.

2 On a lightly floured surface, roll pizza dough into a 10×8-inch rectangle. Spread filling across half of the dough. Fold remaining half of dough over filling; press lightly to seal edges. Cut lengthwise into ten 8×½-inch strips. Fold each strip in half and twist two or three times. Place 1 inch apart on prepared baking sheet.

3 Bake in a 350° oven for 12 to 15 minutes or until golden. Cool on a wire rack.

Nutrition Facts per serving: 113 cal., 3 g total fat (1 g sat. fat), 3 mg chol., 263 mg sodium, 18 g carbo., 1 g fiber, 5 g pro. **Daily Values:** 1% vit. A, 5% vit. C, 3% calcium, 5% iron

For an alternative to bread, try these nicely seasoned chips. They also make good dippers for salsa.

ITALIAN-STYLE CHIPS

²/₃ cup finely chopped onion

2 tablespoons butter or margarine

1 teaspoon dried Italian seasoning, crushed

4 8-inch flour tortillas

Bottled salsa (optional)

PREP:
15 minutes
BAKE:
8 minutes
OVEN:
350°F
MAKES:
8 servings

1 In a small skillet cook onion in hot butter for 3 to 5 minutes or until tender. Stir in Italian seasoning. Carefully brush onion mixture evenly over one side of tortillas. Cut each tortilla into 8 wedges.

2 Spread wedges in an ungreased 15×10×1-inch baking pan. Bake in a 350° oven for 8 to 10 minutes or until chips are crisp and edges are light brown. If desired, serve chips with salsa.

Nutrition Facts per serving: 105 cal., 7 g total fat (2 g sat. fat), 8 mg chol., 127 mg sodium, 9 g carbo., 0 g fiber, 1 g pro. Daily Values: 1% vit. C, 1% calcium, 4% iron

Rich, smooth, buttery, and tart, lemon curd brings something gourmet to the renowned shortcake. Look for it alongside jams and jellies in the supermarket.

QUICK STRAWBERRY SHORTCAKES

PREP:

10 minutes

BAKE:

per package directions

OVEN:

per package directions

MAKES:

4 servings

4   frozen unbaked buttermilk biscuits

$1/3$ cup strawberry jelly

1   pint (2 cups) strawberries, sliced

$1/3$ cup lemon or strawberry curd

    Sweetened whipped cream

1 Bake biscuits according to package directions. Cool completely.

2 In a small saucepan heat strawberry jelly just until melted. In a medium bowl place strawberries. Add jelly; toss gently to coat. Set aside.

3 Split biscuits horizontally. Spread bottoms of biscuits with lemon curd; replace tops of biscuits. Place each biscuit on a dessert plate. Spoon strawberry mixture over biscuits and top with whipped cream.

Nutrition Facts per serving: 472 cal., 22 g total fat (10 g sat. fat), 61 mg chol., 619 mg sodium, 48 g carbo., 5 g fiber, 5 g pro. **Daily Values:** 9% vit. A, 69% vit. C, 5% calcium, 8% iron

Fruit crisp is always an easy dessert to make, but it's even easier when you use granola instead of a combination of crispy ingredients.

EASY FRUIT CRISP

5 cups peeled and sliced apples, pears, or peaches or frozen unsweetened peach slices, thawed

¼ cup dried cherries, dried cranberries, or mixed dried fruit bits

2 tablespoons sugar

1½ cups granola

3 tablespoons butter, melted
Vanilla ice cream (optional)

PREP:
20 minutes
BAKE:
30 minutes
OVEN:
350°F
MAKES:
6 servings

1 In a 2-quart square baking dish combine sliced fruit and dried fruit; sprinkle with sugar. In a small bowl combine granola and melted butter; sprinkle over fruit.

2 Bake in a 350° oven for 30 to 35 minutes or until fruit is tender. Serve warm. If desired, serve with ice cream.

Nutrition Facts per serving: 306 cal., 13 g total fat (5 g sat. fat), 16 mg chol., 66 mg sodium, 46 g carbo., 5 g fiber, 3 g pro. **Daily Values:** 8% vit. A, 7% vit. C, 3% calcium, 6% iron

These adorable cheesecakes are irresistible—they provide just the right amount of "tah-dah!" for a lively gathering.

CHOCOLATE COOKIE CHEESECAKES

PREP:

20 minutes

BAKE:

20 minutes

CHILL:

1 hour

OVEN:

325°F

MAKES:

12 servings

12	chocolate sandwich cookies with white filling
2	8-ounce packages cream cheese, softened
½	cup sugar
1	teaspoon vanilla
2	eggs

1 Line twelve 2½-inch muffin cups with foil bake cups. Split each cookie, keeping filling intact on one cookie half. Place a cookie half with filling in each cup, filling side up.

2 In a medium mixing bowl beat cream cheese, sugar, and vanilla with an electric mixer on low to medium speed until smooth. Add eggs. Beat on low speed just until combined. Spoon mixture into cups. Crush remaining cookies; sprinkle on top of cream cheese mixture.

3 Bake in a 325° oven for 20 to 25 minutes or until set (tops may indent slightly). Cool. Cover and chill for 1 to 24 hours. To serve, remove bake cups.

Nutrition Facts per serving: 223 cal., 16 g total fat (9 g sat. fat), 77 mg chol., 183 mg sodium, 16 g carbo., 0 g fiber, 4 g pro. **Daily Values:** 12% vit. A, 4% calcium, 5% iron

When you need a quick dessert, the ubiquitous purchased pound cake can be dressed to your liking. This one features chocolate and nuts.

CRUNCHY POUND CAKE SLICES

4   ½-inch slices purchased pound cake

¼   cup chocolate-hazelnut spread

½   cup roasted mixed nuts, coarsely chopped

1   pint (2 cups) caramel or cinnamon ice cream

1 Preheat broiler. On an ungreased baking sheet place pound cake slices. Broil 3 to 4 inches from the heat about 2 minutes or until light brown, turning once halfway through broiling. Cool slightly.

2 Spread one side of each cake slice with 1 tablespoon chocolate-hazelnut spread. Sprinkle with nuts; pat gently to form an even layer. Transfer each slice to a dessert plate and top with a scoop of ice cream. Serve immediately.

Nutrition Facts per serving: 763 cal., 45 g total fat (22 g sat. fat), 206 mg chol., 421 mg sodium, 82 g carbo., 2 g fiber, 12 g pro. **Daily Values:** 19% vit. A, 19% calcium, 11% iron

PREP:
15 minutes
BROIL:
2 minutes
MAKES:
4 servings

Like tiramisu—a fancy Italian dessert—but so much easier, these light and frothy parfaits provide a fanciful finish to a slow cooked meal.

COFFEE ANGEL DESSERT

PREP:
20 minutes
CHILL:
4 hours
MAKES:
4 servings

1 cup whipping cream

¼ cup sifted powdered sugar

⅓ cup coffee liqueur or strong coffee

½ of an 8- or 10-inch purchased angel food cake

¼ cup shaved semisweet chocolate (1 ounce)

1 In a chilled medium mixing bowl beat whipping cream, powdered sugar, and 1 tablespoon of the coffee liqueur with an electric mixer until stiff peaks form (tips stand straight). Set aside.

2 Cut cake into bite-size cubes. In four parfait glasses place half of the cake cubes. Drizzle with half of the remaining coffee liqueur. Spoon half of the whipping cream over cake in glasses; top with half of the shaved chocolate. Repeat layers. Cover and chill for 4 to 24 hours.

Nutrition Facts per serving: 466 cal., 25 g total fat (15 g sat. fat), 82 mg chol., 396 mg sodium, 48 g carbo., 1 g fiber, 5 g pro. **Daily Values:** 18% vit. A, 1% vit. C, 11% calcium, 4% iron

This no-bake cheese pie comes together in minutes. Keep the ingredients on hand so you'll always be ready to wow guests.

STRAWBERRY-CHOCOLATE PIE

- 1 cup semisweet chocolate pieces (6 ounces)
- 1 8-ounce package cream cheese
- 3 tablespoons honey
- 1 baked 9-inch pastry shell, cooled
- 4 cups whole strawberries, stems and caps removed

1 In a small heavy saucepan heat chocolate pieces over low heat until melted and smooth, stirring constantly. Cool.

2 In a medium mixing bowl beat cream cheese with an electric mixer on low speed until softened. Gradually beat in melted chocolate and honey. Spread mixture in pastry shell.

3 Cover and chill for 1 to 2 hours. Arrange strawberries on top of pie. If desired, drizzle with additional melted semisweet chocolate. Serve immediately.

Nutrition Facts per serving: 387 cal., 25 g total fat (12 g sat. fat), 31 mg chol., 160 mg sodium, 40 g carbo., 3 g fiber, 5 g pro. **Daily Values:** 9% vit. A, 68% vit. C, 4% calcium, 12% iron

PREP:
20 minutes
CHILL:
1 hour
MAKES:
8 servings

How does a fancy French dessert qualify as swift? It starts with frozen puff pastry, an amazingly easy-to-use ingredient that turns out amazing layers of flaky pastry.

FRUIT-FILLED NAPOLEONS

PREP:

20 minutes

BAKE:

20 minutes

OVEN:

375°F

MAKES:

8 servings

½ of a 17.3-ounce package (1 sheet) frozen puff pastry sheets, thawed

2 cups prepared pudding, fruit yogurt, sweetened whipped cream, or softened ice cream

1 cup peeled and sliced kiwifruit, halved seedless red grapes, berries, and/or halved orange slices

Sifted powdered sugar (optional)

① On a lightly floured surface, unfold puff pastry sheet. Using a small sharp knife, cut pastry into 8 rectangles. Place pastry rectangles on an ungreased baking sheet. Bake in a 375° oven about 20 minutes or until puffed and golden. Transfer to wire racks; cool.

② Just before serving, split each pastry rectangle in half horizontally. Spoon pudding onto bottoms of pastry. Add fruit; replace tops of pastry. If desired, sprinkle with powdered sugar. Serve immediately.

Nutrition Facts per serving: 266 cal., 13 g total fat (0 g sat. fat), 1 mg chol., 184 mg sodium, 35 g carbo., 1 g fiber, 3 g pro. **Daily Values:** 4% vit. A, 67% vit. C, 8% calcium, 2% iron

SLOW COOKED DESSERTS

9

With its caramel and apple "pudding" on the bottom and moist walnut cake on top, this dessert has an irresistibly homespun appeal.

DUTCH APPLE PUDDING CAKE

PREP:

25 minutes

COOK:

2 to 2¹/₂ hours (high)

COOL:

30 minutes

MAKES:

6 to 8 servings

**SWEETENED
WHIPPED CREAM**

Chill a small mixing bowl and the beaters of an electric mixer. In chilled bowl combine ¹/₂ cup whipping cream and 2 teaspoons brown sugar. Beat with an electric mixer on medium speed until soft peaks form (tips curl).

Nonstick cooking spray

1   20- or 21-ounce can apple pie filling

¹/₂   cup dried cherries, dried cranberries, or raisins

1   cup all-purpose flour

¹/₄   cup granulated sugar

1   teaspoon baking powder

¹/₄   teaspoon salt

¹/₂   cup milk

2   tablespoons butter or margarine, melted

¹/₂   cup chopped walnuts, toasted

1¹/₄   cups apple juice

¹/₃   cup packed brown sugar

1   tablespoon butter or margarine

1   recipe Sweetened Whipped Cream (optional)

1   Lightly coat a 3¹/₂- or 4-quart slow cooker with cooking spray; set aside. In a small saucepan bring apple pie filling to boiling. Stir in dried cherries. Transfer apple mixture to prepared cooker.

2   In a medium bowl stir together flour, granulated sugar, baking powder, and salt. Add milk and melted butter; stir just until combined. Stir in walnuts. Pour over apple mixture in cooker, spreading evenly.

3   In the same small saucepan combine apple juice, brown sugar, and the 1 tablespoon butter. Bring to boiling. Boil gently, uncovered, for 2 minutes. Carefully pour apple juice mixture over batter in cooker.

4   Cover and cook on high-heat setting for 2 to 2¹/₂ hours or until a wooden toothpick inserted into center of cake comes out clean. Remove liner from cooker, if possible, or turn off cooker. Let stand, uncovered, for 30 to 45 minutes to cool slightly before serving.

5   To serve, spoon warm cake and sauce into dessert dishes. If desired, top with Sweetened Whipped Cream and additional toasted chopped walnuts.

Nutrition Facts per serving: 435 cal., 13 g total fat (5 g sat. fat), 18 mg chol., 284 mg sodium, 77 g carbo., 3 g fiber, 5 g pro. **Daily Values:** 6% vit. A, 3% vit. C, 10% calcium, 11% iron

This decadent dessert is a classic combination of tender cake smothered in rich caramel sauce. Serve in bowls topped with cream.

ORANGE PUDDING CAKE & CARAMEL SAUCE

1   cup all-purpose flour

1/3   cup granulated sugar

1   teaspoon baking powder

1/2   teaspoon ground cinnamon

1/4   teaspoon salt

1/2   cup milk

2   tablespoons butter or margarine, melted

1/2   cup chopped pecans

1/4   cup dried currants or raisins

3/4   cup water

1/2   teaspoon finely shredded orange peel

3/4   cup orange juice

2/3   cup packed brown sugar

1   tablespoon butter or margarine

       Half-and-half or light cream

PREP:

25 minutes

COOK:

2 1/2 hours (high)

COOL:

30 minutes

MAKES:

6 servings

1 In a medium bowl stir together flour, granulated sugar, baking powder, cinnamon, and salt. Add milk and melted butter; stir just until combined. Stir in pecans and currants. Spread batter evenly in the bottom of a 3 1/2- or 4-quart slow cooker.

2 In a medium saucepan combine water, orange peel, orange juice, brown sugar, and the 1 tablespoon butter. Bring to boiling. Boil gently, uncovered, for 2 minutes. Carefully pour orange juice mixture over batter in cooker.

3 Cover and cook on high-heat setting for 2 1/2 hours (center may appear moist but will set upon standing). Remove liner from cooker, if possible, or turn off cooker. Let stand, uncovered, about 30 minutes to cool slightly before serving.

4 To serve, spoon warm cake and sauce into dessert dishes. Serve with half-and-half.

Nutrition Facts per serving: 390 cal., 15 g total fat (6 g sat. fat), 23 mg chol., 255 mg sodium, 61 g carbo., 2 g fiber, 5 g pro. **Daily Values:** 8% vit. A, 27% vit. C, 12% calcium, 11% iron

Your friends are sure to be impressed with all the nifty things your slow cooker can do when you present this rich cake topped with its own warm sauce.

CHOCOLATE~PEANUT BUTTER PUDDING CAKE

PREP:

20 minutes

COOK:

2 to 2½ hours (high)

COOL:

30 minutes

MAKES:

8 servings

Nonstick cooking spray

1 cup all-purpose flour

⅓ cup sugar

2 tablespoons unsweetened cocoa powder

1½ teaspoons baking powder

½ cup chocolate milk or milk

2 tablespoons cooking oil

2 teaspoons vanilla

½ cup peanut butter-flavored pieces

½ cup semisweet chocolate pieces

½ cup chopped peanuts

¾ cup sugar

2 tablespoons unsweetened cocoa powder

1½ cups boiling water

Vanilla ice cream (optional)

1 Lightly coat a 3½- or 4-quart slow cooker with cooking spray; set aside. In a medium bowl stir together flour, the ⅓ cup sugar, 2 tablespoons cocoa powder, and baking powder. Add chocolate milk, oil, and vanilla; stir just until combined. Stir in peanut butter pieces, chocolate pieces, and peanuts. Spread batter evenly in the bottom of prepared cooker.

2 In another medium bowl combine the ¾ cup sugar and 2 tablespoons cocoa powder. Gradually stir in boiling water. Carefully pour cocoa mixture over batter in cooker.

3 Cover and cook on high-heat setting for 2 to 2½ hours or until a wooden toothpick inserted 1 inch deep into center of cake comes out clean. Remove liner from cooker, if possible, or turn off cooker. Let stand, uncovered, for 30 to 40 minutes to cool slightly before serving.

4 To serve, spoon warm cake and sauce into dessert dishes. If desired, top with ice cream.

Nutrition Facts per serving: 372 cal., 15 g total fat (6 g sat. fat), 3 mg chol., 125 mg sodium, 52 g carbo., 3 g fiber, 5 g pro. **Daily Values:** 10% calcium, 7% iron

Slow cookers are much loved in the winter months, as they're great for simmering up soups, stews, and ample meat dishes. They make great sense in summer, too, when you want to make a sweet fruit cobbler without heating up your kitchen.

CHERRY & RHUBARB COBBLER

Nonstick cooking spray

1 cup all-purpose flour

1 cup packed brown sugar

1 teaspoon ground cinnamon

½ teaspoon baking powder

¼ teaspoon baking soda

¼ teaspoon salt

2 slightly beaten eggs

3 tablespoons butter or margarine, melted

2 tablespoons milk

5 cups fresh or frozen sliced rhubarb

1 30-ounce can cherry pie filling

1 tablespoon granulated sugar

Vanilla ice cream (optional)

PREP:
20 minutes

COOK:
2 hours (high)

COOL:
30 minutes

MAKES:
8 to 10 servings

① Lightly coat a 3½- or 4-quart slow cooker with cooking spray; set aside.

② In a medium bowl combine flour, ⅔ cup of the brown sugar, ½ teaspoon of the cinnamon, the baking powder, baking soda, and salt. In a small bowl combine eggs, melted butter, and milk. Add egg mixture to flour mixture; stir just until combined. Set aside.

③ In a large saucepan combine the remaining ⅓ cup brown sugar, ¼ teaspoon of the cinnamon, the rhubarb, and cherry pie filling. Cook and stir until mixture comes to boiling. Transfer hot fruit mixture to prepared cooker. Immediately spoon batter over top of fruit mixture. Combine remaining ¼ teaspoon cinnamon and the granulated sugar; sprinkle on top of batter.

④ Cover and cook on high-heat setting about 2 hours or until a wooden toothpick inserted into center of cake comes out clean. Remove liner from cooker, if possible, or turn off cooker. Let stand, uncovered, for 30 to 45 minutes to cool slightly before serving.

⑤ To serve, spoon warm cobbler into dessert dishes. If desired, top with ice cream.

Nutrition Facts per serving: 374 cal., 6 g total fat (3 g sat. fat), 66 mg chol., 235 mg sodium, 76 g carbo., 3 g fiber, 4 g pro. **Daily Values:** 11% vit. A, 15% vit. C, 14% calcium, 11% iron

When summer is here, it's berry time and that means cobbler—warmed jewels of sun-kissed flavor covered with a soft, sweet bread that soaks up the juice. For the ultimate cobbler experience, top with ice cream.

DOUBLE-BERRY COBBLER

PREP:

25 minutes

COOK:

1³/₄ to 2 hours (high)

COOL:

1 hour

MAKES:

6 servings

1   cup all-purpose flour

³/₄   cup sugar

1   teaspoon baking powder

¹/₄   teaspoon salt

¹/₄   teaspoon ground cinnamon

¹/₄   teaspoon ground nutmeg

2   slightly beaten eggs

3   tablespoons cooking oil

2   tablespoons milk

3   cups fresh or one 16-ounce package frozen unsweetened blueberries

3   cups fresh or one 16-ounce package frozen unsweetened blackberries

1   cup sugar

1   cup water

3   tablespoons quick-cooking tapioca

Vanilla ice cream, whipped cream, half-and-half, or light cream (optional)

1 In a medium bowl stir together flour, the ³/₄ cup sugar, the baking powder, salt, cinnamon, and nutmeg. In a small bowl combine eggs, oil, and milk. Add egg mixture to flour mixture; stir just until combined. Set aside.

2 In a large saucepan combine blueberries, blackberries, the 1 cup sugar, the water, and tapioca. Bring to boiling. Transfer hot fruit mixture to a 3¹/₂- or 4-quart slow cooker. Immediately spoon batter over top of fruit mixture.

3 Cover and cook on high-heat setting for 1³/₄ to 2 hours or until a wooden toothpick inserted into center of cake comes out clean. Remove liner from cooker, if possible, or turn off cooker. Let stand, uncovered, about 1 hour to cool slightly before serving.

4 To serve, spoon warm cobbler into dessert dishes. If desired, top with ice cream.

Nutrition Facts per serving: 478 cal., 10 g total fat (2 g sat. fat), 71 mg chol., 194 mg sodium, 97 g carbo., 6 g fiber, 6 g pro. **Daily Values:** 6% vit. A, 41% vit. C, 9% calcium, 11% iron

For a taste of spring, surprise your gang with ginger-kissed fruits spooned over mounds of cake and drizzled with cream.

STRAWBERRY-RHUBARB COBBLER

1	cup all-purpose flour
1	cup sugar
1	teaspoon baking powder
1	teaspoon finely shredded lemon peel
½	teaspoon ground cinnamon
¼	teaspoon salt
2	slightly beaten eggs
2	tablespoons cooking oil
2	tablespoons milk
3	cups fresh or frozen whole strawberries
3	cups fresh or frozen sliced rhubarb
¾	cup sugar
½	cup water
1	tablespoon finely chopped crystallized ginger or ½ teaspoon ground ginger
	Half-and-half, light cream, whipped cream, or vanilla ice cream (optional)

PREP:
20 minutes

COOK:
2 to 2½ hours (high)

COOL:
30 minutes

MAKES:
8 to 10 servings

1 In a medium bowl stir together flour, the 1 cup sugar, the baking powder, lemon peel, cinnamon, and salt. In a small bowl combine eggs, oil, and milk. Add egg mixture to flour mixture; stir just until combined. Spread batter evenly in bottom of a 3½- or 4-quart slow cooker.

2 In a large saucepan combine strawberries, rhubarb, the ¾ cup sugar, the water, and ginger. Bring to boiling. Carefully spoon hot fruit mixture over batter in cooker.

3 Cover and cook on high-heat setting for 2 to 2½ hours or until a wooden toothpick inserted into center of cake comes out clean. Remove liner from cooker, if possible, or turn off cooker. Let stand, uncovered, about 30 minutes to cool slightly before serving.

4 To serve, spoon warm cobbler into dessert dishes. If desired, serve with half-and-half.

Nutrition Facts per serving: 294 cal., 5 g total fat (1 g sat. fat), 53 mg chol., 144 mg sodium, 60 g carbo., 3 g fiber, 4 g pro. **Daily Values:** 3% vit. A, 58% vit. C, 9% calcium, 7% iron

Brown sugar brings depth to the sweetness in this fruity compote. Serve it over vanilla ice cream for an irresistible hot/cold effect.

MIXED FRUIT COMPOTE WITH GINGER

PREP:

15 minutes

COOK:

*6 to 8 hours (low)
or 3 to 4 hours (high)*

MAKES:

10 to 12 servings

1	15½-ounce can pineapple chunks, undrained
3	medium pears, peeled (if desired), cored, and cubed
2	cups frozen unsweetened pitted dark sweet cherries
1	cup dried apricots, quartered
3	tablespoons frozen orange juice concentrate
2	tablespoons brown sugar
1	tablespoon quick-cooking tapioca
1	teaspoon grated fresh ginger or ½ teaspoon ground ginger
	Vanilla ice cream
½	cup flaked coconut, toasted
¼	cup macadamia nuts or pecans, chopped and toasted

1 In a 3½- or 4-quart slow cooker combine pineapple, pears, cherries, dried apricots, orange juice concentrate, brown sugar, tapioca, and ginger.

2 Cover and cook on low-heat setting for 6 to 8 hours or on high-heat setting for 3 to 4 hours.

3 To serve, spoon warm compote into dessert dishes. Top with ice cream, coconut, and nuts.

Nutrition Facts per serving: 362 cal., 17 g total fat (10 g sat. fat), 45 mg chol., 63 mg sodium, 53 g carbo., 4 g fiber, 5 g pro. **Daily Values:** 31% vit. A, 28% vit. C, 12% calcium, 7% iron

**TOASTING NUTS
OR COCONUT**

Spread the nuts or coconut in a single layer in a shallow baking pan. Bake in a 350°F oven for 5 to 10 minutes or until light golden brown, watching carefully and stirring once or twice so the nuts or coconut doess not burn.

Here's an easygoing finale to a relaxed Sunday dinner.

ORANGE-APPLE-RUM COMPOTE

6	medium cooking apples, peeled, cored, and cut into ½-inch slices (6 cups)
1	7-ounce package mixed dried fruit bits
2	teaspoons finely shredded orange peel
¾	cup orange juice or apple juice
¼	cup sugar
3	tablespoons rum (optional)
1	tablespoon quick-cooking tapioca
¾	cup whipping cream
¾	cup sliced almonds, toasted

PREP:

15 minutes

COOK:

*7 to 8 hours (low)
or 3½ to 4 hours (high)*

MAKES:

12 servings

1 In a 3½- or 4-quart slow cooker combine apples, dried fruit bits, orange peel, orange juice, sugar, rum (if desired), and tapioca.

2 Cover and cook on low-heat setting for 7 to 8 hours or on high-heat setting for 3½ to 4 hours. To serve, spoon warm compote into dessert dishes. Top with cream and almonds.

Nutrition Facts per serving: 210 cal., 10 g total fat (4 g sat. fat), 21 mg chol., 18 mg sodium, 30 g carbo., 2 g fiber, 3 g pro. **Daily Values:** 5% vit. A, 17% vit. C, 4% calcium, 3% iron

As it stands, this velvety, lemony, very pretty dessert makes a captivating, light finish to a dinner party. For something more substantial, serve it over angel food or pound cake.

PEARS IN LEMON CREAM SAUCE

PREP:
20 minutes

COOK:
1 1/2 to 2 hours (high)

MAKES:
6 to 8 servings

6	medium pears
1	teaspoon finely shredded lemon peel
2	tablespoons lemon juice
1/3	cup packed brown sugar
1/4	teaspoon ground nutmeg
1/2	of an 8-ounce package cream cheese, cubed and softened
1/4	cup whipping cream
3	tablespoons broken pecans, toasted

1 Peel and core pears. Cut each pear into 8 wedges; place in a medium bowl. Add lemon peel and lemon juice; toss gently to coat. Add brown sugar and nutmeg; toss gently to coat. Transfer to a 3 1/2- or 4-quart slow cooker.

2 Cover and cook on high-heat setting for 1 1/2 to 2 hours or until pears are tender. Using a slotted spoon, transfer pears to dessert dishes.

3 Add cream cheese and whipping cream to juices in cooker. Whisk until cream cheese is melted. Spoon cream cheese mixture over pears. Sprinkle with pecans.

Nutrition Facts per serving: 273 cal., 13 g total fat (7 g sat. fat), 34 mg chol., 65 mg sodium, 40 g carbo., 4 g fiber, 3 g pro. **Daily Values:** 9% vit. A, 13% vit. C, 5% calcium, 5% iron

THE MULTIUSE COOKER
During the holidays, oven and cooktop space fill up quickly. Use your slow cooker to make a tantalizing dessert or vegetable side dish from this book. Slow cookers also provide a handy way to keep food warm on a party buffet table.

If you're serving pound cake, try toasting the slices.
Doing so brings out extra flavor and creates an interesting texture.

MOCK CHERRIES JUBILEE

2	16-ounce packages frozen unsweetened pitted tart red cherries
½	cup packed brown sugar
½	cup cherry cider, apple cider, or apple juice
2	tablespoons quick-cooking tapioca
1	vanilla bean, split lengthwise, or 2 teaspoons vanilla
2	to 3 tablespoons cherry or almond liqueur or cherry cider
	Purchased pound cake slices, angel food cake slices, or vanilla ice cream
	Whipped cream (optional)

PREP:
15 minutes
COOK:
4 to 5 hours (high)
MAKES:
8 servings

1 In a 3½- or 4-quart slow cooker combine frozen cherries, brown sugar, cider, tapioca, and, if using, vanilla bean.

2 Cover and cook on high-heat setting for 4 to 5 hours. Remove vanilla bean, if using, or stir in vanilla. Stir in liqueur.

3 To serve, place cake slices in dessert dishes. Spoon warm cherry mixture over cake. If desired, top with whipped cream.

Nutrition Facts per serving: 428 cal., 15 g total fat (9 g sat. fat), 166 mg chol., 307 mg sodium, 68 g carbo., 2 g fiber, 5 g pro. **Daily Values:** 24% vit. A, 3% vit. C, 5% calcium, 11% iron

Rife with raisins, or dried cranberries, cherries, or currants, this creamy old-fashioned dessert is ready to make a comeback as one of your household's favorite treats.

OLD-FASHIONED RICE PUDDING

PREP:

10 minutes

COOK:

2 to 3 hours (low)

MAKES:

12 to 14 servings

Nonstick cooking spray

4   cups cooked rice

1   12-ounce can (1½ cups) evaporated milk

1   cup raisins, dried cranberries, dried cherries, or dried currants

1   cup milk

⅓   cup sugar

¼   cup water

3   tablespoons butter or margarine, softened

1   tablespoon vanilla

1   teaspoon ground cinnamon

1   Lightly coat a 3½- or 4-quart slow cooker with cooking spray; set aside.

2   In a large bowl combine cooked rice, evaporated milk, raisins, milk, sugar, water, butter, vanilla, and cinnamon. Transfer rice mixture to prepared cooker.

3   Cover and cook on low-heat setting for 2 to 3 hours. Stir well before serving.

Nutrition Facts per serving: 204 cal., 6 g total fat (3 g sat. fat), 18 mg chol., 73 mg sodium, 34 g carbo., 1 g fiber, 4 g pro. **Daily Values:** 5% vit. A, 2% vit. C, 11% calcium, 6% iron

Kids will go wild over this gooey, chocolate and cherry-studded activity.

MALT SHOP FONDUE

1   14-ounce can (1¼ cups) sweetened condensed milk

1   12-ounce jar chocolate fudge ice cream topping

¼   cup malted milk powder

1   cup pecans, toasted and finely chopped

1   cup drained maraschino cherries, chopped

     Assorted dippers (such as strawberries, large marshmallows, sliced bananas, pineapple chunks, and/or pound cake cubes)

     Milk

1 In a 1½-quart slow cooker stir together sweetened condensed milk, ice cream topping, and malted milk powder. Cover and cook for 1½ hours. Stir in pecans and maraschino cherries. Serve immediately or keep warm for up to 45 minutes.

2 To serve, spear dippers with fondue forks. Dip into chocolate mixture, swirling as you dip. If the mixture thickens, stir in enough milk to make fondue of desired consistency.

Nutrition Facts per serving: 305 cal., 11 g total fat (3 g sat. fat), 13 mg chol., 125 mg sodium, 48 g carbo., 2 g fiber, 4 g pro. **Daily Values:** 3% vit. A, 2% vit. C, 12% calcium, 4% iron

PREP:

10 minutes

COOK:

1½ hours

MAKES:

12 servings

COMING CLEAN

Be sure to unplug your slow cooker before you clean it, and never immerse the cooker or the cord in water. To clean the ceramic lining, use a soft cloth and warm, soapy water. If your slow cooker has a removable insert, you can usually wash it in the dishwasher. Don't use abrasive cleaners and cleansing pads. To avoid cracking the crockery insert, let it cool completely before washing it. Be sure to check your manufacturer's directions as well.

Tell guests that it's important to swirl as they dip to keep the chocolate mixture from setting up.

CHOCOLATE-CARAMEL FONDUE

PREP:

10 minutes

COOK:

1½ hours

MAKES:

12 servings

1   14-ounce can (1¼ cups) sweetened condensed milk

1   12-ounce jar caramel ice cream topping

9   ounces semisweet chocolate, coarsely chopped, or 1½ cups semisweet chocolate pieces

Assorted dippers (such as angel food cake cubes, pound cake cubes, brownie squares, large marshmallows, dried apricots, strawberries, banana slices, and/or pineapple chunks)

Milk

1 In a 1½-quart slow cooker stir together sweetened condensed milk, ice cream topping, and chocolate.

2 Cover and cook for 1½ hours. Stir until chocolate is melted. Serve immediately or keep warm for up to 45 minutes. (Chocolate mixture will become grainy if held longer.)

3 To serve, spear dippers with fondue forks. Dip into chocolate mixture, swirling as you dip. If the mixture thickens, stir in enough milk to make fondue of desired consistency.

Nutrition Facts per serving: 295 cal., 10 g total fat (6 g sat. fat), 11 mg chol., 104 mg sodium, 50 g carbo., 2 g fiber, 6 g pro. **Daily Values:** 2% vit. A, 1% vit. C, 14% calcium, 6% iron

A small slow cooker doubles as a fondue pot for the irresistible chocolate sauce. If there are any leftovers, you can reheat them and serve over ice cream.

CANDY BAR FONDUE

4 1.76-ounce bars chocolate-coated almond nougat bars, chopped

1 7-ounce bar milk chocolate, chopped

1 7-ounce jar marshmallow creme

¾ cup whipping cream, half-and-half, or light cream

¼ cup finely chopped almonds, toasted

2 to 3 tablespoons almond, hazelnut, or raspberry liqueur (optional)

Assorted dippers (such as filled sugar wafers, pound cake cubes, strawberries, cherries, and/or pineapple pieces)

Finely chopped almonds, toasted; coconut, toasted; and/or almond toffee pieces (optional)

1 In a 3½-quart slow cooker combine nougat bars, milk chocolate bar, marshmallow creme, and whipping cream.

2 Cover and cook on low-heat setting for 2 to 2½ hours. Stir until smooth. Stir in the ¼ cup almonds and, if desired, liqueur.

3 To serve, if desired, transfer chocolate mixture to a 16-ounce slow cooker. Spear dippers with fondue forks. Dip into chocolate mixture, swirling as you dip. If desired, dip into additional almonds, coconut, and/or toffee pieces to coat.

Nutrition Facts per serving: 294 cal., 16 g total fat (8 g sat. fat), 25 mg chol., 55 mg sodium, 34 g carbo., 1 g fiber, 3 g pro. Daily Values: 5% vit. A, 7% calcium, 2% iron

PREP:
15 minutes

COOK:
2 to 2½ hours (low)

MAKES:
12 servings

Here's a comforting, but none-too-heavy dessert to serve after a warming winter meal.

SPICED FRUIT SOUP

PREP:

10 minutes

COOK:

*6 to 8 hours (low)
or 3 to 4 hours (high)*

MAKES:

8 servings

1	16-ounce package frozen unsweetened peach slices
1½	cups frozen unsweetened pitted dark sweet cherries
½	cup sugar
½	cup golden raisins
2	tablespoons quick-cooking tapioca, ground
2	teaspoons finely shredded lemon peel
2	tablespoons lemon juice
3	inches stick cinnamon, broken into 1-inch pieces
3	cups apple cider or apple juice
	Whipped cream (optional)

1 In a 3½- or 4-quart slow cooker combine frozen peach slices, frozen cherries, sugar, raisins, tapioca, lemon peel, lemon juice, and stick cinnamon. Pour apple cider over mixture in cooker.

2 Cover and cook on low-heat setting for 6 to 8 hours or on high-heat setting for 3 to 4 hours. Remove stick cinnamon.

3 To serve, spoon warm or chilled fruit soup into small dessert bowls. If desired, top with whipped cream.

Nutrition Facts per serving: 177 cal., 0 g total fat (0 g sat. fat), 0 mg chol., 4 mg sodium, 45 g carbo., 3 g fiber, 1 g pro. **Daily Values:** 7% vit. A, 15% vit. C, 2% calcium, 4% iron

STOCKING THE PANTRY

10

When you have some extra time, roast a chicken in your slow cooker and freeze the meat for use in future soup, stew, or casserole recipes. Thaw meat in the refrigerator before using.

ROASTED CHICKEN

PREP:

15 minutes

COOK:

7 to 8 hours (low)
or 3 1/2 to 4 hours (high)

MAKES:

4 servings

1	teaspoon dried rosemary or thyme, crushed
1/2	teaspoon salt
1/4	teaspoon black pepper
3	cloves garlic, minced
1	3- to 4-pound whole broiler-fryer chicken, cut into 4 pieces
1	tablespoon olive oil
1/2	cup water

1 In a small bowl combine rosemary, salt, pepper, and garlic. Rub skin of chicken with olive oil. Sprinkle rosemary mixture evenly over chicken; rub in with your fingers.

2 In a 3 1/2- to 4 1/2-quart slow cooker place water. Add chicken pieces, skin side up. Cover and cook on low-heat setting for 7 to 8 hours or on high-heat setting for 3 1/2 to 4 hours.

3 If storing chicken for later use, remove chicken from bones. Discard skin and bones. Chop chicken and place in an airtight container; seal. Chill for up to 4 days or freeze for up to 3 months.

Nutrition Facts per serving: 356 cal., 22 g total fat (6 g sat. fat), 118 mg chol., 402 mg sodium, 1 g carbo., 0 g fiber, 37 g pro. **Daily Values:** 1% vit. C, 3% calcium, 10% iron

Stock your freezer with this big-flavored, smoky marinara sauce and a package of frozen meatballs, and you'll always have a quick and interesting answer to the dinnertime dilemma.

CHUNKY MARINARA SAUCE

4	medium carrots, chopped
2	cups fresh mushrooms, quartered
1	large onion, chopped
1	tablespoon olive oil
3	14½-ounce cans fire-roasted diced tomatoes, undrained
1	cup dry red wine or water
1	6-ounce can tomato paste
½	cup water
1	tablespoon balsamic vinegar
2	teaspoons dried Italian seasoning, crushed
¾	teaspoon salt
½	teaspoon black pepper
¼	teaspoon crushed red pepper (optional)
3	cloves garlic, minced
2	teaspoons sugar (optional)

PREP:
25 minutes

COOK:
8 to 10 hours (low) or 4 to 5 hours (high)

MAKES:
10 servings

1 Preheat broiler. In a 15×10×1-inch baking pan combine carrots, mushrooms, and onion. Drizzle with olive oil; toss to coat. Broil vegetables 4 to 6 inches from the heat for 8 to 10 minutes or until browned, stirring once.

2 In a 3½- or 4-quart slow cooker combine broiled vegetables, tomatoes, wine, tomato paste, water, balsamic vinegar, Italian seasoning, salt, black pepper, crushed red pepper (if desired), and garlic. Cover and cook on low-heat setting for 8 to 10 hours or on high-heat setting for 4 to 5 hours. If desired, stir in sugar.

3 If storing sauce for later use, pour into airtight containers; seal. Chill for up to 4 days or freeze for up to 3 months. Thaw frozen sauce overnight in the refrigerator. Reheat in a saucepan over medium heat, stirring frequently.

Nutrition Facts per serving: 107 cal., 2 g total fat (0 g sat. fat), 0 mg chol., 421 mg sodium, 16 g carbo., 2 g fiber, 3 g pro. **Daily Values:** 123% vit. A, 38% vit. C, 7% calcium, 9% iron

This versatile beef broth will bring a rich, homemade flavor to your homemade soup and stew recipes. Use the meat in sandwiches, soups, stews, or casseroles.

BEEF BROTH

PREP:

20 minutes

COOK:

10 to 12 hours (low) or 5 to 6 hours (high)

MAKES:

5 to 5¹/₂ cups broth and 2¹/₂ to 3¹/₂ cups cooked meat

2	large onions, sliced
8	sprigs fresh parsley
4	large bay leaves
8	whole black peppercorns
1¹/₂	teaspoons salt
4	cloves garlic, halved
3	pounds meaty beef soup bones (beef shank crosscuts or short ribs)
5	cups water
1	egg white (optional)
1	eggshell, crushed (optional)
¹/₄	cup water (optional)

1 In a 4- to 6-quart slow cooker combine onions, parsley, bay leaves, peppercorns, salt, and garlic. Add soup bones and the 5 cups water.

2 Cover and cook on low-heat setting for 10 to 12 hours or on high-heat setting for 5 to 6 hours.

3 Remove bones from cooker. Strain broth through a large sieve or colander lined with two layers of 100-percent-cotton cheesecloth. Discard solids in cheesecloth. If desired, clarify broth by combining egg white, eggshell, and the ¹/₄ cup water in a large saucepan; add hot broth. Bring to boiling. Let stand for 5 minutes. Strain broth through two layers of 100-percent-cotton cheesecloth.

4 If using broth right away, skim off fat. If storing broth for later use, chill broth in a bowl for 6 to 24 hours. Lift off fat. Pour broth into an airtight container, discarding residue in bottom of bowl; seal. Chill for up to 3 days or freeze for up to 3 months.

5 When bones are cool enough to handle, remove meat from bones. Discard bones. Place meat in an airtight container; seal. Chill for up to 3 days or freeze for up to 3 months.

Nutrition Facts per 1 cup of broth: 0 cal., 0 g total fat (0 g sat. fat), 0 mg chol., 705 mg sodium, 0 g carbo., 0 g fiber, 0 g pro. **Daily Values:** 1% calcium

Lower in sodium than canned versions, this flavorful bouillon works in any recipe that calls for chicken broth; it makes an especially good chicken noodle soup.

CHICKEN BROTH

4   to 4½ pounds meaty chicken pieces (breast halves, thighs, and/or drumsticks)

4   stalks celery with leaves, cut up

1   small onion, sliced

2   sprigs fresh parsley

1   bay leaf

¾   teaspoon salt

½   teaspoon dried thyme or marjoram, crushed

¼   teaspoon black pepper

4   cups water

PREP:

20 minutes

COOK:

7 to 10 hours (low)
or 3½ to 5 hours (high)

MAKES:

5 to 6 cups broth and
4 to 5 cups cooked chicken

1 In a 5- to 6-quart slow cooker combine chicken, celery, onion, parsley, bay leaf, salt, thyme, and pepper. Add the water.

2 Cover and cook on low-heat setting for 7 to 10 hours or on high-heat setting for 3½ to 5 hours.

3 Remove chicken from cooker. Strain broth through a large sieve or colander lined with two layers of 100-percent-cotton cheesecloth. Discard solids in cheesecloth.

4 If using broth right away, skim off fat. If storing broth for later use, chill broth in a bowl for 6 to 24 hours. Lift off fat. Pour broth into an airtight container; seal. Chill for up to 3 days or freeze for up to 3 months.

5 When chicken is cool enough to handle, remove chicken from bones. Discard skin and bones. Place chicken in an airtight container; seal. Chill for up to 3 days or freeze for up to 3 months.

Nutrition Facts per 1 cup of broth: 0 cal., 0 g total fat (0 g sat. fat), 0 mg chol., 354 mg sodium, 0 g carbo., 0 g fiber, 0 g pro.

If your recipes usually call for canned vegetable broth, freeze this vegetable stock in 1¾-cup portions—the equivalent of 14-ounce cans.

VEGETABLE STOCK

PREP:

30 minutes

COOK:

12 to 14 hours (low) or 6 to 7 hours (high)

MAKES:

about 6 cups stock

4	medium carrots, cut up
2	tomatoes, cut up
2	medium onions, cut up
1	turnip or 2 parsnips, cut up
1	medium potato, halved lengthwise and cut into ½-inch slices
1	stalk celery with leaves, cut up
6	sprigs fresh parsley
1	bay leaf
1	teaspoon salt
½	teaspoon dried thyme, crushed
¼	teaspoon whole black peppercorns
6	cloves garlic, halved
6	cups water

1 In a 3½- to 5-quart slow cooker combine carrots, tomatoes, onions, turnip, potato, celery, parsley, bay leaf, salt, thyme, peppercorns, and garlic. Add the water.

2 Cover and cook on low-heat setting for 12 to 14 hours or on high-heat setting for 6 to 7 hours. Strain stock through a large sieve or colander lined with two layers of 100-percent-cotton cheesecloth. Discard solids in cheesecloth.

3 If storing stock for later use, pour into an airtight container; seal. Chill for up to 3 days or freeze for up to 3 months.

Nutrition Facts per 1 cup of stock: 44 cal., 0 g total fat (0 g sat. fat), 0 mg chol., 319 mg sodium, 10 g carbo., 0 g fiber, 1 g pro.

It's possible to end up with too many homegrown tomatoes after a bountiful summer season. When that happens, cook up this recipe and stash it in your freezer. Use it in place of canned tomatoes in soups, chilis, stews, and casseroles.

SLOW COOKER MEXICAN TOMATOES

4	pounds tomatoes, peeled and quartered
½	cup sugar
1	medium onion, chopped
¼	cup lemon juice
2	to 3 teaspoons chipotle or regular chili powder
2	teaspoons salt
¼	teaspoon crushed red pepper

PREP:
25 minutes

COOK:
*8 to 10 hours (low)
or 4 to 5 hours (high)*

MAKES:
16 servings

1 In a 4- or 4½-quart slow cooker combine tomatoes, sugar, onion, lemon juice, chili powder, salt, and crushed red pepper. Cover and cook on low-heat setting for 8 to 10 hours or on high-heat setting for 4 to 5 hours. Using a potato masher, coarsely mash tomatoes.

2 If storing tomatoes for later use, cool slightly. Place 1¾-cup portions in airtight containers; seal. Chill for up to 4 days or freeze for up to 3 months.

Nutrition Facts per serving: 49 cal., 0 g total fat (0 g sat. fat), 0 mg chol., 303 mg sodium, 12 g carbo., 1 g fiber, 1 g pro. **Daily Values:** 14% vit. A, 32% vit. C, 1% calcium, 3% iron

SLOW COOKER ITALIAN TOMATOES
Prepare Crockery Mexican Tomatoes as directed, except omit the chili powder and crushed red pepper. Add 2 teaspoons dried Italian seasoning, crushed.

SLOW COOKER CAJUN TOMATOES
Prepare Crockery Mexican Tomatoes as directed, except omit the chili powder and crushed red pepper. Add 2 teaspoons Cajun seasoning.

Make this big batch of caramelized onions for your next family barbecue.
They'll taste great over grilled steaks, burgers, or hot dogs.

SLOW COOKED CARAMELIZED ONIONS

PREP:

20 minutes

COOK:

12 to 14 hours (low)
or 6 to 7 hours (high)

MAKES:

22 servings

3 pounds sweet onions (such as Vidalia or Walla Walla), sliced

$^1/_3$ cup butter or margarine, cut up

2 tablespoons brown sugar

1 tablespoon balsamic vinegar

1 teaspoon salt

1 In a 3$^1/_2$- to 4$^1/_2$-quart slow cooker combine onions, butter, brown sugar, vinegar, and salt. Cover and cook on low-heat setting for 12 to 14 hours or on high-heat for 6 to 7 hours.

2 If storing onions for later use, place in airtight containers; seal. Chill for up to 4 days or freeze for up to 3 months.

Nutrition Facts per serving: 52 cal., 3 g total fat (2 g sat. fat), 8 mg chol., 138 mg sodium, 6 g carbo., 1 g fiber, 1 g pro. **Daily Values:** 2% vit. A, 5% vit. C, 1% calcium, 1% iron

*Granny Smith apples are a good candidate for this homemade applesauce
that you can stash in your freezer for up to 8 months.*

APPLE-Y CHUNKY APPLESAUCE

3	pounds tart cooking apples, peeled, cored, and sliced
1	cup snipped dried apples
½	cup packed brown sugar
½	cup water
¼	cup frozen apple juice concentrate, thawed
1	teaspoon finely shredded lemon peel
3	tablespoons lemon juice
6	inches stick cinnamon, broken into 1-inch pieces

PREP:

20 minutes

COOK:

*6 to 8 hours (low)
or 3 to 4 hours (high)*

MAKES:

10 servings

1 In a 3½- or 4-quart slow cooker combine sliced apples, dried apples, brown sugar, water, apple juice concentrate, lemon peel, lemon juice, and stick cinnamon. Cover and cook on low-heat setting for 6 to 8 hours or on high-heat setting for 3 to 4 hours. Remove stick cinnamon. Using a potato masher, coarsely mash apples.

2 If storing applesauce for later use, cool slightly. Ladle into airtight containers; seal. Chill for up to 1 week or freeze for up to 8 months.

Nutrition Facts per serving: 141 cal., 0 g total fat (0 g sat. fat), 0 mg chol., 14 mg sodium, 37 g carbo., 3 g fiber, 0 g pro. **Daily Values:** 1% vit. A, 10% vit. C, 2% calcium, 3% iron

Though it's wonderful made with frozen fruit, this dessert is a real treat when rhubarb and strawberries are in season. Serve over ice cream or frozen yogurt.

STRAWBERRY-RHUBARB SAUCE

PREP:

10 minutes

COOK:

*5$\frac{1}{2}$ to 6 hours (low)
or 2$\frac{1}{2}$ to 3 hours (high),
plus 15 minutes (high)*

MAKES:

10 servings

6 cups fresh rhubarb, cut into 1-inch pieces
(about 2 pounds), or two 16-ounce packages
frozen unsweetened sliced rhubarb

1 cup sugar

$\frac{1}{2}$ cup white grape juice or apple juice

3 inches stick cinnamon, broken into 1-inch pieces

$\frac{1}{2}$ teaspoon finely shredded orange peel

$\frac{1}{4}$ teaspoon ground ginger

2 cups strawberries, halved

1 In a 3$\frac{1}{2}$- or 4-quart slow cooker combine rhubarb, sugar, grape juice, stick cinnamon, orange peel, and ginger.

2 Cover and cook on low-heat setting for 5$\frac{1}{2}$ to 6 hours or on high-heat setting for 2$\frac{1}{2}$ to 3 hours. Remove stick cinnamon.

3 If using low-heat setting, turn to high-heat setting. Stir in strawberries. Cover and cook for 15 minutes more.

4 If storing sauce for later use, cool slightly. Ladle into airtight containers; seal. Chill for up to 1 week or freeze for up to 3 months.

Nutrition Facts per serving: 103 cal., 0 g total fat (0 g sat. fat), 0 mg chol., 4 mg sodium, 26 g carbo., 2 g fiber, 1 g pro. **Daily Values:** 2% vit. A, 44% vit. C, 7% calcium, 2% iron

This rich caramel sauce is delectable over ice cream or pound cake. Or serve it as a luscious dip for fruits.

DULCE DE LECHE

2   14-ounce cans (2½ cups total) sweetened condensed milk

¼   teaspoon apple pie spice, pumpkin pie spice, or vanilla

2   teaspoons brandy

1 In a 1½-quart slow cooker combine sweetened condensed milk and apple pie spice. Cover and cook for 2 to 2½ hours, stirring twice. (Mixture will be lumpy.)

2 Whisk until smooth. Remove liner from cooker, if possible, or turn off cooker. Let stand, uncovered, for 30 minutes to cool slightly. Whisk in brandy.

3 If storing sauce for later use, pour into an airtight container; seal. Chill for up to 1 week.

Nutrition Facts per serving: 143 cal., 4 g total fat (2 g sat. fat), 15 mg chol., 56 mg sodium, 24 g carbo., 0 g fiber, 3 g pro. **Daily Values:** 3% vit. A, 2% vit. C, 13% calcium, 1% iron

PREP:

5 minutes

COOK:

2 to 2½ hours

COOL:

30 minutes

MAKES:

18 servings

INDEX

METRIC INFORMATION

The charts on this page provide a guide for converting measurements from the U.S. customary system, which is used throughout this book, to the metric system.

Product Differences

Most of the ingredients called for in the recipes in this book are available in most countries. However, some are known by different names. Here are some common American ingredients and their possible counterparts:

- Sugar (white) is granulated, fine granulated, or castor sugar.
- Powdered sugar is icing sugar.
- All-purpose flour is enriched, bleached or unbleached white household flour. When self-rising flour is used in place of all-purpose flour in a recipe that calls for leavening, omit the leavening agent (baking soda or baking powder) and salt.
- Light-colored corn syrup is golden syrup.
- Cornstarch is cornflour.
- Baking soda is bicarbonate of soda.
- Vanilla or vanilla extract is vanilla essence.
- Green, red, or yellow sweet peppers are capsicums or bell peppers.
- Golden raisins are sultanas.

Volume and Weight

The United States traditionally uses cup measures for liquid and solid ingredients. The chart below shows the approximate imperial and metric equivalents. If you are accustomed to weighing solid ingredients, the following approximate equivalents will be helpful.

- 1 cup butter, castor sugar, or rice = 8 ounces = ¹/₂ pound = 250 grams
- 1 cup flour = 4 ounces = ¹/₄ pound = 125 grams
- 1 cup icing sugar = 5 ounces = 150 grams

Canadian and U.S. volume for a cup measure is 8 fluid ounces (237 ml), but the standard metric equivalent is 250 ml.

1 British imperial cup is 10 fluid ounces.

In Australia, 1 tablespoon equals 20 ml, and there are 4 teaspoons in the Australian tablespoon.

Spoon measures are used for smaller amounts of ingredients. Although the size of the tablespoon varies slightly in different countries, for practical purposes and for recipes in this book, a straight substitution is all that's necessary. Measurements made using cups or spoons always should be level unless stated otherwise.

Common Weight Range Replacements

Imperial / U.S.	Metric
¹/₂ ounce	15 g
1 ounce	25 g or 30 g
4 ounces (¹/₄ pound)	115 g or 125 g
8 ounces (¹/₂ pound)	225 g or 250 g
16 ounces (1 pound)	450 g or 500 g
1¹/₄ pounds	625 g
1¹/₂ pounds	750 g
2 pounds or 2¹/₄ pounds	1,000 g or 1 Kg

Oven Temperature Equivalents

Fahrenheit Setting	Celsius Setting*	Gas Setting
300°F	150°C	Gas Mark 2 (very low)
325°F	160°C	Gas Mark 3 (low)
350°F	180°C	Gas Mark 4 (moderate)
375°F	190°C	Gas Mark 5 (moderate)
400°F	200°C	Gas Mark 6 (hot)
425°F	220°C	Gas Mark 7 (hot)
450°F	230°C	Gas Mark 8 (very hot)
475°F	240°C	Gas Mark 9 (very hot)
500°F	260°C	Gas Mark 10 (extremely hot)
Broil	Broil	Grill

*Electric and gas ovens may be calibrated using celsius. However, for an electric oven, increase celsius setting 10 to 20 degrees when cooking above 160°C. For convection or forced air ovens (gas or electric) lower the temperature setting 25°F/10°C when cooking at all heat levels.

Baking Pan Sizes

Imperial / U.S.	Metric
9×1¹/₂-inch round cake pan	22- or 23×4-cm (1.5 L)
9×1¹/₂-inch pie plate	22- or 23×4-cm (1 L)
8×8×2-inch square cake pan	20×5-cm (2 L)
9×9×2-inch square cake pan	22- or 23×4.5-cm (2.5 L)
11×7×1¹/₂-inch baking pan	28×17×4-cm (2 L)
2-quart rectangular baking pan	30×19×4.5-cm (3 L)
13×9×2-inch baking pan	34×22×4.5-cm (3.5 L)
15×10×1-inch jelly roll pan	40×25×2-cm
9×5×3-inch loaf pan	23×13×8-cm (2 L)
2-quart casserole	2 L

U.S. / Standard Metric Equivalents

¹/₈ teaspoon = 0.5 ml	
¹/₄ teaspoon = 1 ml	
¹/₂ teaspoon = 2 ml	
1 teaspoon = 5 ml	
1 tablespoon = 15 ml	
2 tablespoons = 25 ml	
¹/₄ cup = 2 fluid ounces = 50 ml	
¹/₃ cup = 3 fluid ounces = 75 ml	
¹/₂ cup = 4 fluid ounces = 125 ml	
²/₃ cup = 5 fluid ounces = 150 ml	
³/₄ cup = 6 fluid ounces = 175 ml	
1 cup = 8 fluid ounces = 250 ml	
2 cups = 1 pint = 500 ml	
1 quart = 1 litre	